Skip·Beat!

Shojo Beat

Skip·Beat!

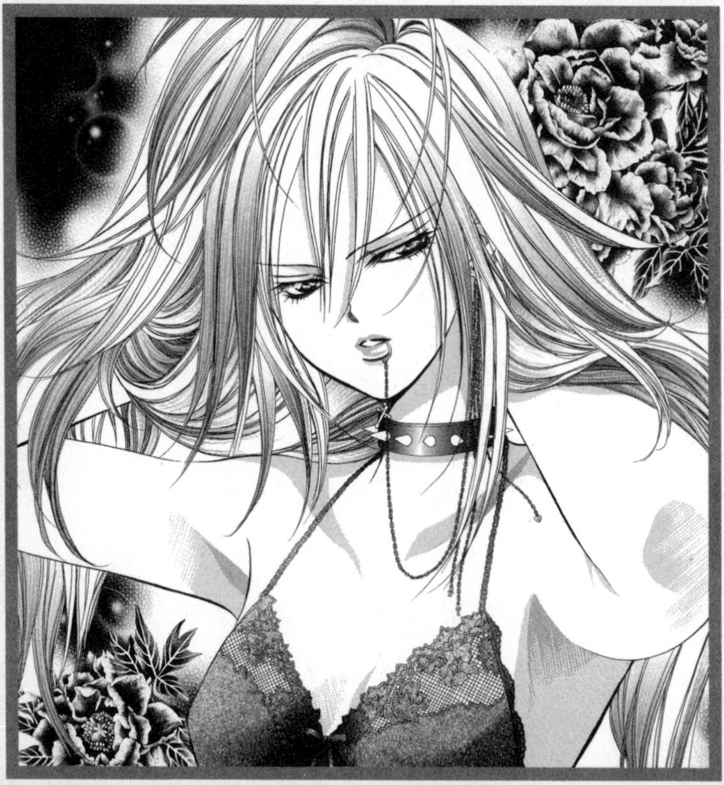

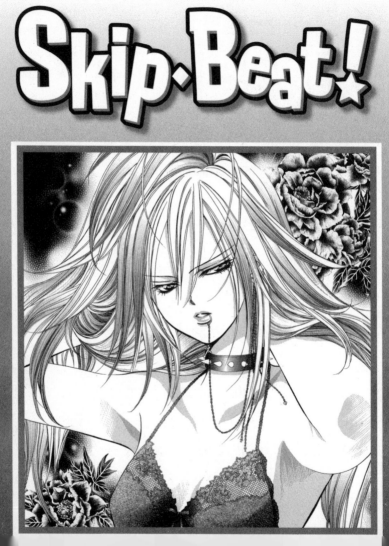

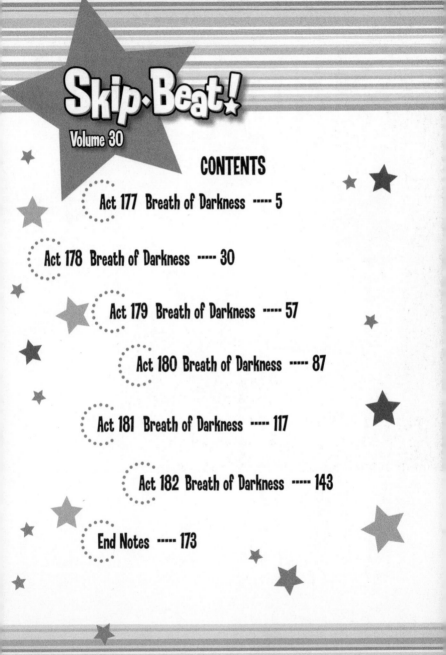

Skip·Beat!

Volume 30

CONTENTS

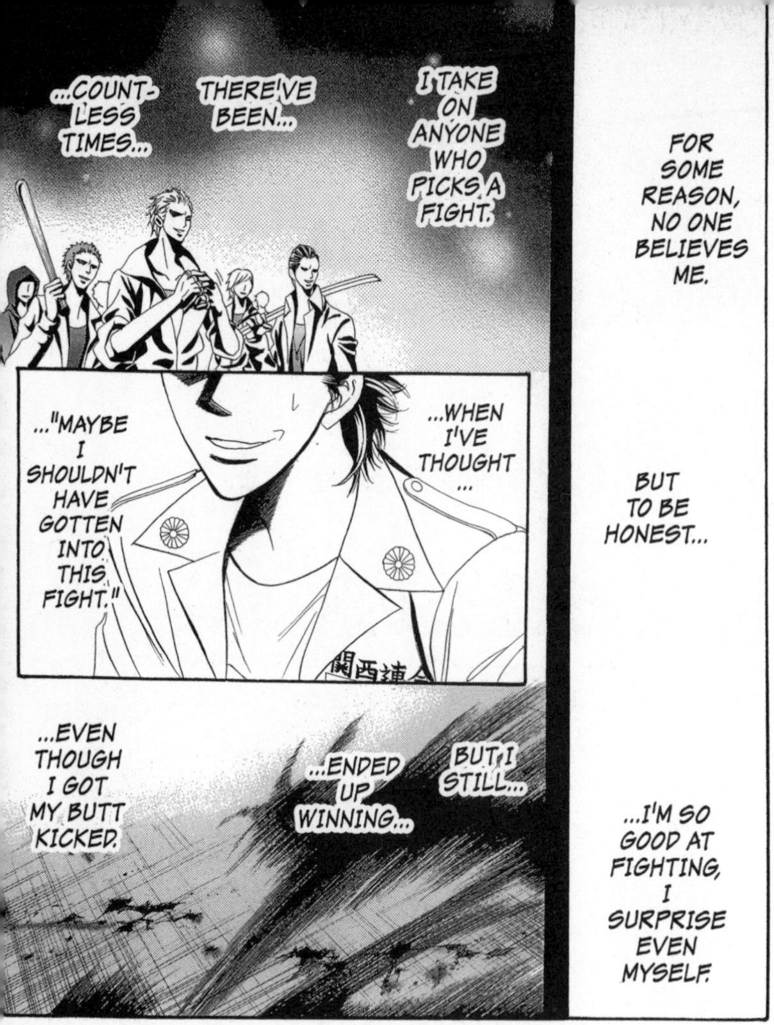
FOR SOME REASON, NO ONE BELIEVES ME.
BUT TO BE HONEST...
...I'M SO GOOD AT FIGHTING, I SURPRISE EVEN MYSELF.
I TAKE ON ANYONE WHO PICKS A FIGHT.
THERE'VE BEEN...
...COUNT-LESS TIMES...
...WHEN I'VE THOUGHT...
..."MAYBE I SHOULDN'T HAVE GOTTEN INTO THIS FIGHT."
BUT I STILL...
...ENDED UP WINNING...
...EVEN THOUGH I GOT MY BUTT KICKED.

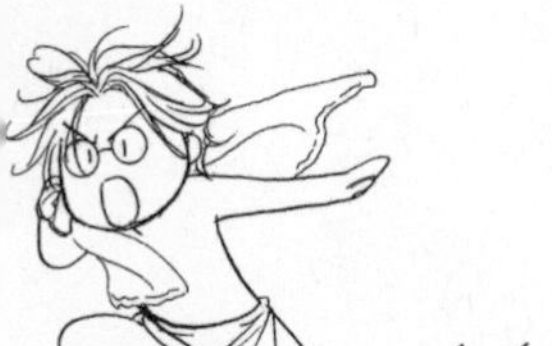

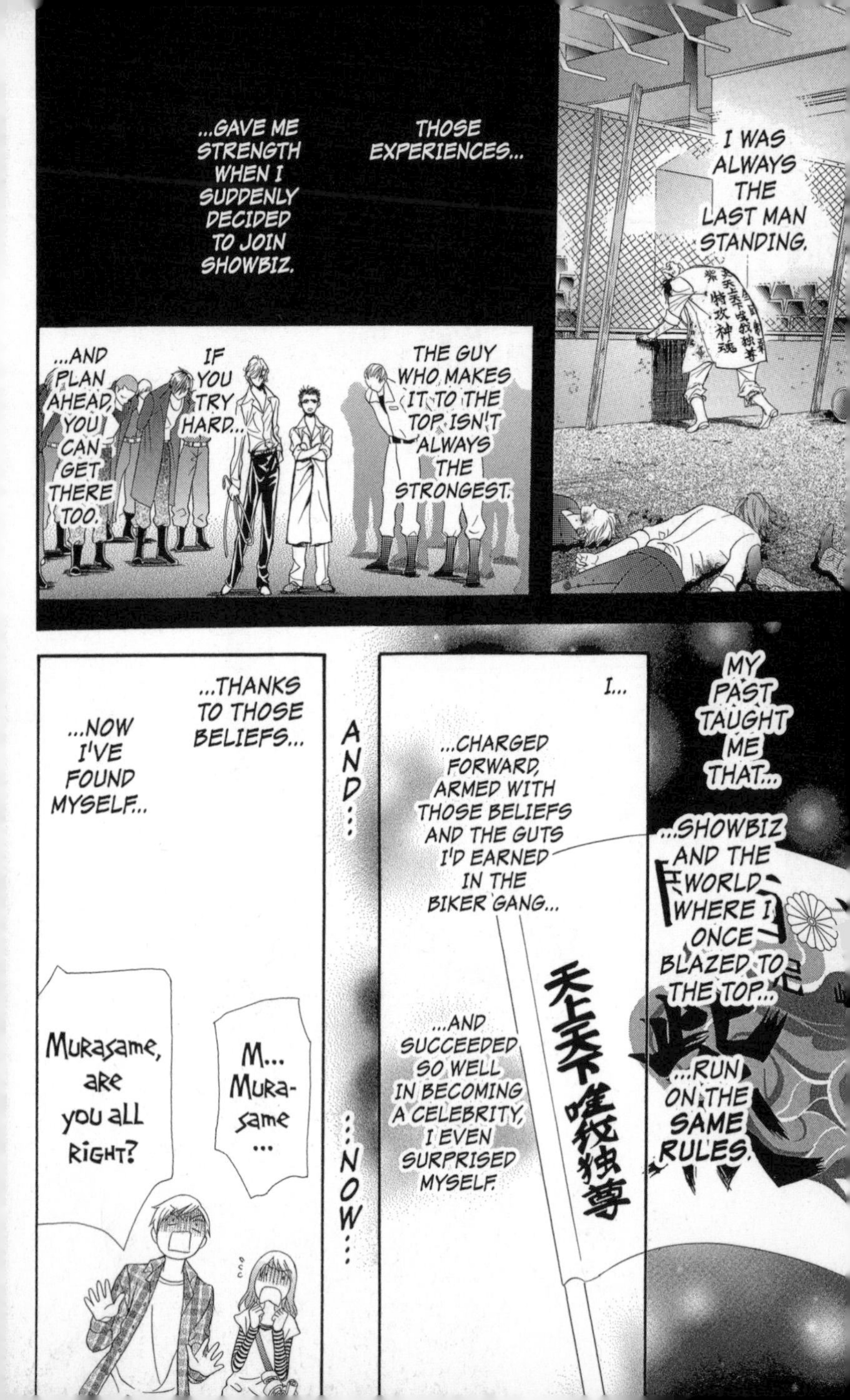
I WAS ALWAYS THE LAST MAN STANDING.
THOSE EXPERIENCES...
...GAVE ME STRENGTH WHEN I SUDDENLY DECIDED TO JOIN SHOWBIZ.
THE GUY WHO MAKES IT TO THE TOP ISN'T ALWAYS THE STRONGEST.
IF YOU TRY HARD...
...AND PLAN AHEAD, YOU CAN GET THERE TOO.
MY PAST TAUGHT ME THAT...
...SHOWBIZ AND THE WORLD WHERE I ONCE BLAZED TO THE TOP...
...RUN ON THE SAME RULES.
I...
...CHARGED FORWARD, ARMED WITH THOSE BELIEFS AND THE GUTS I'D EARNED IN THE BIKER GANG...
天上天下唯我独尊
...AND SUCCEEDED SO WELL IN BECOMING A CELEBRITY, I EVEN SURPRISED MYSELF.
AND...
...NOW...
...THANKS TO THOSE BELIEFS...
...NOW I'VE FOUND MYSELF...
M... Murasame...
Murasame, are you all right?

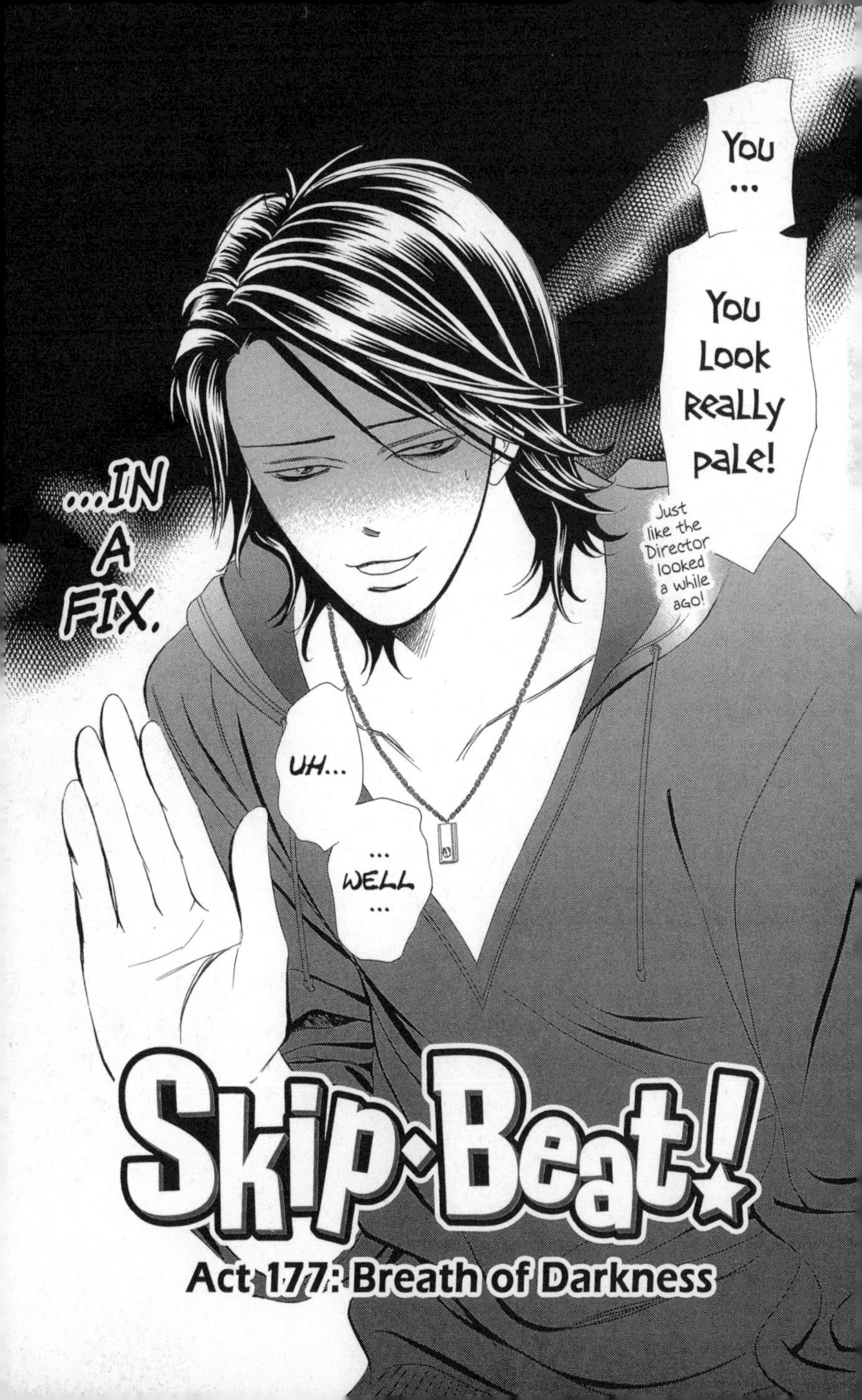
You...
You look really pale!
Just like the Director looked a while ago!
...In a fix.
Uh...
...Well...

Skip·Beat!

Act 177: Breath of Darkness

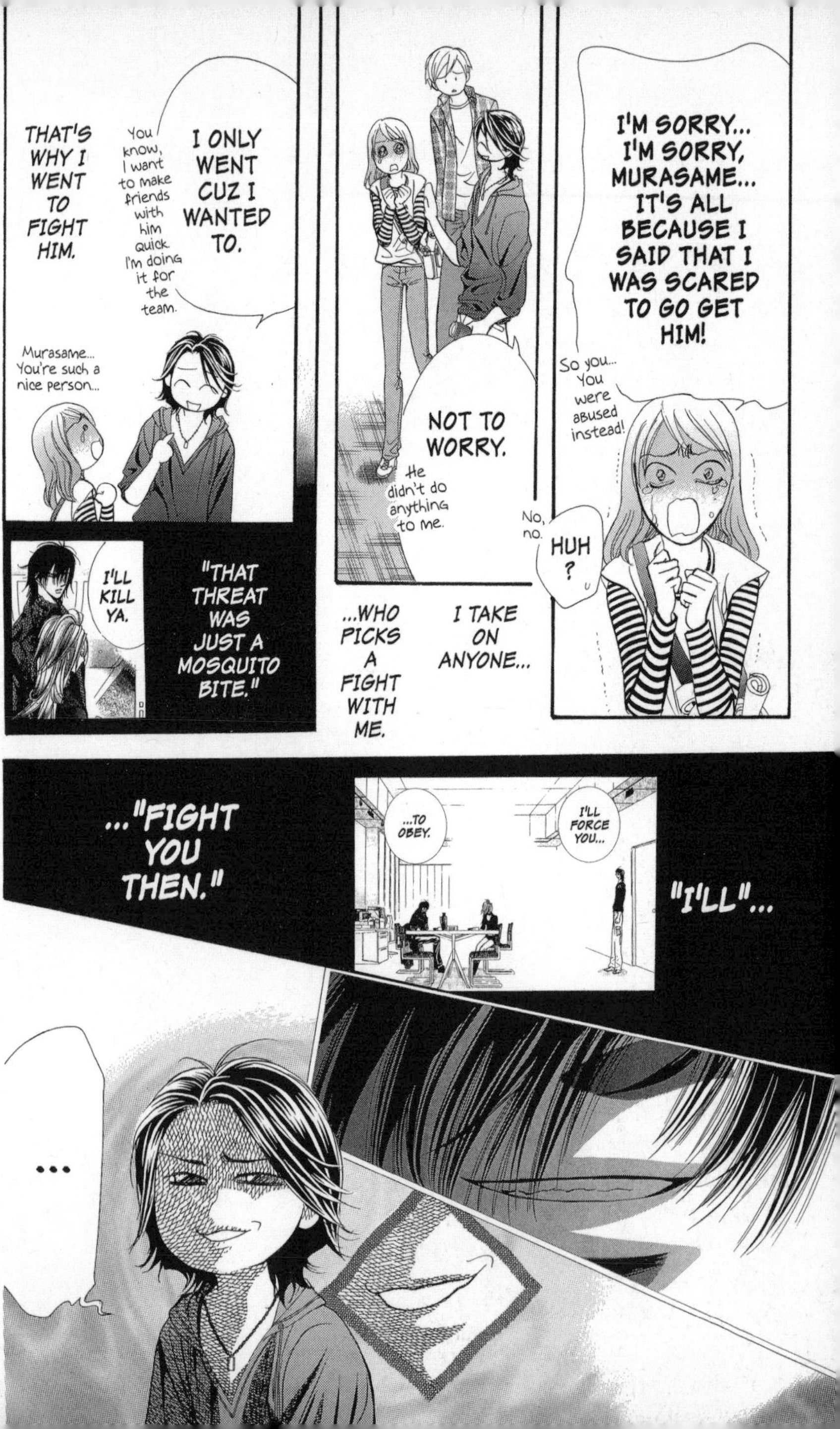
I'M SORRY... I'M SORRY, MURASAME... IT'S ALL BECAUSE I SAID THAT I WAS SCARED TO GO GET HIM!
So you... You were abused instead!
HUH?
No, no.
NOT TO WORRY.
He didn't do anything to me.
I TAKE ON ANYONE...
...WHO PICKS A FIGHT WITH ME.
I ONLY WENT CUZ I WANTED TO.
You know, I want to make friends with him quick. I'm doing it for the team.
THAT'S WHY I WENT TO FIGHT HIM.
Murasame... You're such a nice person...
"THAT THREAT WAS JUST A MOSQUITO BITE."
I'LL KILL YA.
"I'LL"...
I'LL FORCE YOU...
...TO OBEY.
..."FIGHT YOU THEN."
...

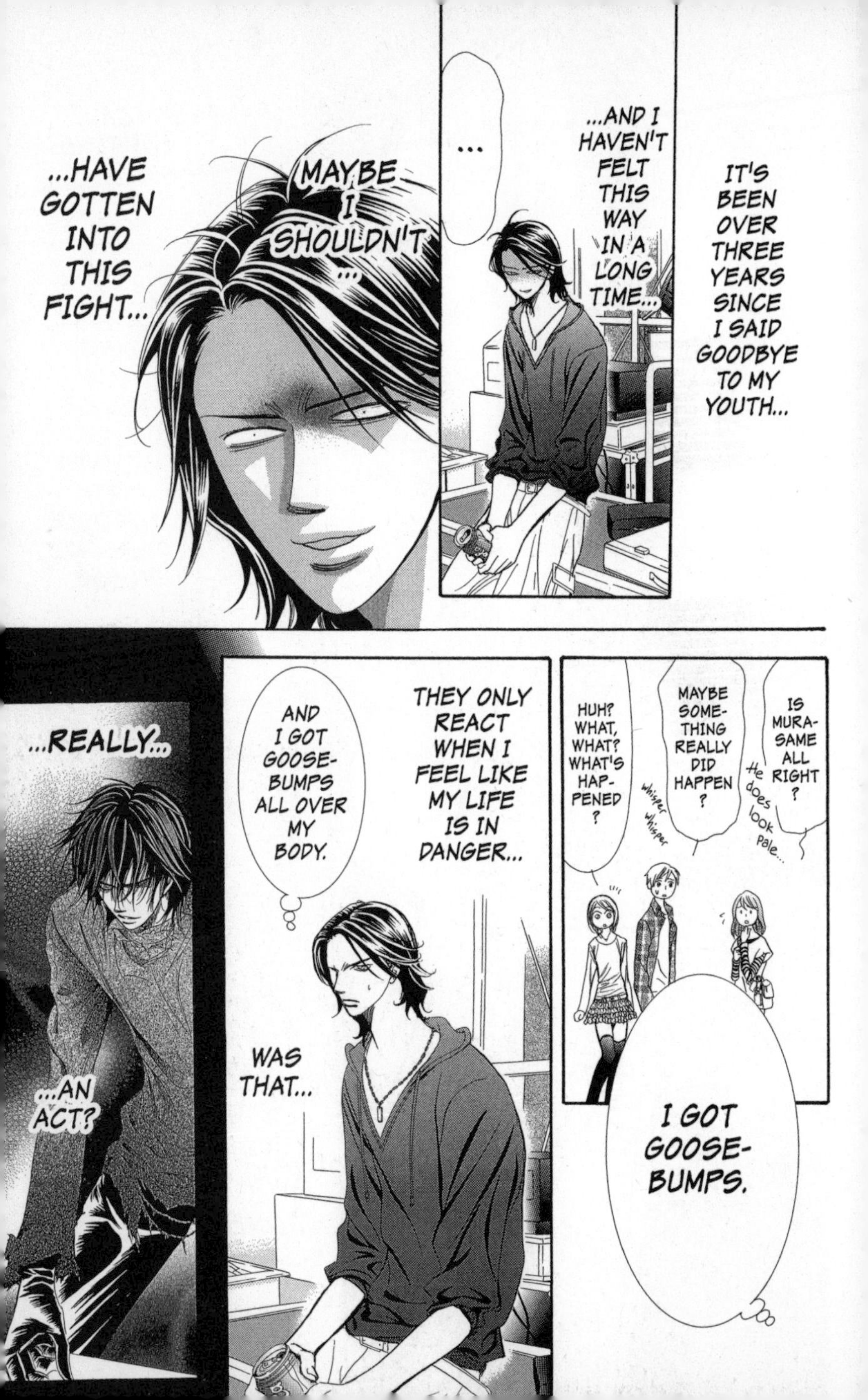
IT'S BEEN OVER THREE YEARS SINCE I SAID GOODBYE TO MY YOUTH...
...AND I HAVEN'T FELT THIS WAY IN A LONG TIME...
...
MAYBE I SHOULDN'T ...
...HAVE GOTTEN INTO THIS FIGHT...
IS MURA-SAME ALL RIGHT?
He does look pale...
MAYBE SOME-THING REALLY DID HAPPEN?
whisper whisper
HUH? WHAT, WHAT? WHAT'S HAP-PENED?
I GOT GOOSE-BUMPS.
THEY ONLY REACT WHEN I FEEL LIKE MY LIFE IS IN DANGER...
AND I GOT GOOSE-BUMPS ALL OVER MY BODY.
WAS THAT...
...REALLY...
...AN ACT?

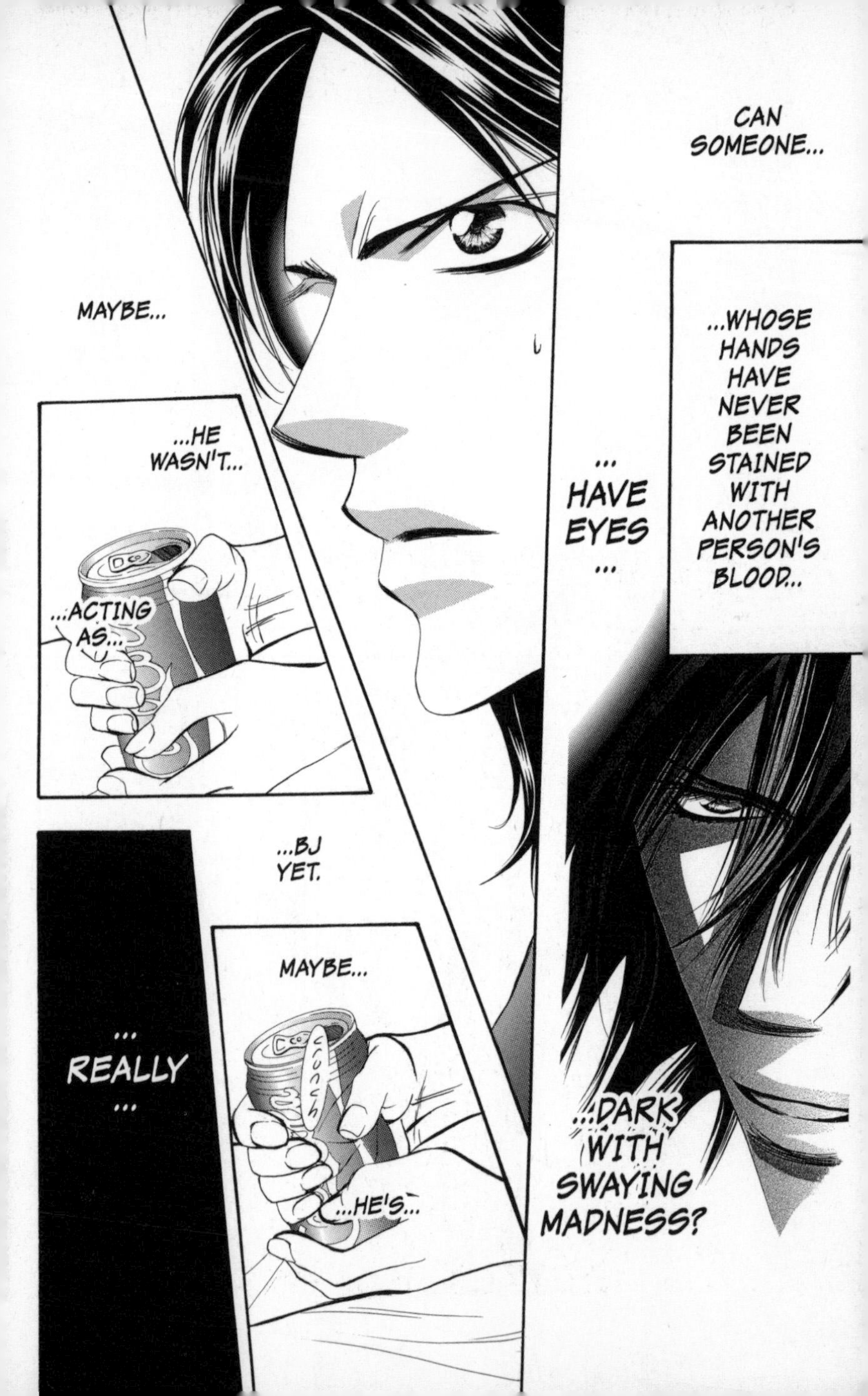
CAN SOMEONE...
...WHOSE HANDS HAVE NEVER BEEN STAINED WITH ANOTHER PERSON'S BLOOD...
...HAVE EYES...
...DARK WITH SWAYING MADNESS?
MAYBE...
...HE WASN'T...
...ACTING AS...
...BJ YET.
MAYBE...
crunch
...HE'S...
...REALLY...

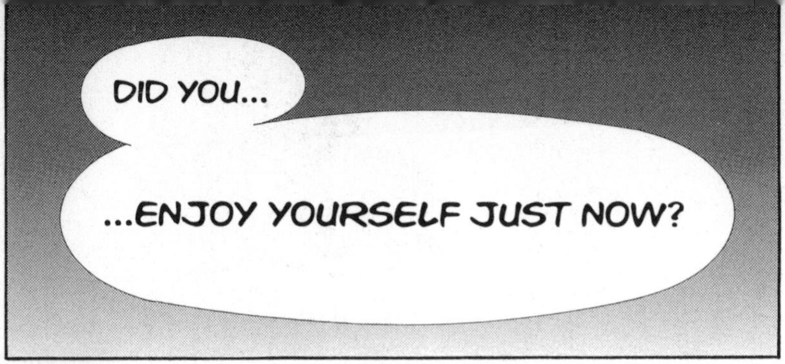
DID YOU...
...ENJOY YOURSELF JUST NOW?

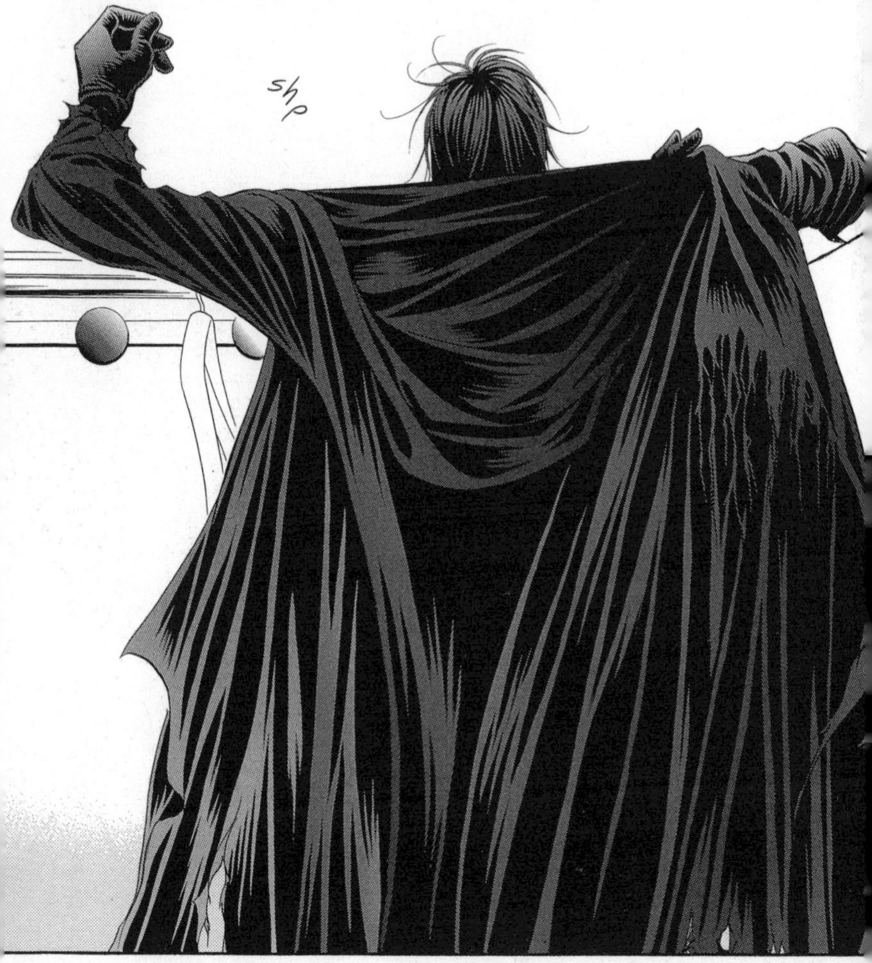
shp

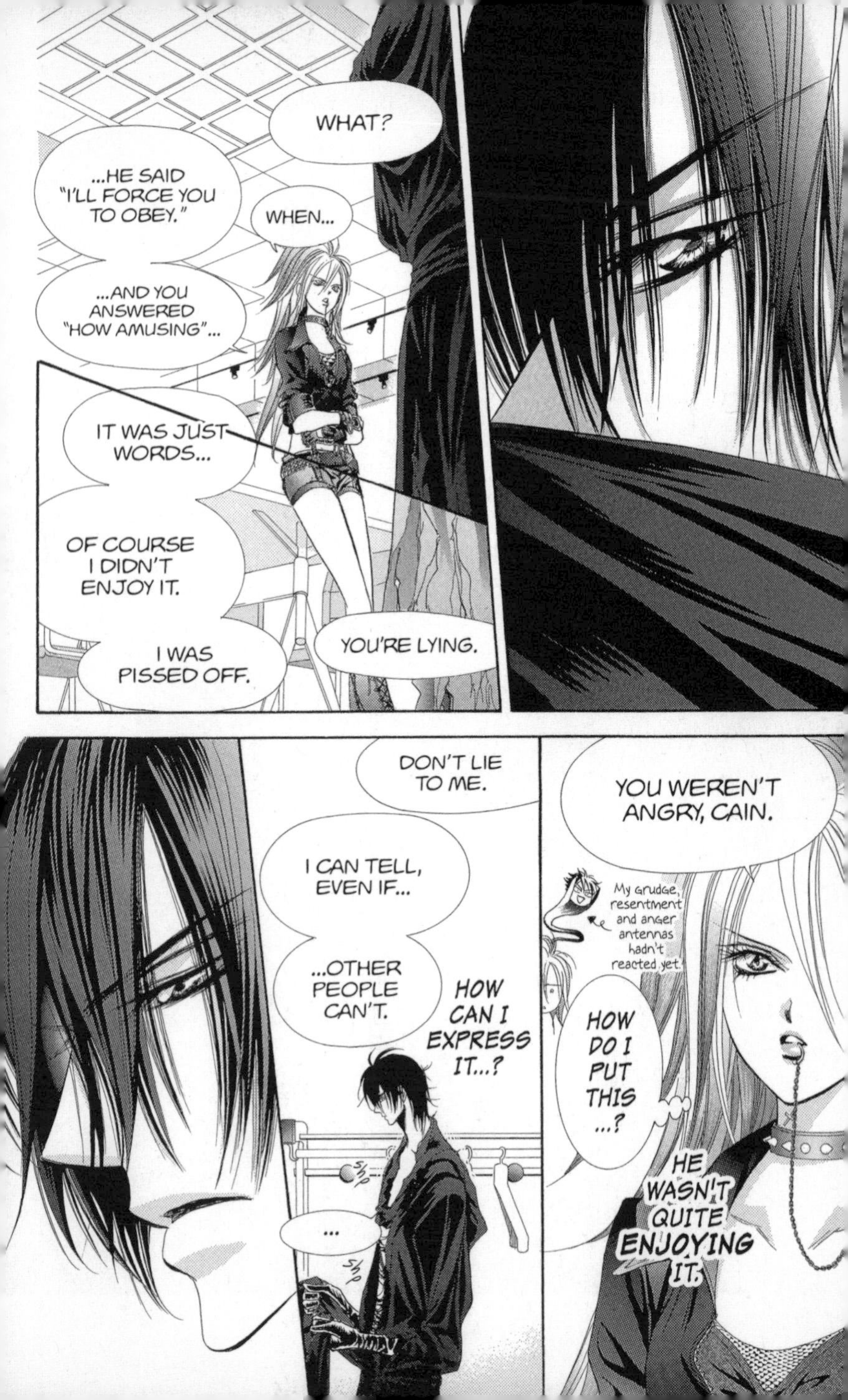
WHAT?
WHEN...
...HE SAID "I'LL FORCE YOU TO OBEY."
...AND YOU ANSWERED "HOW AMUSING"...
IT WAS JUST WORDS...
OF COURSE I DIDN'T ENJOY IT.
I WAS PISSED OFF.
YOU'RE LYING.
YOU WEREN'T ANGRY, CAIN.
My grudge, resentment and anger antennas hadn't reacted yet.
HOW DO I PUT THIS ...?
HE WASN'T QUITE ENJOYING IT.
DON'T LIE TO ME.
I CAN TELL, EVEN IF...
...OTHER PEOPLE CAN'T.
HOW CAN I EXPRESS IT...?
shp
...
shp

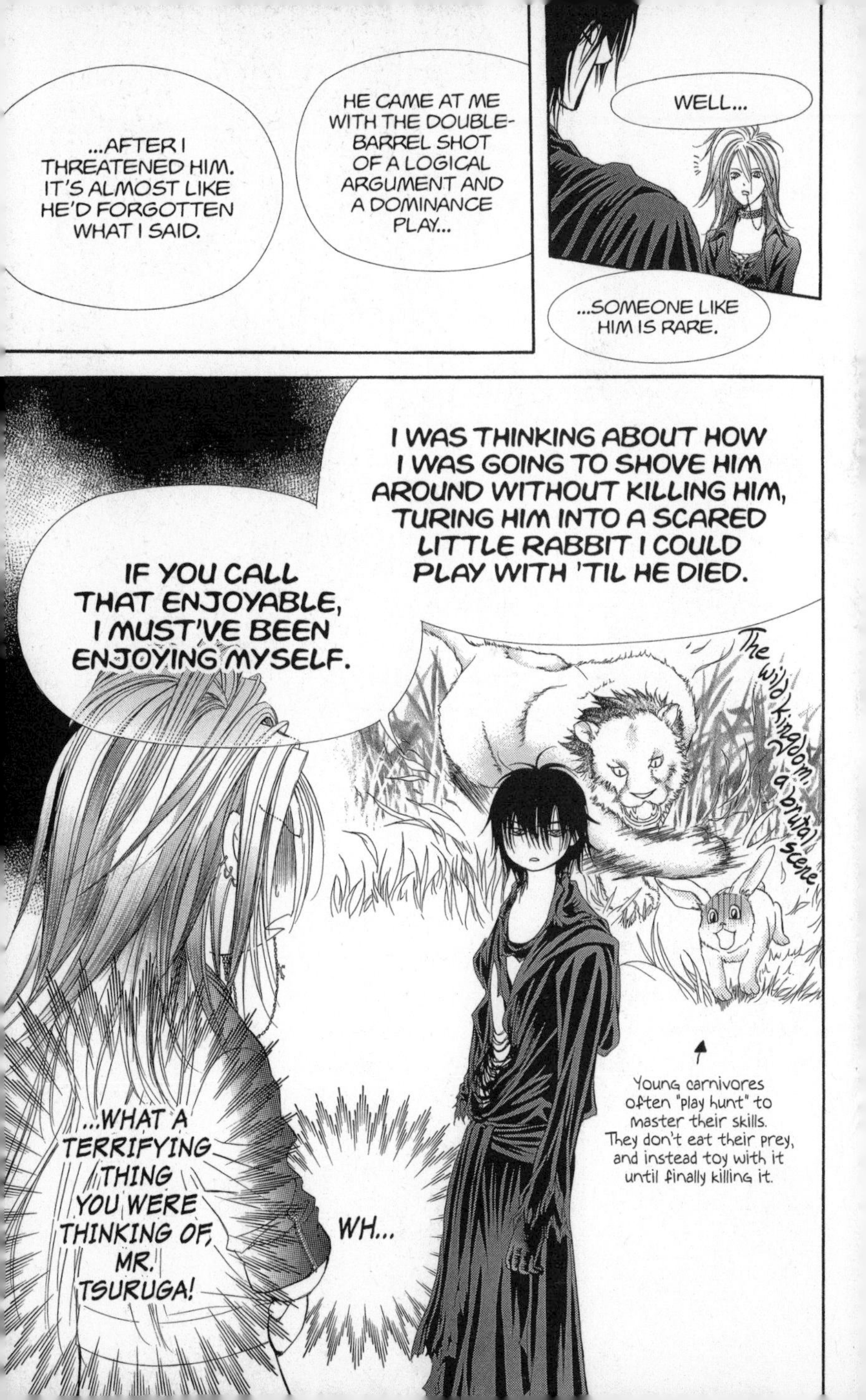
WELL...
...SOMEONE LIKE HIM IS RARE.
HE CAME AT ME WITH THE DOUBLE-BARREL SHOT OF A LOGICAL ARGUMENT AND A DOMINANCE PLAY...
...AFTER I THREATENED HIM. IT'S ALMOST LIKE HE'D FORGOTTEN WHAT I SAID.
I WAS THINKING ABOUT HOW I WAS GOING TO SHOVE HIM AROUND WITHOUT KILLING HIM, TURING HIM INTO A SCARED LITTLE RABBIT I COULD PLAY WITH 'TIL HE DIED.
IF YOU CALL THAT ENJOYABLE, I MUST'VE BEEN ENJOYING MYSELF.
The wild kingdom, a brutal scene.
Young carnivores often "play hunt" to master their skills. They don't eat their prey, and instead toy with it until finally killing it.
WH...
...WHAT A TERRIFYING THING YOU WERE THINKING OF, MR. TSURUGA!

Whoa!
UH.
NO, NO ...
HE'S NOT MR. TSURUGA. HE'S MY BROTHER, CAIN.
OH DEAR. I...
...WAS ACTUALLY A LITTLE APPALLED WHEN HE WAS JUST STATING...
...HIS THOUGHTS AS CAIN HEEL.
It was wonderful. That line symbolizes Cain Heel perfectly!
COMPARED TO THAT, I'M...
Still inexperienced...
SETSU WOULD'VE RESPONDED RIGHT AWAY...
..."SOUNDS FUN. I'LL HELP!"
Hmm...
I GOTTA BANISH "COMMON SENSE" FROM SETSU'S SOUL...
Otherwise I can't be like Cain...

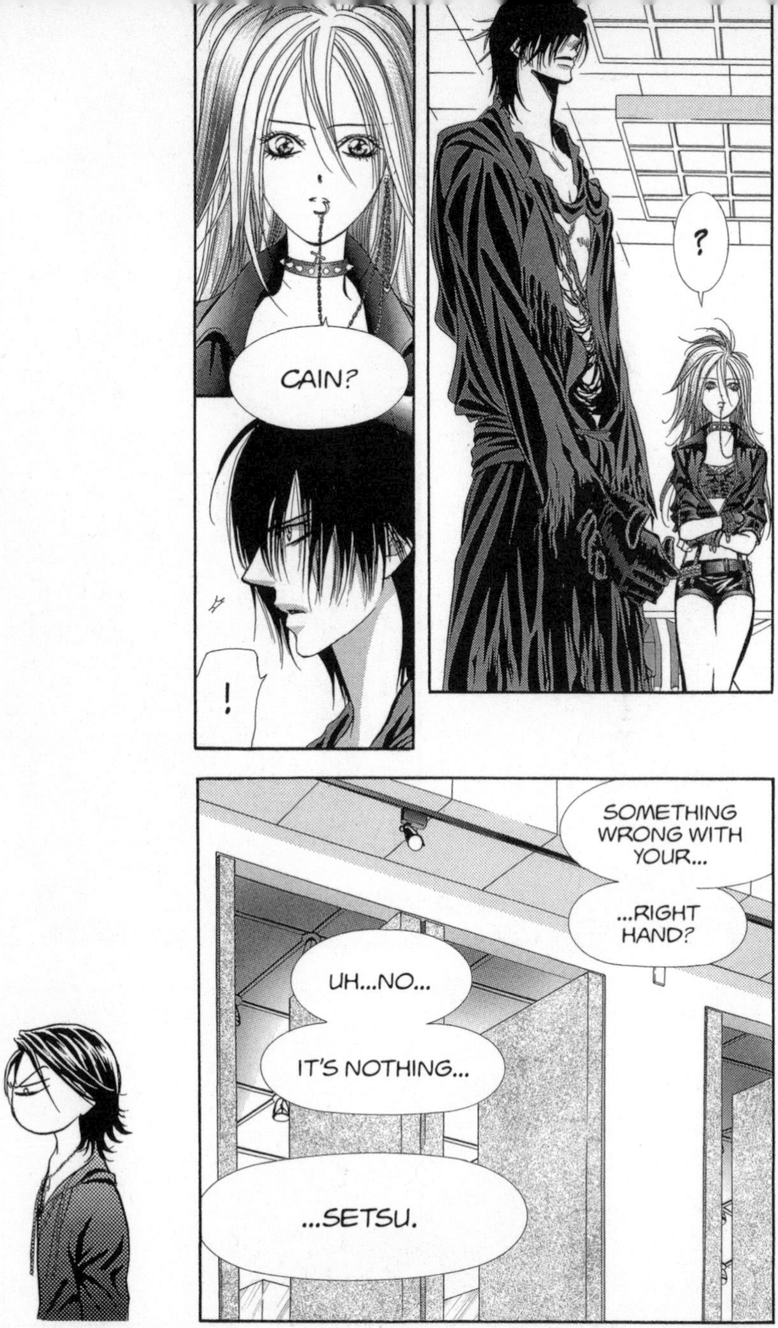
?
CAIN?
!
SOMETHING WRONG WITH YOUR...
...RIGHT HAND?
UH...NO...
IT'S NOTHING...
...SETSU.

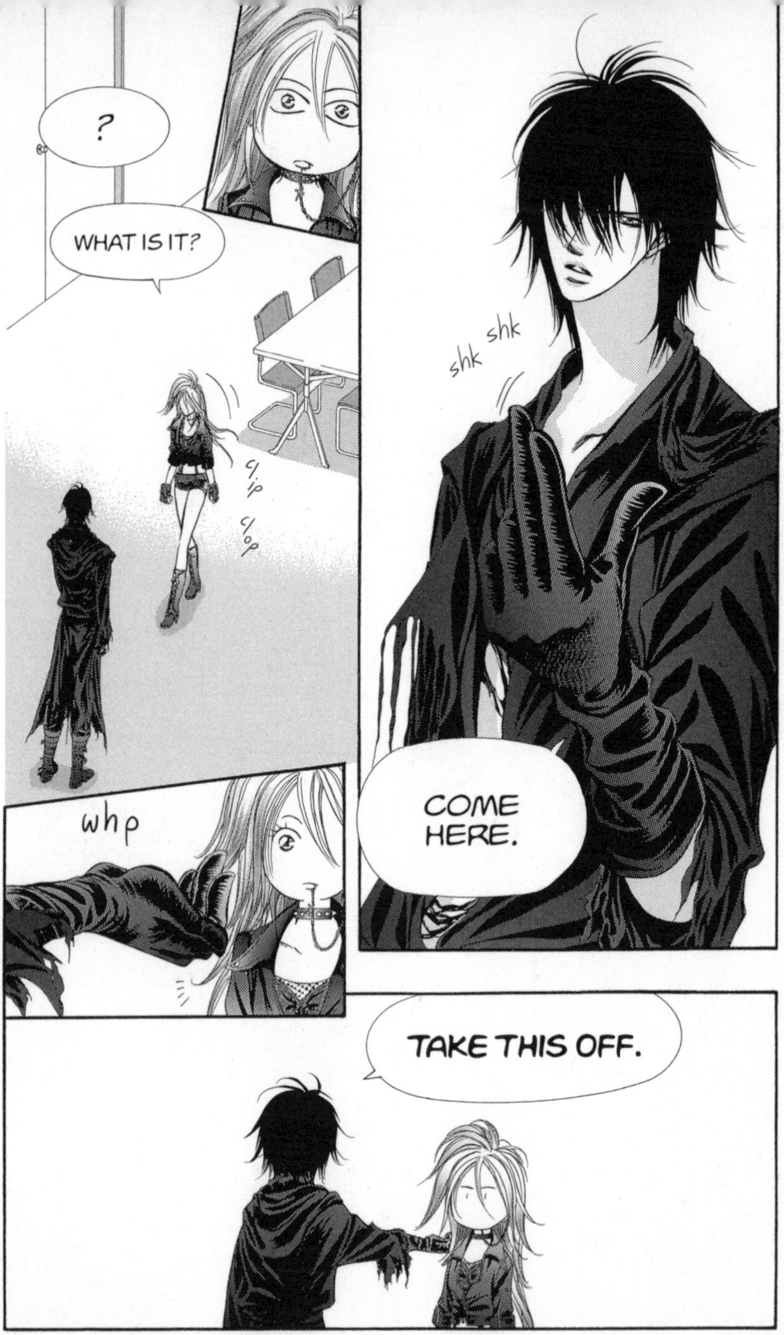
shk shk
COME HERE.
?
WHAT IS IT?
clip clop
whp
TAKE THIS OFF.

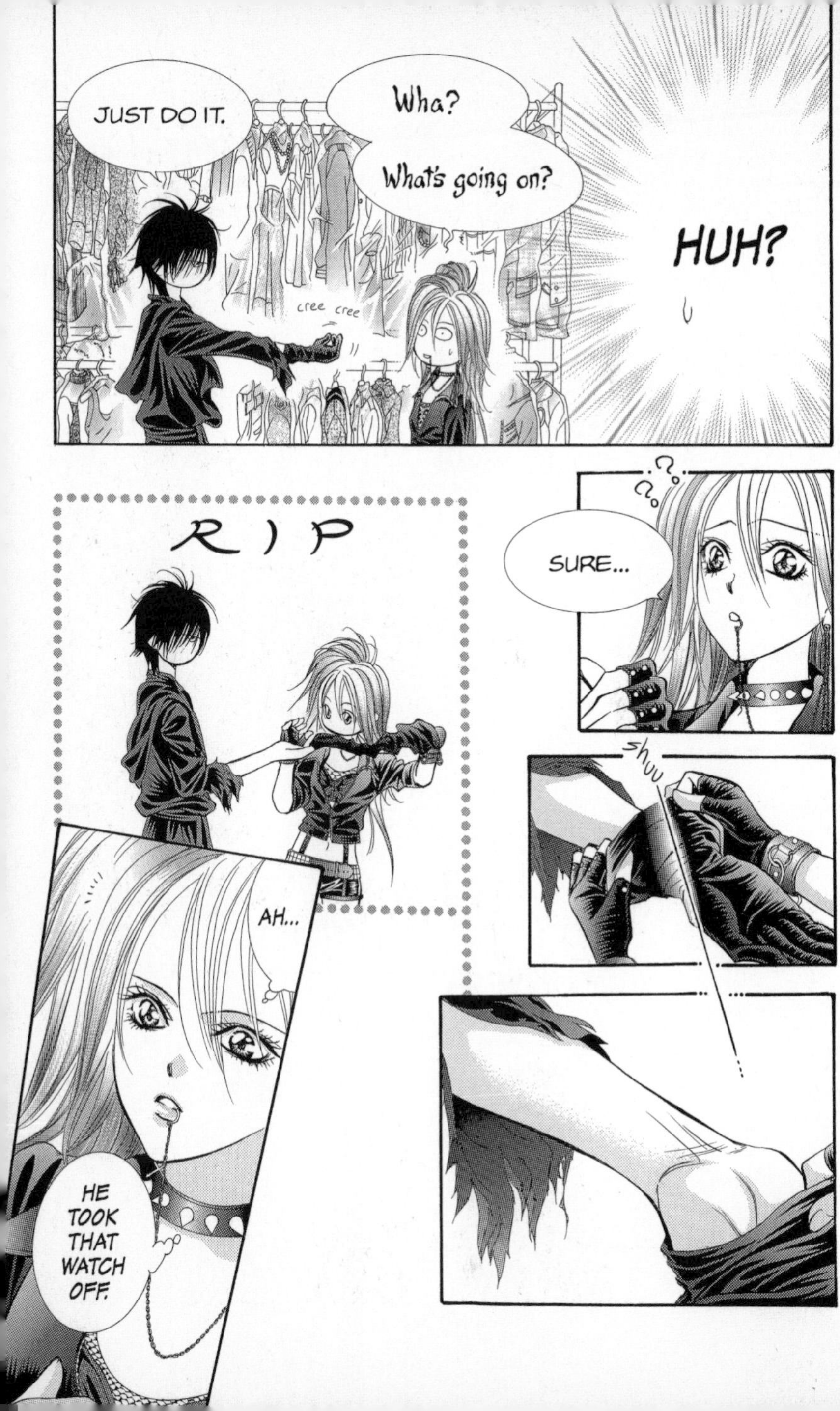
HUH?
Wha?
What's going on?
JUST DO IT.
cree cree
SURE...
shuu
RIP
AH...
HE TOOK THAT WATCH OFF.

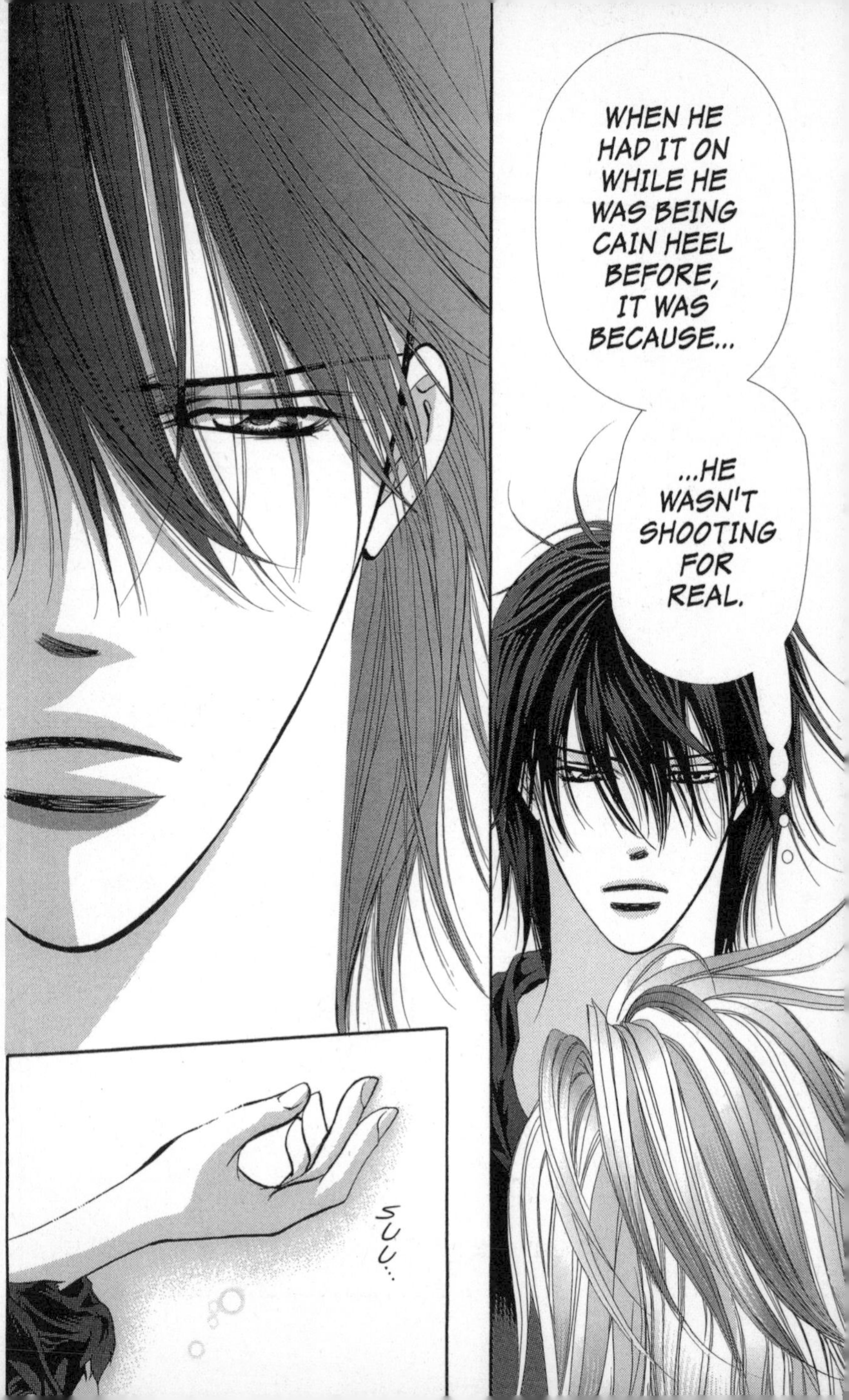
WHEN HE HAD IT ON WHILE HE WAS BEING CAIN HEEL BEFORE, IT WAS BECAUSE...
...HE WASN'T SHOOTING FOR REAL.
SUU...

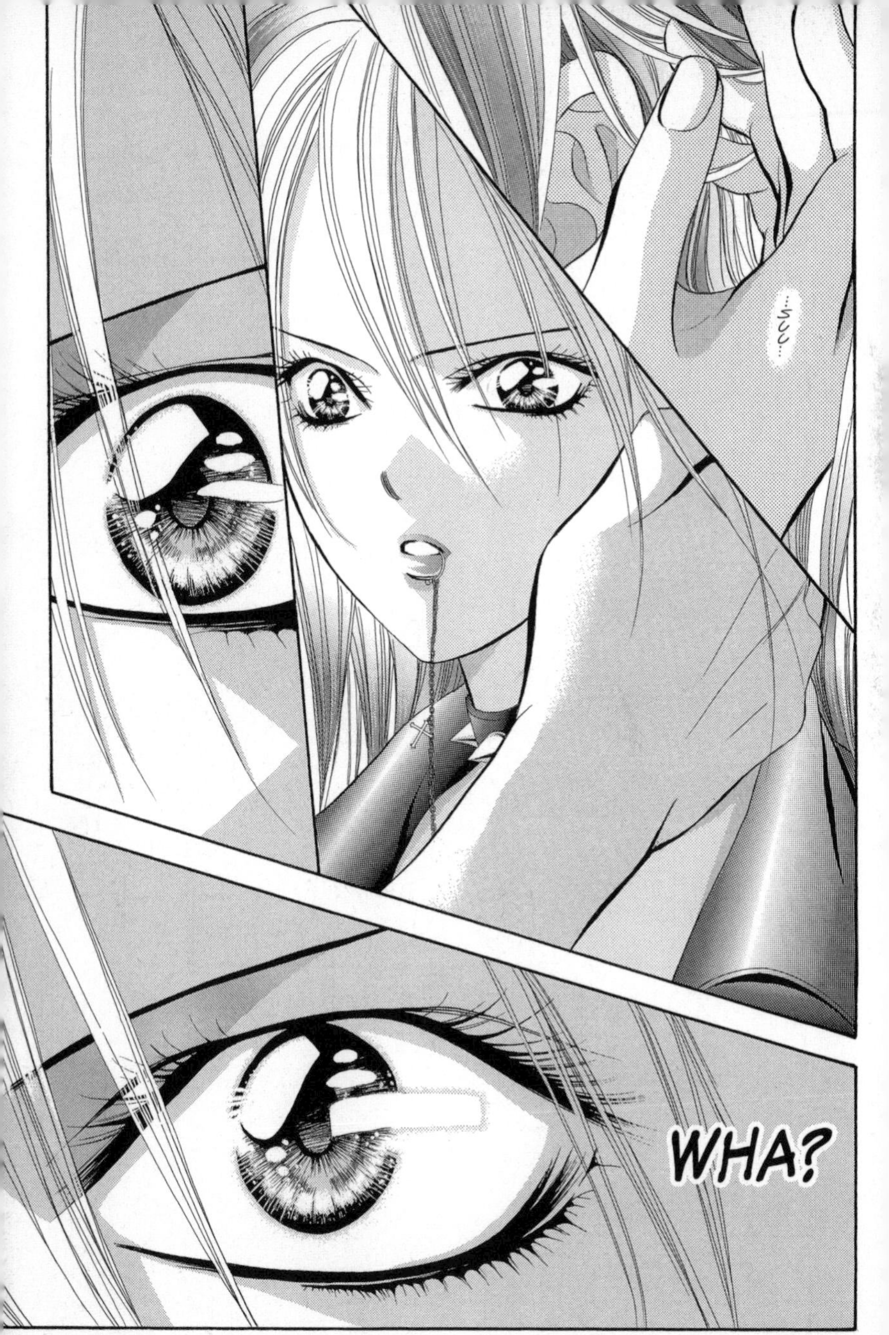
...SUU...
WHA?

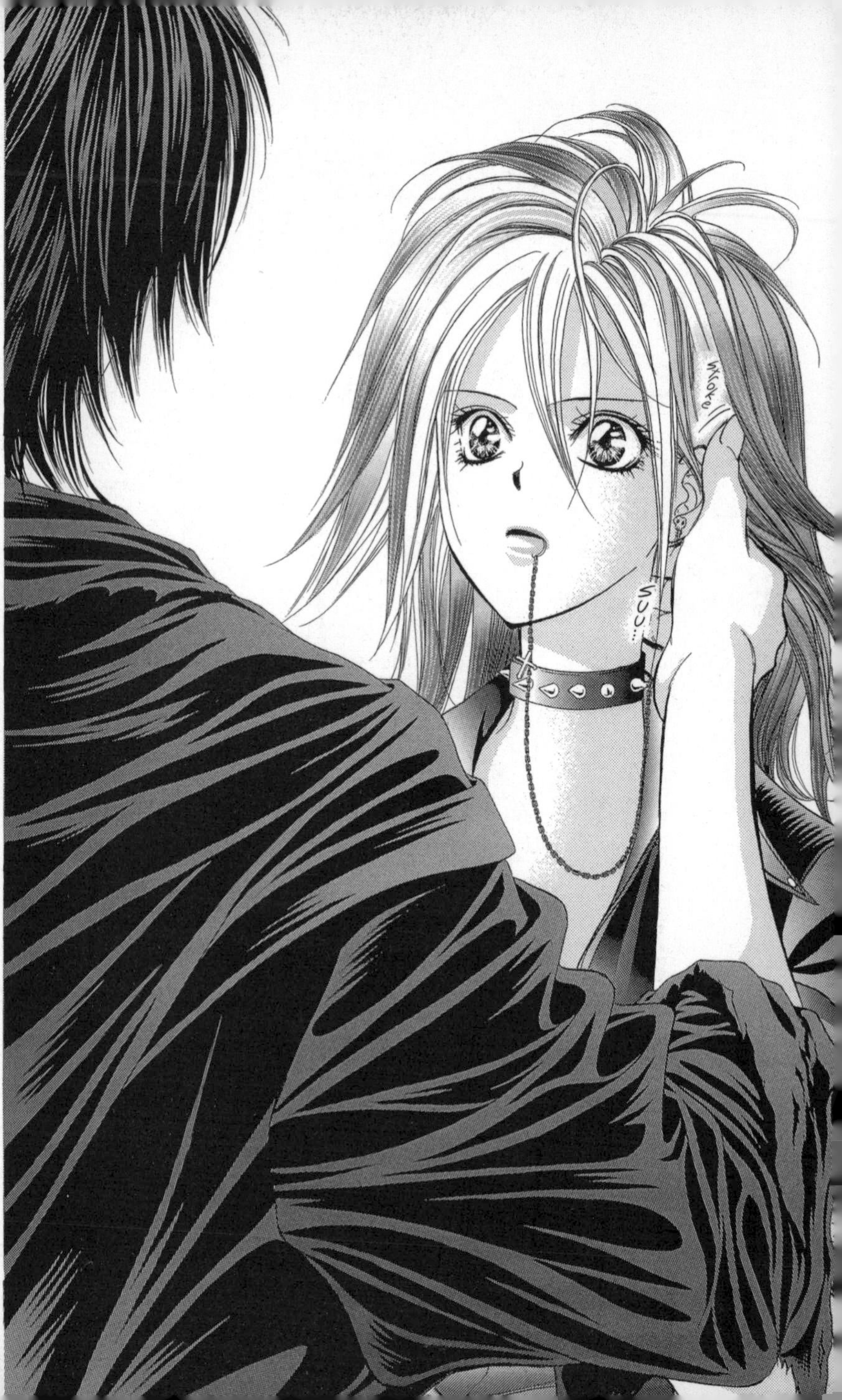
SUU...

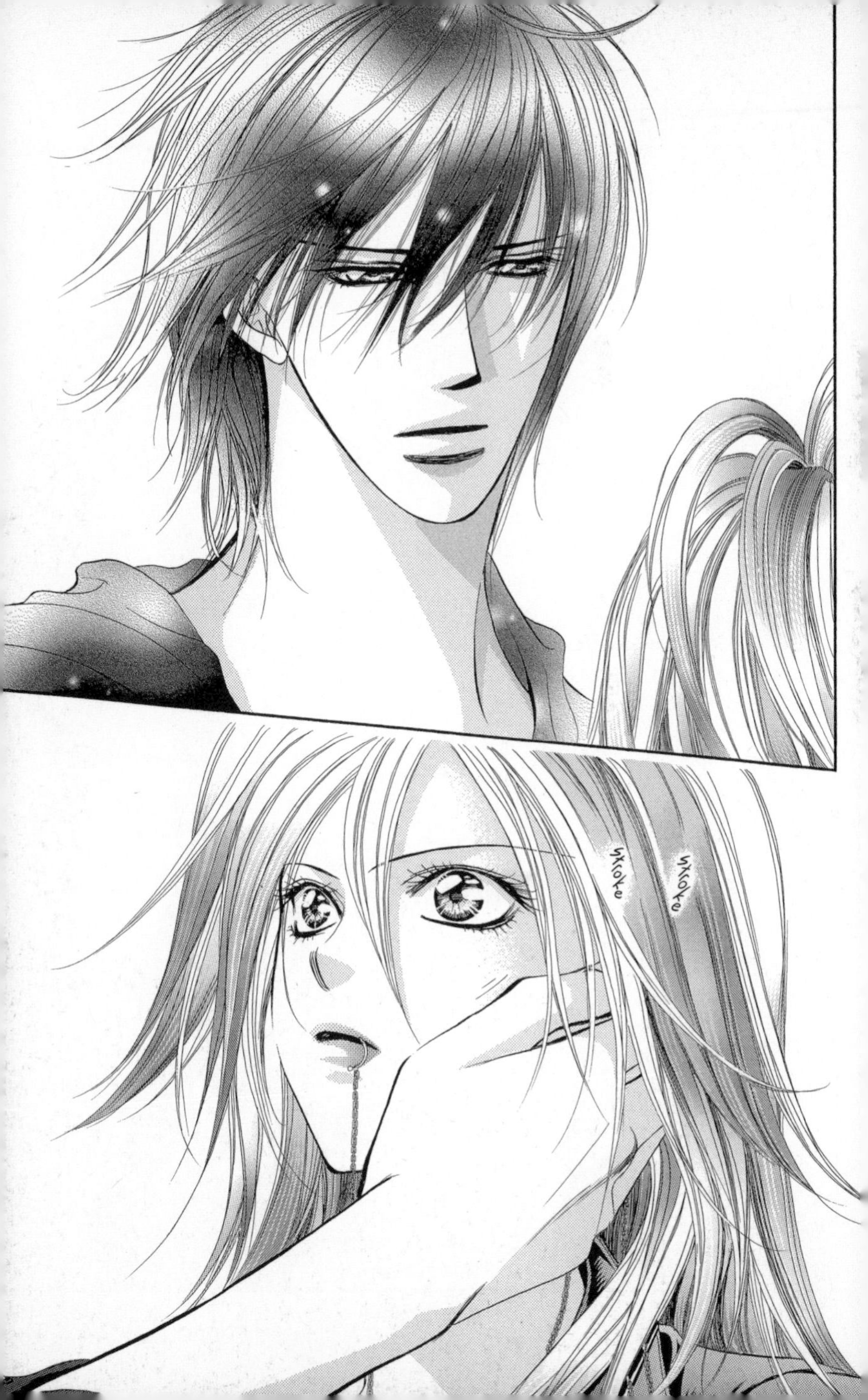
stroke
stroke

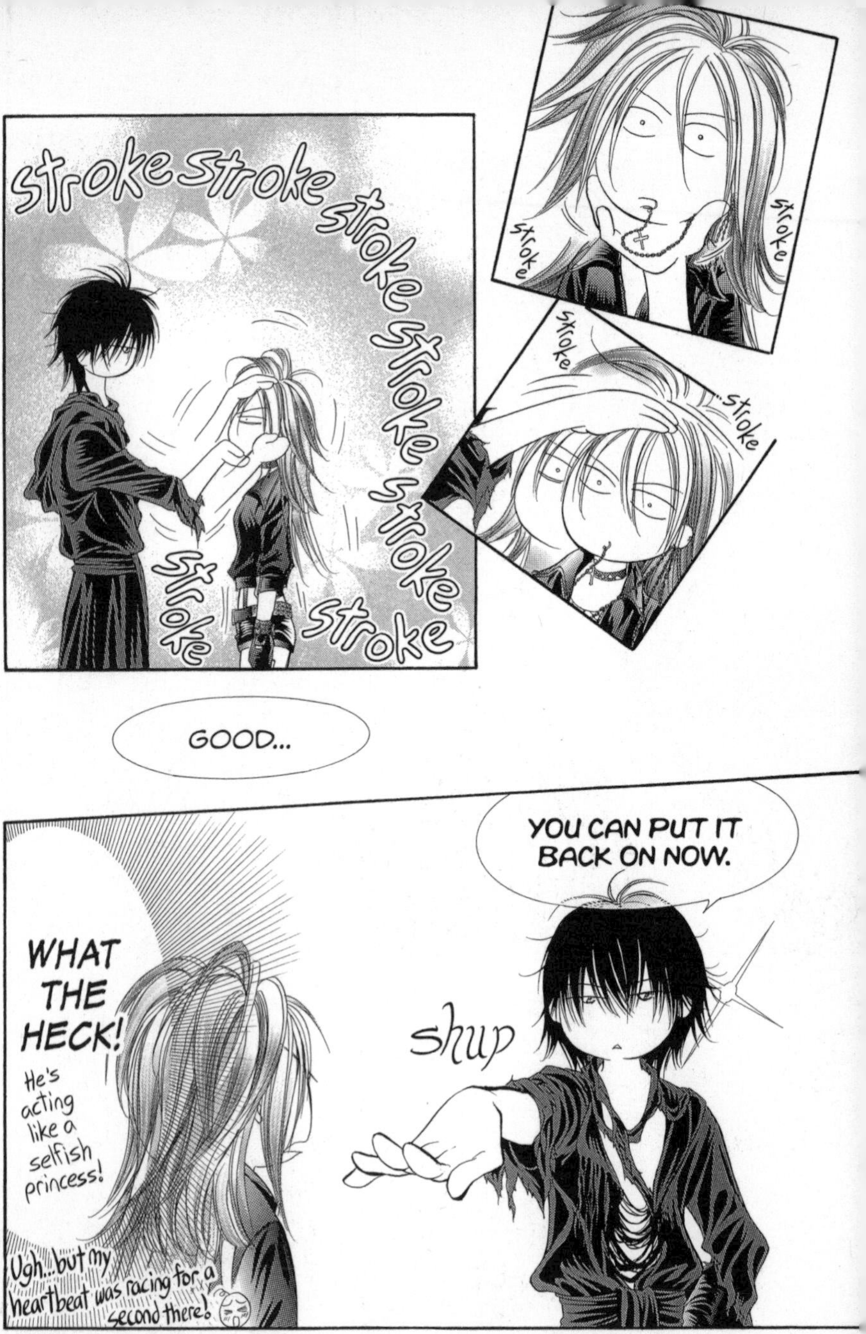

stroke
stroke
stroke
...stroke
stroke stroke stroke stroke stroke stroke stroke stroke
GOOD...
YOU CAN PUT IT BACK ON NOW.
shup
WHAT THE HECK!
He's acting like a selfish princess!
Ugh...but my heartbeat was racing for a second there!

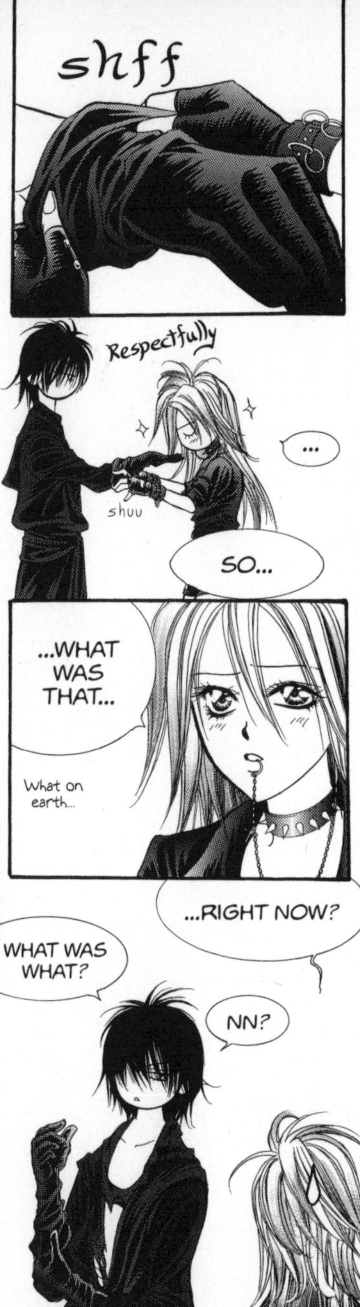
shff
Respectfully
...
shuu
SO...
...WHAT WAS THAT...
What on earth...
...RIGHT NOW?
WHAT WAS WHAT?
NN?
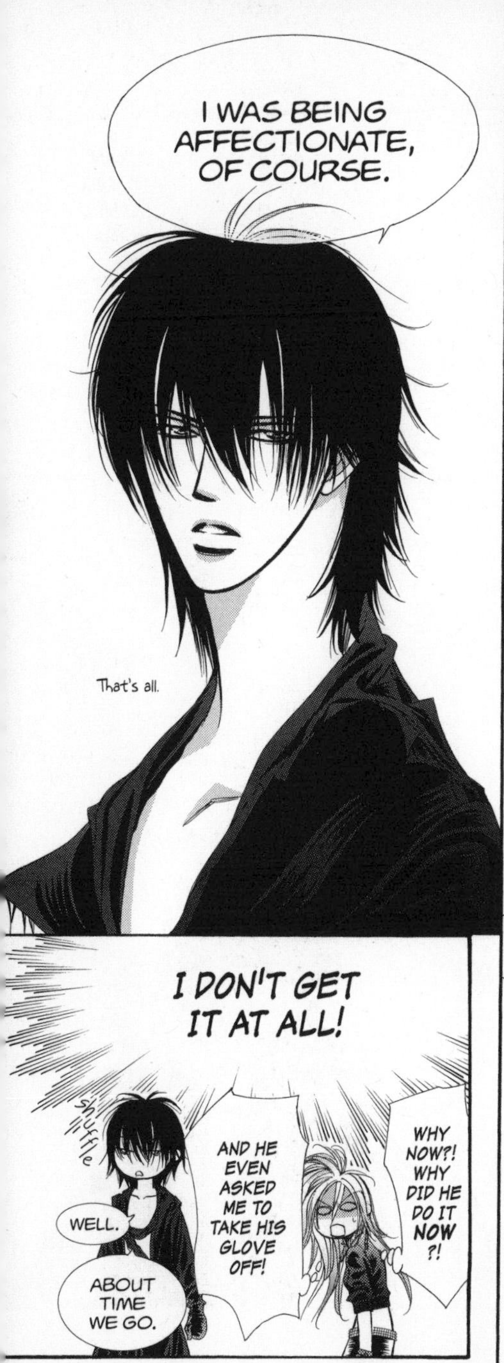
I WAS BEING AFFECTIONATE, OF COURSE.
That's all.
I DON'T GET IT AT ALL!
WHY NOW?! WHY DID HE DO IT NOW?!
AND HE EVEN ASKED ME TO TAKE HIS GLOVE OFF!
shuffle
WELL.
ABOUT TIME WE GO.

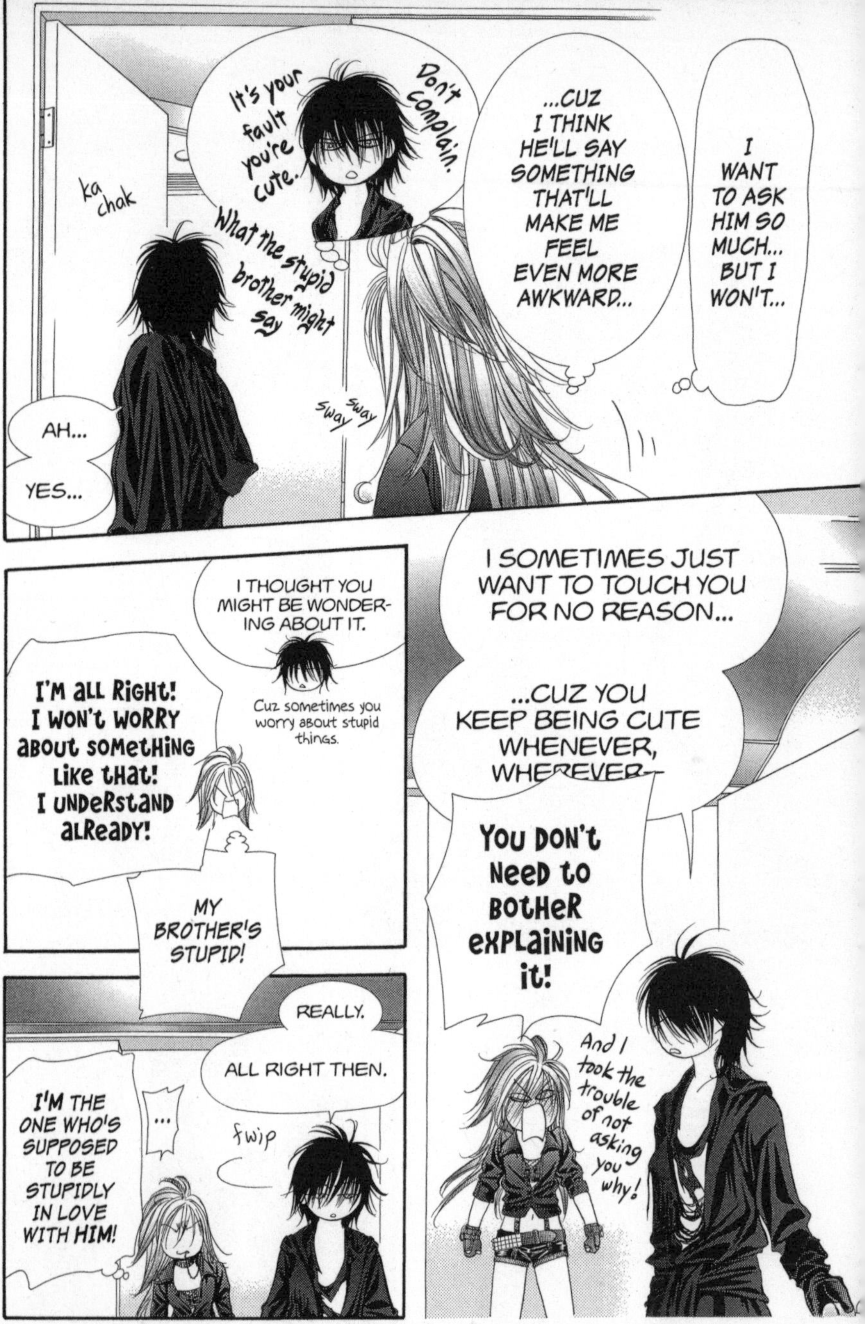
I WANT TO ASK HIM SO MUCH... BUT I WON'T...
...CUZ I THINK HE'LL SAY SOMETHING THAT'LL MAKE ME FEEL EVEN MORE AWKWARD...
Don't complain.
It's your fault you're cute.
What the stupid brother might say
sway sway
ka chak
AH...
YES...
I SOMETIMES JUST WANT TO TOUCH YOU FOR NO REASON...
...CUZ YOU KEEP BEING CUTE WHENEVER, WHEREVER—
YOU DON'T NEED TO BOTHER EXPLAINING IT!
And I took the trouble of not asking you why!
I THOUGHT YOU MIGHT BE WONDERING ABOUT IT.
Cuz sometimes you worry about stupid things.
I'M ALL RIGHT! I WON'T WORRY ABOUT SOMETHING LIKE THAT! I UNDERSTAND ALREADY!
MY BROTHER'S STUPID!
REALLY.
ALL RIGHT THEN.
fwip
...
I'M THE ONE WHO'S SUPPOSED TO BE STUPIDLY IN LOVE WITH HIM!

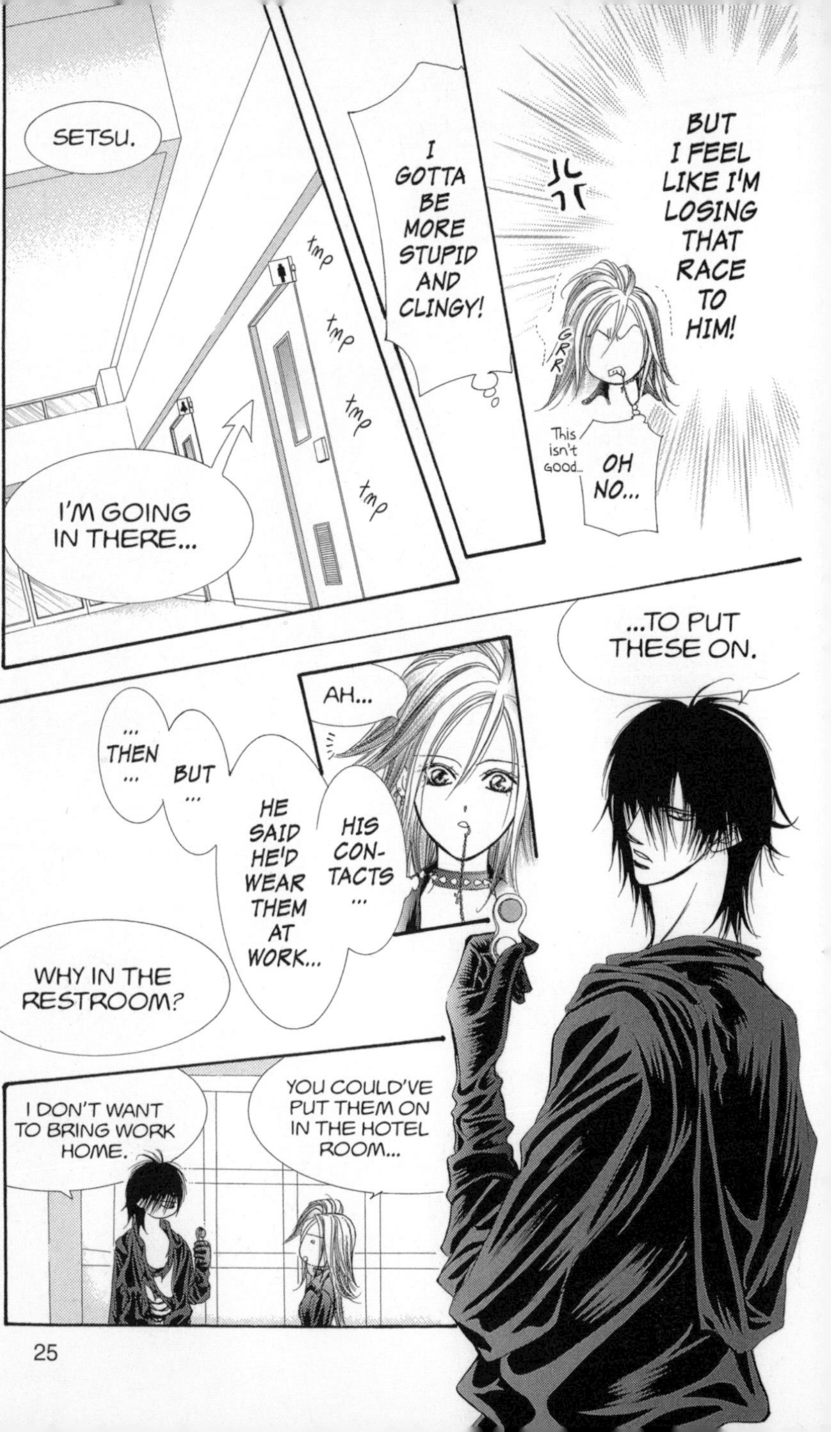
BUT I FEEL LIKE I'M LOSING THAT RACE TO HIM!
GRR
OH NO...
This isn't good...
I GOTTA BE MORE STUPID AND CLINGY!
SETSU.
tmp tmp tmp tmp
I'M GOING IN THERE...
...TO PUT THESE ON.
AH...
HIS CONTACTS...
HE SAID HE'D WEAR THEM AT WORK...
BUT...
...THEN...
WHY IN THE RESTROOM?
YOU COULD'VE PUT THEM ON IN THE HOTEL ROOM...
I DON'T WANT TO BRING WORK HOME.

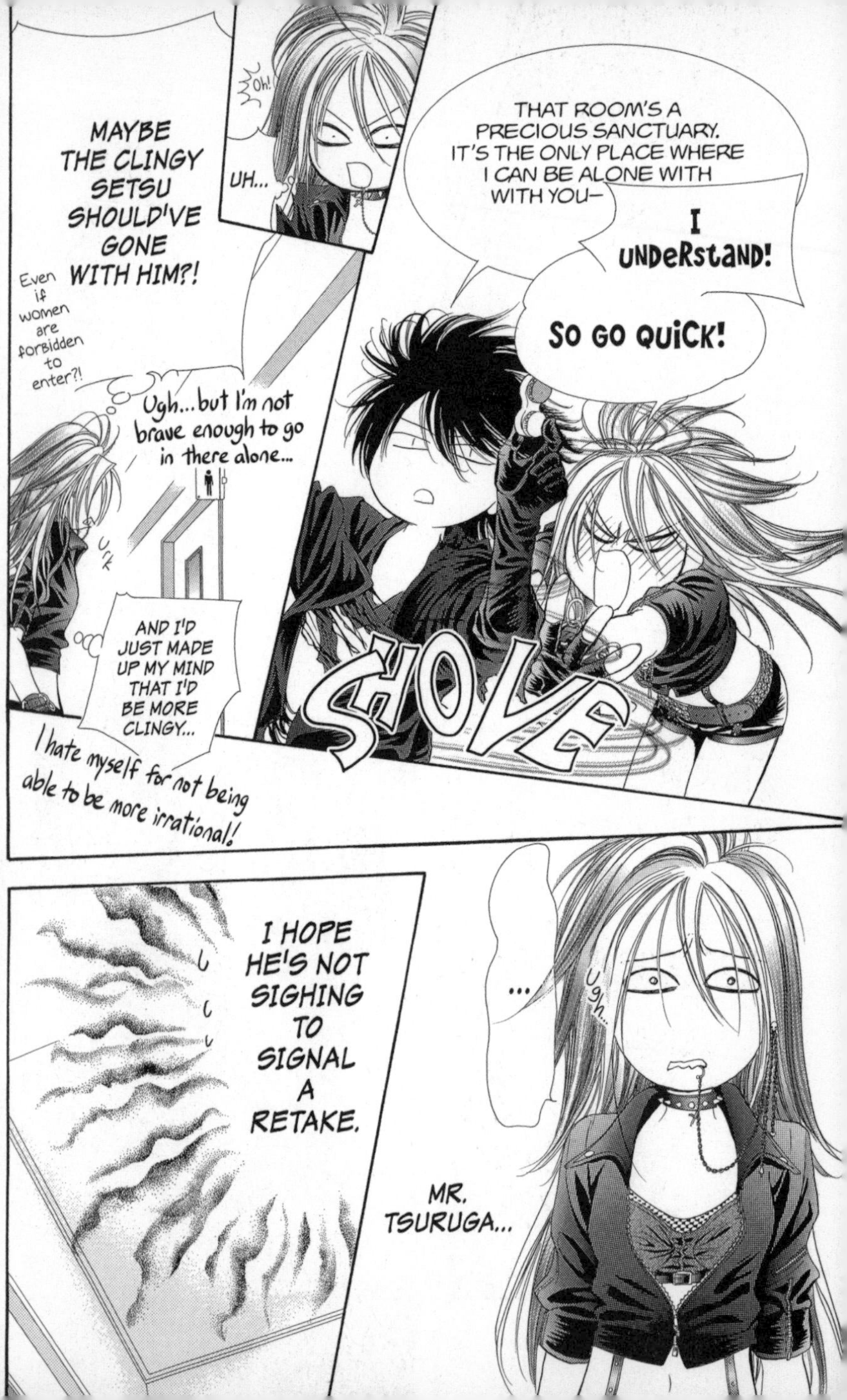
THAT ROOM'S A PRECIOUS SANCTUARY. IT'S THE ONLY PLACE WHERE I CAN BE ALONE WITH WITH YOU–
I UNDERSTAND!
SO GO QUICK!
SHOVE
Oh!
UH...
MAYBE THE CLINGY SETSU SHOULD'VE GONE WITH HIM?!
Even if women are forbidden to enter?!
Ugh... but I'm not brave enough to go in there alone...
Urk
AND I'D JUST MADE UP MY MIND THAT I'D BE MORE CLINGY...
I hate myself for not being able to be more irrational!
...
Ugh...
MR. TSURUGA...
I HOPE HE'S NOT SIGHING TO SIGNAL A RETAKE.

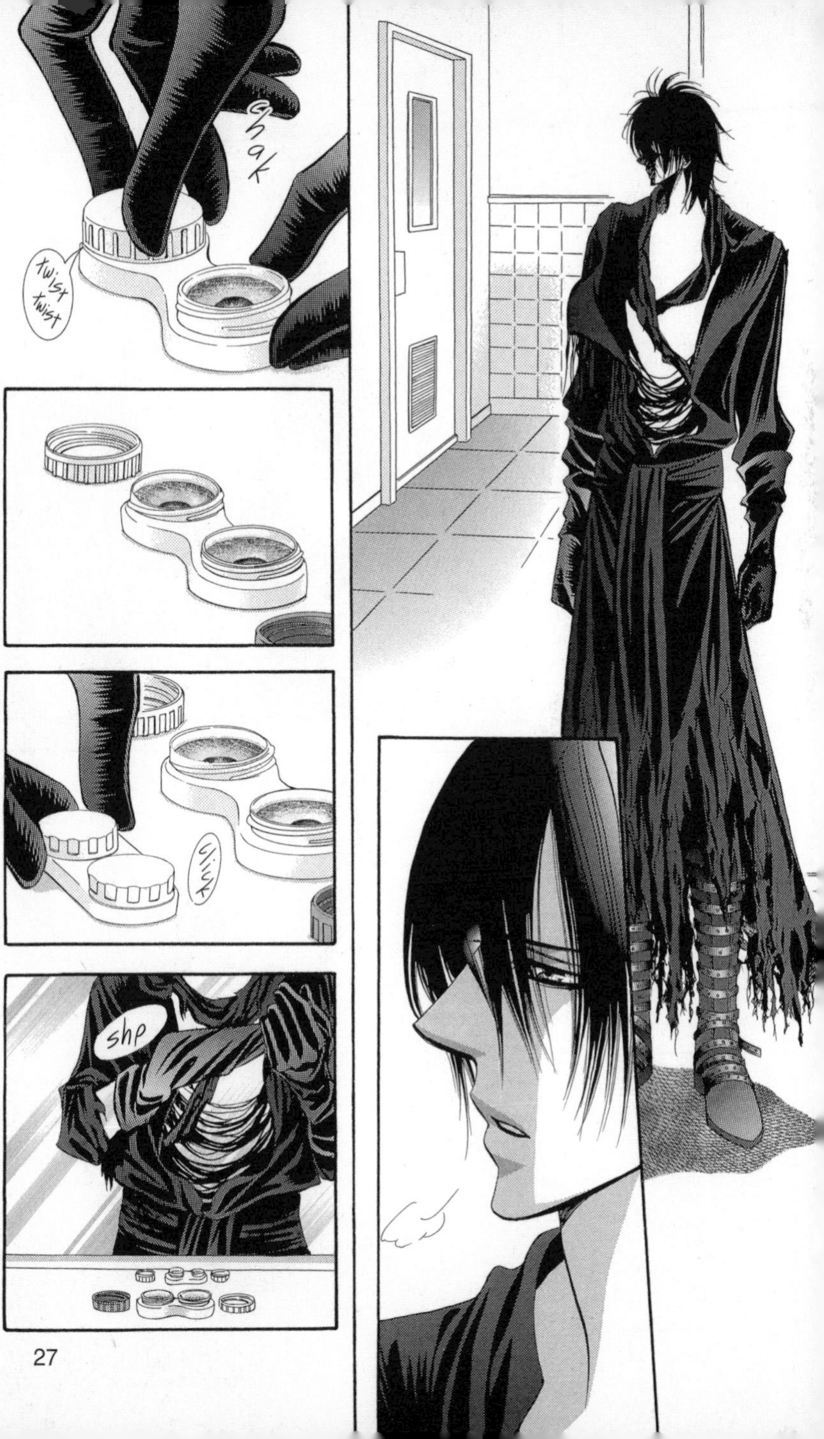
chak
twist twist
click
shp

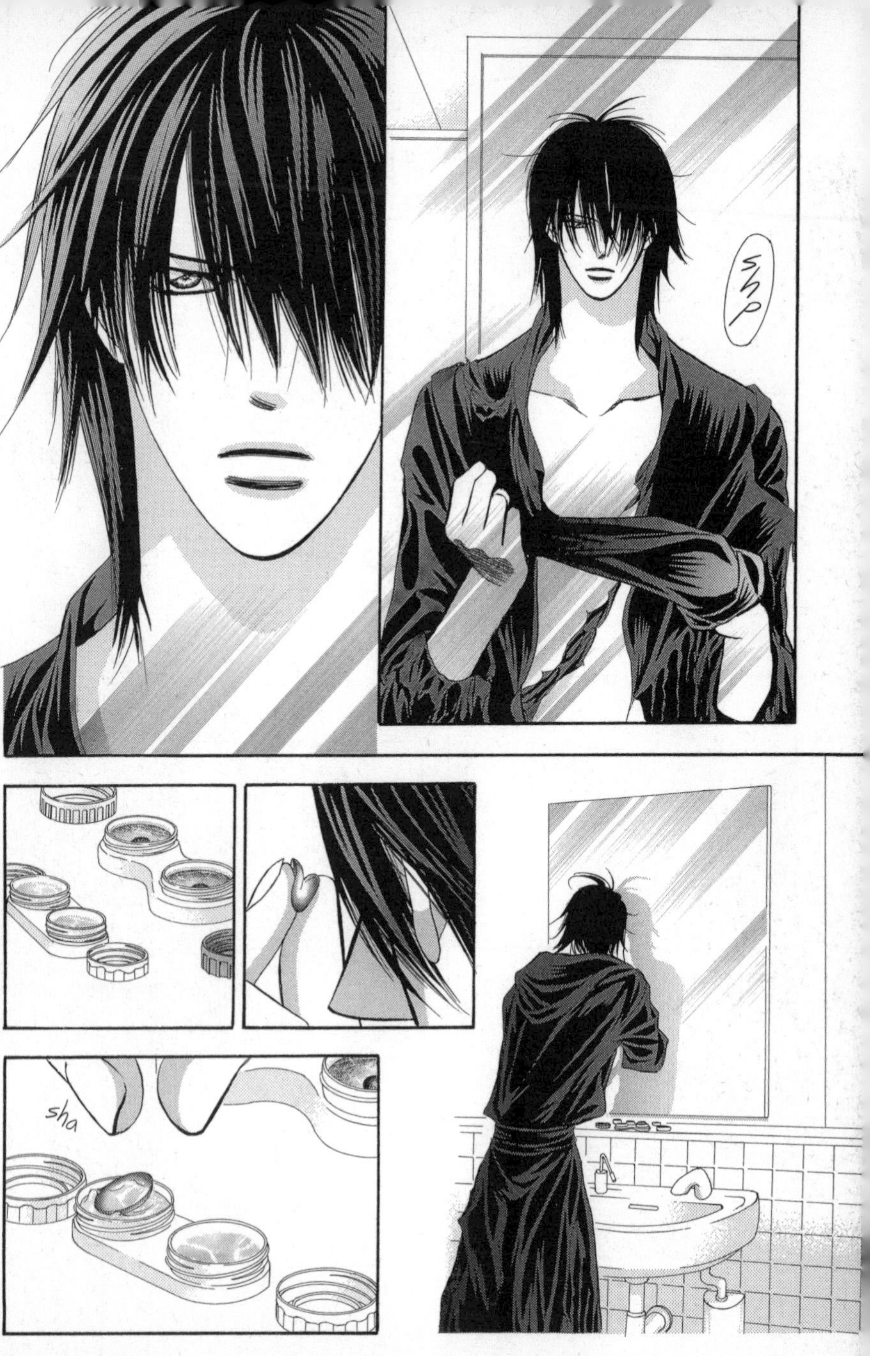
shp
sha

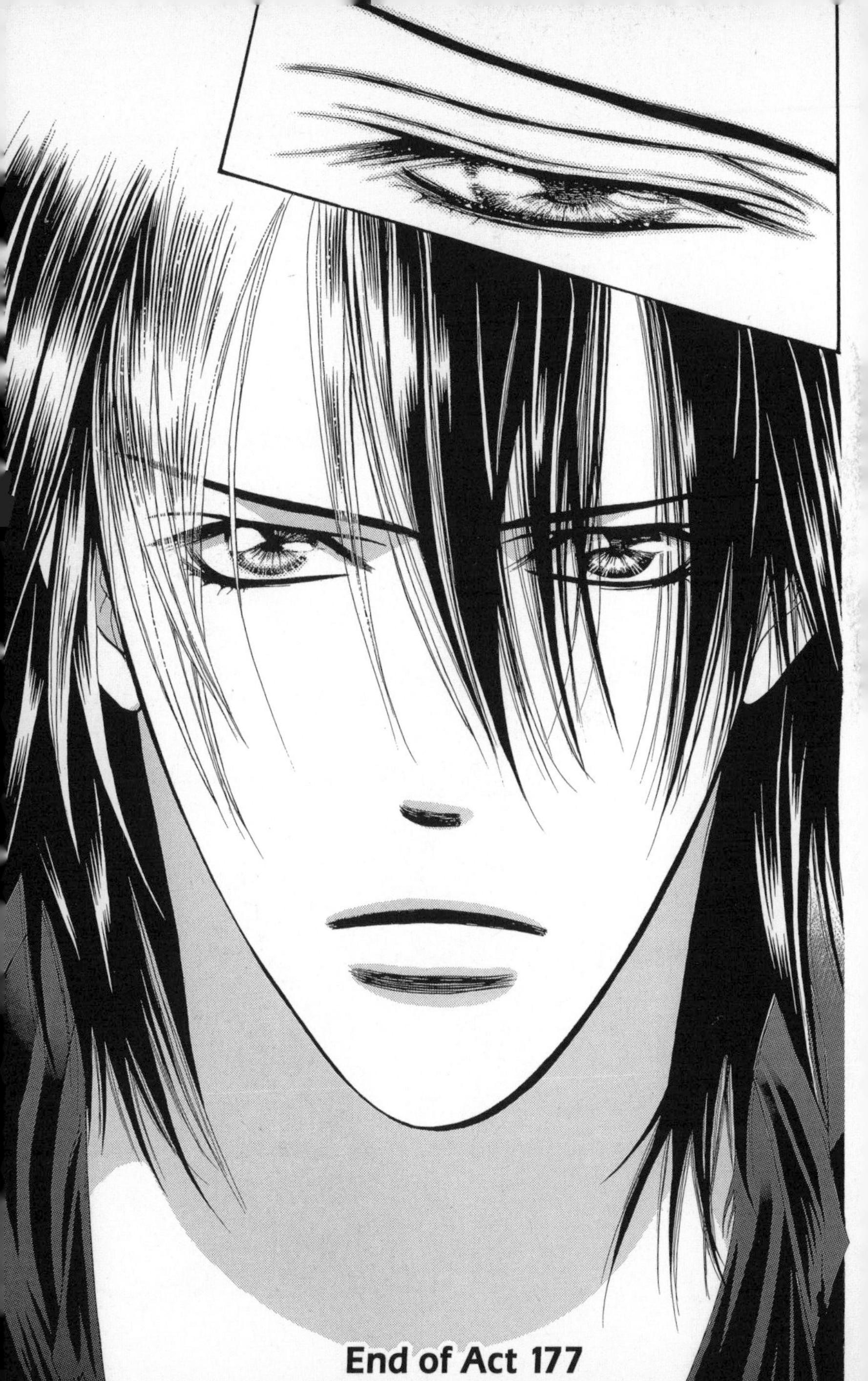

End of Act 177

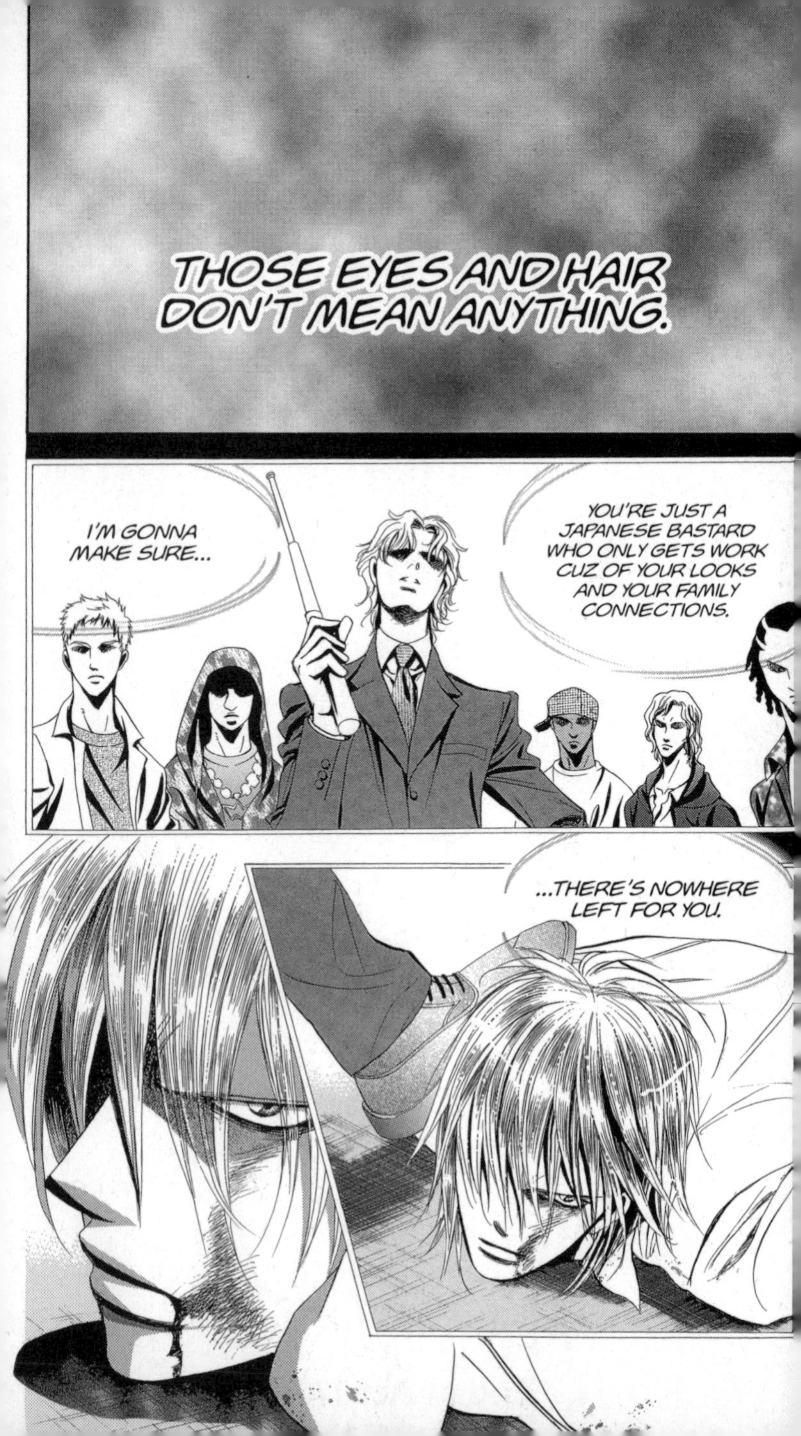
THOSE EYES AND HAIR DON'T MEAN ANYTHING.
YOU'RE JUST A JAPANESE BASTARD WHO ONLY GETS WORK CUZ OF YOUR LOOKS AND YOUR FAMILY CONNECTIONS.
I'M GONNA MAKE SURE...
...THERE'S NOWHERE LEFT FOR YOU.

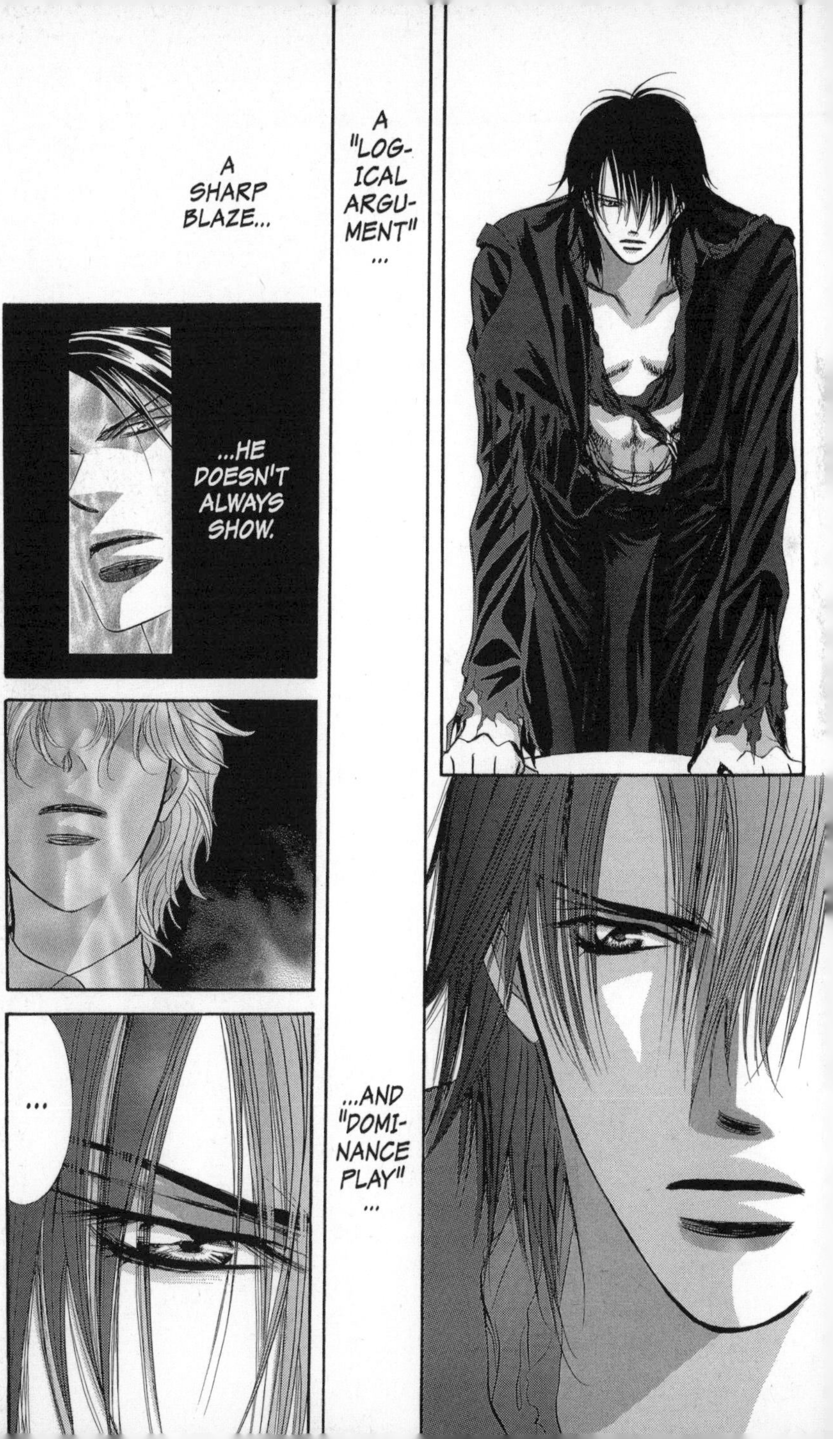
A "LOG-ICAL ARGU-MENT" ...
A SHARP BLAZE...
...AND "DOMI-NANCE PLAY" ...
...HE DOESN'T ALWAYS SHOW.
...

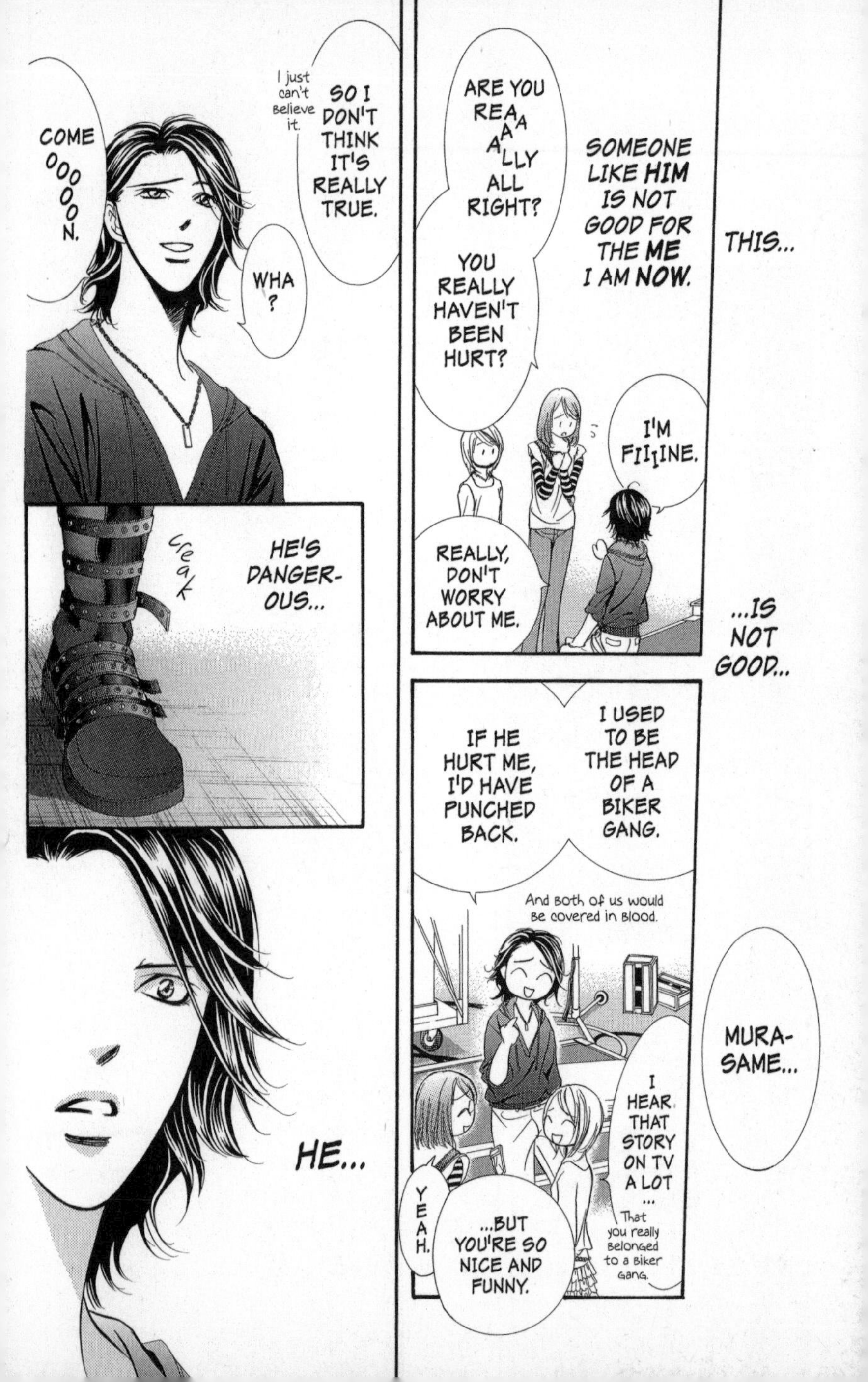
THIS...
SOMEONE LIKE HIM IS NOT GOOD FOR THE ME I AM NOW.
ARE YOU REAAAALLY ALL RIGHT?
YOU REALLY HAVEN'T BEEN HURT?
I'M FIIIINE.
REALLY, DON'T WORRY ABOUT ME.
...IS NOT GOOD...
I USED TO BE THE HEAD OF A BIKER GANG.
IF HE HURT ME, I'D HAVE PUNCHED BACK.
And both of us would be covered in blood.
MURA-SAME...
I HEAR THAT STORY ON TV A LOT...
That you really belonged to a biker gang.
...BUT YOU'RE SO NICE AND FUNNY.
YEAH.
SO I DON'T THINK IT'S REALLY TRUE.
I just can't believe it.
WHA?
COMEOOOOOON.
creak
HE'S DANGEROUS...
HE...

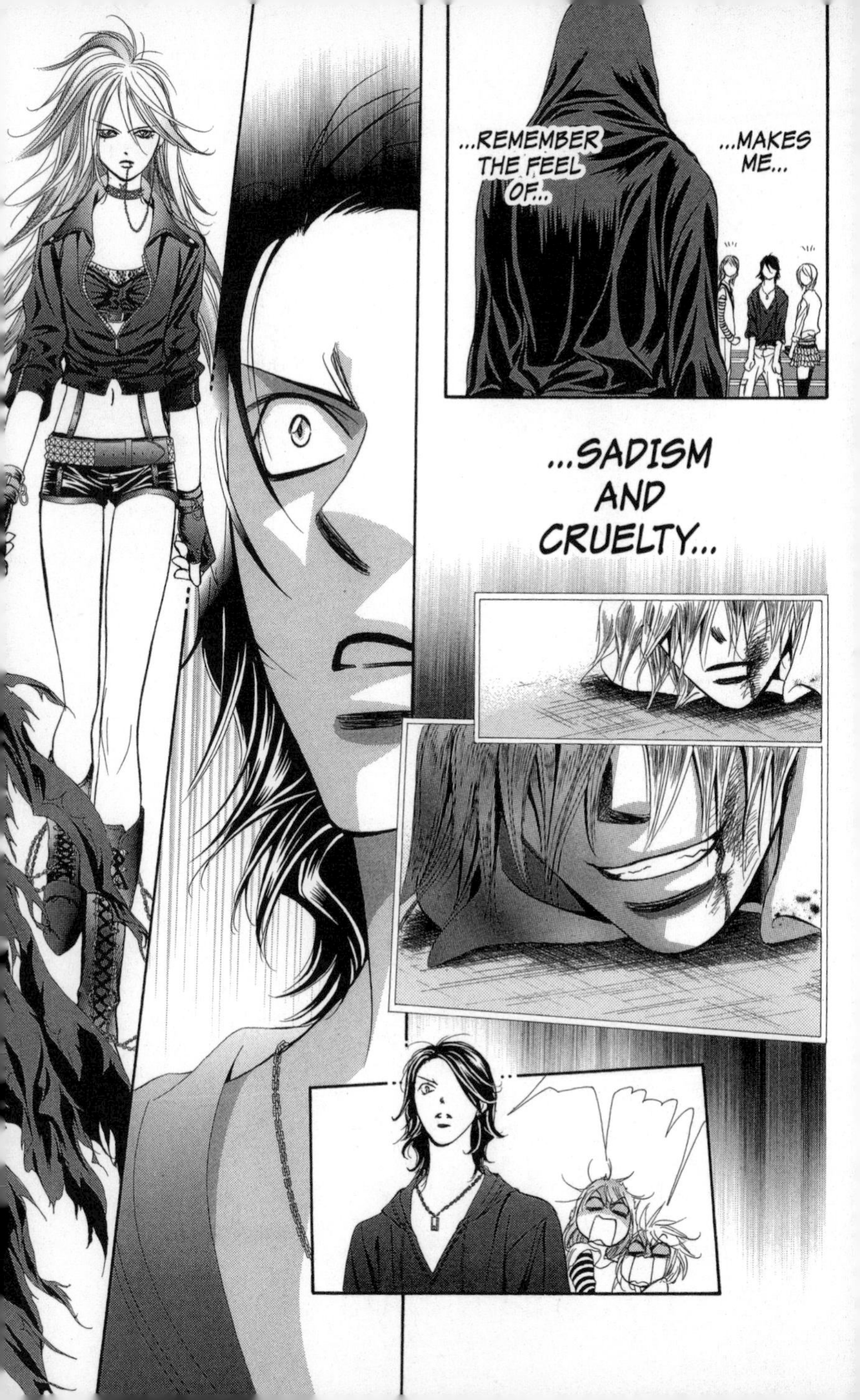
...REMEMBER THE FEEL OF...
...MAKES ME...
...SADISM AND CRUELTY...

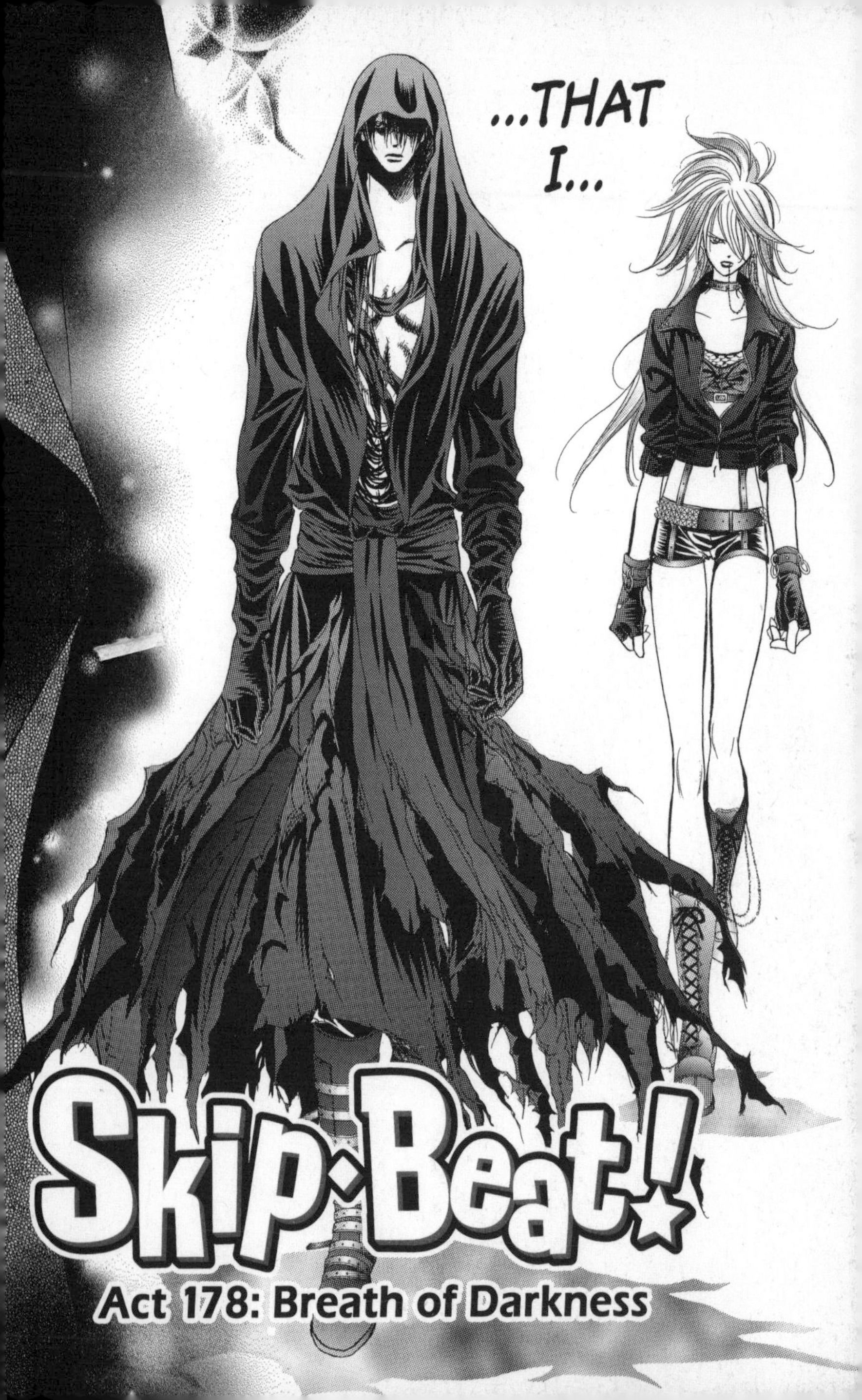
...THAT I...
Skip·Beat!
Act 178: Breath of Darkness

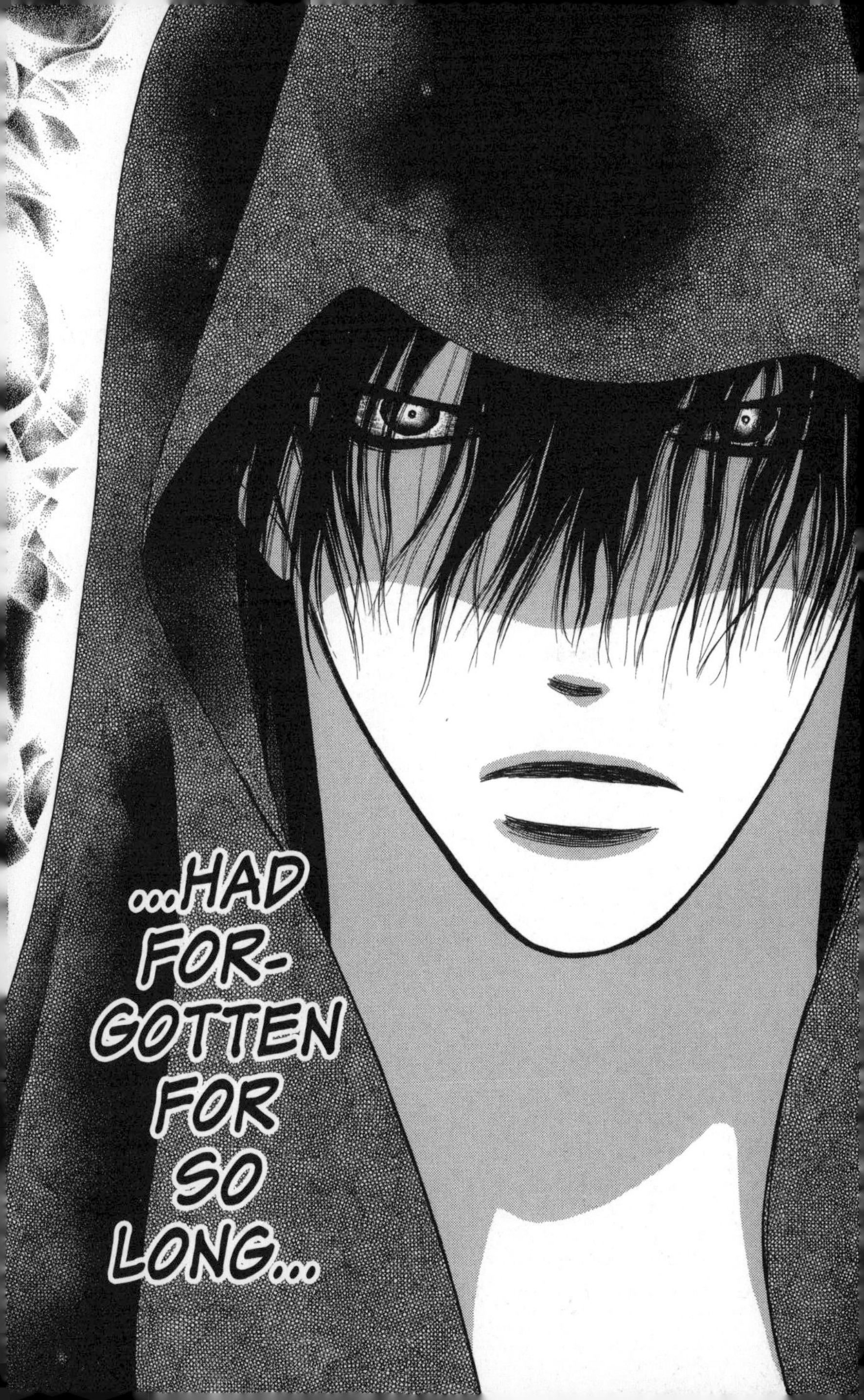
...HAD FOR-GOTTEN FOR SO LONG...

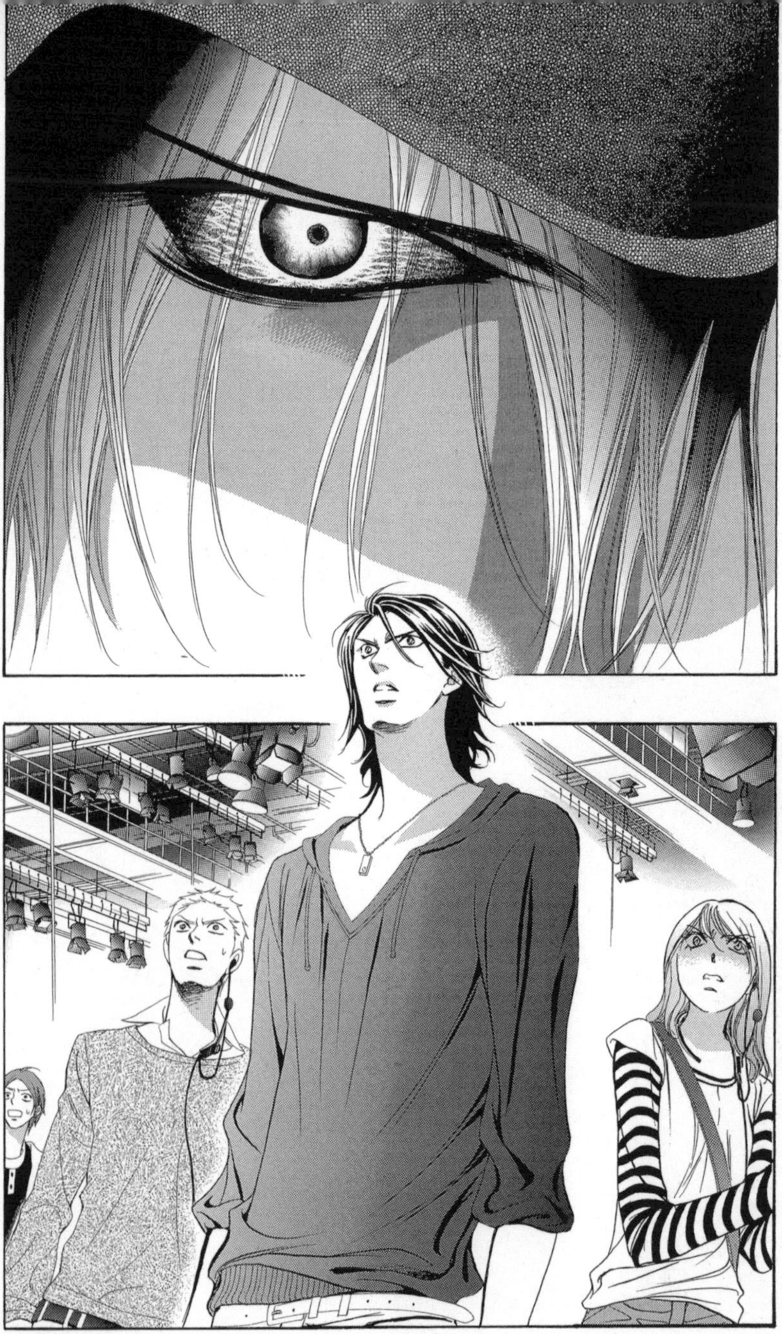

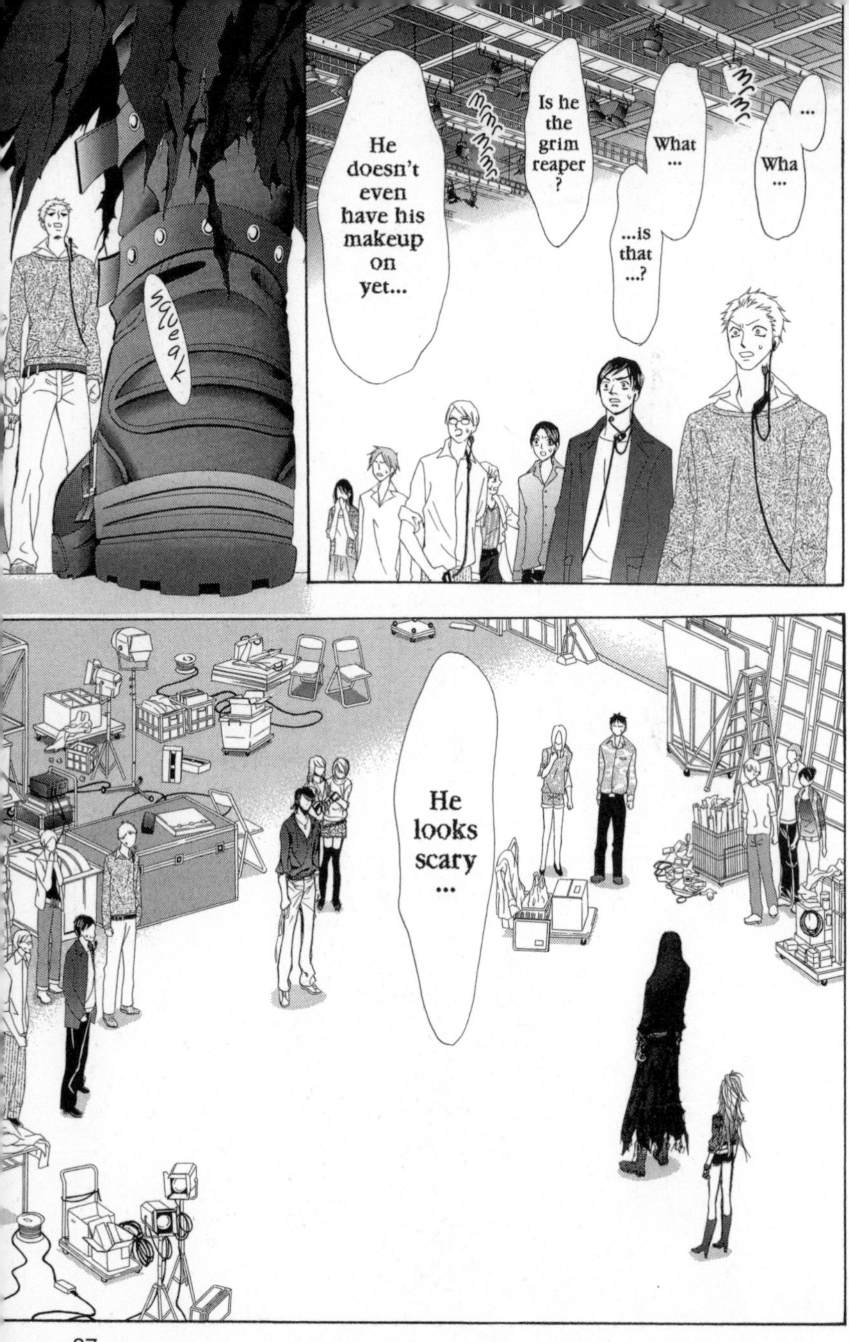
... Wha...
mrmr
What... ...is that...?
Is he the grim reaper?
mrmr
He doesn't even have his makeup on yet...
squeak
He looks scary...

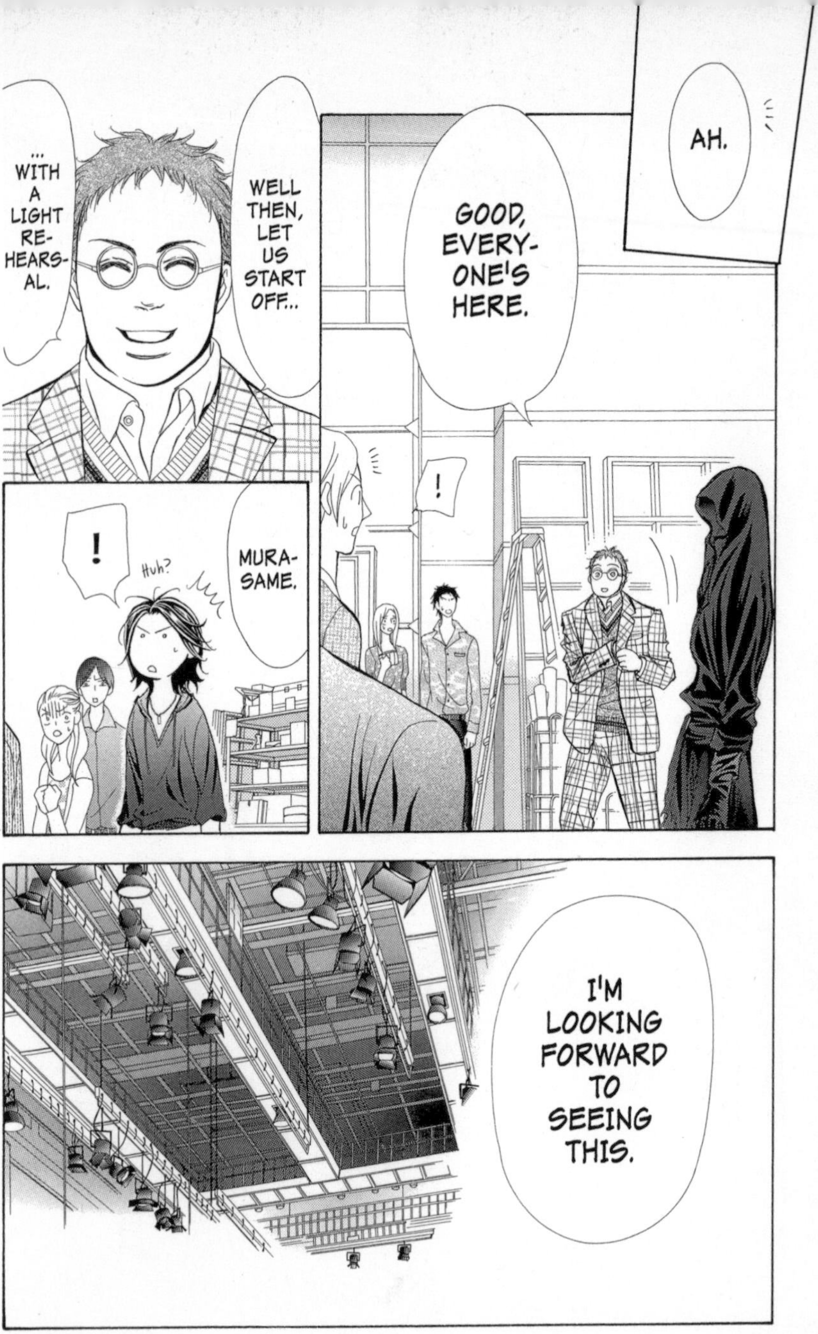
AH.
GOOD, EVERYONE'S HERE.
!
WELL THEN, LET US START OFF...
... WITH A LIGHT REHEARSAL.
MURASAME.
!
Huh?
I'M LOOKING FORWARD TO SEEING THIS.

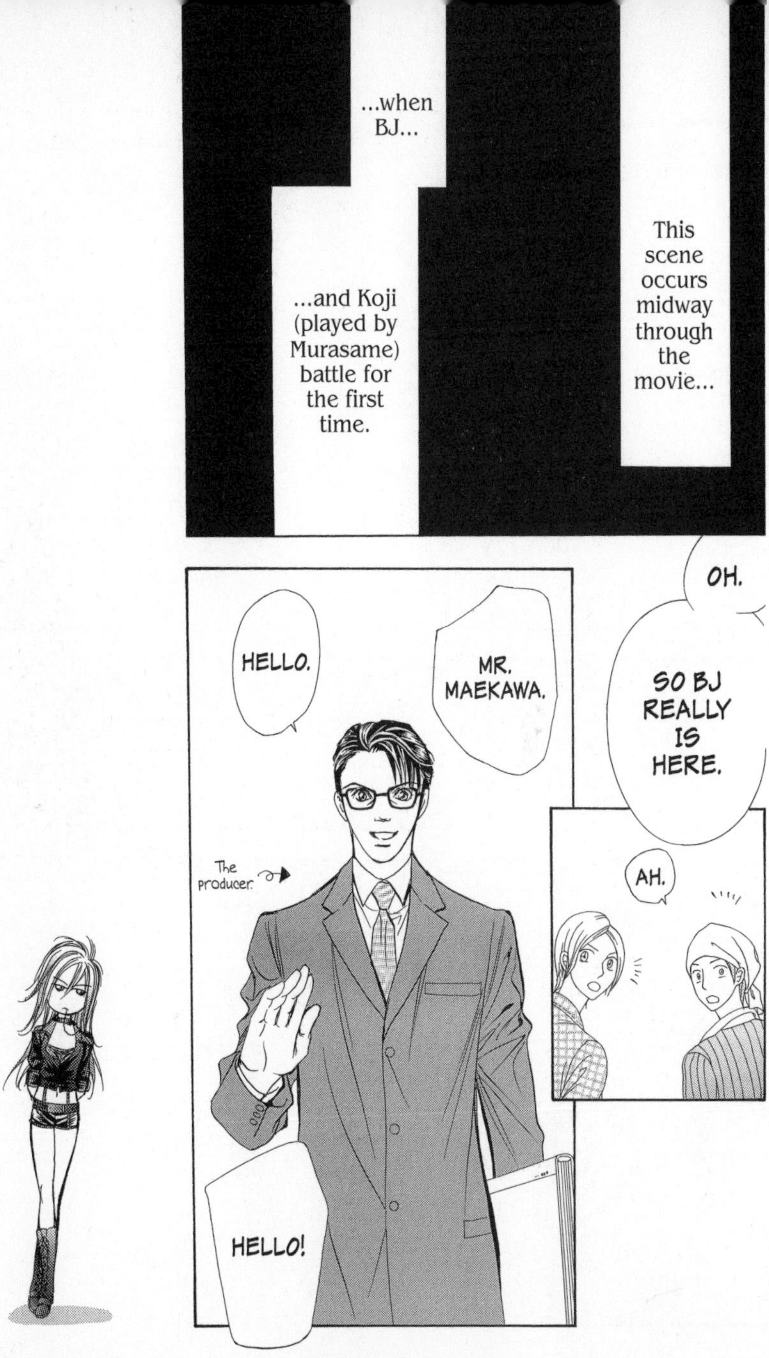
This scene occurs midway through the movie...
...when BJ...
...and Koji (played by Murasame) battle for the first time.
OH.
SO BJ REALLY IS HERE.
AH.
MR. MAEKAWA.
HELLO.
The producer.
HELLO!

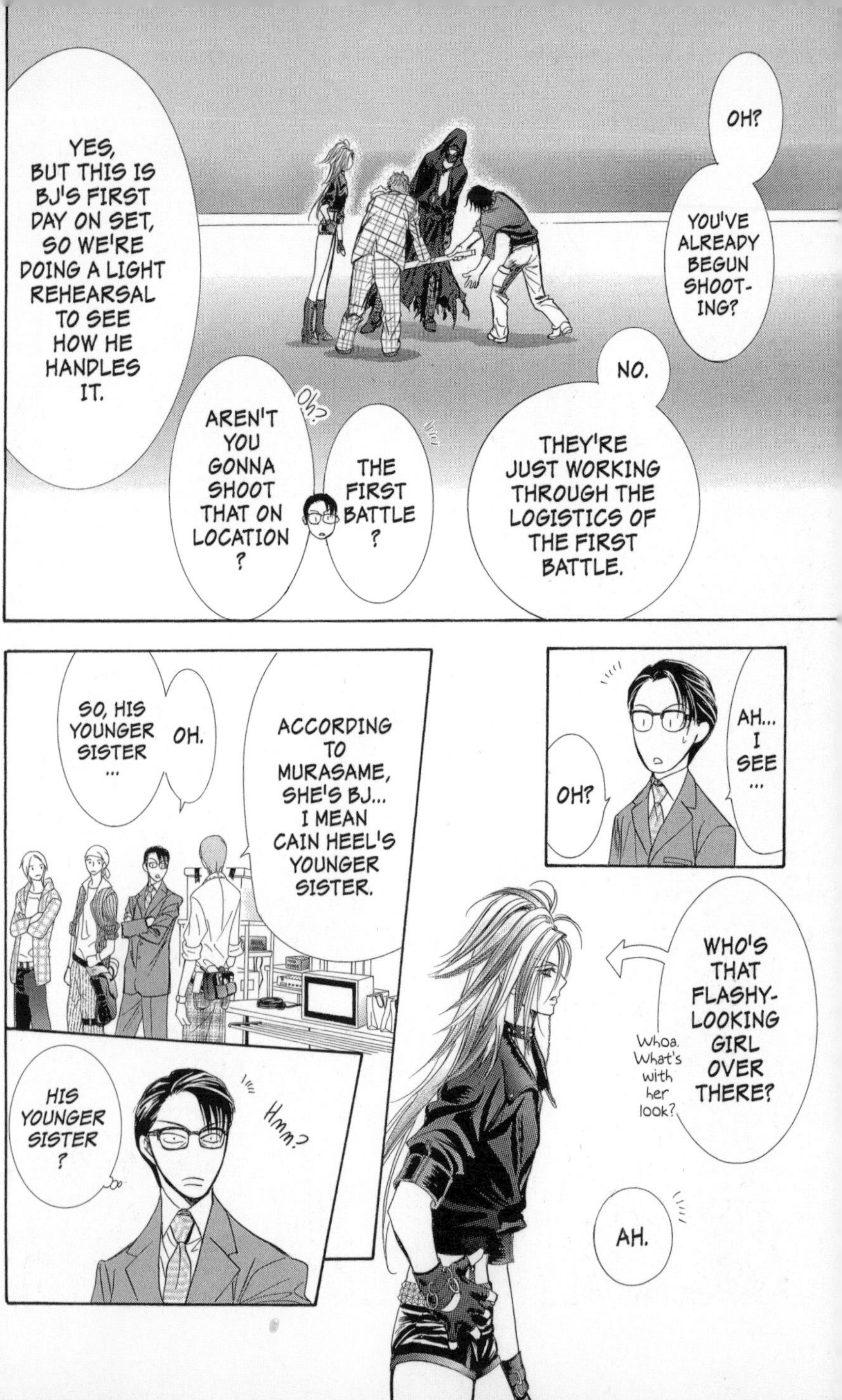
OH?
YOU'VE ALREADY BEGUN SHOOT-ING?
NO.
THEY'RE JUST WORKING THROUGH THE LOGISTICS OF THE FIRST BATTLE.
THE FIRST BATTLE?
Oh?
AREN'T YOU GONNA SHOOT THAT ON LOCATION?
YES, BUT THIS IS BJ'S FIRST DAY ON SET, SO WE'RE DOING A LIGHT REHEARSAL TO SEE HOW HE HANDLES IT.
AH... I SEE...
OH?
ACCORDING TO MURASAME, SHE'S BJ... I MEAN CAIN HEEL'S YOUNGER SISTER.
OH.
SO, HIS YOUNGER SISTER...
WHO'S THAT FLASHY-LOOKING GIRL OVER THERE?
Whoa. What's with her look?
AH.
Hmm?
HIS YOUNGER SISTER?

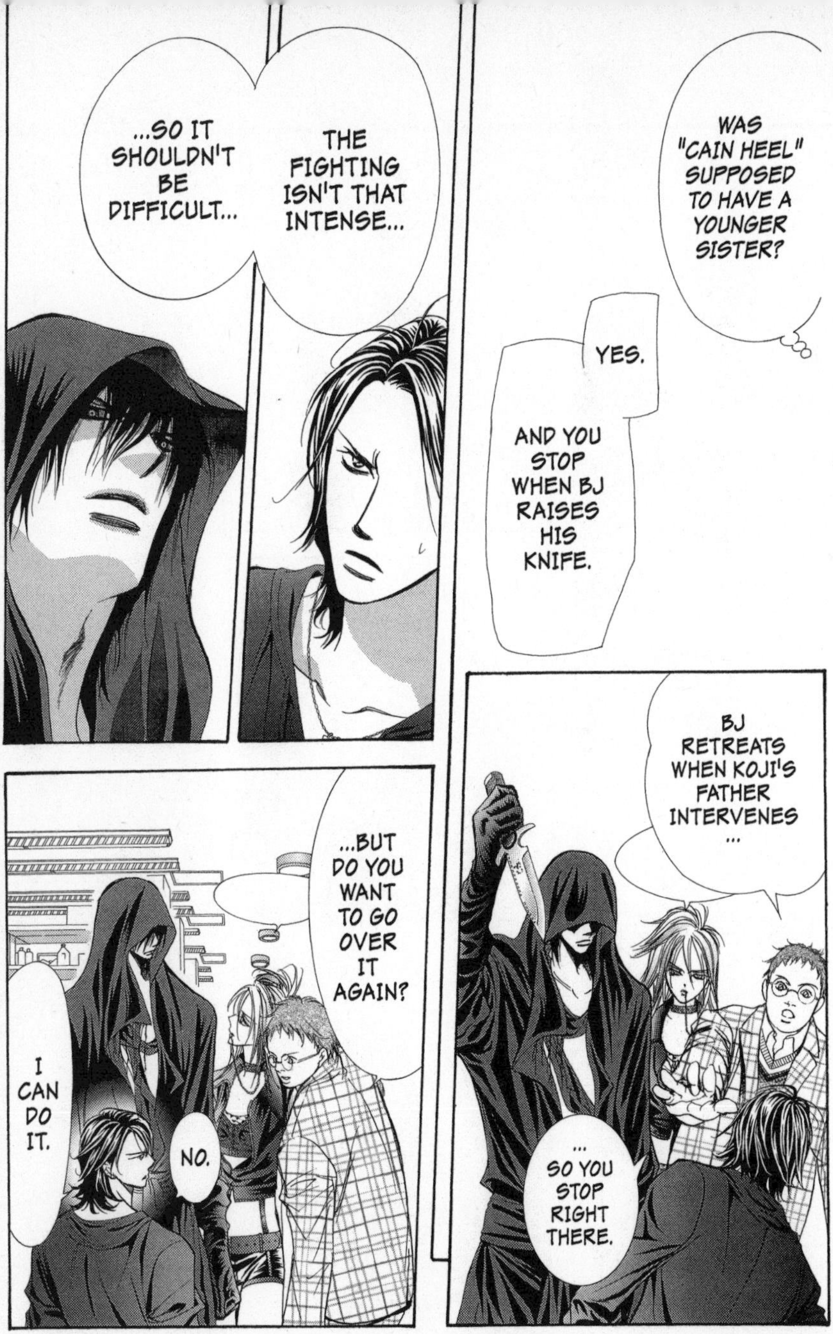
WAS "CAIN HEEL" SUPPOSED TO HAVE A YOUNGER SISTER?
YES.
AND YOU STOP WHEN BJ RAISES HIS KNIFE.
THE FIGHTING ISN'T THAT INTENSE...
...SO IT SHOULDN'T BE DIFFICULT...
BJ RETREATS WHEN KOJI'S FATHER INTERVENES ...
... SO YOU STOP RIGHT THERE.
...BUT DO YOU WANT TO GO OVER IT AGAIN?
I CAN DO IT.
NO.

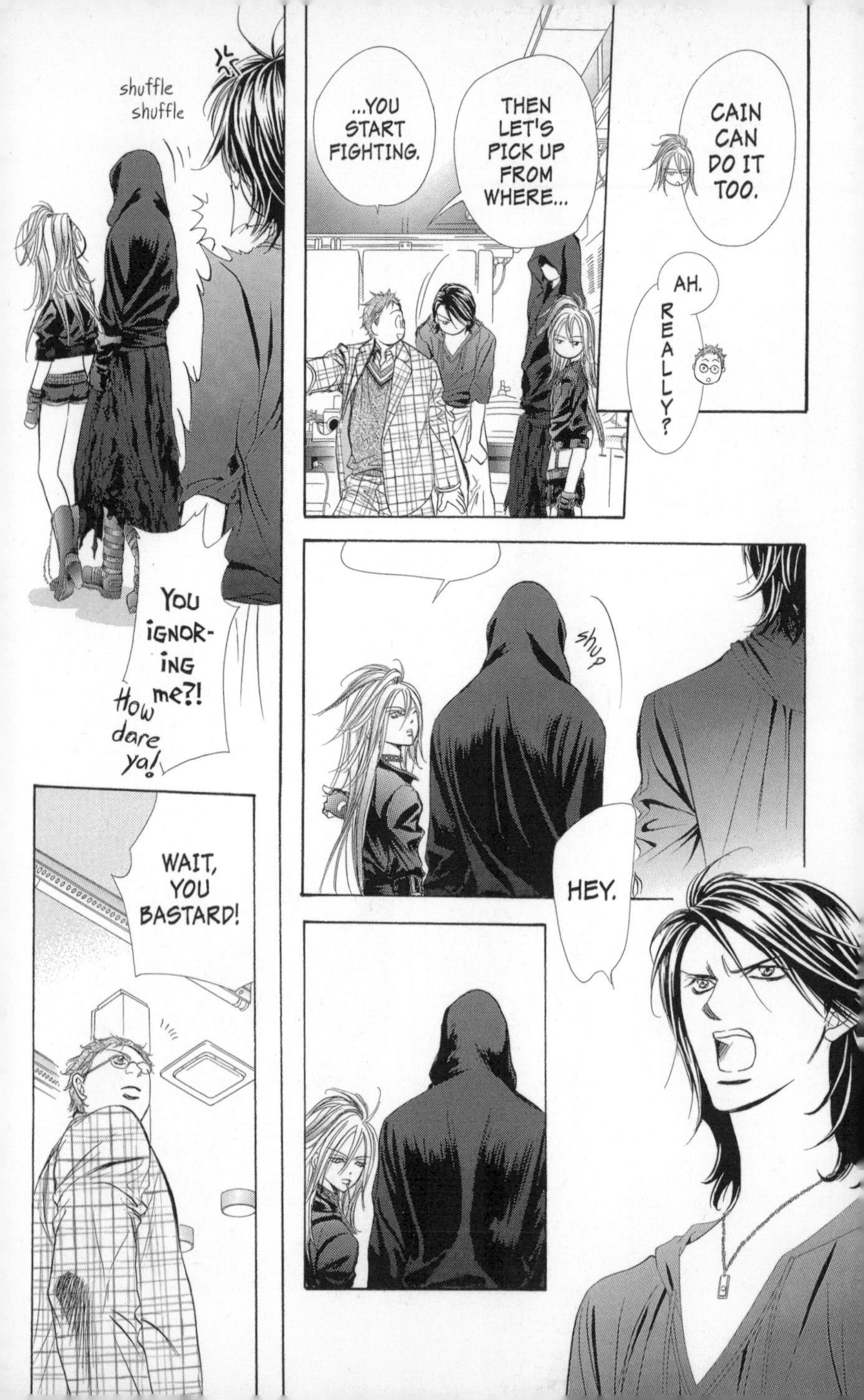
CAIN CAN DO IT TOO.
AH. REALLY?
THEN LET'S PICK UP FROM WHERE...
...YOU START FIGHTING.
shuffle shuffle
YOU iGNOR-ING me?!
How dare ya!
WAIT, YOU BASTARD!
shup
HEY.

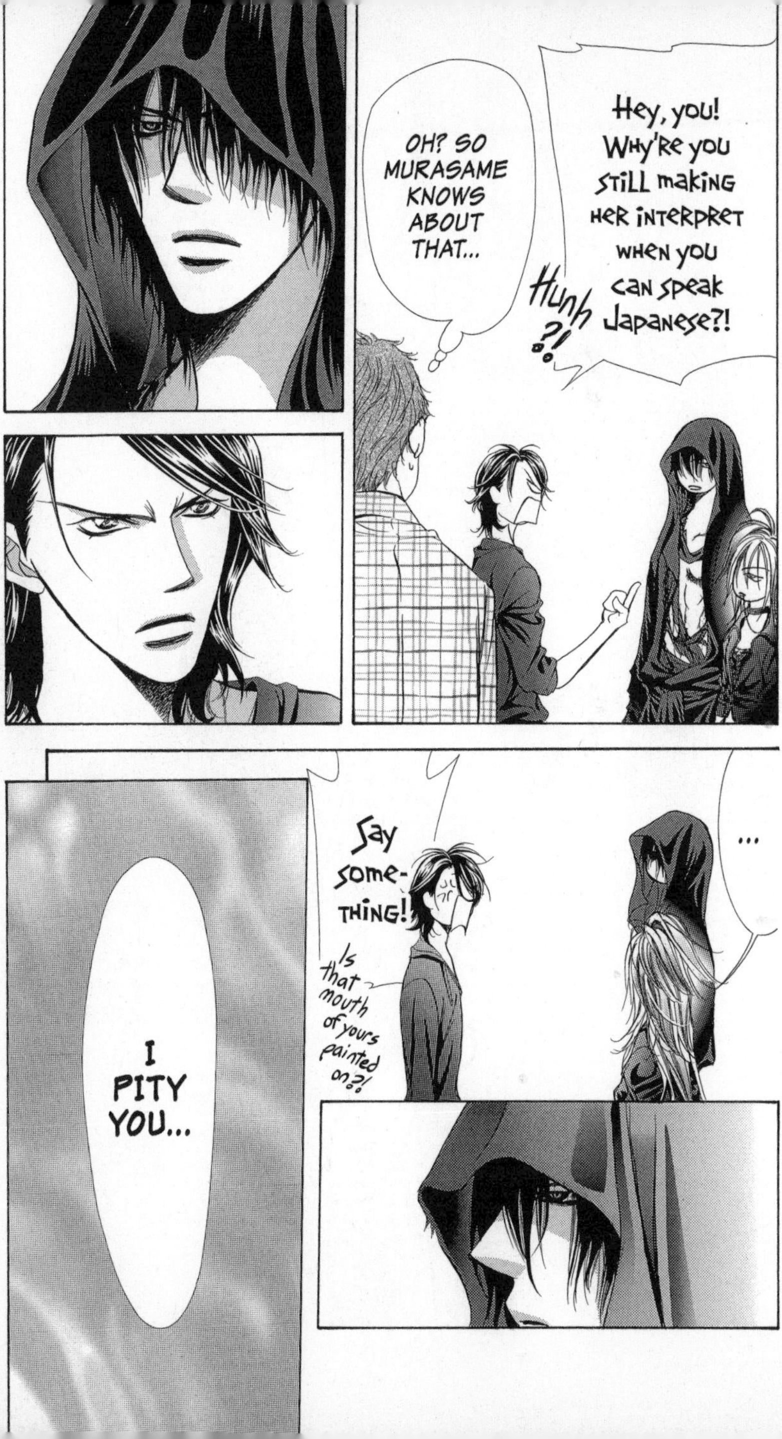
Hey, you! Why're you still making her interpret when you can speak Japanese?!
Hunh ?!
OH? SO MURASAME KNOWS ABOUT THAT...
...
Say some-thing!
Is that mouth of yours painted on?!
I PITY YOU...

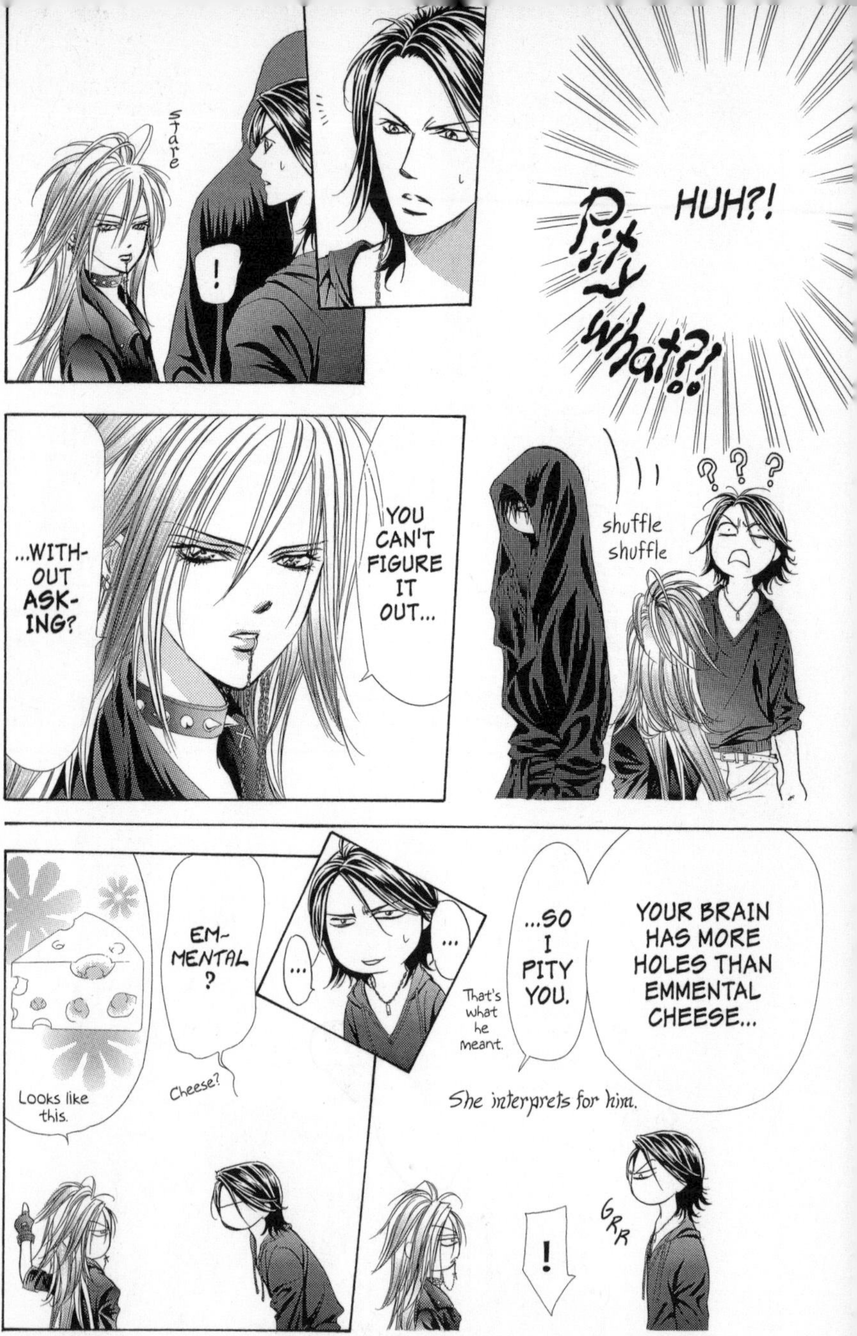
HUH?!
Pity what?!
Stare
!
shuffle shuffle
YOU CAN'T FIGURE IT OUT...
...WITH-OUT ASK-ING?
YOUR BRAIN HAS MORE HOLES THAN EMMENTAL CHEESE...
...SO I PITY YOU.
That's what he meant.
She interprets for him.
...
...
EM-MENTAL?
Cheese?
Looks like this.
GRR
!

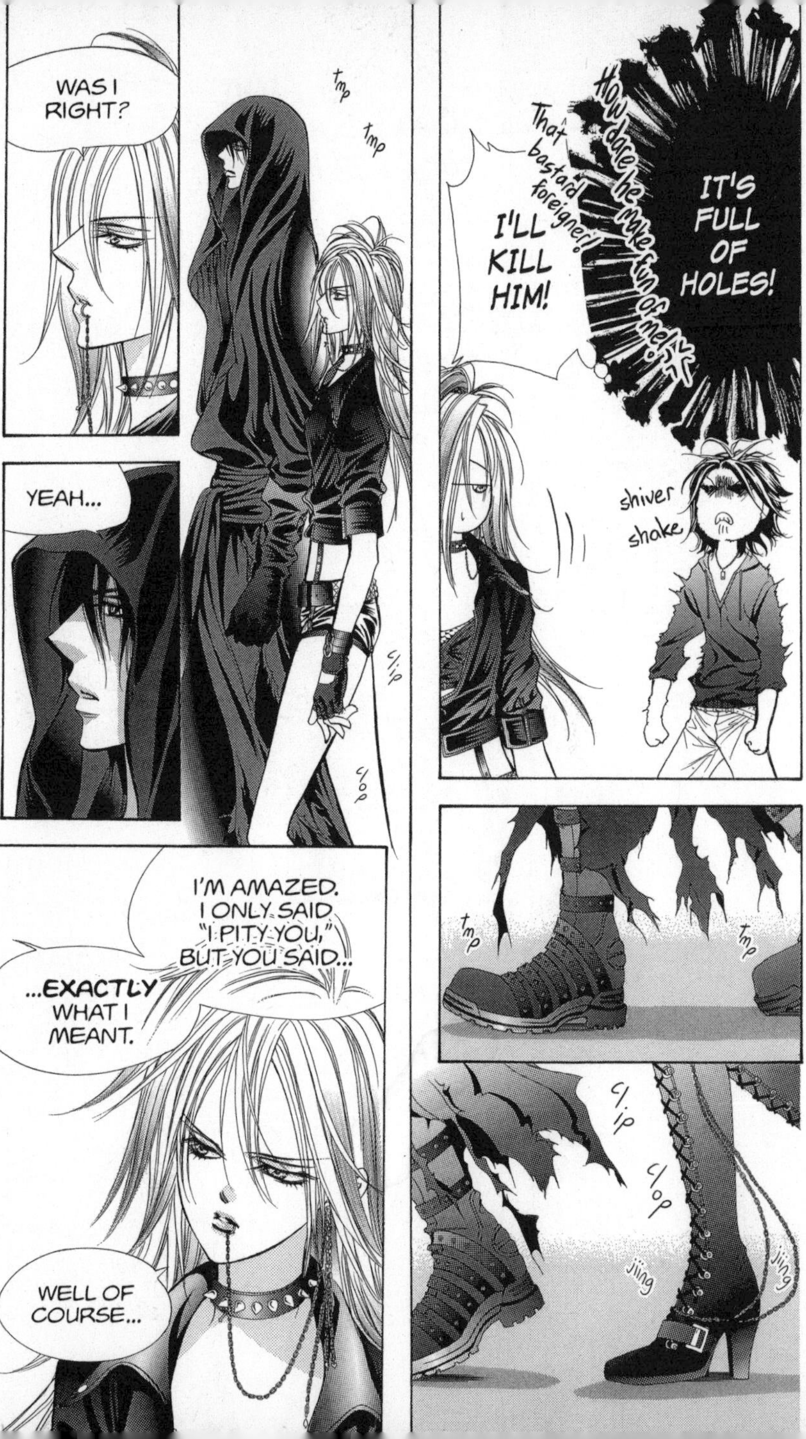

IT'S FULL OF HOLES!
How dare he make fun of me!
That bastard foreigner!
I'LL KILL HIM!
shiver
shake
WAS I RIGHT?
tmp
tmp
YEAH...
clip
clop
tmp
tmp
clip
clop
jiing
jiing
I'M AMAZED. I ONLY SAID "I PITY YOU," BUT YOU SAID...
...EXACTLY WHAT I MEANT.
WELL OF COURSE...

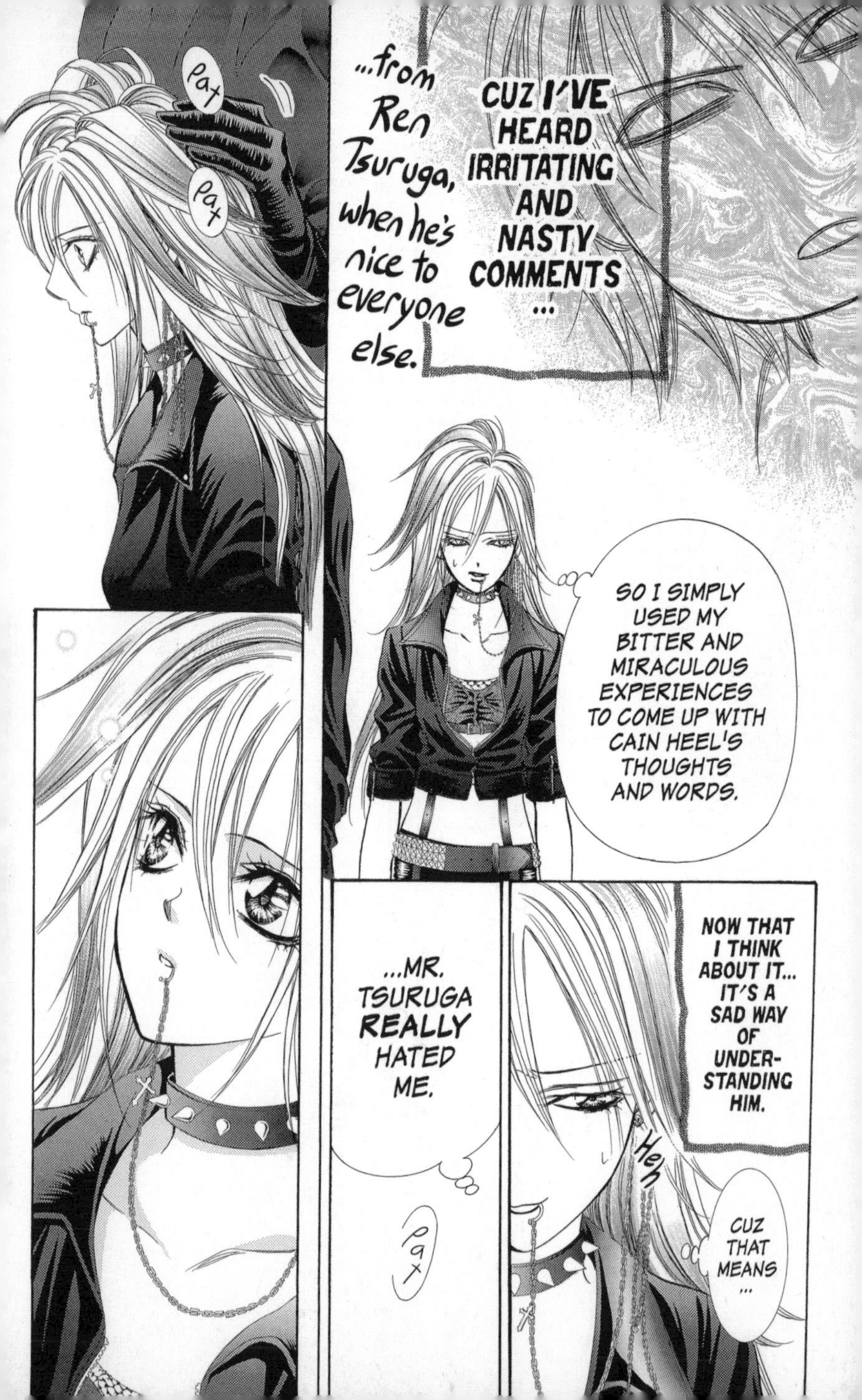
CUZ I'VE HEARD IRRITATING AND NASTY COMMENTS...
...from Ren Tsuruga, when he's nice to everyone else.
SO I SIMPLY USED MY BITTER AND MIRACULOUS EXPERIENCES TO COME UP WITH CAIN HEEL'S THOUGHTS AND WORDS.
Pat
Pat
NOW THAT I THINK ABOUT IT... IT'S A SAD WAY OF UNDER-STANDING HIM.
Heh
CUZ THAT MEANS ...
...MR. TSURUGA REALLY HATED ME.
Pat

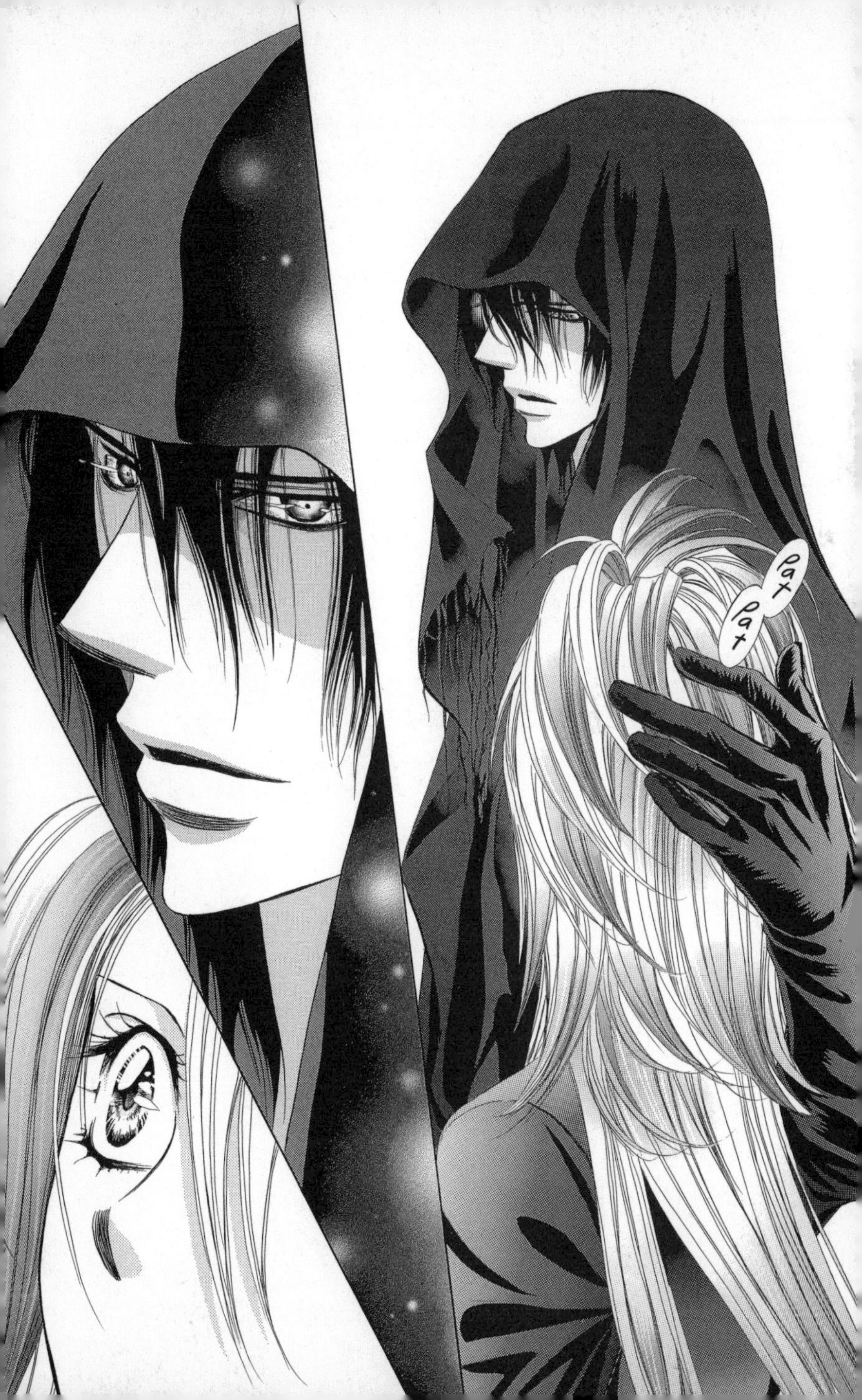
pat pat

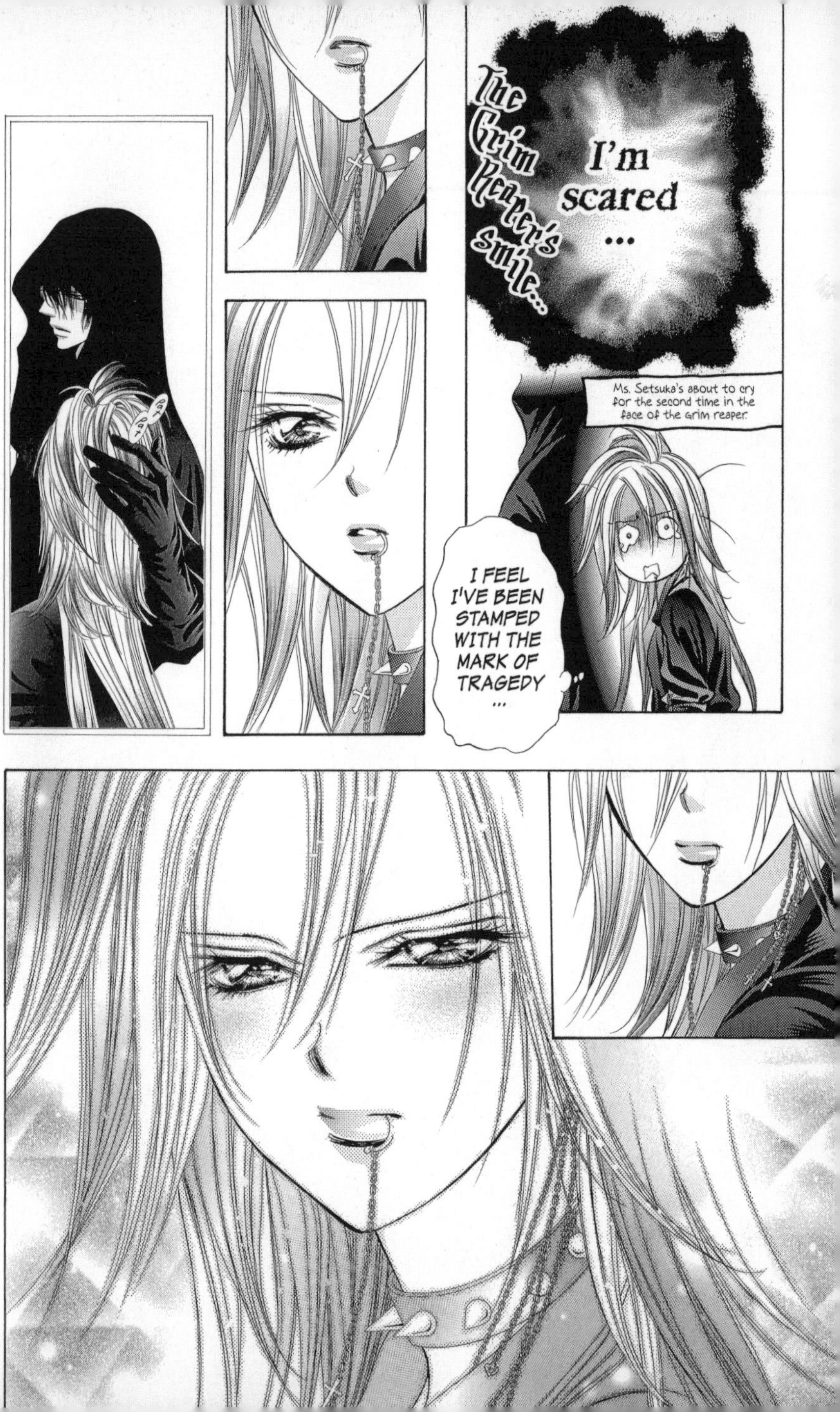
I'm scared ...
The Grim Reaper's smile...
Ms. Setsuka's about to cry for the second time in the face of the grim reaper.
I FEEL I'VE BEEN STAMPED WITH THE MARK OF TRAGEDY ...

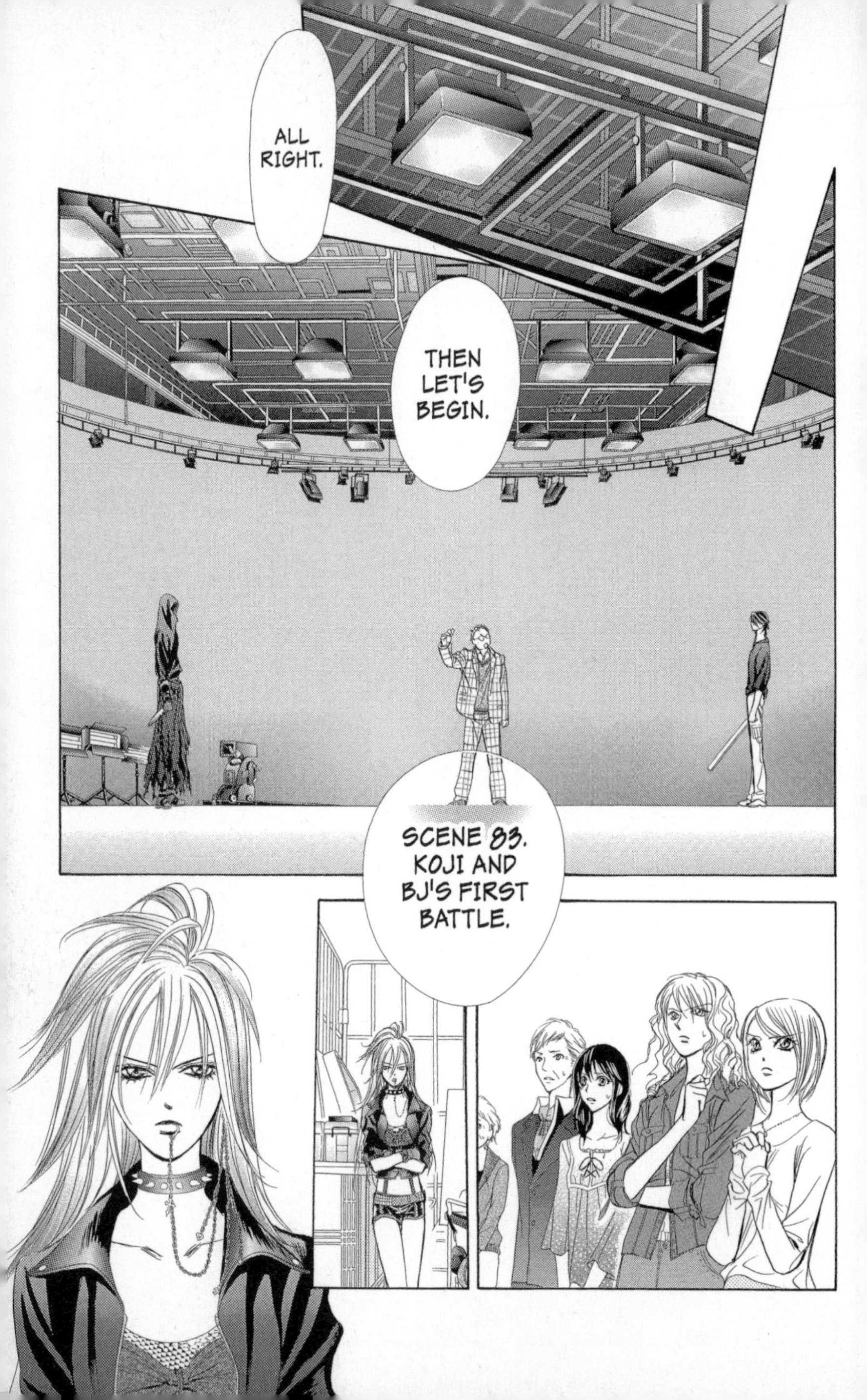
ALL RIGHT.
THEN LET'S BEGIN.
SCENE 83. KOJI AND BJ'S FIRST BATTLE.

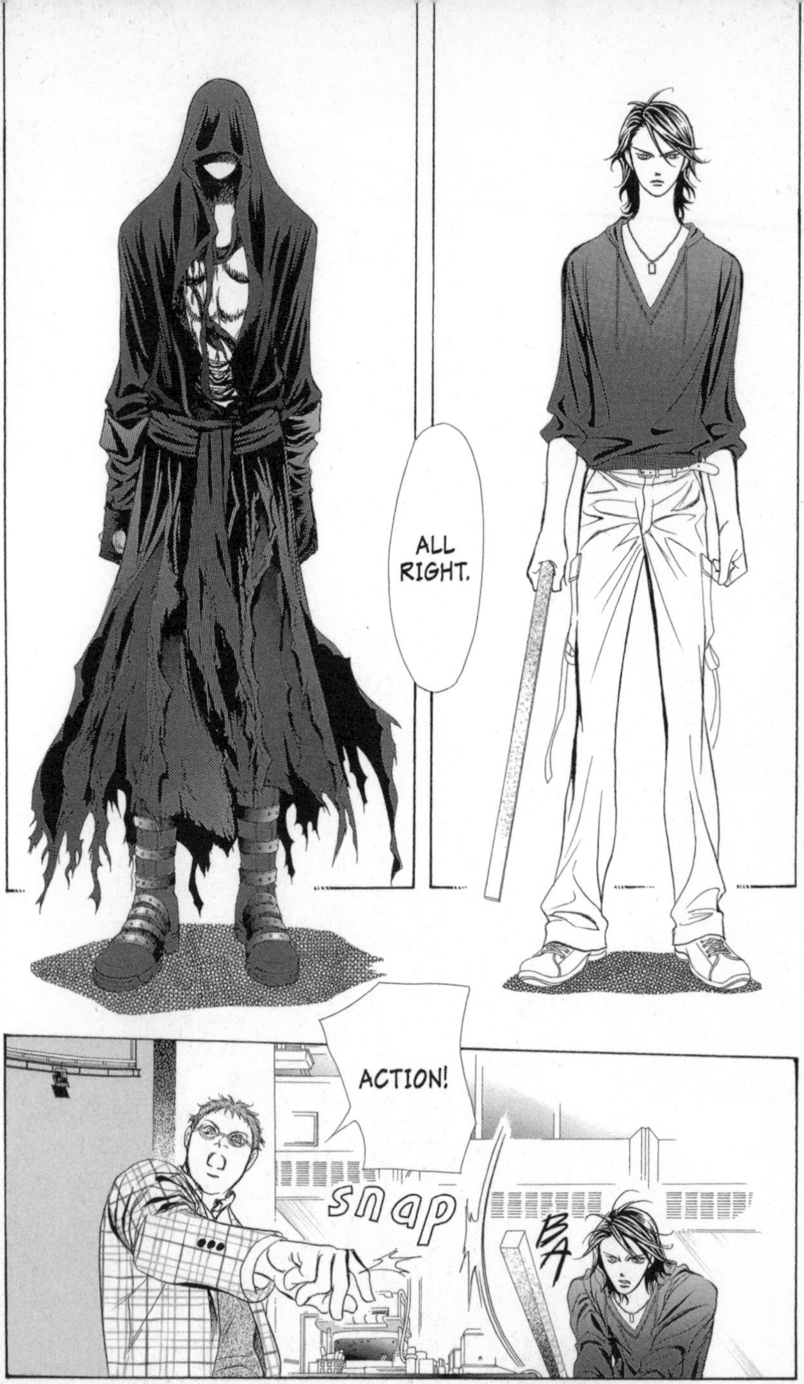
ALL RIGHT.
ACTION!
snap
BA

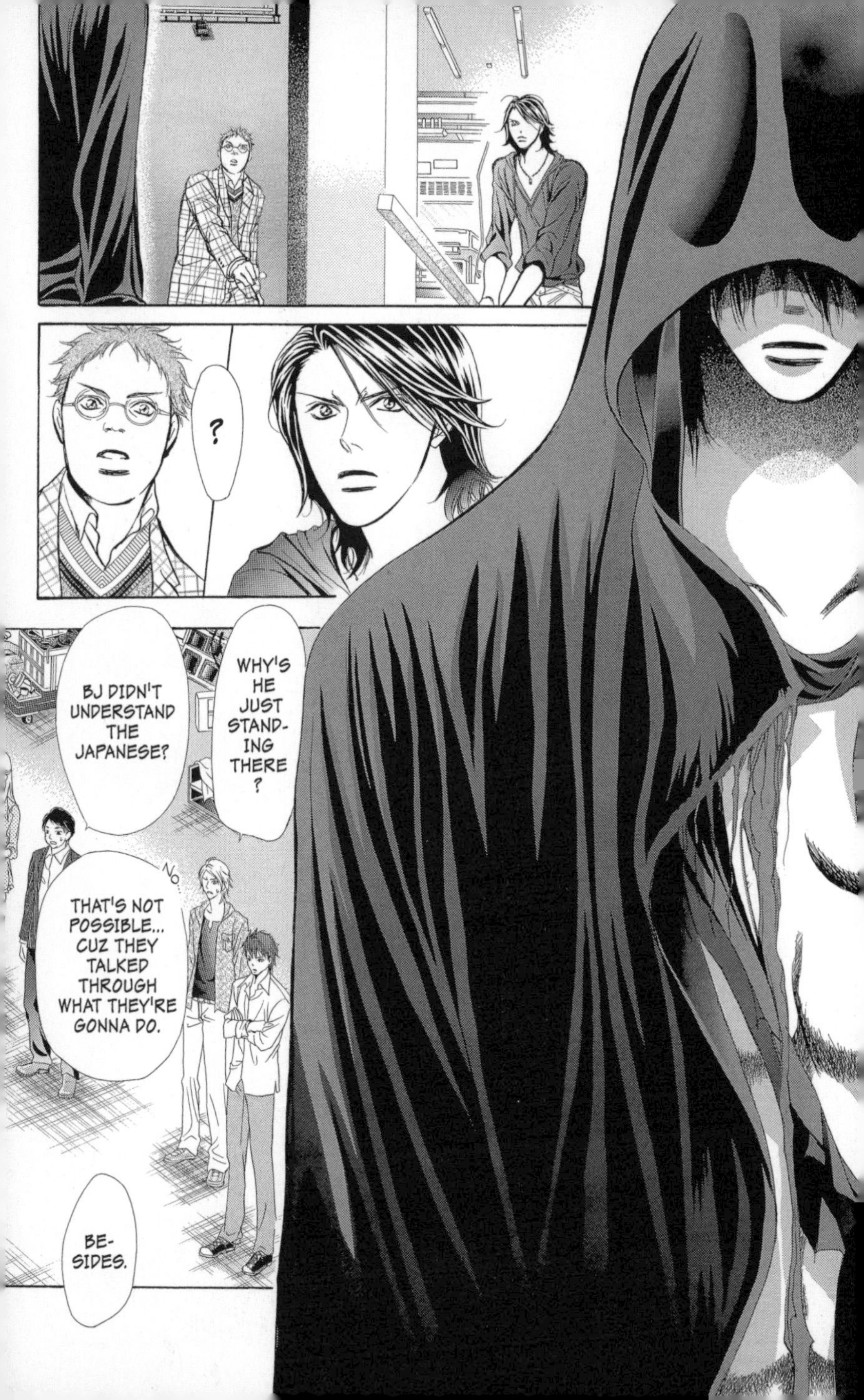
?
WHY'S HE JUST STAND-ING THERE?
BJ DIDN'T UNDERSTAND THE JAPANESE?
NO...
THAT'S NOT POSSIBLE... CUZ THEY TALKED THROUGH WHAT THEY'RE GONNA DO.
BE-SIDES.

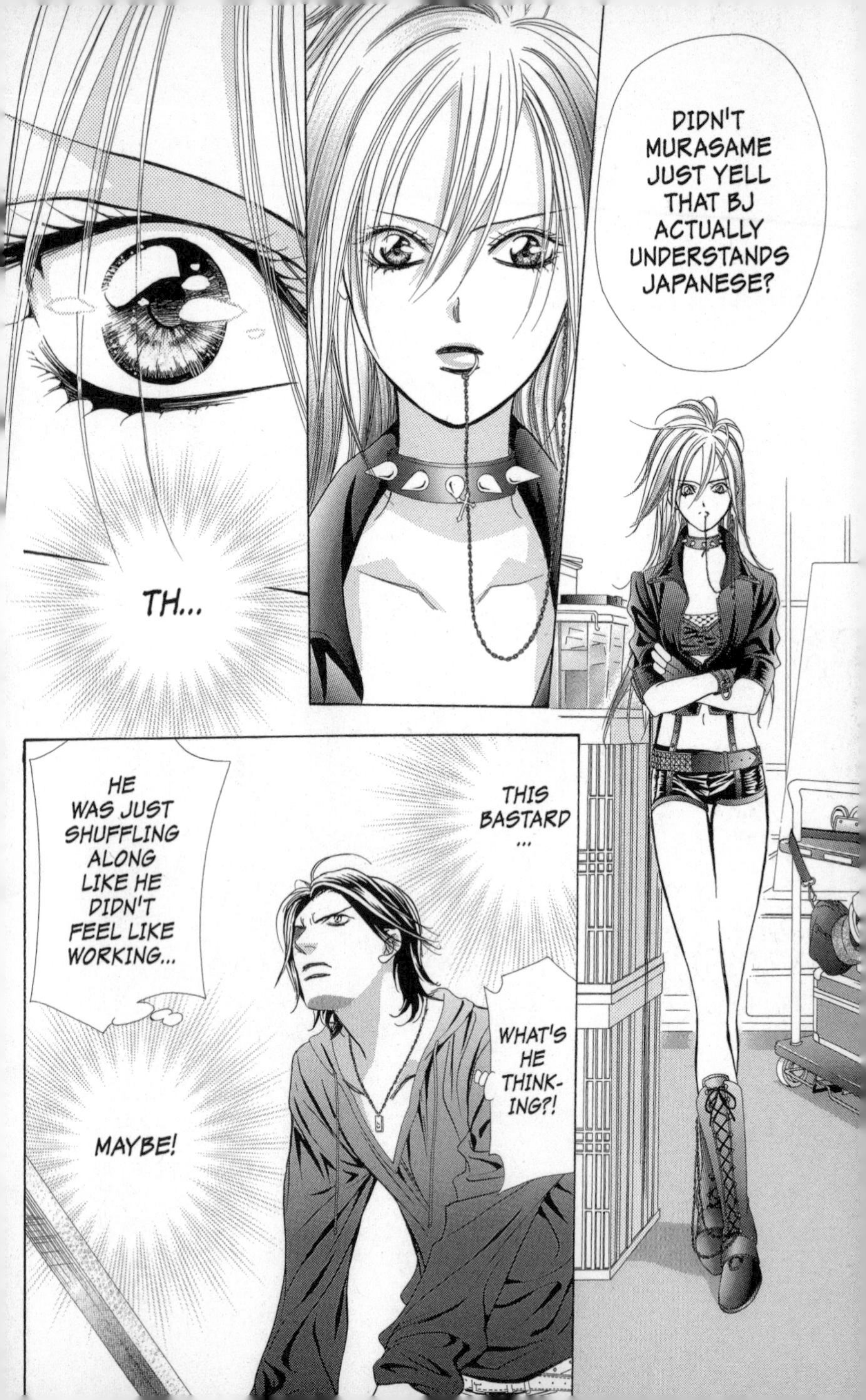
DIDN'T MURASAME JUST YELL THAT BJ ACTUALLY UNDERSTANDS JAPANESE?
TH...
THIS BASTARD ...
HE WAS JUST SHUFFLING ALONG LIKE HE DIDN'T FEEL LIKE WORKING...
WHAT'S HE THINK-ING?!
MAYBE!

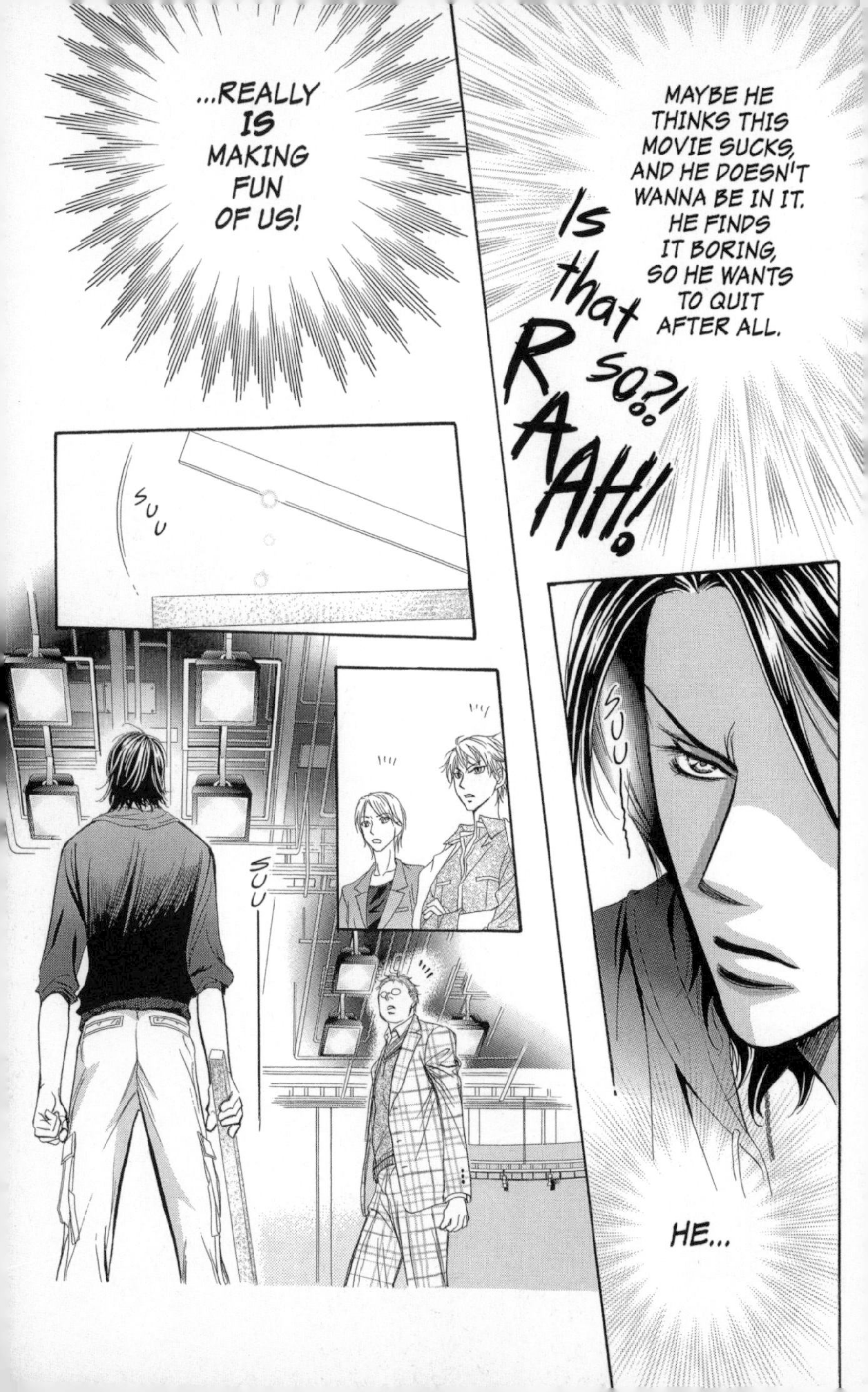
MAYBE HE THINKS THIS MOVIE SUCKS, AND HE DOESN'T WANNA BE IN IT. HE FINDS IT BORING, SO HE WANTS TO QUIT AFTER ALL.
Is that so?!
RAAH!
SUU
HE...
...REALLY IS MAKING FUN OF US!
SUU
SUU

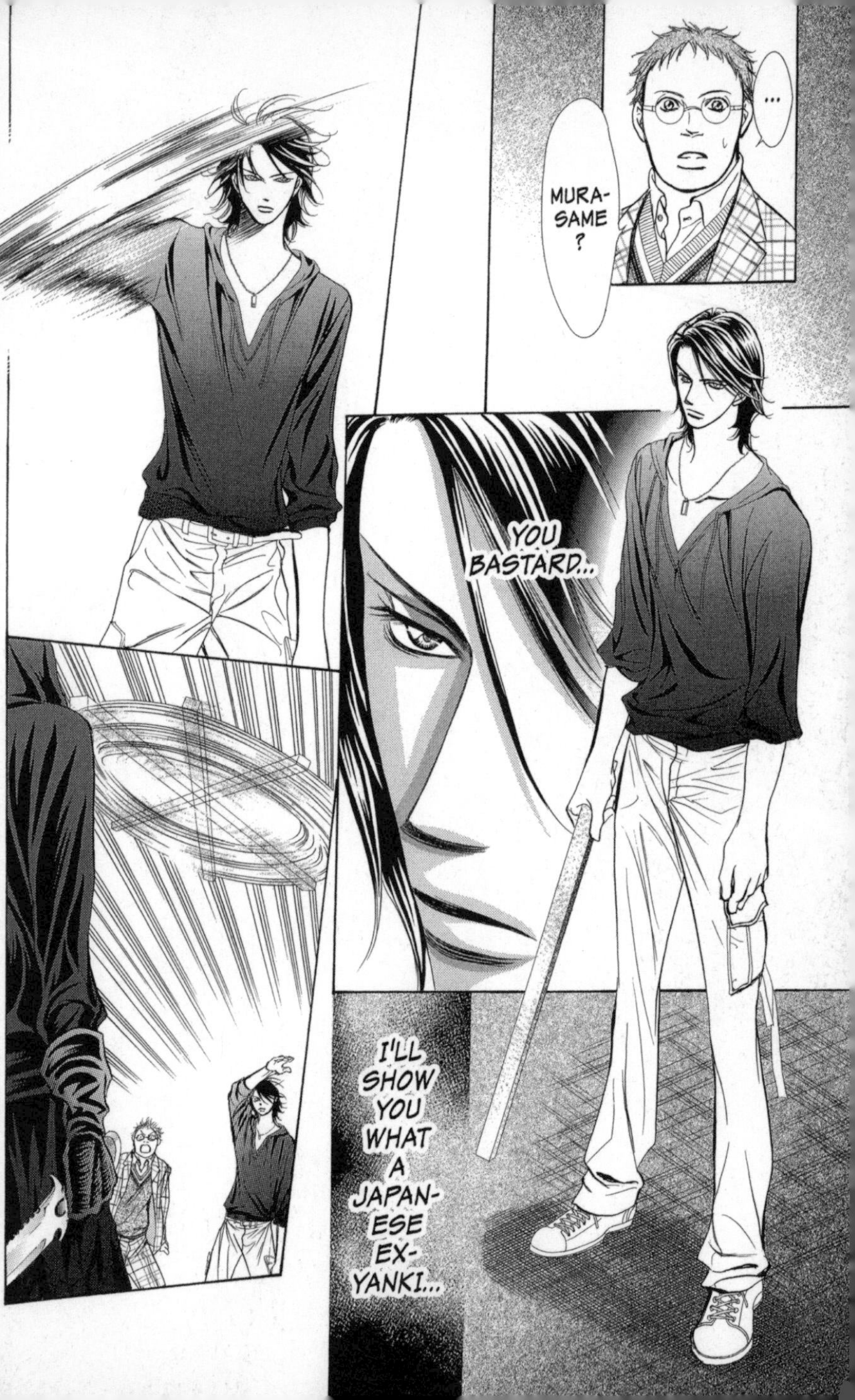
...
MURA-SAME?
YOU BASTARD...
I'LL SHOW YOU WHAT A JAPANESE EX-YANKI...

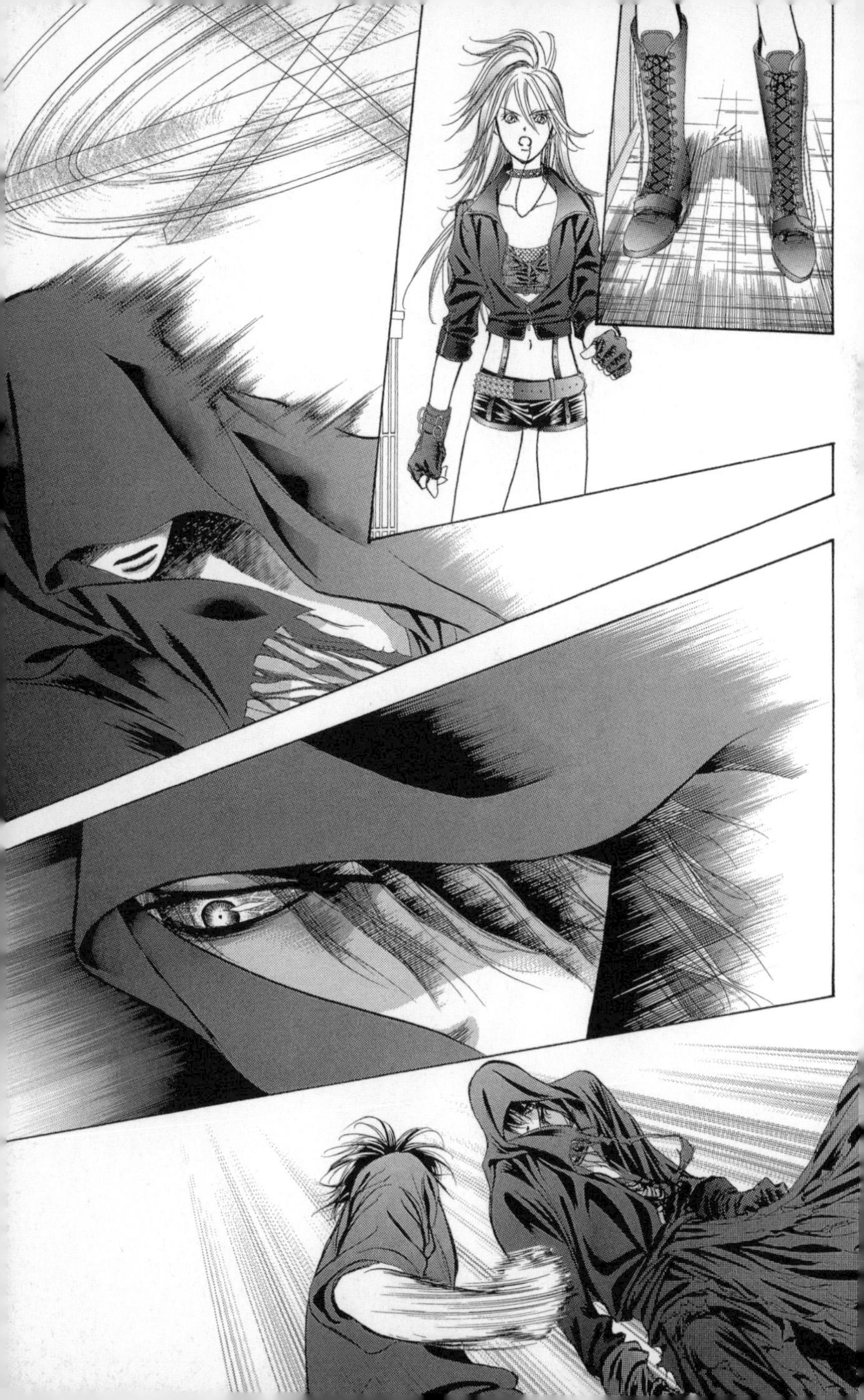

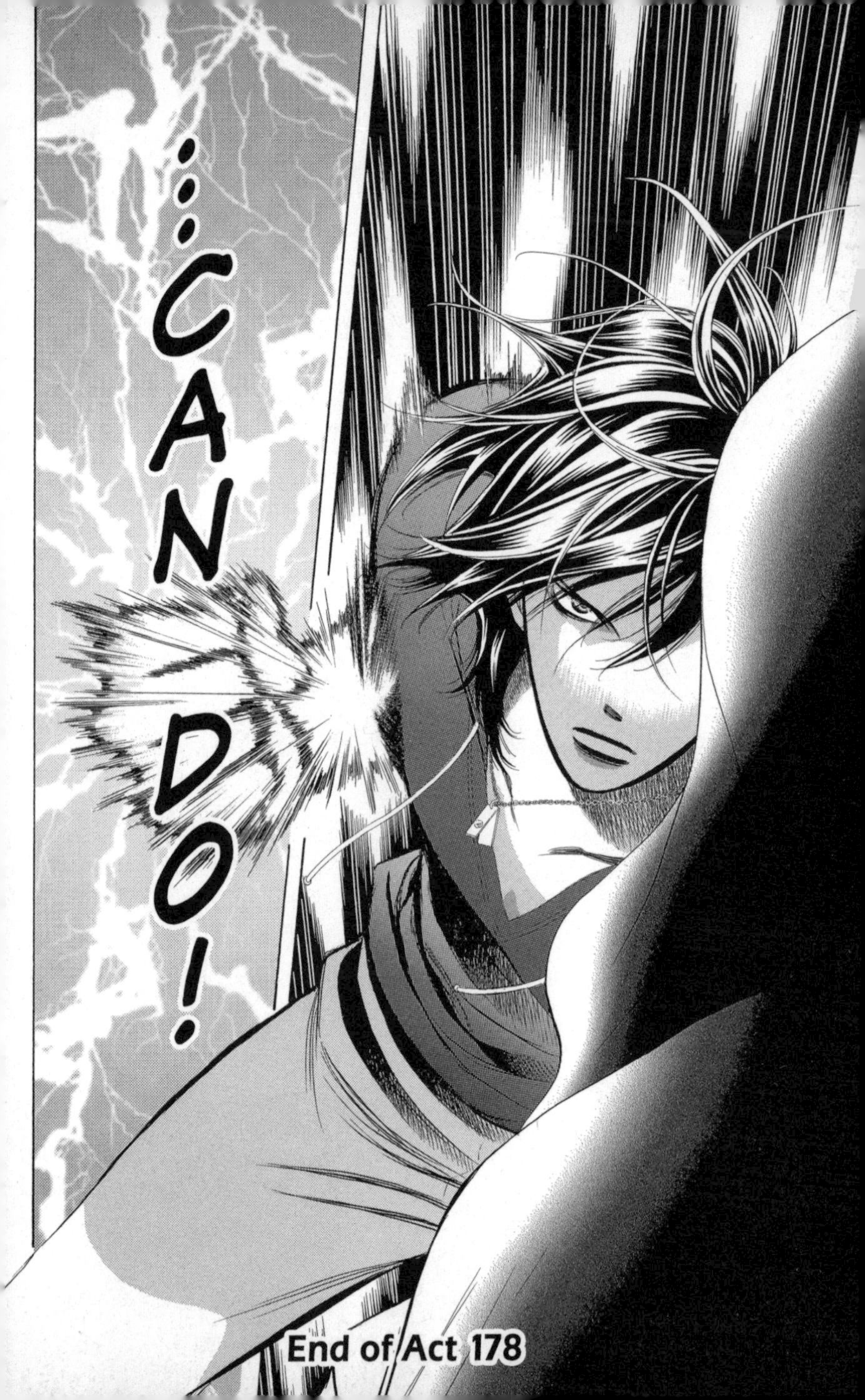
...CAN DO!
End of Act 178

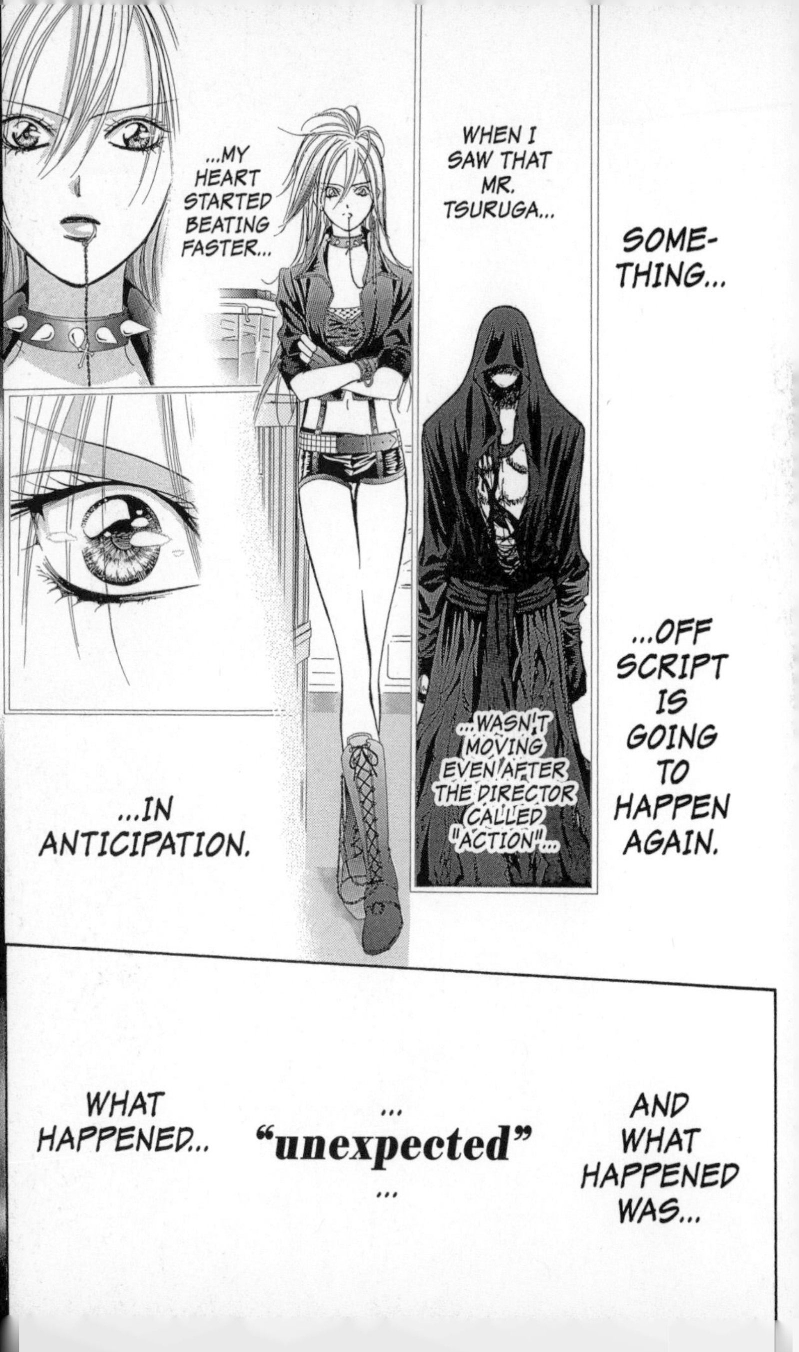
SOME-THING...
...OFF SCRIPT IS GOING TO HAPPEN AGAIN.
WHEN I SAW THAT MR. TSURUGA...
...WASN'T MOVING EVEN AFTER THE DIRECTOR CALLED "ACTION"...
...MY HEART STARTED BEATING FASTER...
...IN ANTICIPATION.
AND WHAT HAPPENED WAS...
... "unexpected" ...
WHAT HAPPENED...

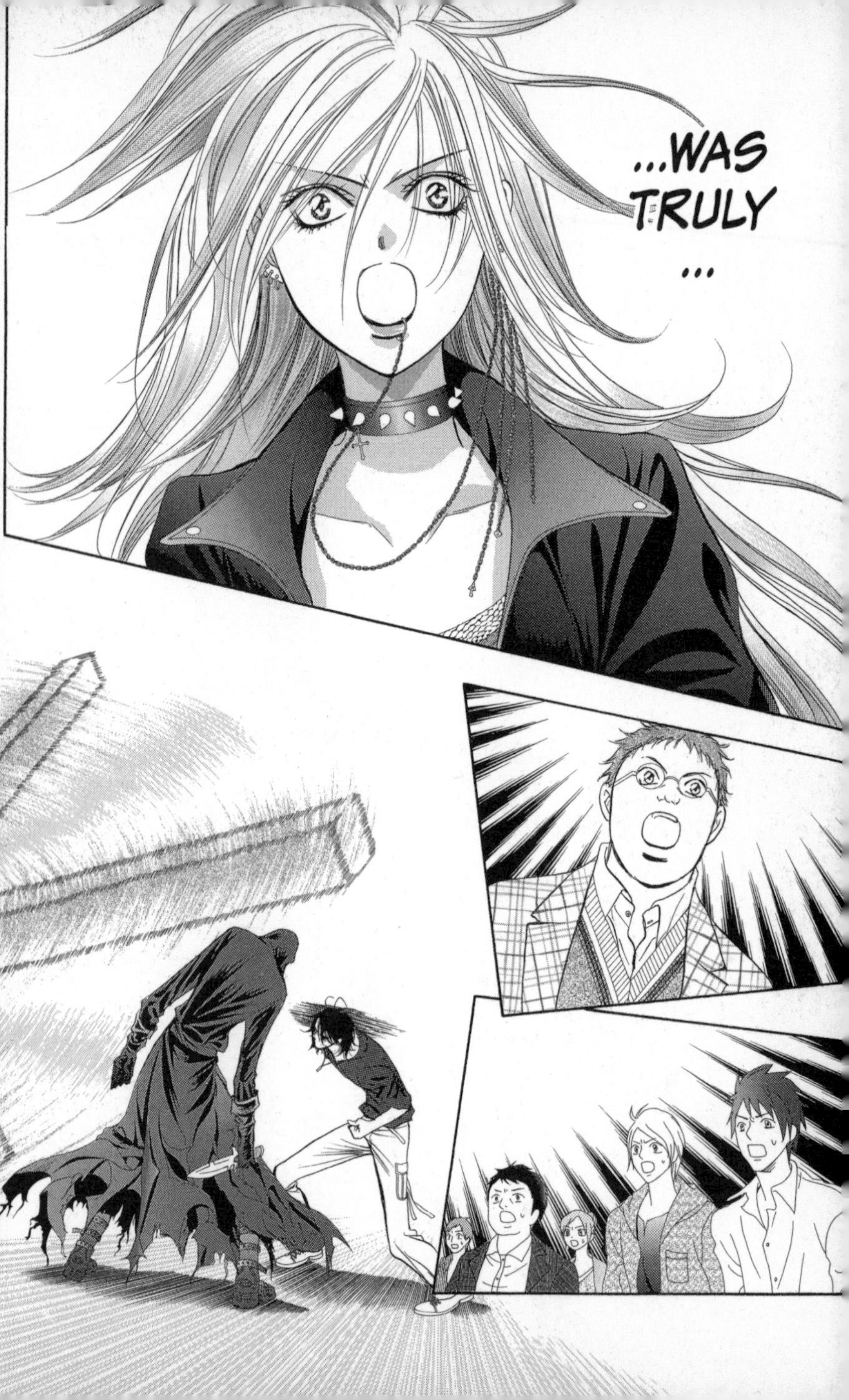
...WAS TRULY ...

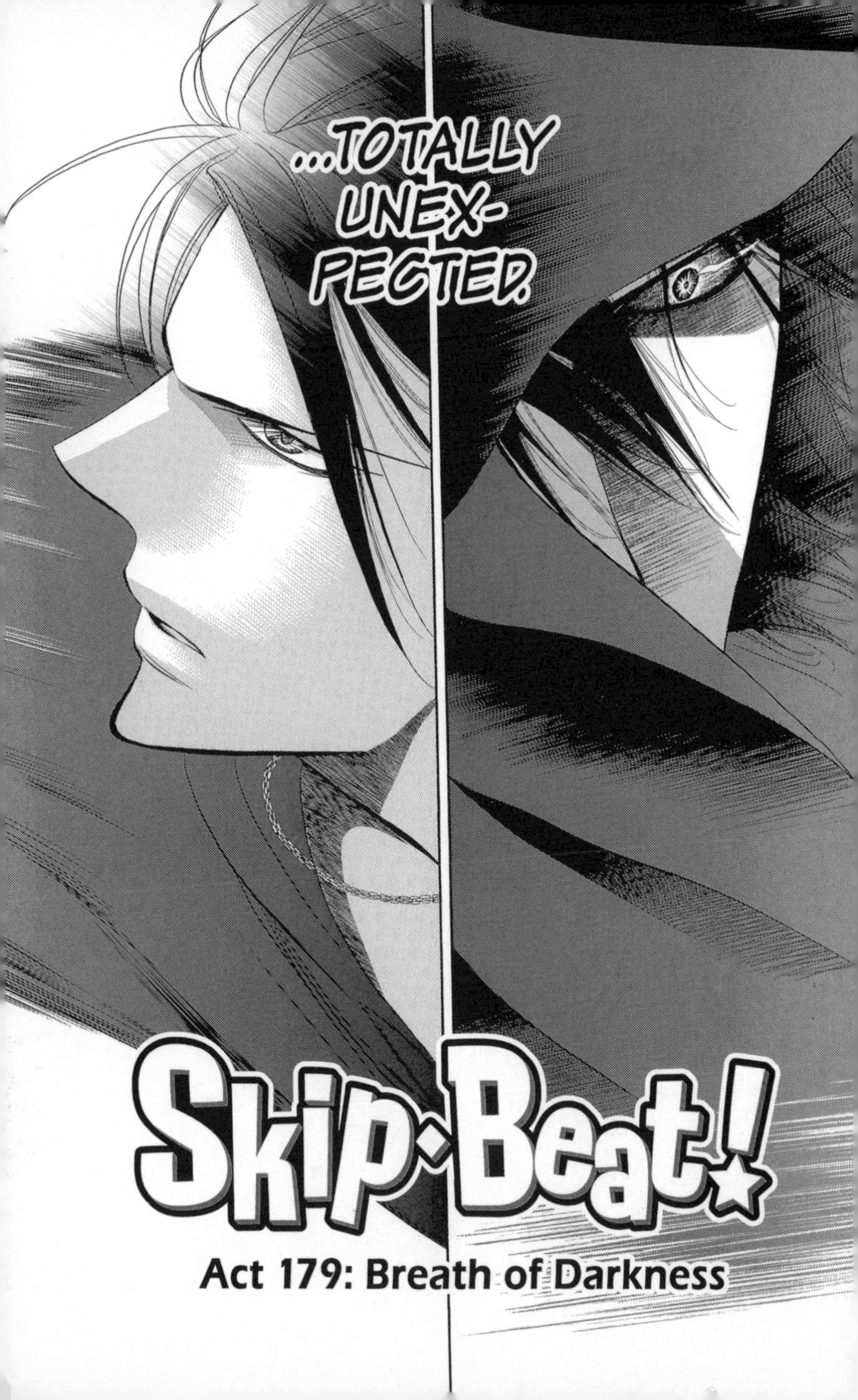
...TOTALLY UNEX-PECTED.
Skip·Beat!
Act 179: Breath of Darkness

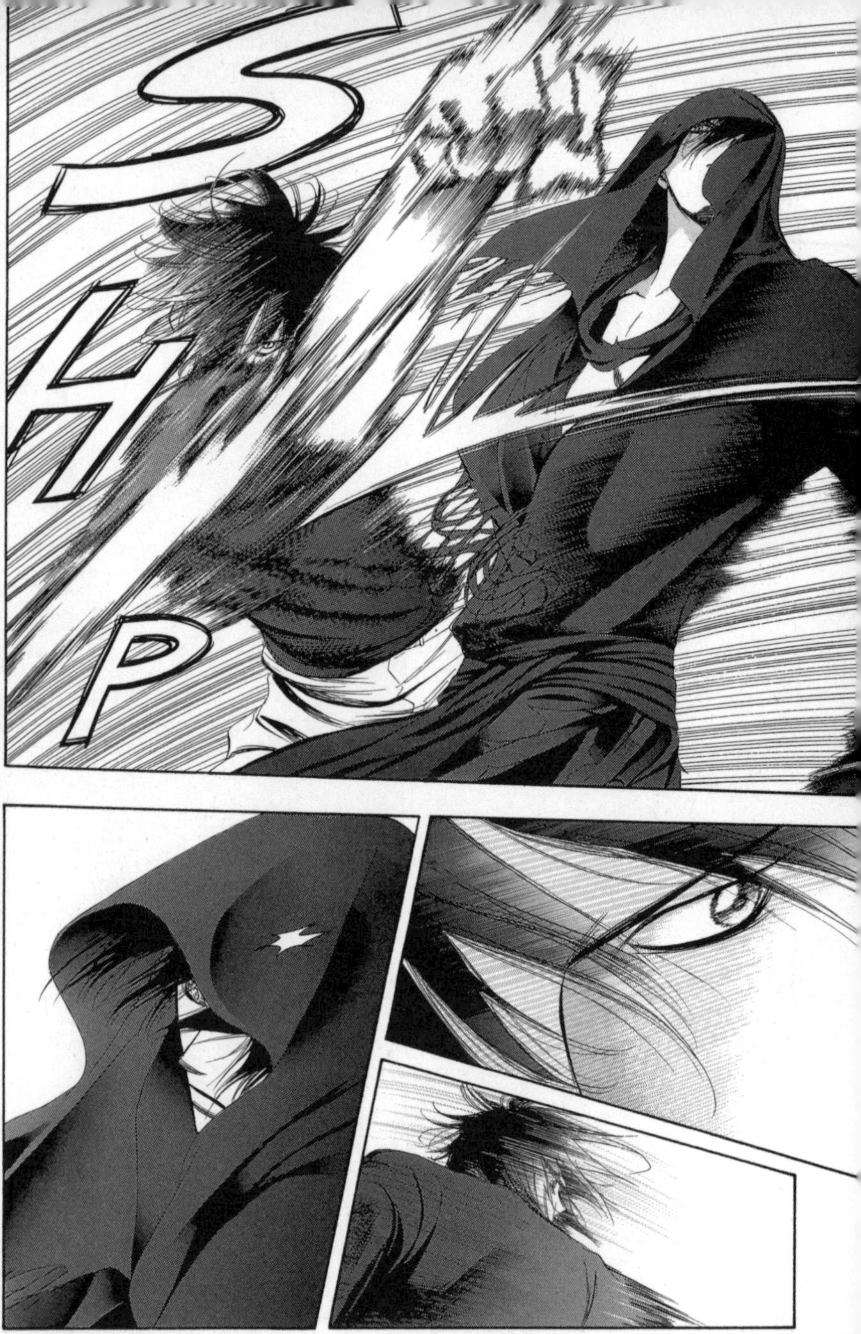
SHP

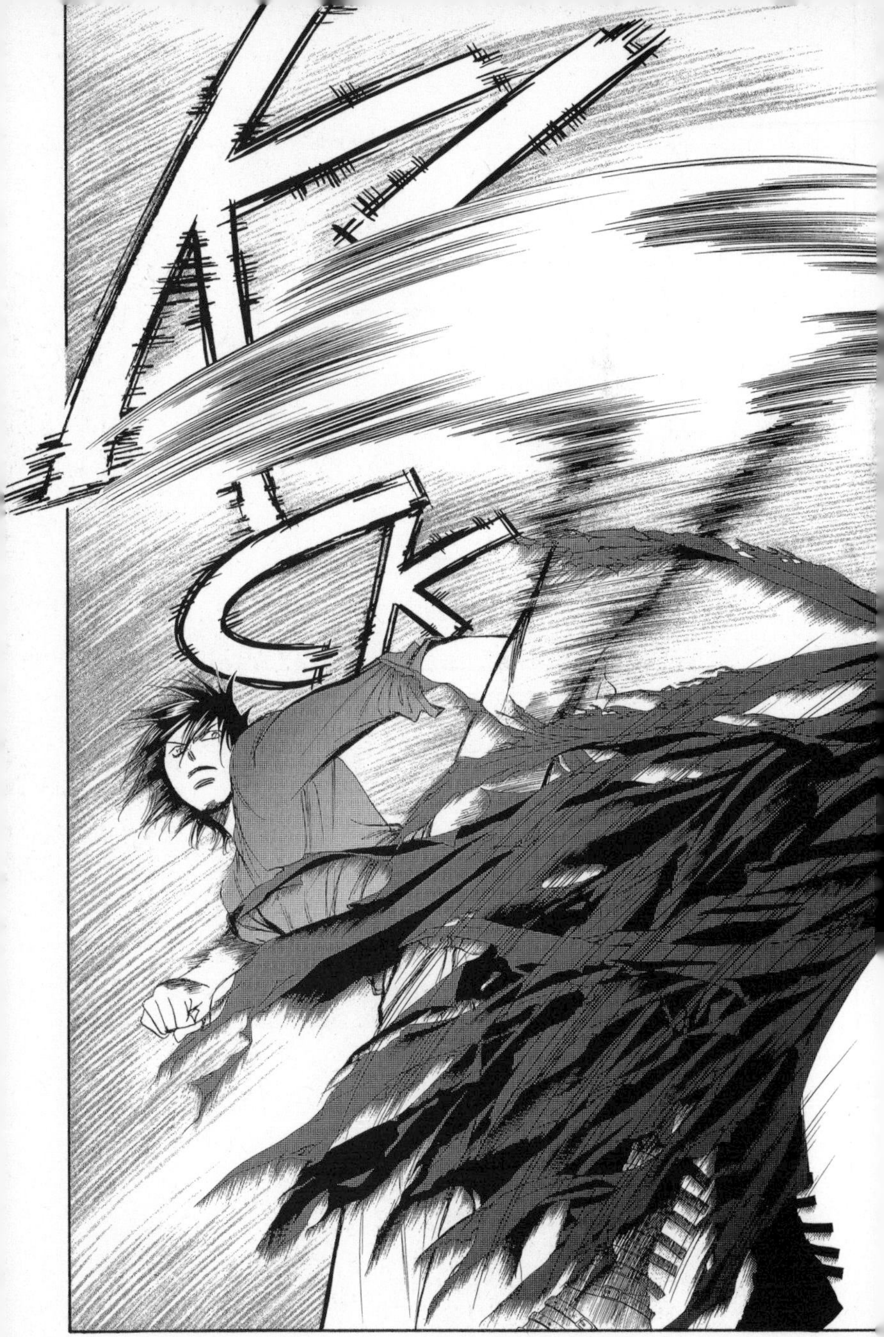
WHACK

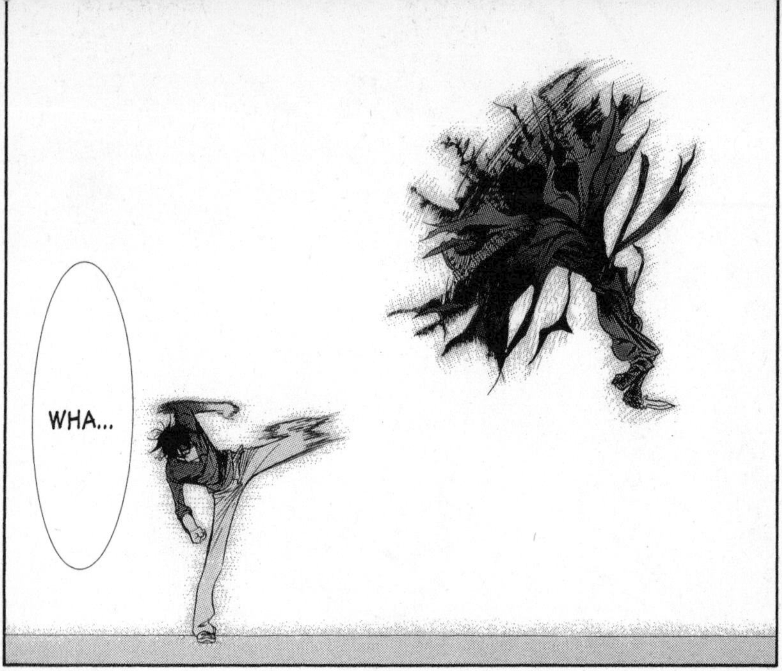
WHA...

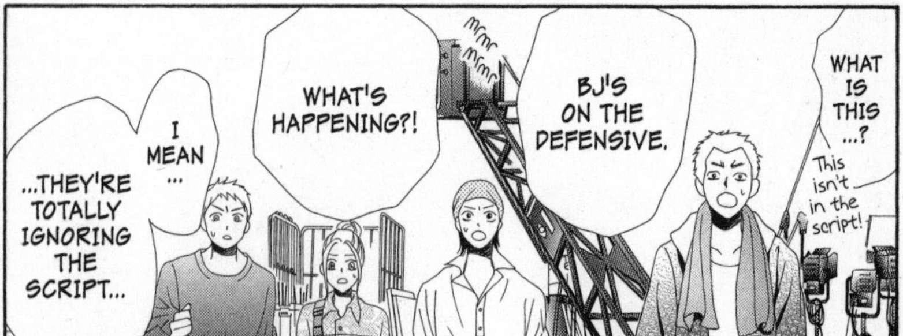
WHAT IS THIS ...?
This isn't in the script!
BJ'S ON THE DEFENSIVE.
mrmr mrmr
WHAT'S HAPPENING?!
I MEAN ...
...THEY'RE TOTALLY IGNORING THE SCRIPT...

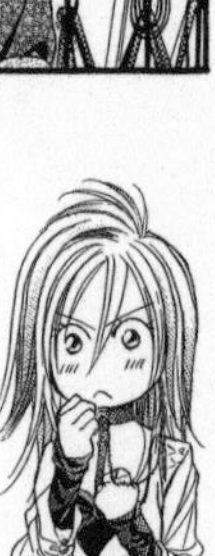

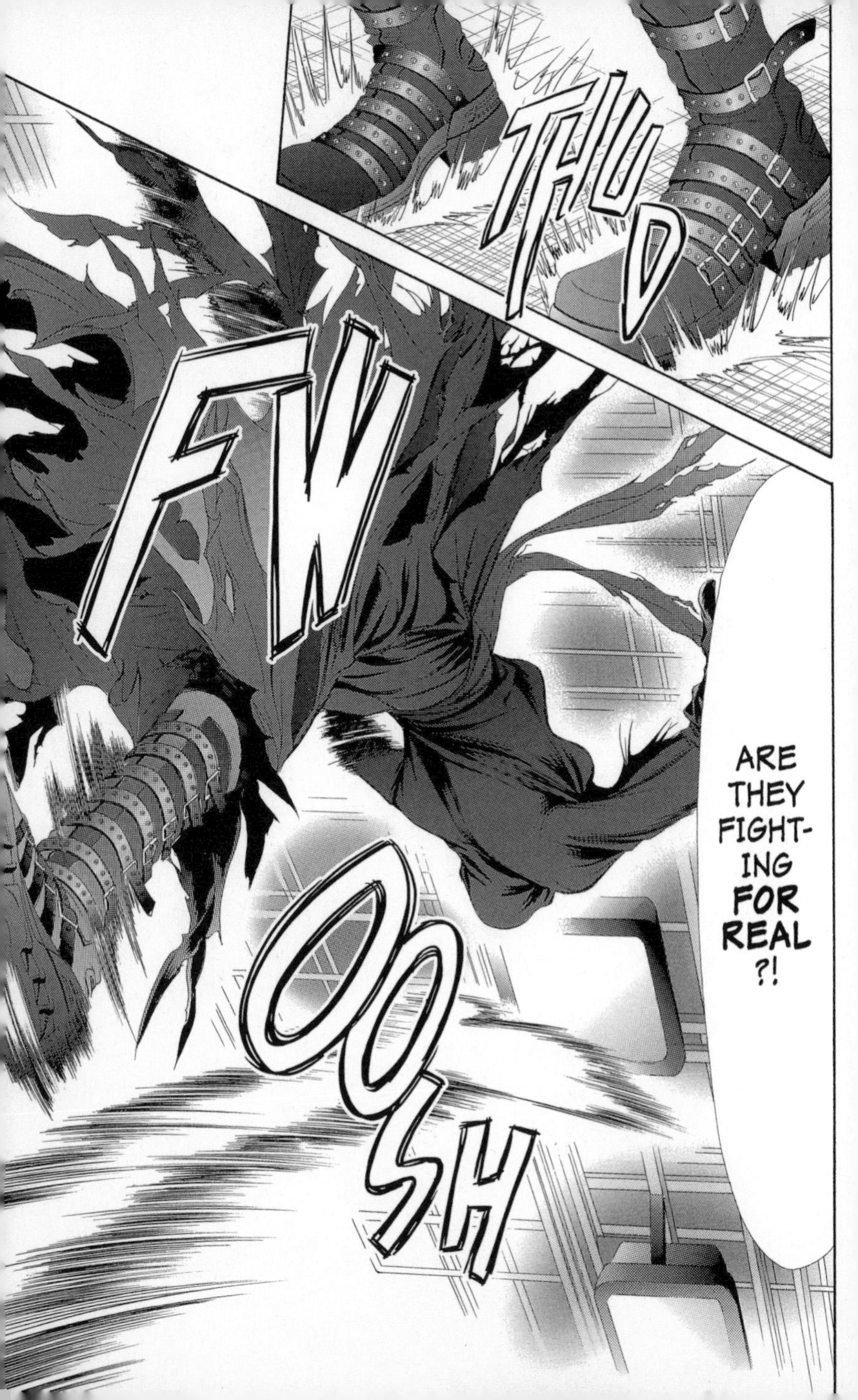
THUD
ARE THEY FIGHT-ING FOR REAL?!
FWOOSH

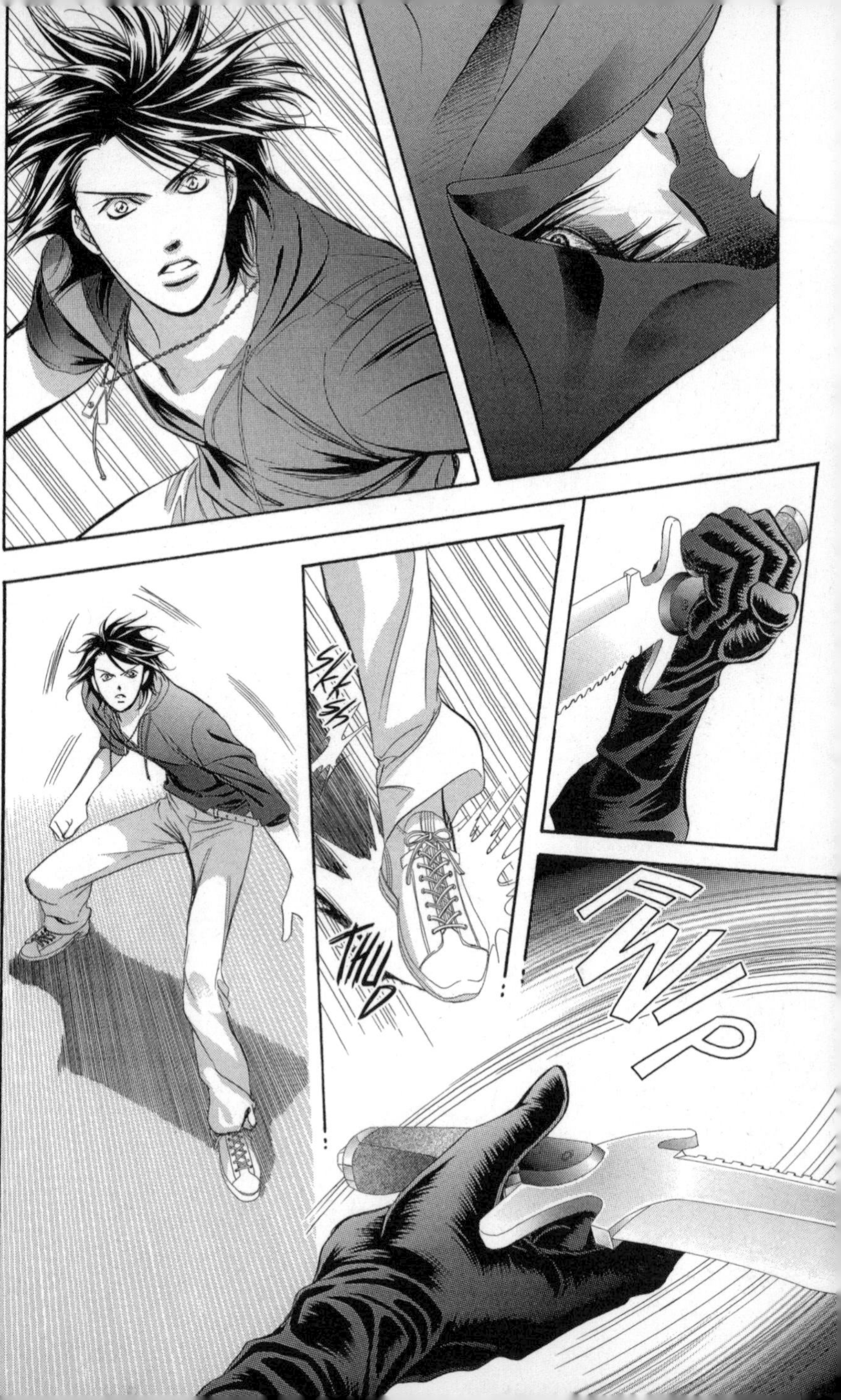
SKKSH
THUD
FWIP

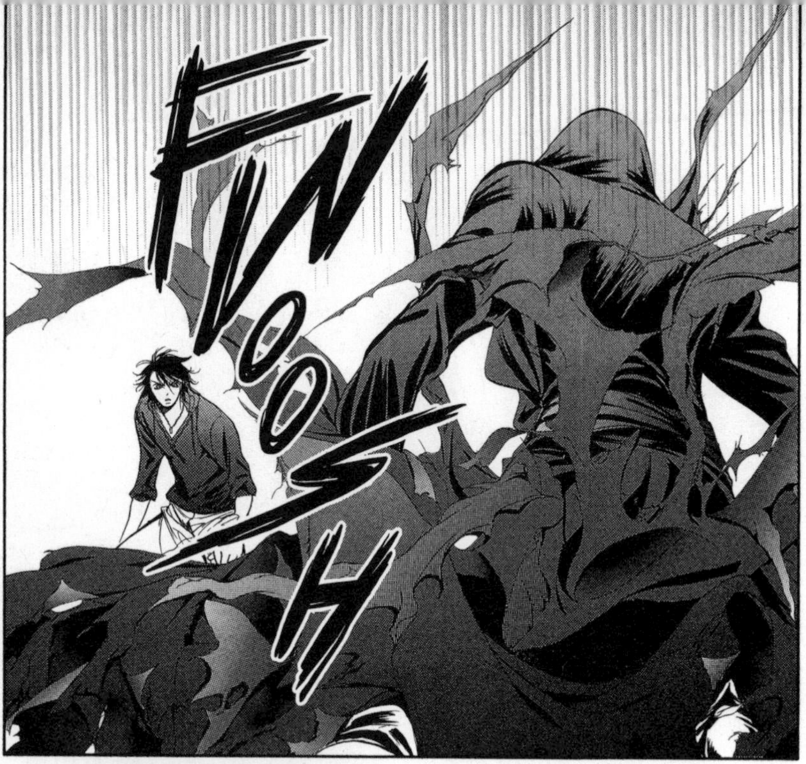
FWOOSH
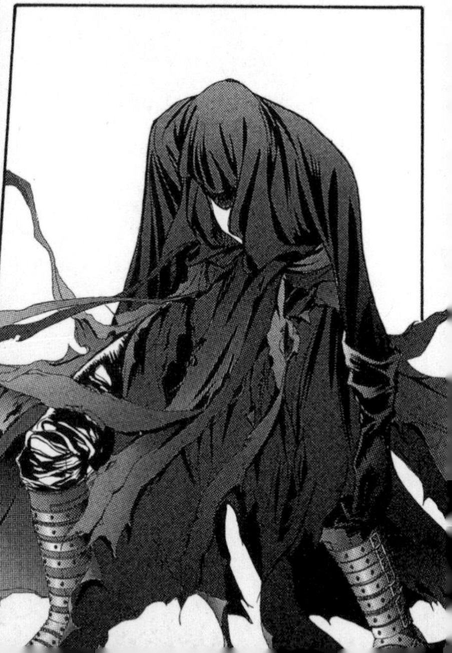
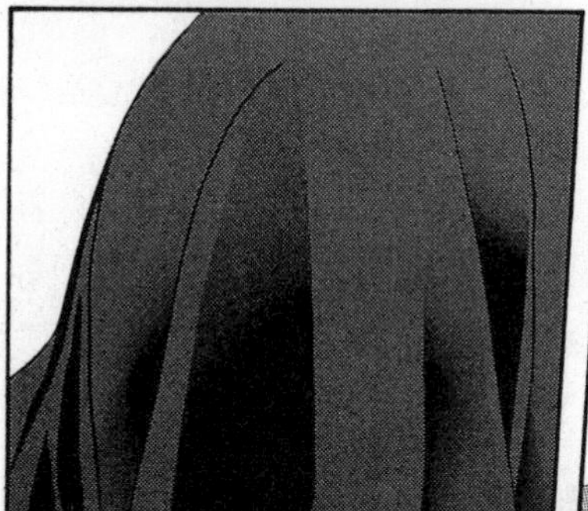

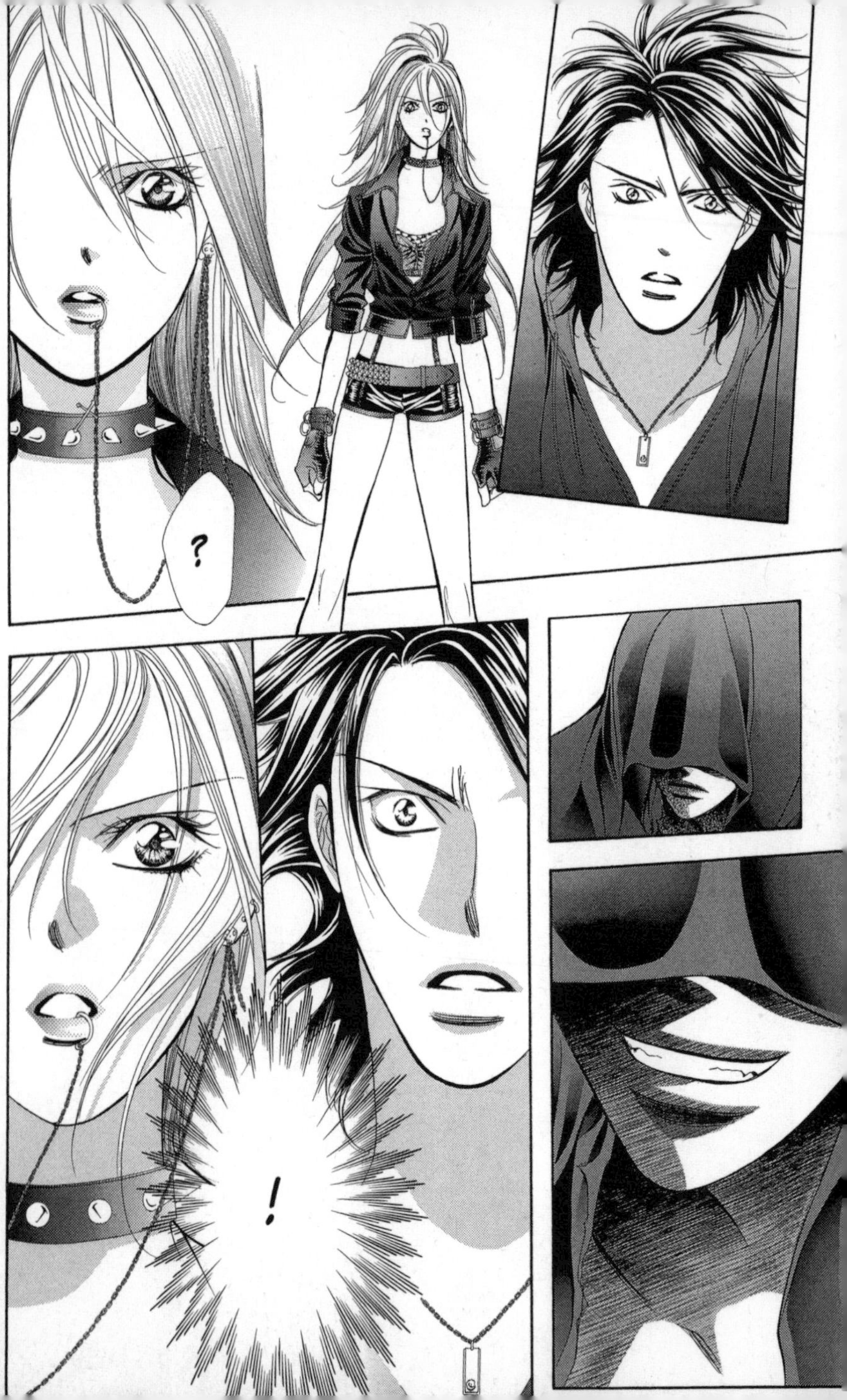
?
!

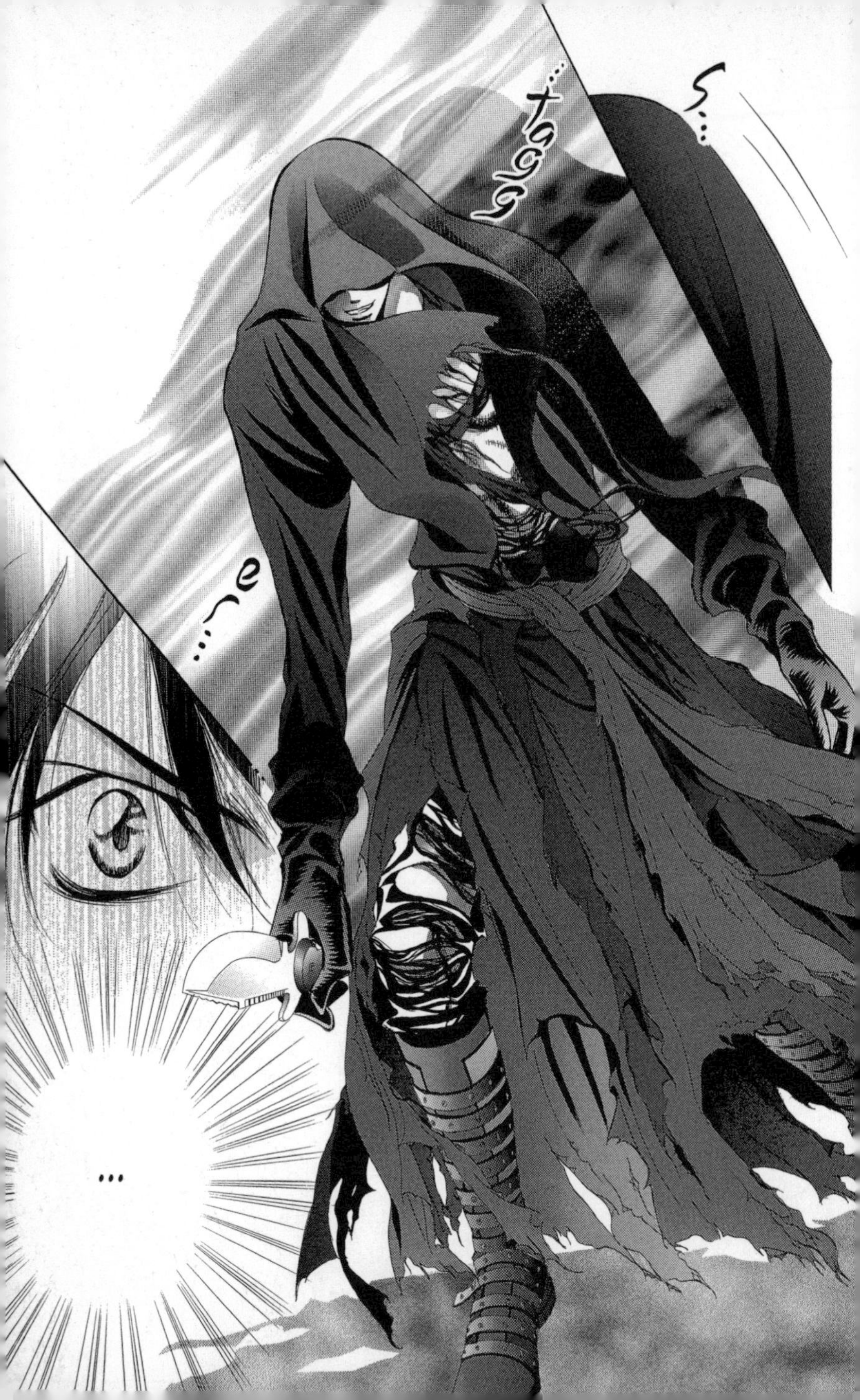

S...
...tagg
er...
...

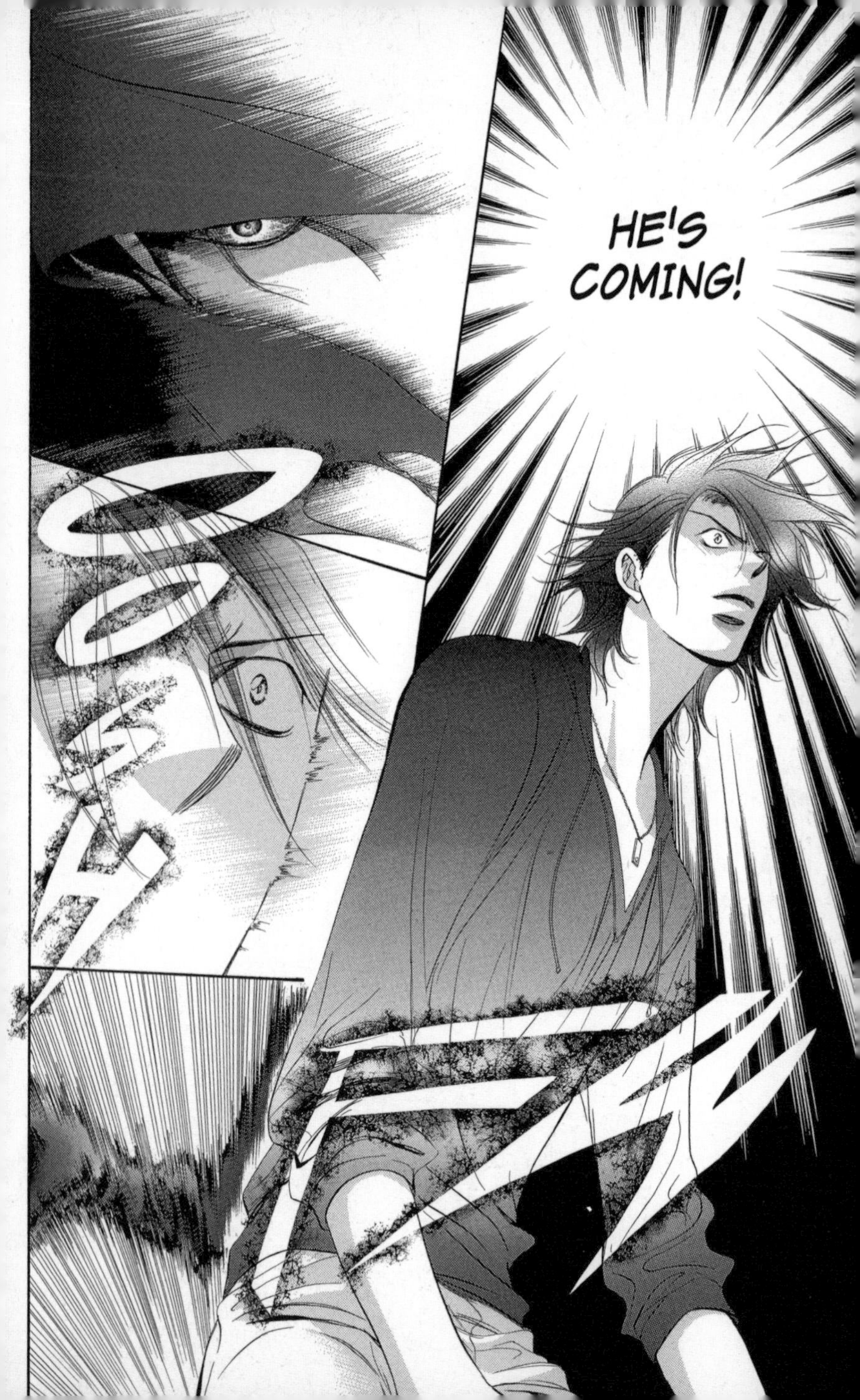
HE'S COMING!

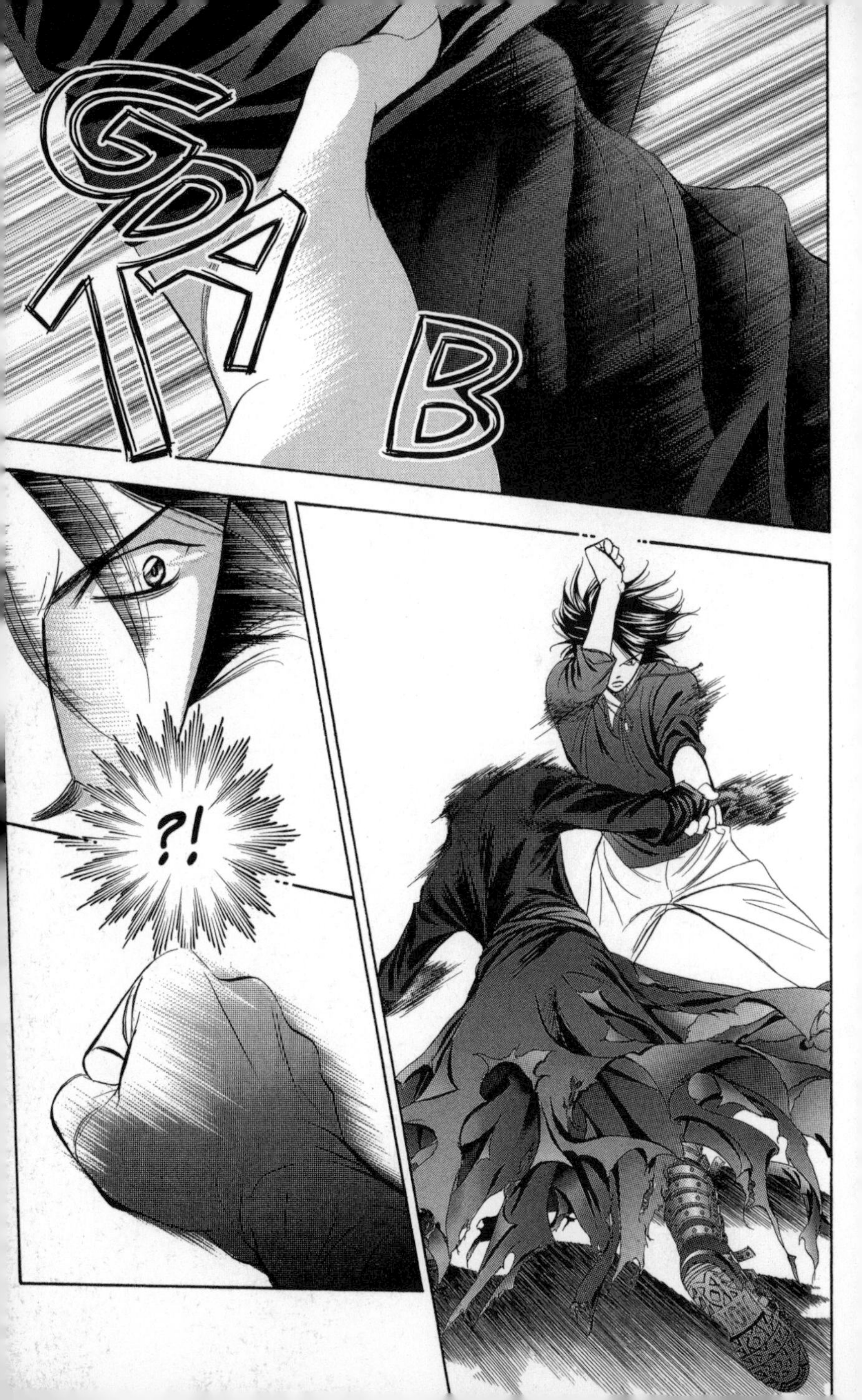
GRAB
?!

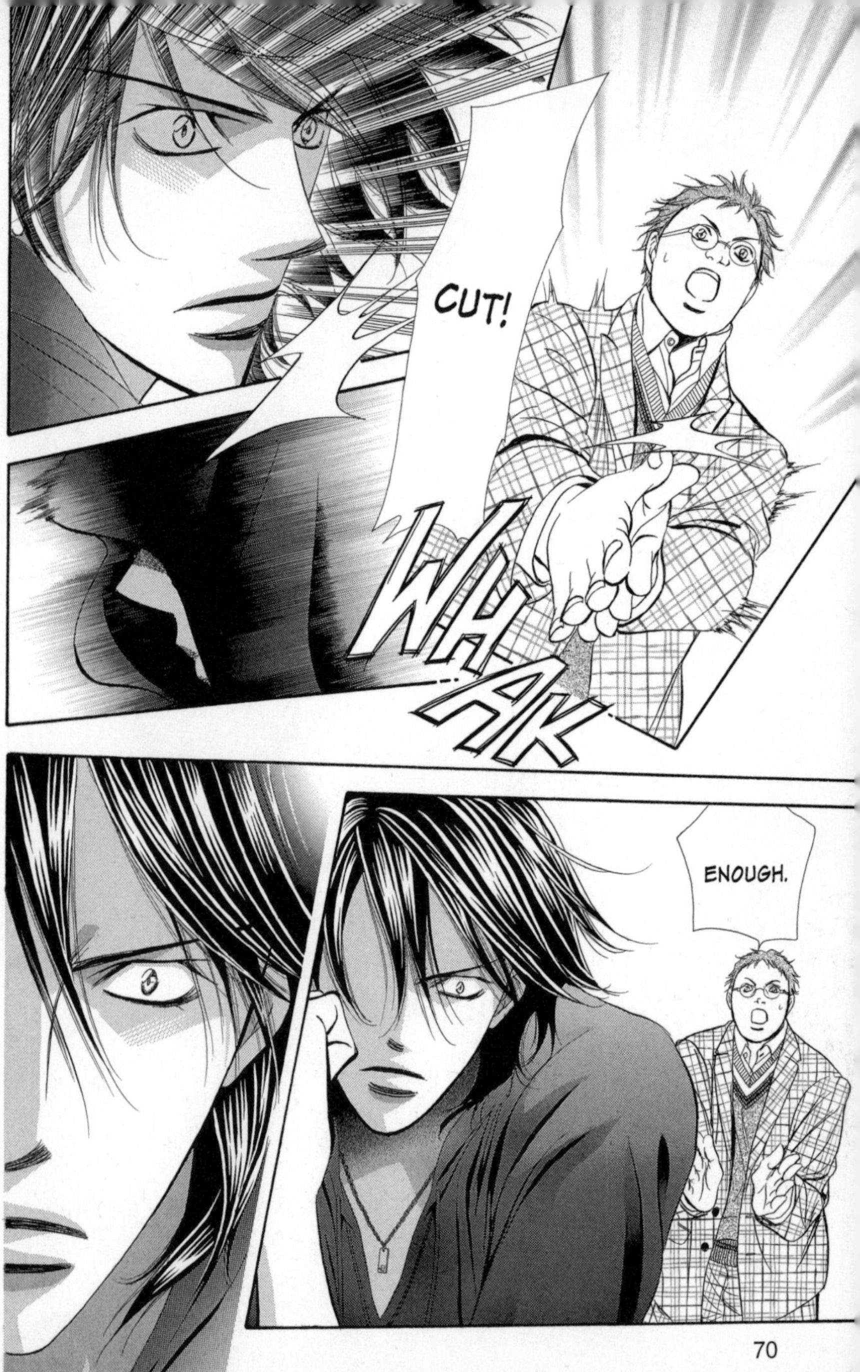
CUT!
WHAK
ENOUGH.

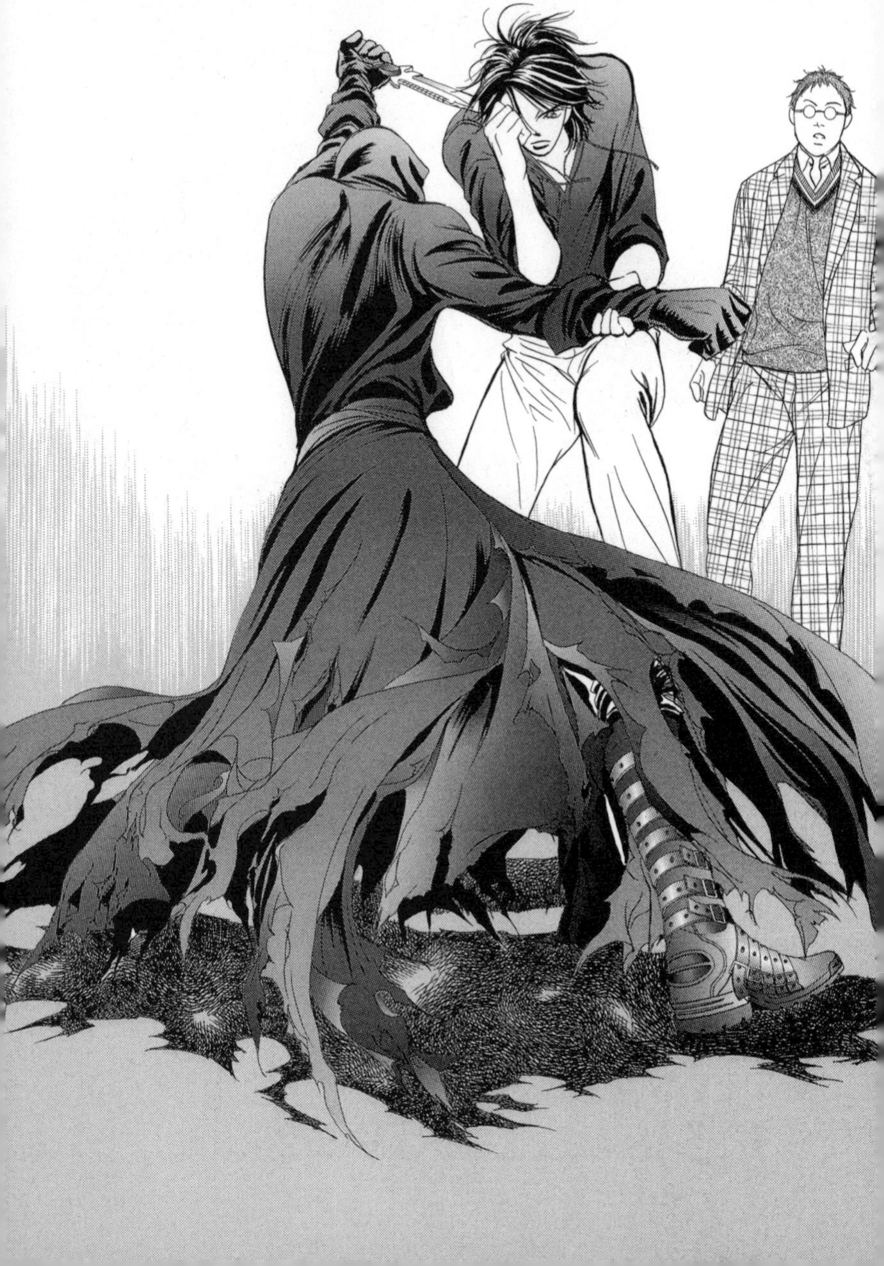

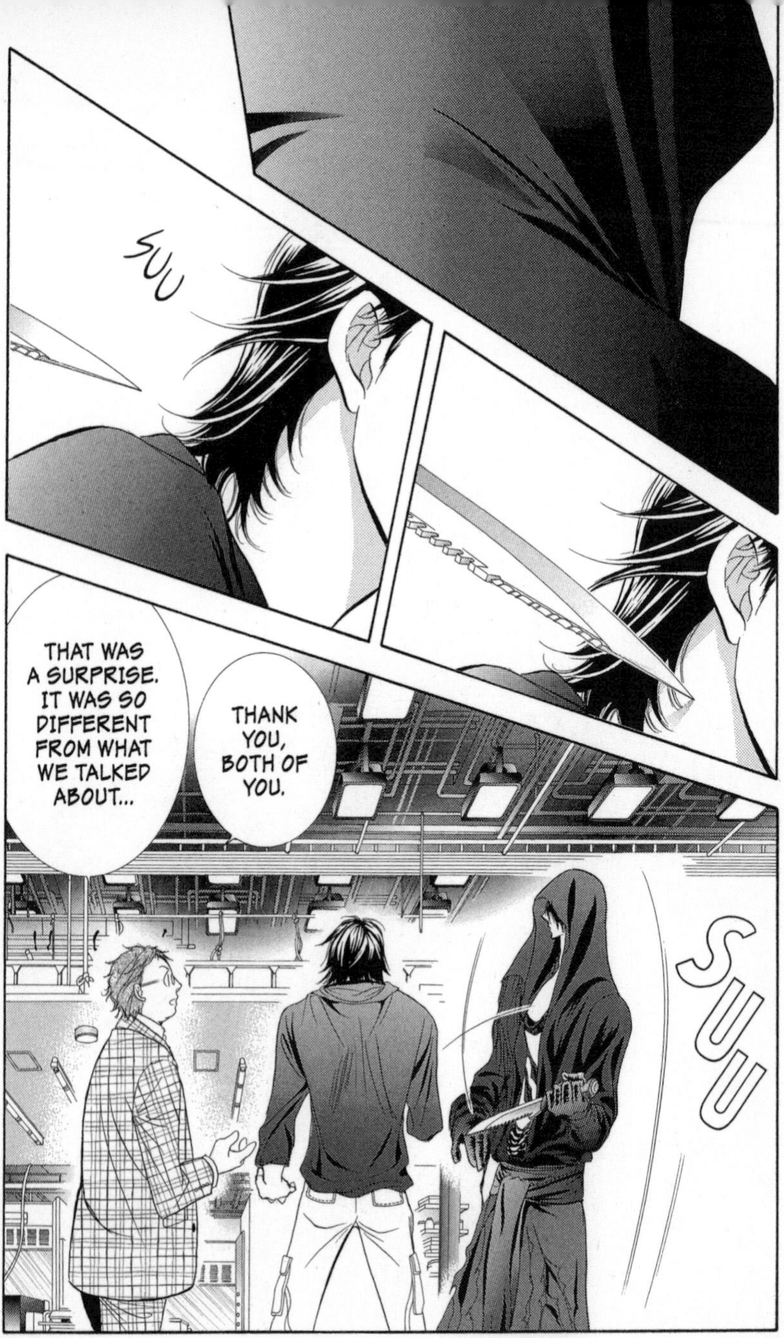
SUU
THANK YOU, BOTH OF YOU.
THAT WAS A SURPRISE. IT WAS SO DIFFERENT FROM WHAT WE TALKED ABOUT...
SUU

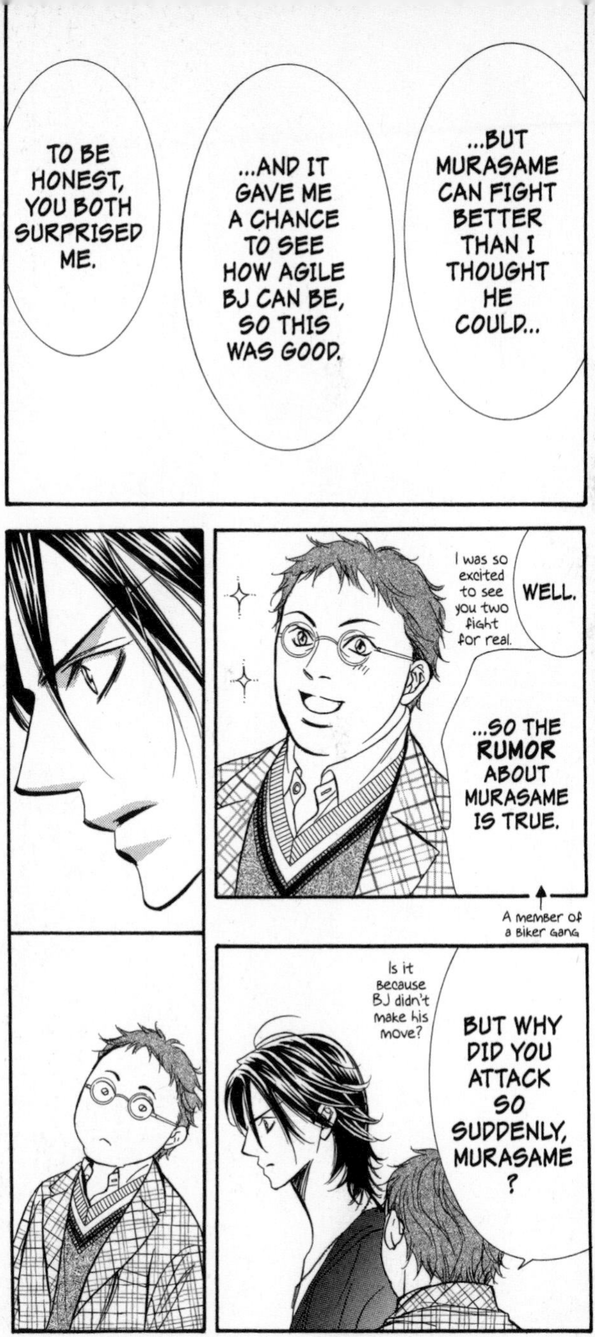
...BUT MURASAME CAN FIGHT BETTER THAN I THOUGHT HE COULD...
...AND IT GAVE ME A CHANCE TO SEE HOW AGILE BJ CAN BE, SO THIS WAS GOOD.
TO BE HONEST, YOU BOTH SURPRISED ME.
WELL.
I was so excited to see you two fight for real.
...SO THE RUMOR ABOUT MURASAME IS TRUE.
A member of a Biker Gang
BUT WHY DID YOU ATTACK SO SUDDENLY, MURASAME?
Is it because BJ didn't make his move?

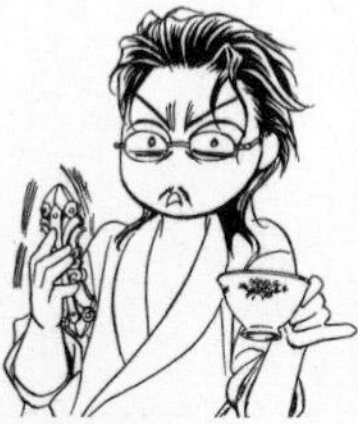

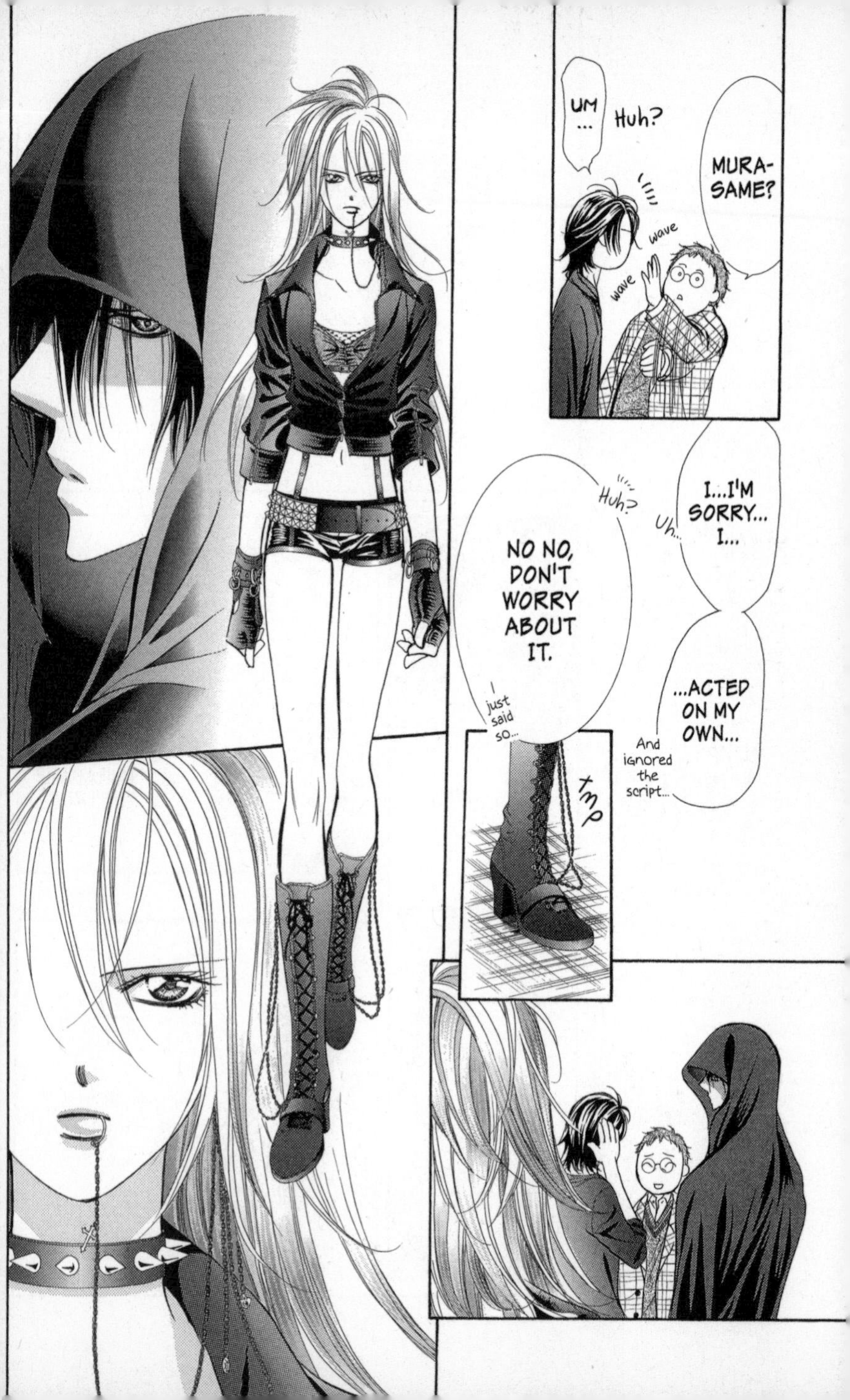
MURA-SAME?
wave
wave
Huh?
UM...
I...I'M SORRY... I...
...ACTED ON MY OWN...
And ignored the script...
Uh...
Huh?
NO NO, DON'T WORRY ABOUT IT.
I just said so...
tmp

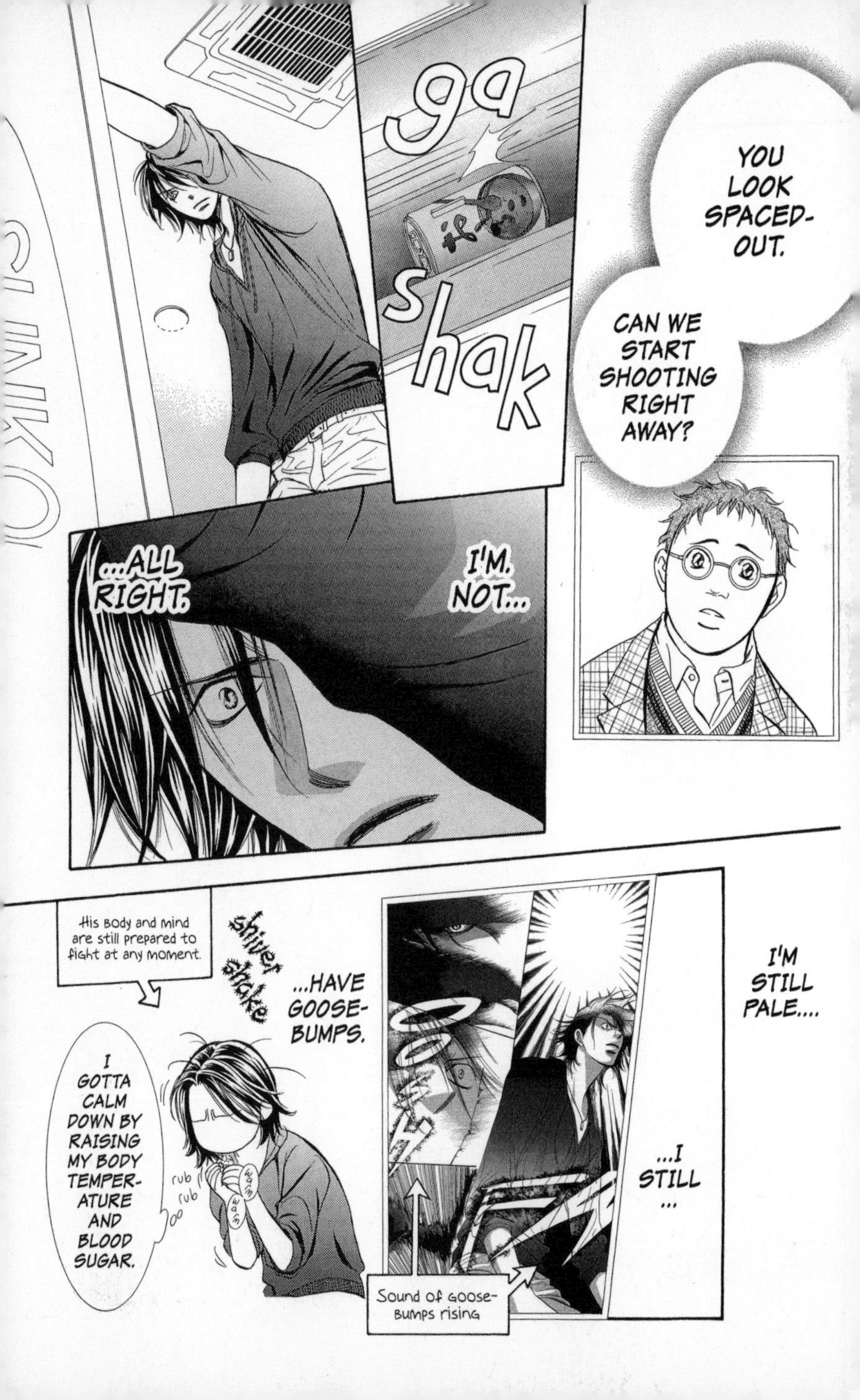
YOU LOOK SPACED-OUT.
CAN WE START SHOOTING RIGHT AWAY?
ga shak
I'M. NOT...
...ALL RIGHT.
I'M STILL PALE....
...I STILL ...
Sound of goose-bumps rising
...HAVE GOOSE-BUMPS.
shiver shake
His body and mind are still prepared to fight at any moment.
I GOTTA CALM DOWN BY RAISING MY BODY TEMPERATURE AND BLOOD SUGAR.
rub rub
warm
warm

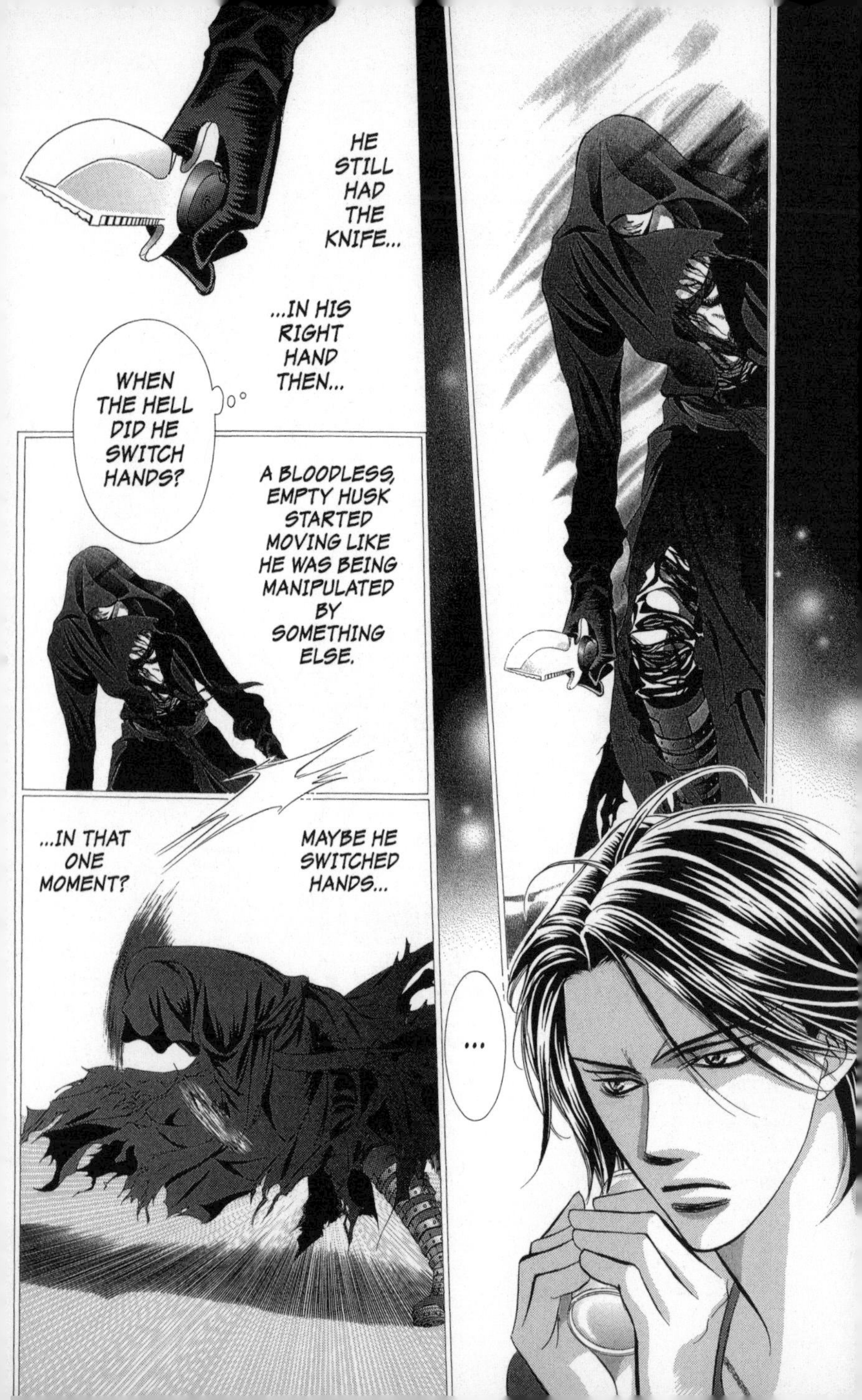
...
HE STILL HAD THE KNIFE...
...IN HIS RIGHT HAND THEN...
WHEN THE HELL DID HE SWITCH HANDS?
A BLOODLESS, EMPTY HUSK STARTED MOVING LIKE HE WAS BEING MANIPULATED BY SOMETHING ELSE.
MAYBE HE SWITCHED HANDS...
...IN THAT ONE MOMENT?

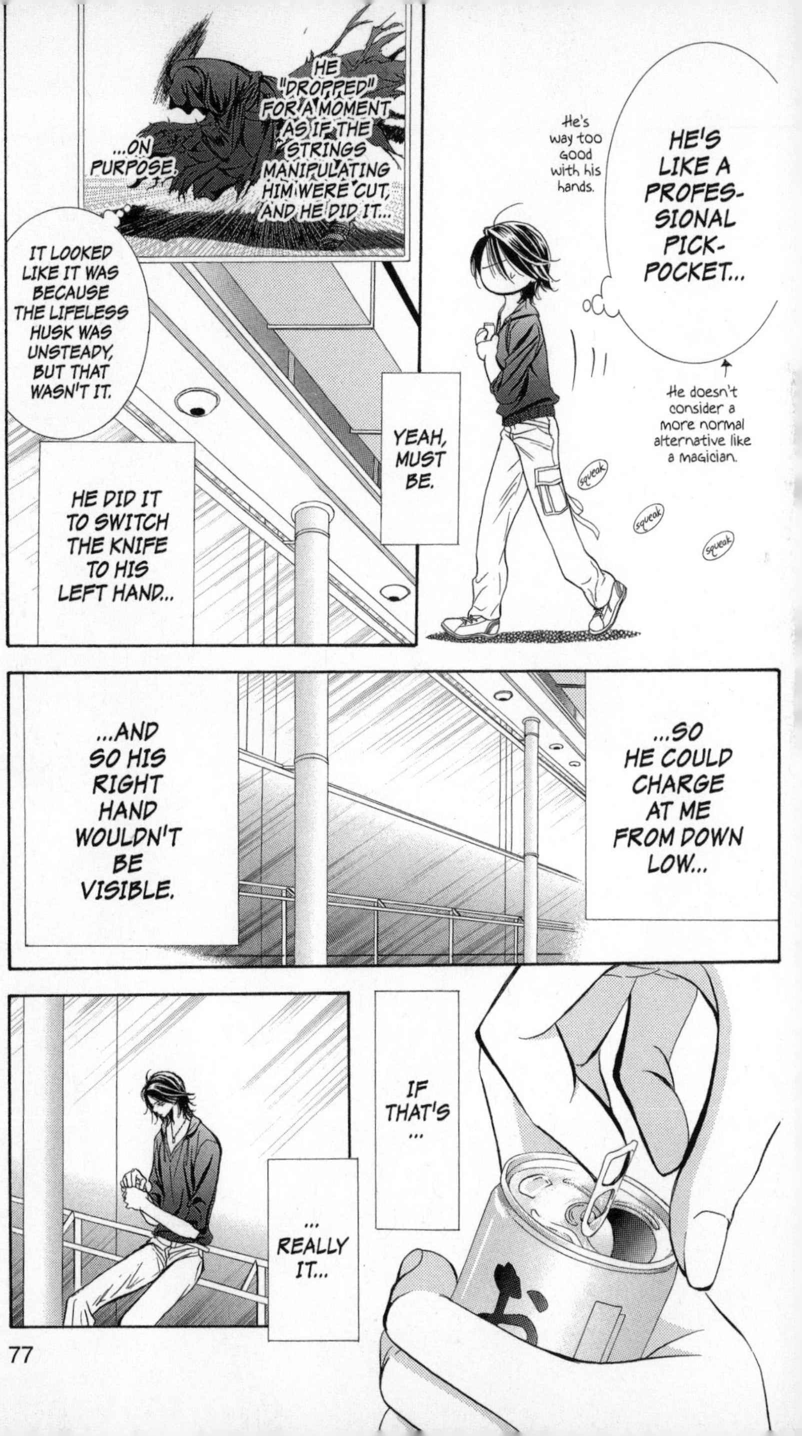
HE'S LIKE A PROFES-SIONAL PICK-POCKET...
He's way too good with his hands.
He doesn't consider a more normal alternative like a magician.
squeak
squeak
squeak
YEAH, MUST BE.
HE "DROPPED" FOR A MOMENT, AS IF THE STRINGS MANIPULATING HIM WERE CUT, AND HE DID IT...
...ON PURPOSE.
IT LOOKED LIKE IT WAS BECAUSE THE LIFELESS HUSK WAS UNSTEADY, BUT THAT WASN'T IT.
HE DID IT TO SWITCH THE KNIFE TO HIS LEFT HAND...
...SO HE COULD CHARGE AT ME FROM DOWN LOW...
...AND SO HIS RIGHT HAND WOULDN'T BE VISIBLE.
IF THAT'S ...
... REALLY IT...

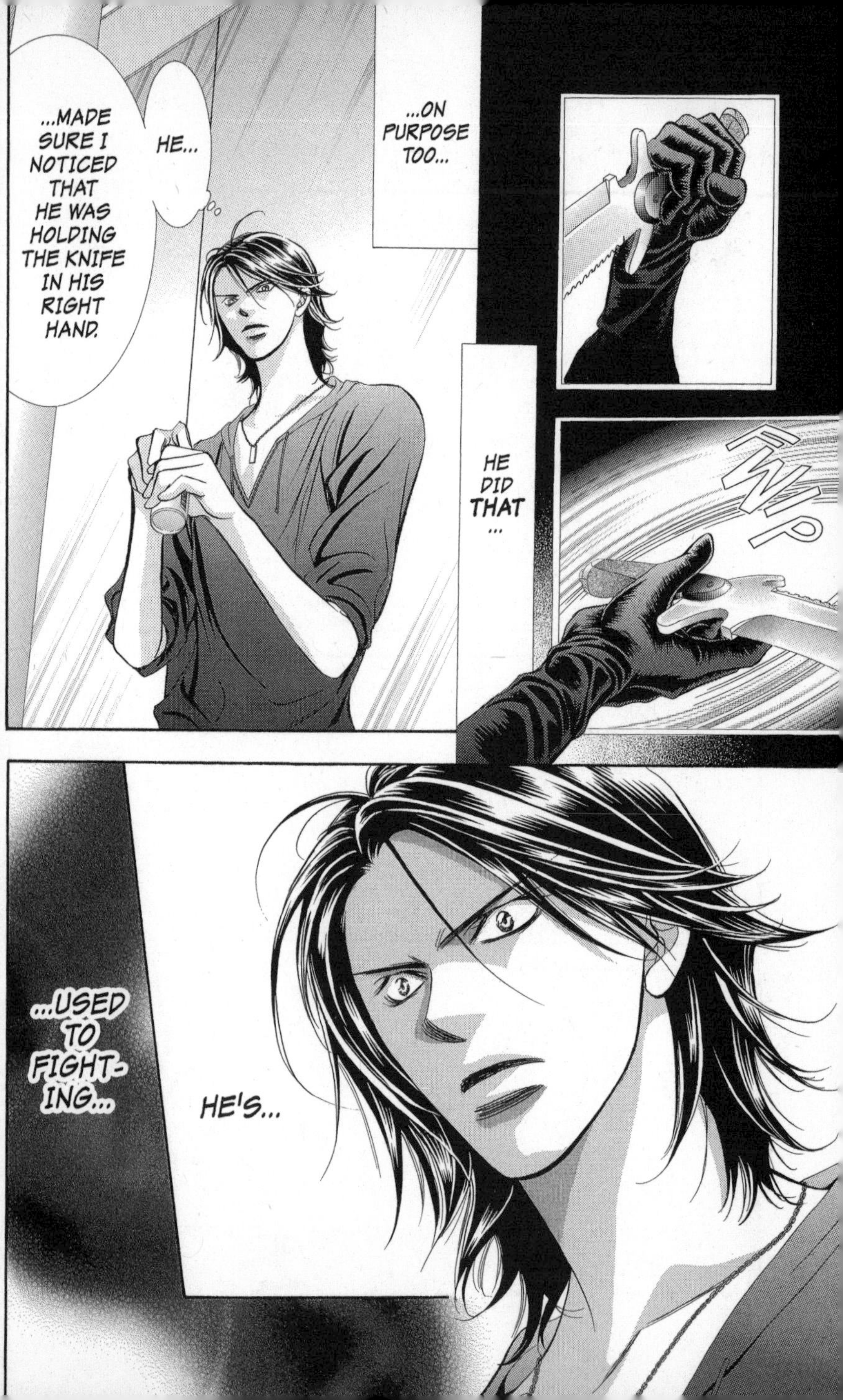
FWIP
HE DID THAT...
...ON PURPOSE TOO...
HE...
...MADE SURE I NOTICED THAT HE WAS HOLDING THE KNIFE IN HIS RIGHT HAND.
HE'S...
...USED TO FIGHTING...

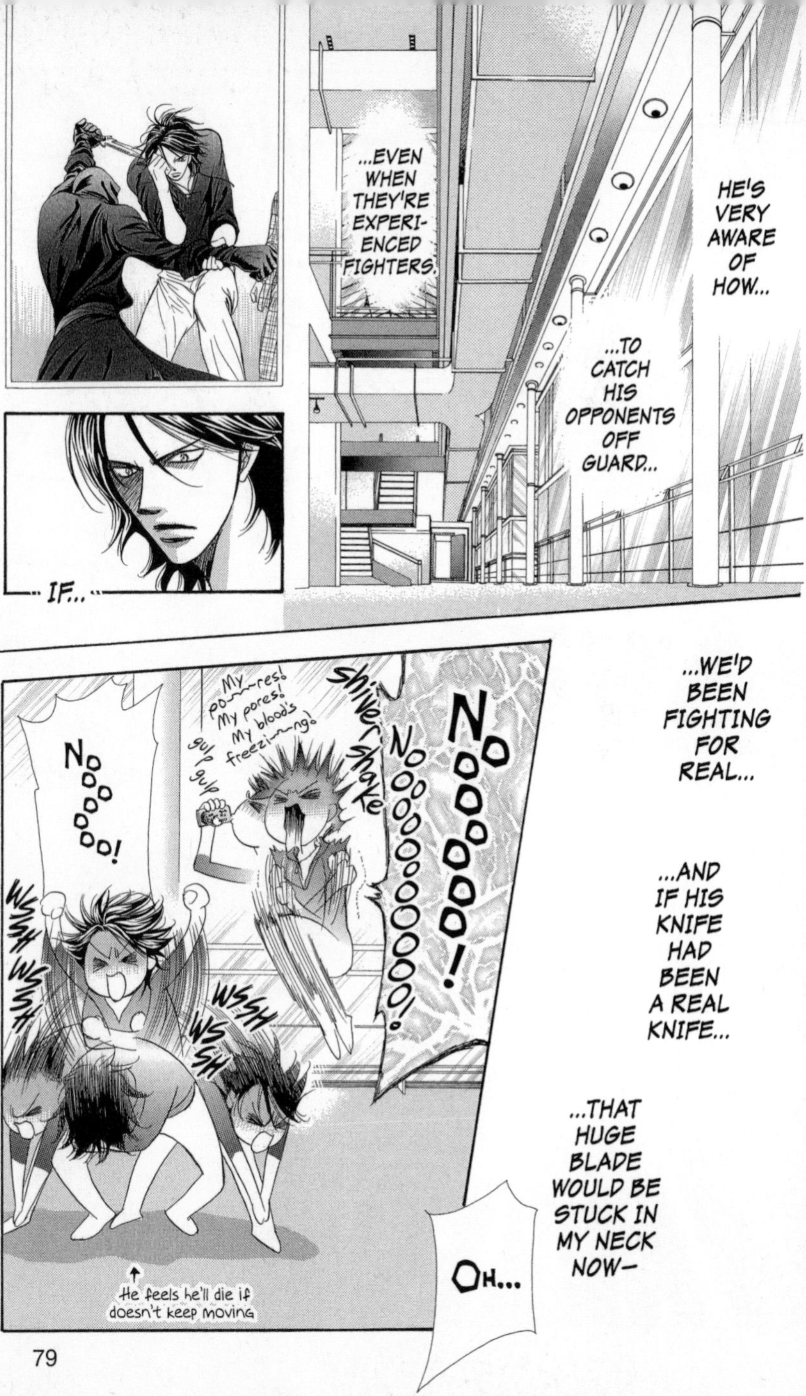
HE'S VERY AWARE OF HOW...
...TO CATCH HIS OPPONENTS OFF GUARD...
...EVEN WHEN THEY'RE EXPERI-ENCED FIGHTERS.
IF...
...WE'D BEEN FIGHTING FOR REAL...
...AND IF HIS KNIFE HAD BEEN A REAL KNIFE...
...THAT HUGE BLADE WOULD BE STUCK IN MY NECK NOW—
OH...
NOOOOOOOO!
NOOOOOOOOOOOOO!
shiver shake
My po~~res! My pores! My blood's freezi~~ng!
gulp gulp
Nooooooo!
WSSH WSSH
WSSH WSSH
↑ He feels he'll die if doesn't keep moving

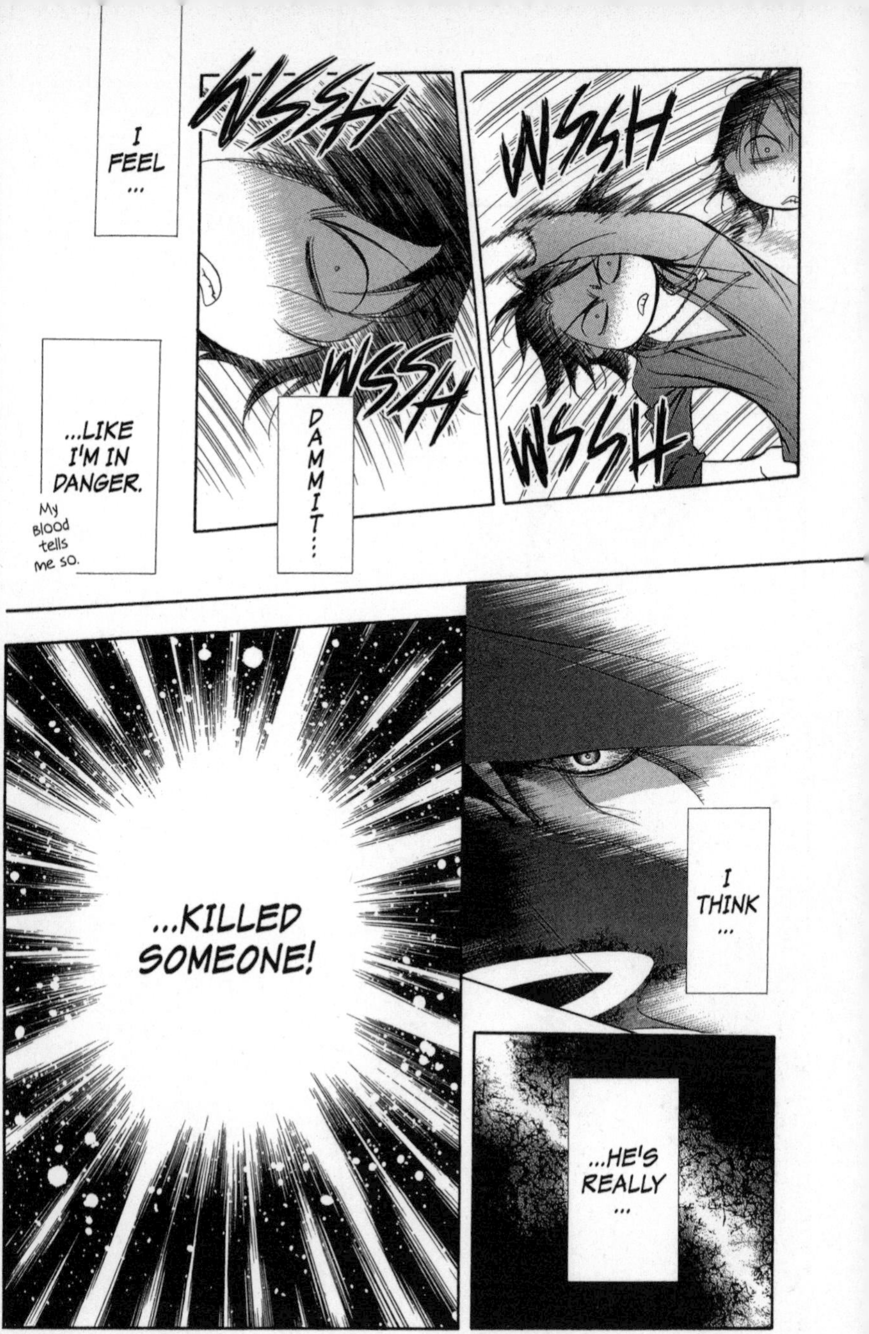
WSSH
WSSH
WSSH
WSSH
DAMMIT...
I FEEL ...
...LIKE I'M IN DANGER.
My blood tells me so.
I THINK ...
...HE'S REALLY ...
...KILLED SOMEONE!

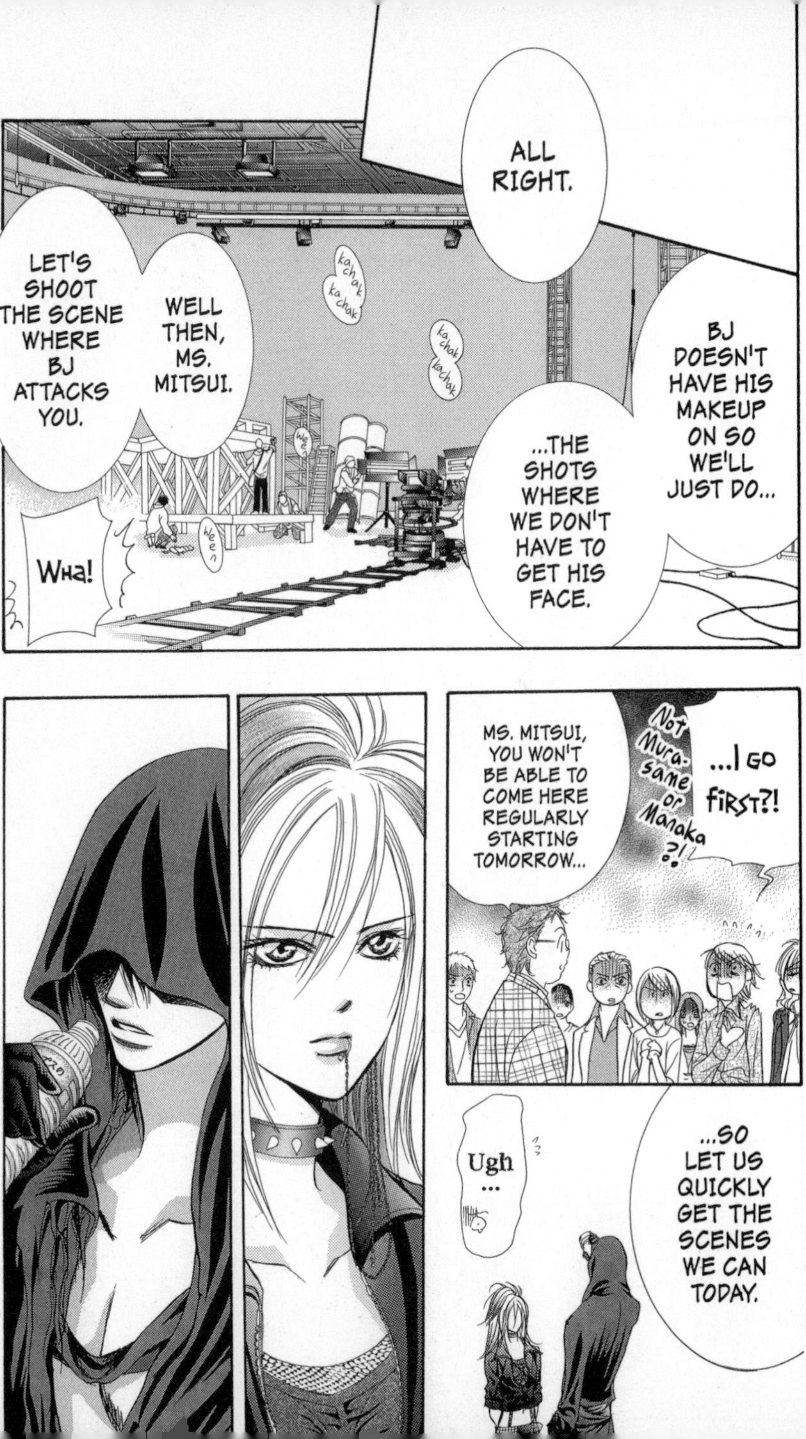
ALL RIGHT.
BJ DOESN'T HAVE HIS MAKEUP ON SO WE'LL JUST DO...
...THE SHOTS WHERE WE DON'T HAVE TO GET HIS FACE.
ka chak ka chak
ka chak kachak
kachak ka chak
Ween
Ween
WELL THEN, MS. MITSUI.
LET'S SHOOT THE SCENE WHERE BJ ATTACKS YOU.
Wha!
MS. MITSUI, YOU WON'T BE ABLE TO COME HERE REGULARLY STARTING TOMORROW...
...I GO FIRST?!
Not Murasame or Manaka?!
...SO LET US QUICKLY GET THE SCENES WE CAN TODAY.
Ugh ...

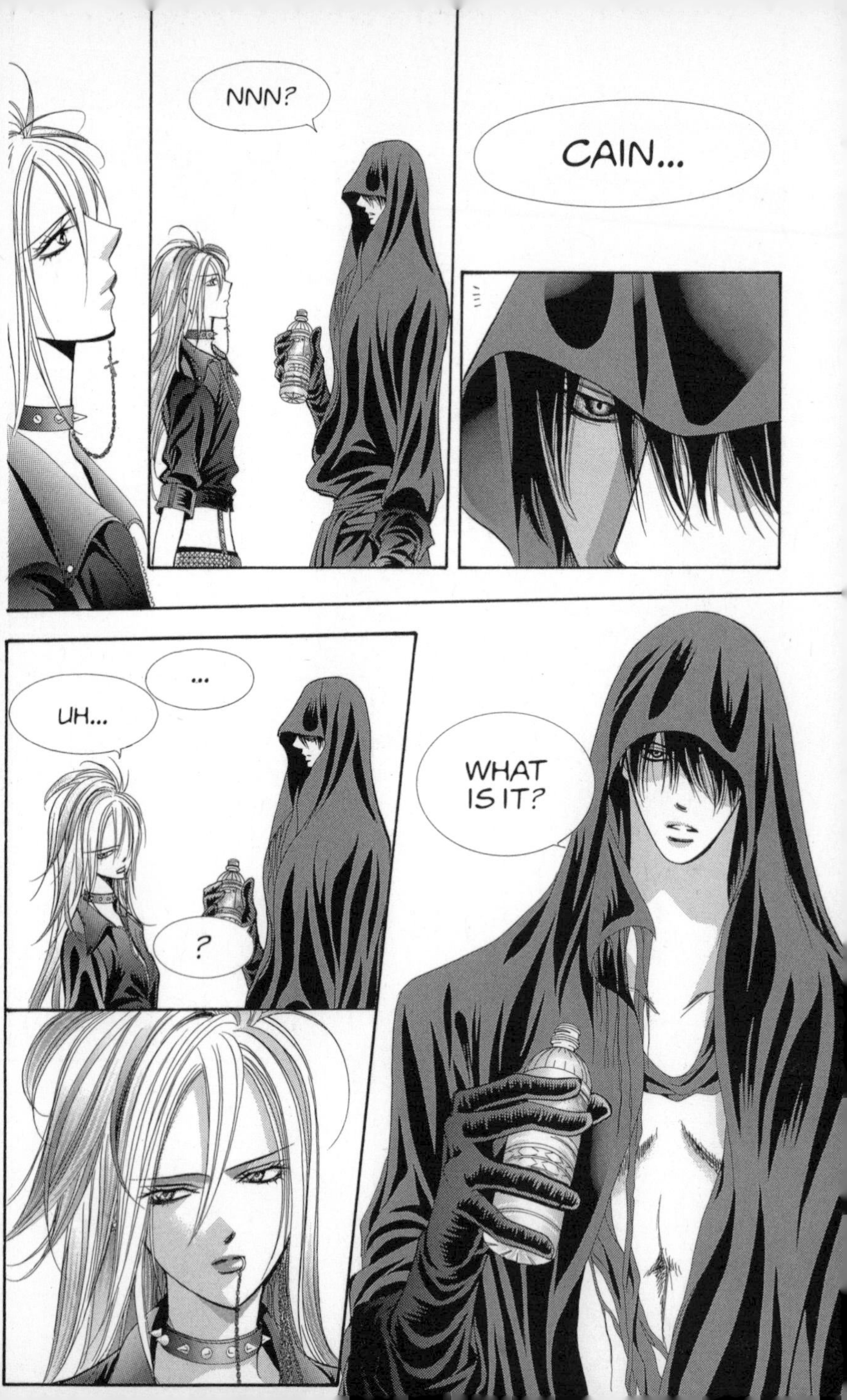
CAIN...
NNN?
WHAT IS IT?
...
UH...
?

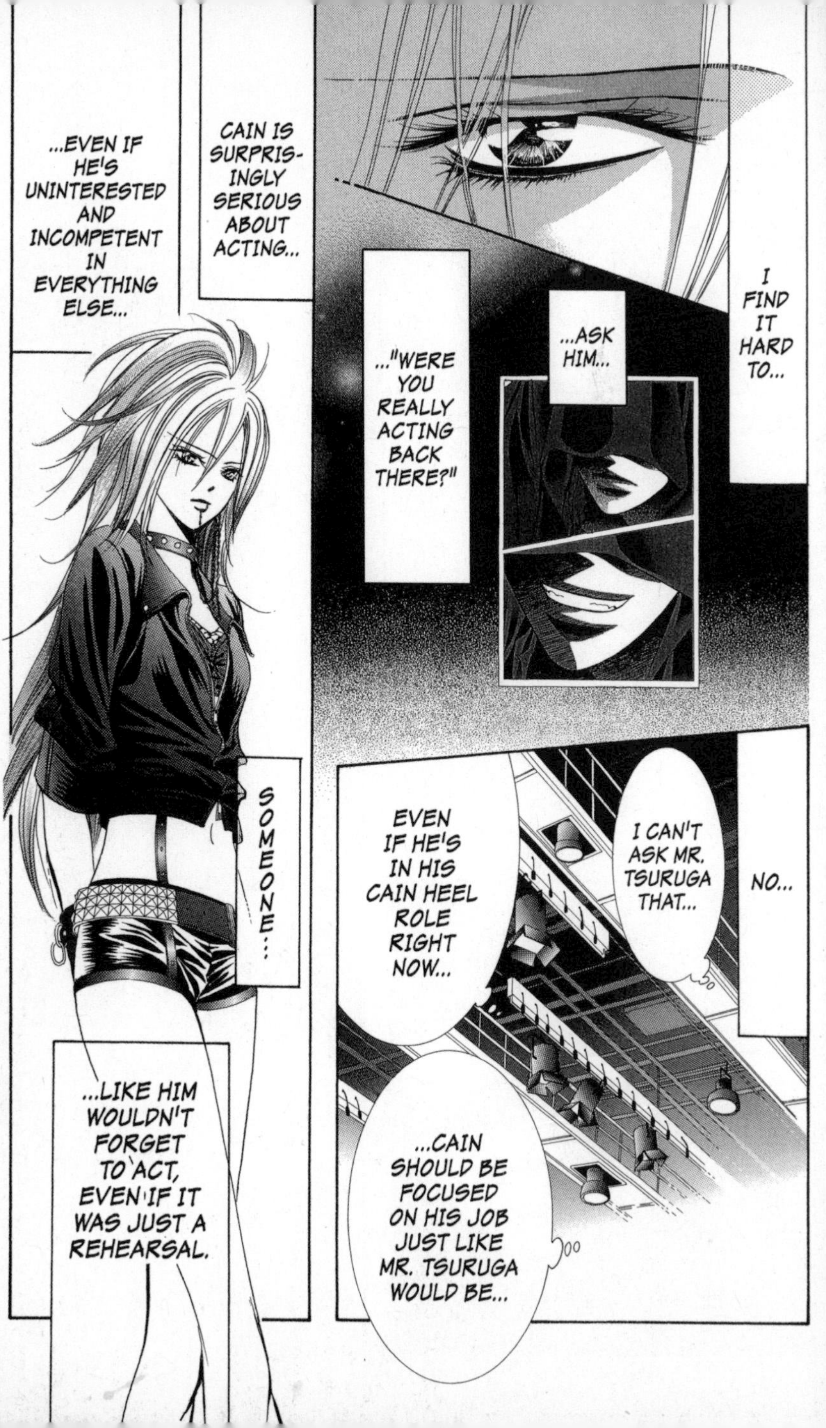

I FIND IT HARD TO...
...ASK HIM...
..."WERE YOU REALLY ACTING BACK THERE?"
NO...
I CAN'T ASK MR. TSURUGA THAT...
EVEN IF HE'S IN HIS CAIN HEEL ROLE RIGHT NOW...
...CAIN SHOULD BE FOCUSED ON HIS JOB JUST LIKE MR. TSURUGA WOULD BE...
CAIN IS SURPRISINGLY SERIOUS ABOUT ACTING...
...EVEN IF HE'S UNINTERESTED AND INCOMPETENT IN EVERYTHING ELSE...
SOMEONE...
...LIKE HIM WOULDN'T FORGET TO ACT, EVEN IF IT WAS JUST A REHEARSAL.

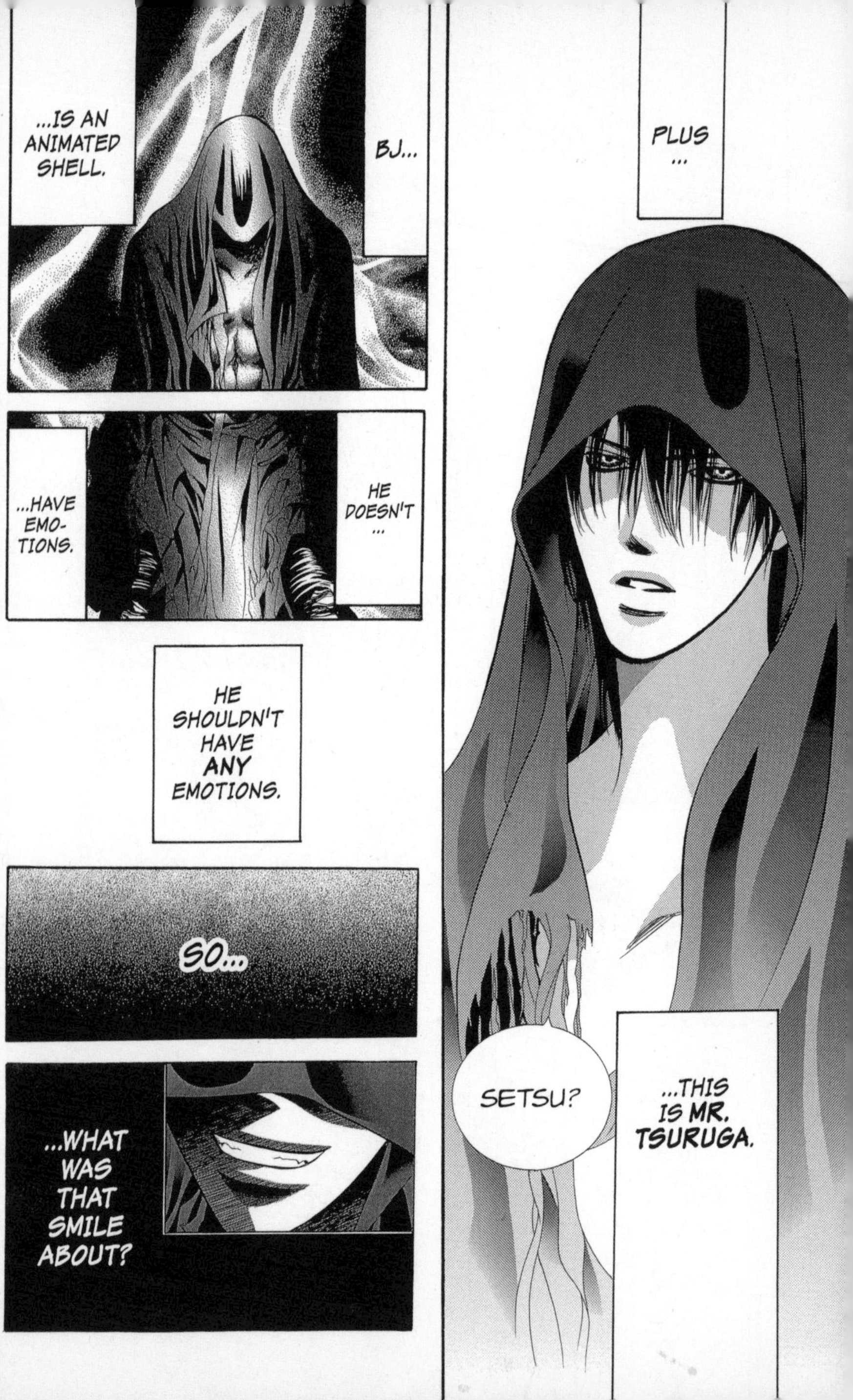
PLUS ...
...THIS IS MR. TSURUGA.
SETSU?
BJ...
...IS AN ANIMATED SHELL.
HE DOESN'T ...
...HAVE EMO- TIONS.
HE SHOULDN'T HAVE ANY EMOTIONS.
SO...
...WHAT WAS THAT SMILE ABOUT?

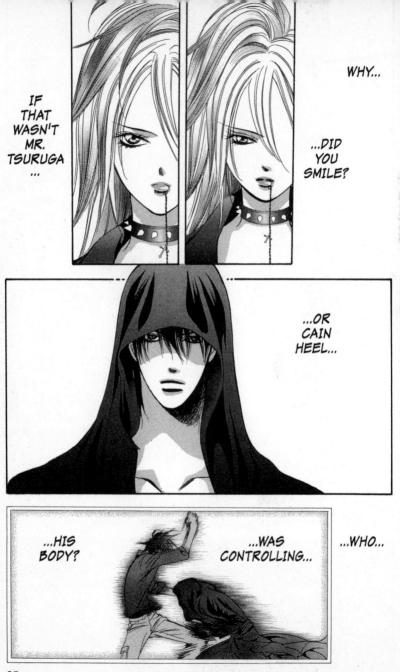

WHY...

IF THAT WASN'T MR. TSURUGA...

...DID YOU SMILE?

...OR CAIN HEEL...

...HIS BODY?

...WAS CONTROLLING...

...WHO...

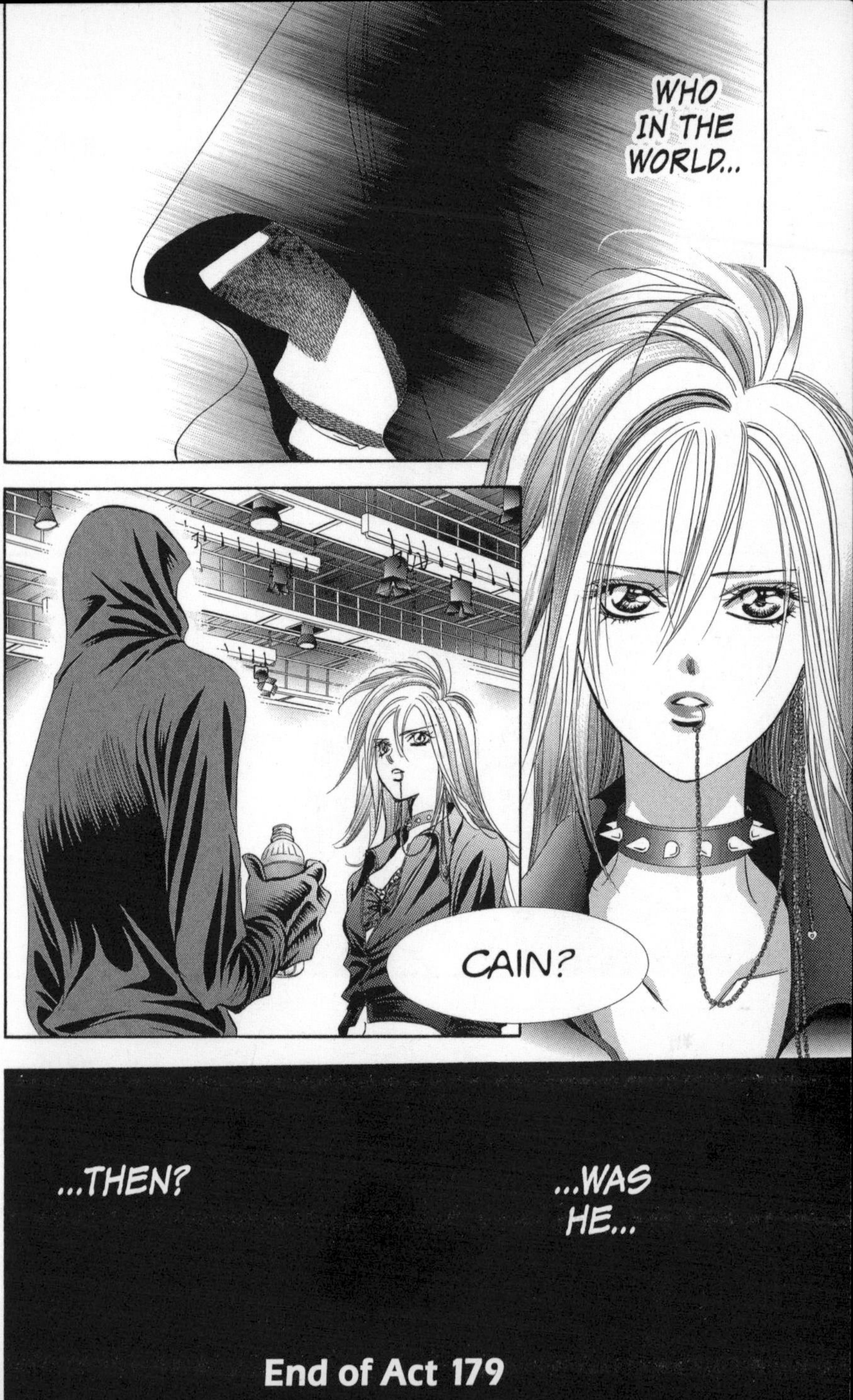
WHO IN THE WORLD...
CAIN?
...WAS HE...
...THEN?
End of Act 179

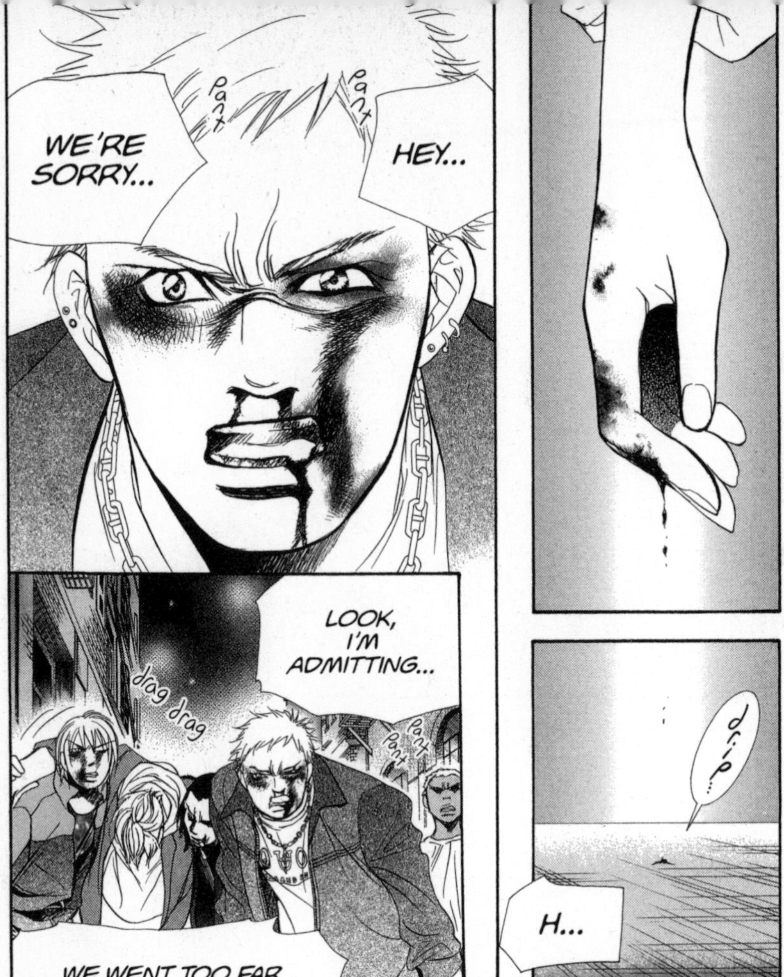
Pant
Pant
HEY...
WE'RE SORRY...
drip...
H...
LOOK, I'M ADMITTING...
Pant Pant
drag drag
...WE WENT TOO FAR...

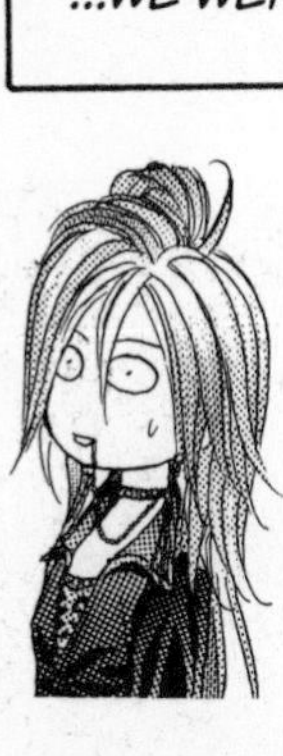

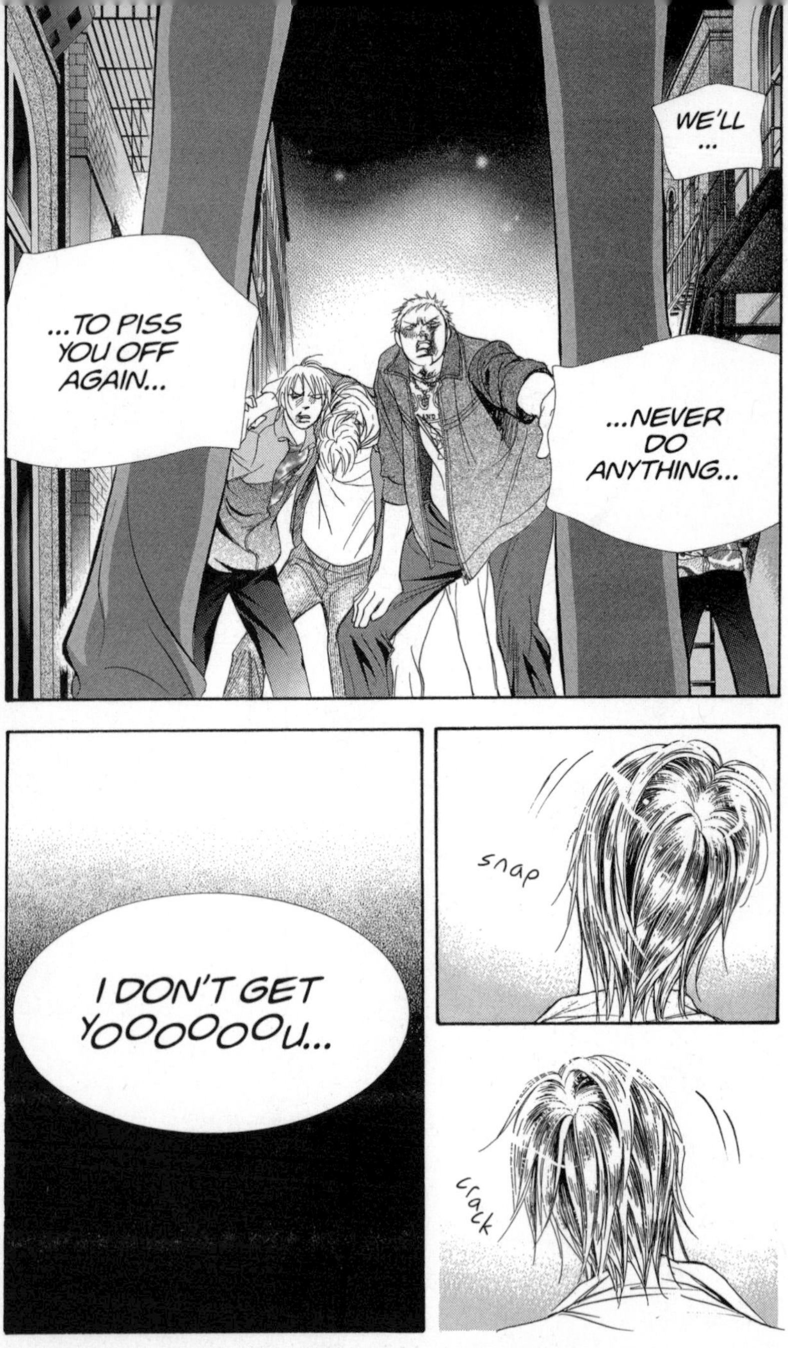
WE'LL ...
...NEVER DO ANYTHING...
...TO PISS YOU OFF AGAIN...
snap
crack
I DON'T GET YOOOOOOU...

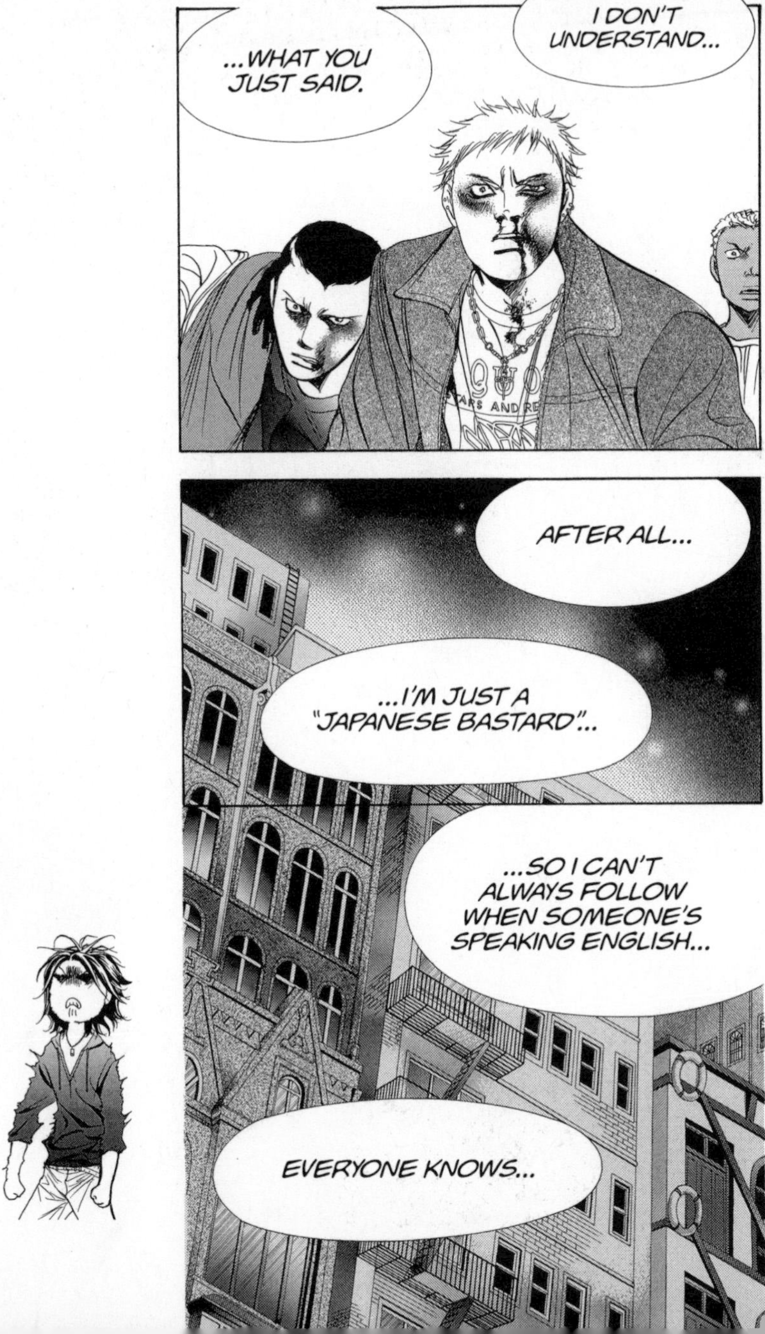
I DON'T UNDERSTAND...
...WHAT YOU JUST SAID.
AFTER ALL...
...I'M JUST A "JAPANESE BASTARD"...
...SO I CAN'T ALWAYS FOLLOW WHEN SOMEONE'S SPEAKING ENGLISH...
EVERYONE KNOWS...

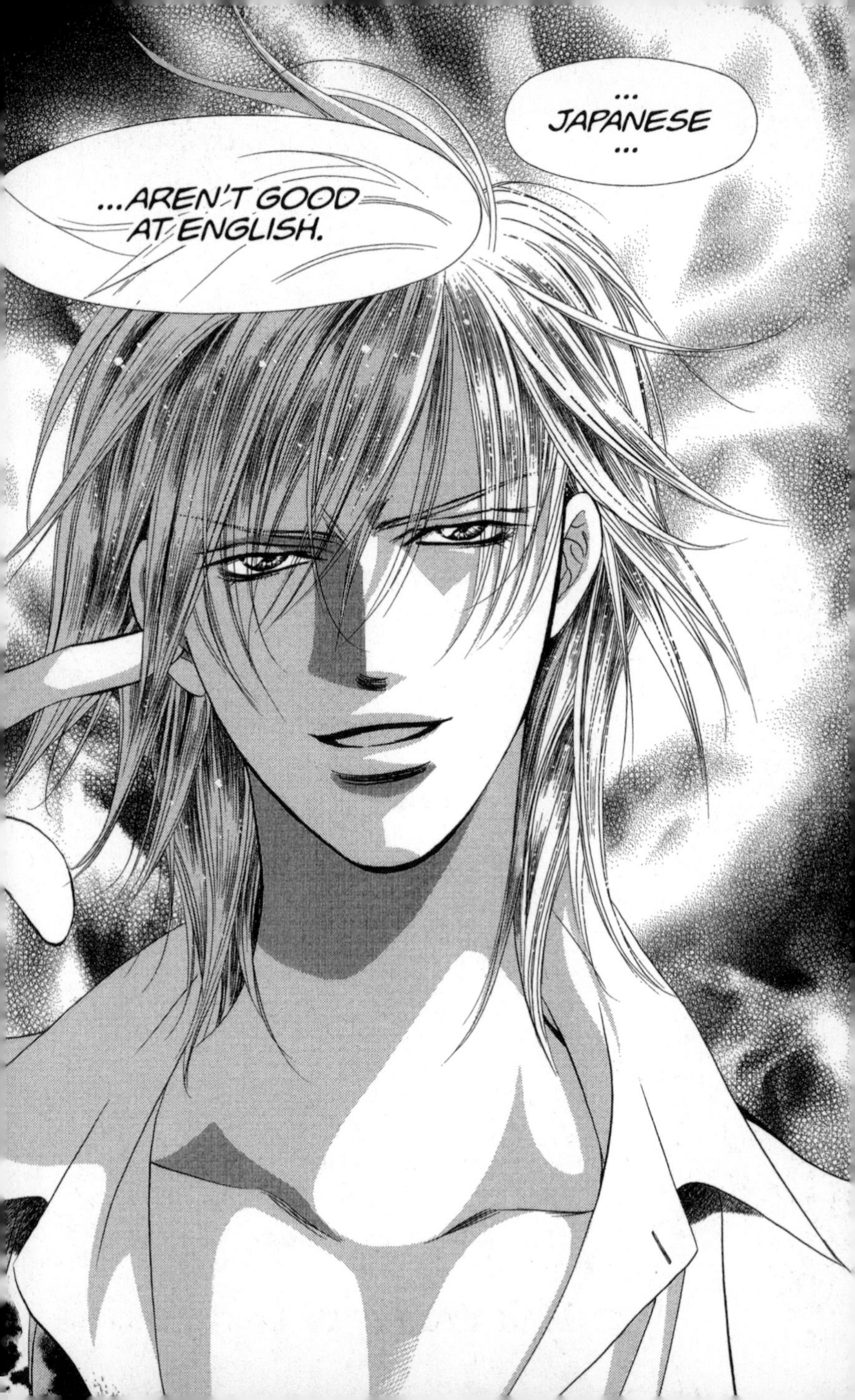
... JAPANESE ...
...AREN'T GOOD AT ENGLISH.

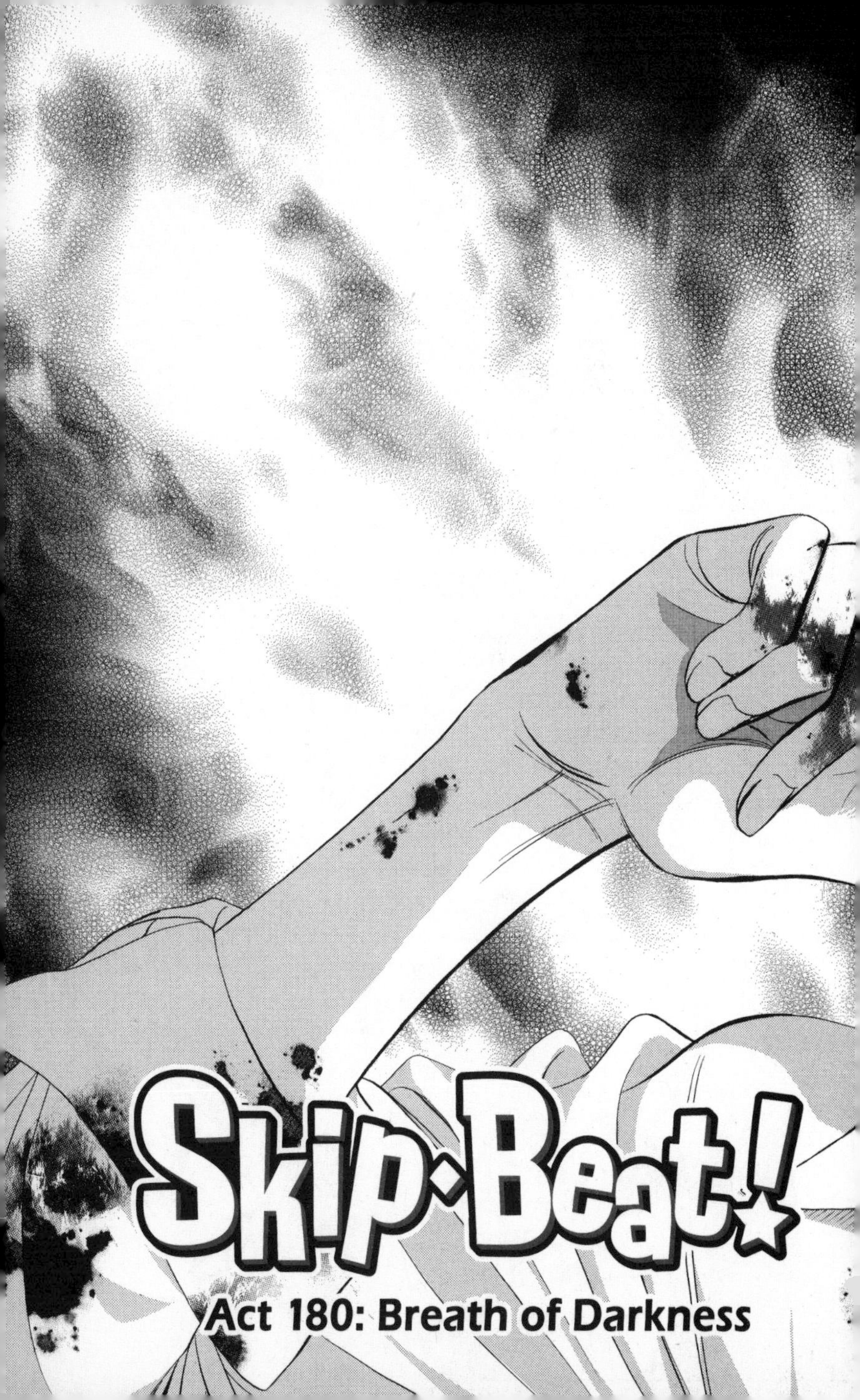
Skip·Beat!
Act 180: Breath of Darkness

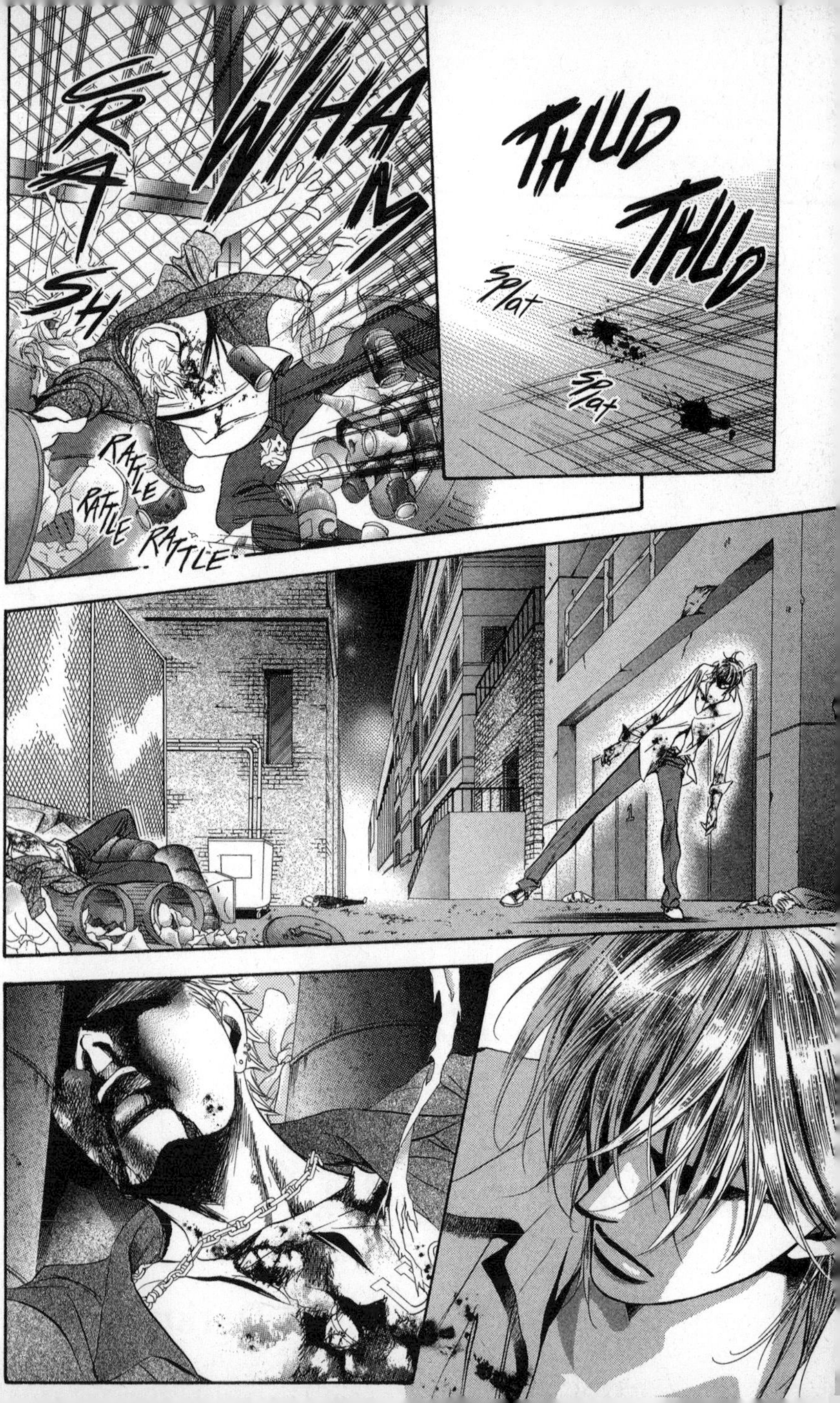
THUD
THUD
SPLAT
SPLAT
WHAM
CRASH
RATTLE
RATTLE
RATTLE

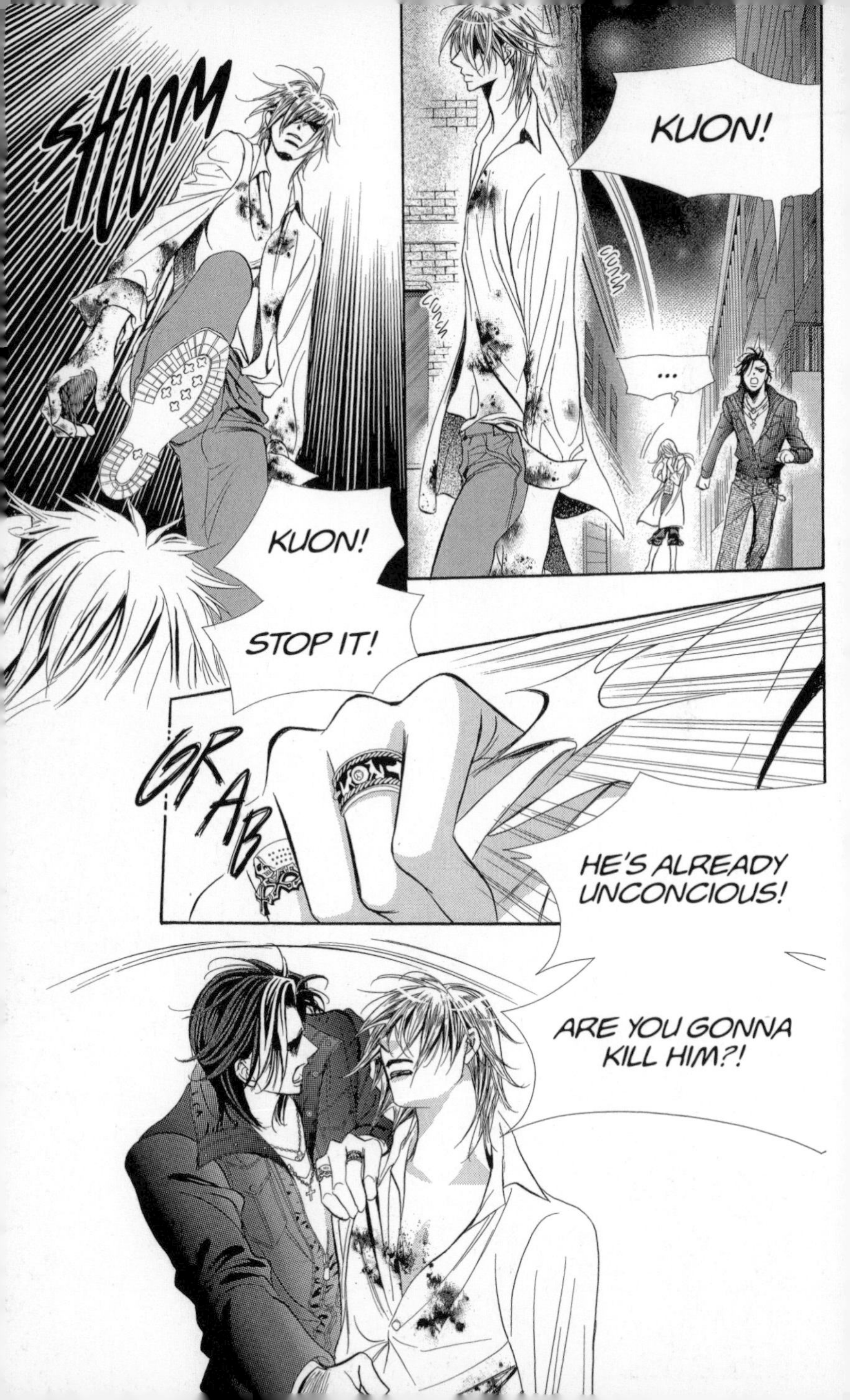
KUON!
crunch
crunch
...
SHOOM
KUON!
STOP IT!
GRAB
HE'S ALREADY UNCONCIOUS!
ARE YOU GONNA KILL HIM?!

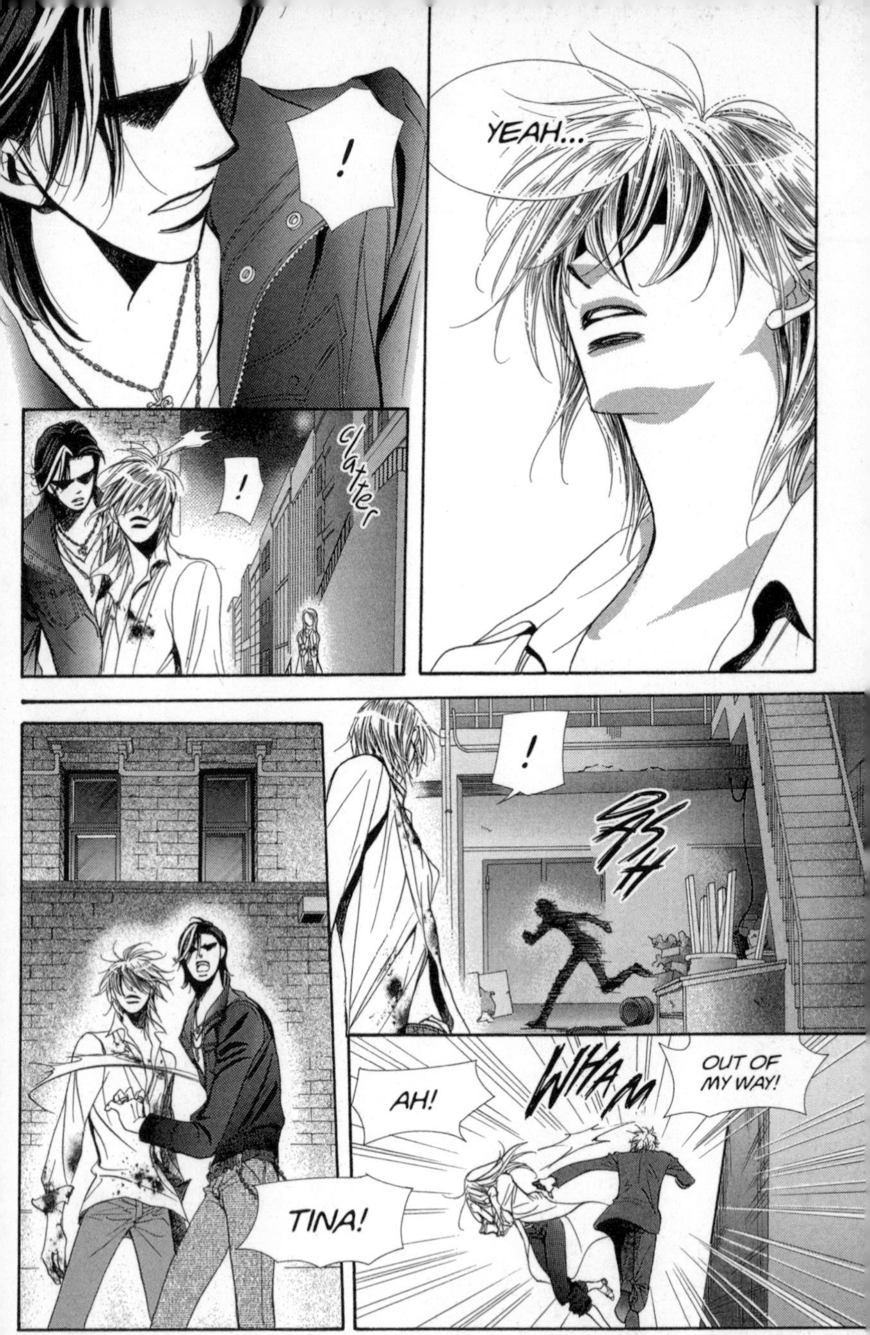
YEAH...
!
!
clatter
!
DASH
OUT OF MY WAY!
WHAM
AH!
TINA!

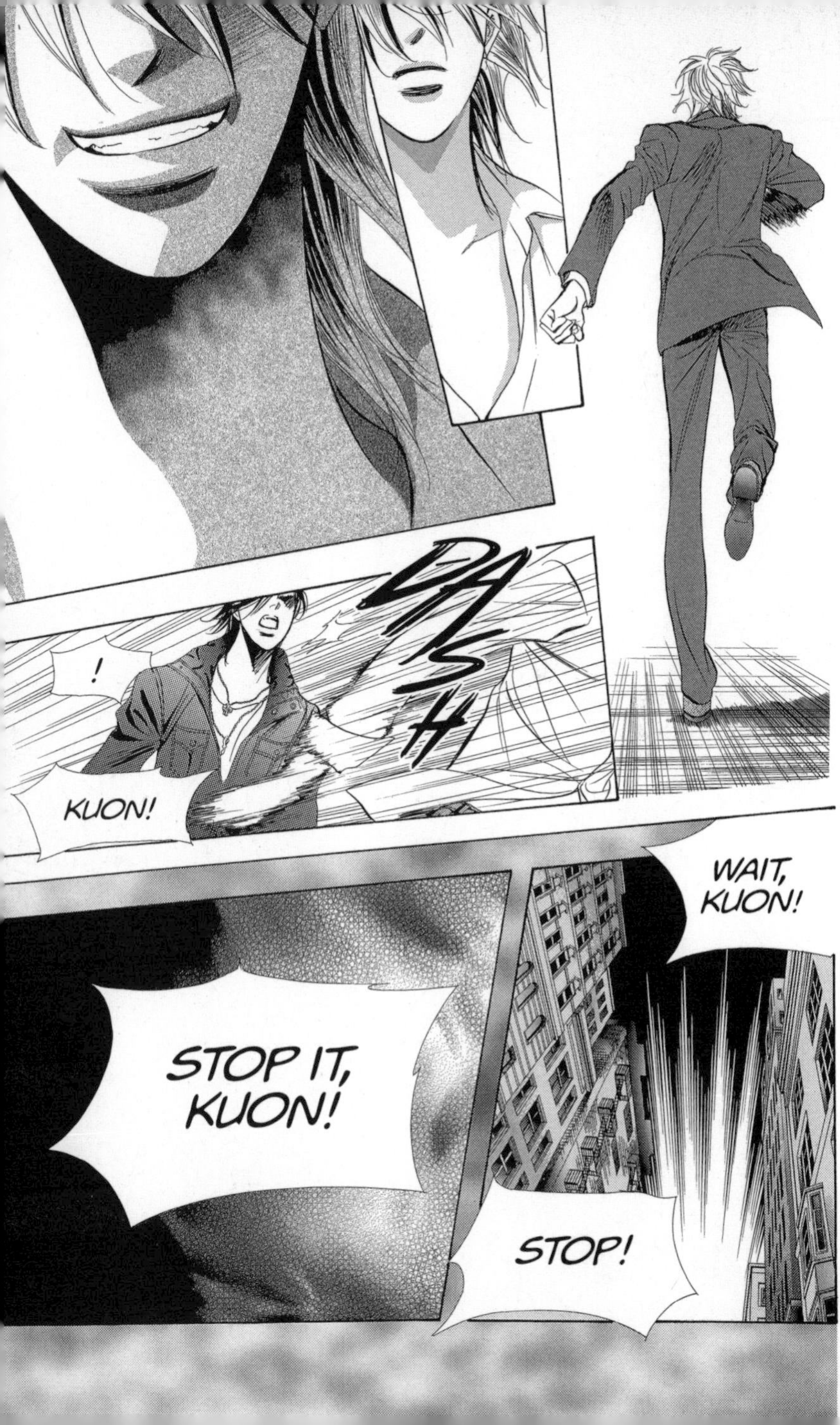
DASH
!
KUON!
WAIT, KUON!
STOP!
STOP IT, KUON!

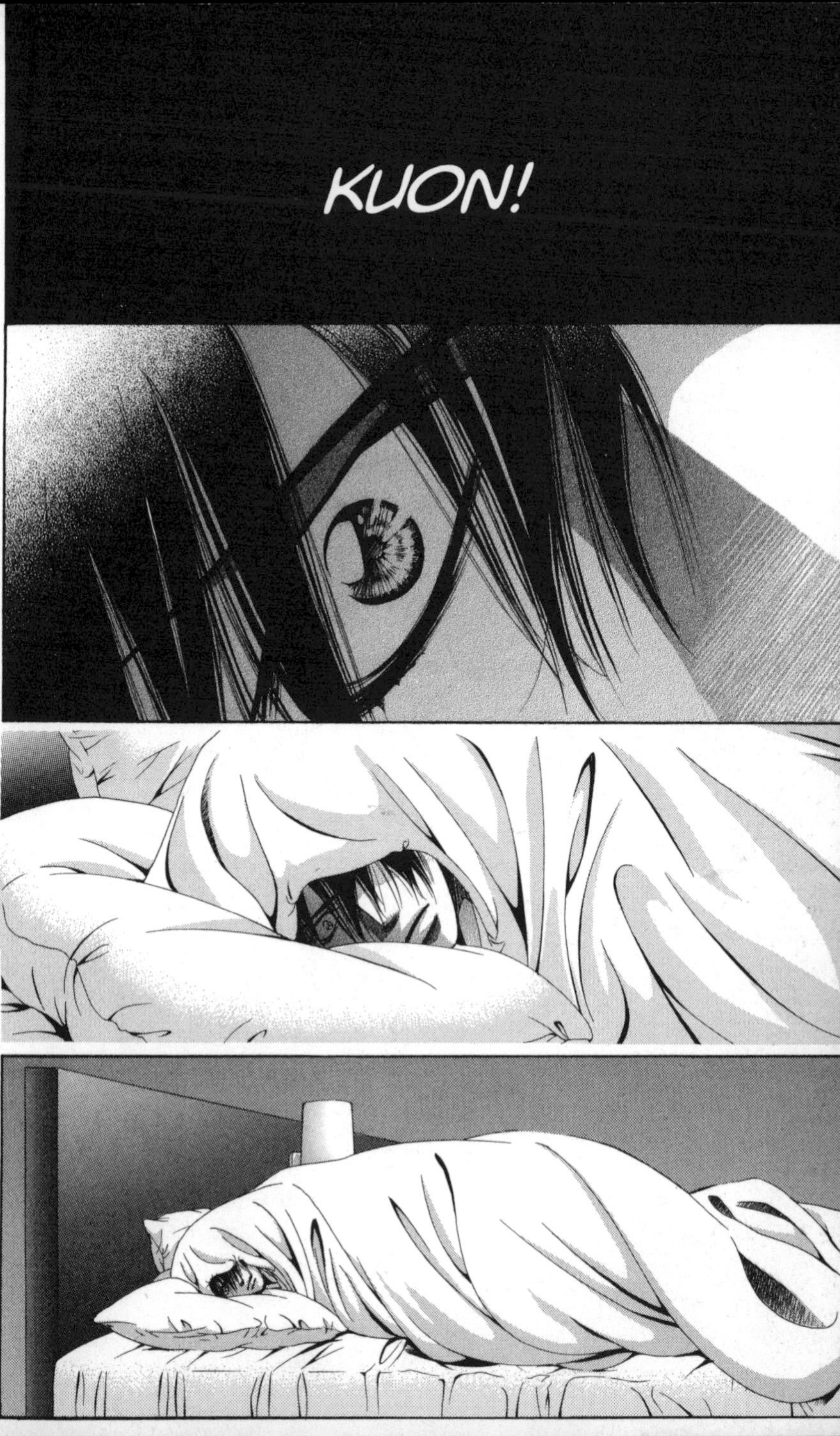
KUON!

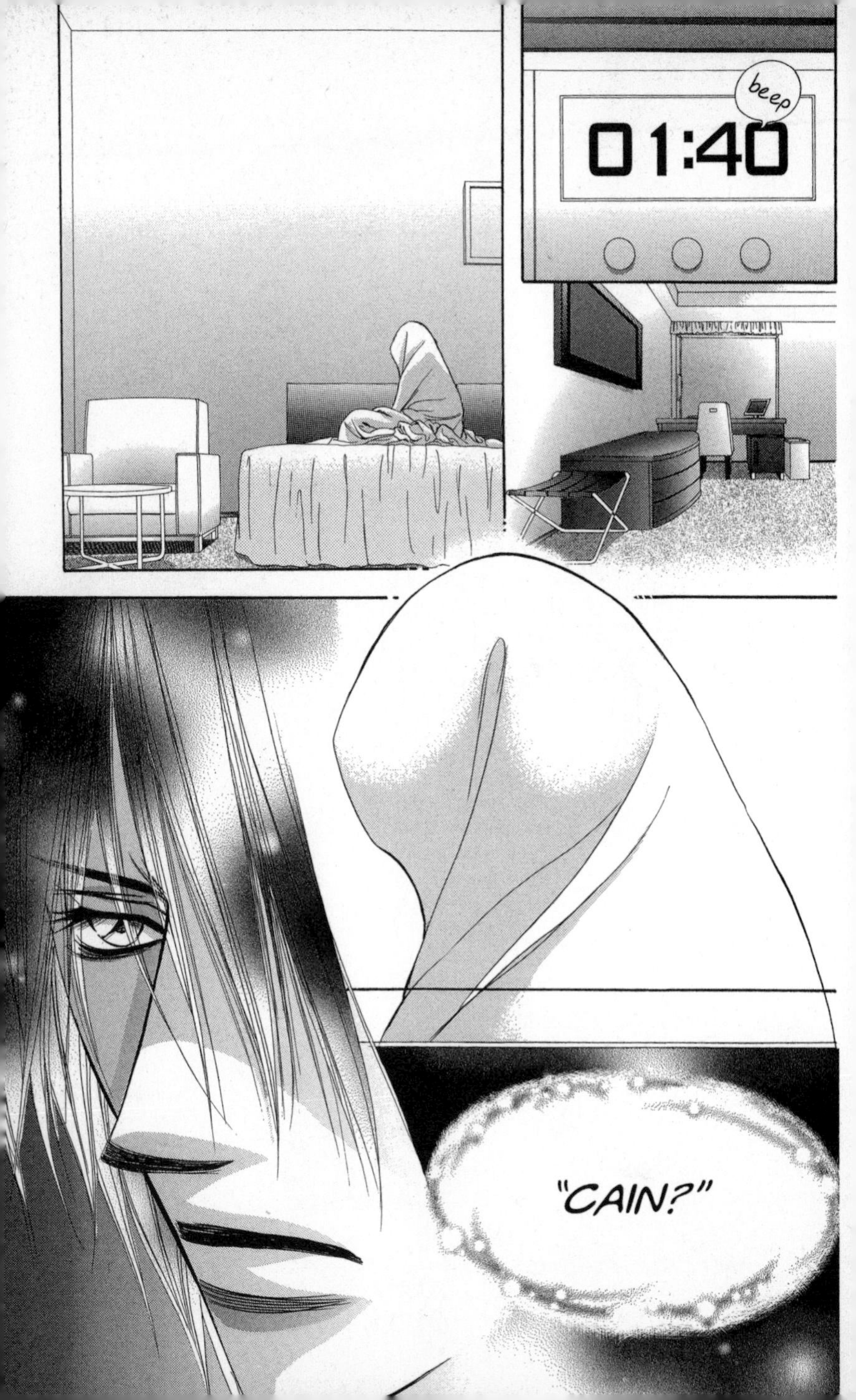
beep
01:40
"CAIN?"

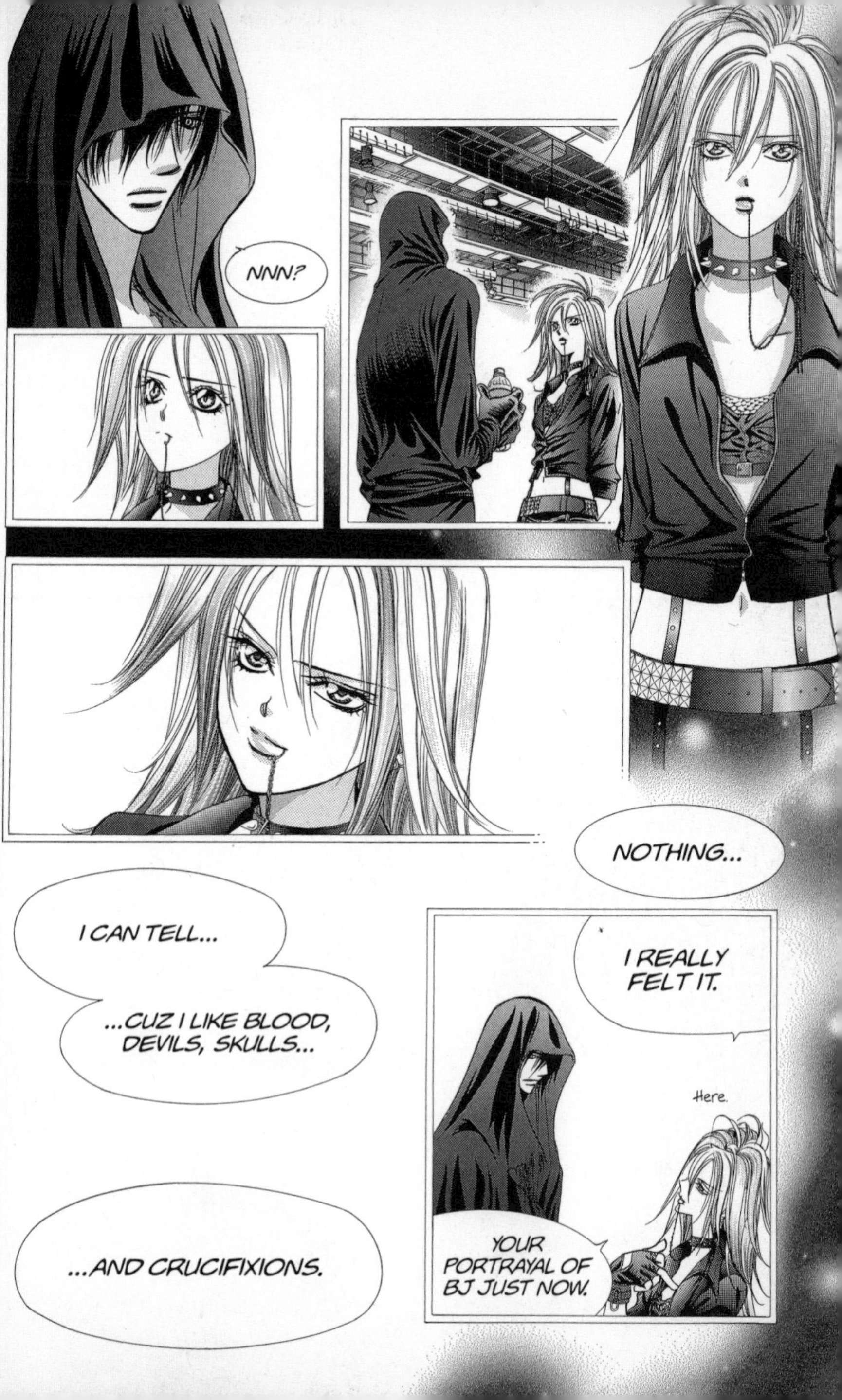
NNN?
NOTHING...
I REALLY FELT IT.
Here.
YOUR PORTRAYAL OF BJ JUST NOW.
I CAN TELL...
...CUZ I LIKE BLOOD, DEVILS, SKULLS...
...AND CRUCIFIXIONS.

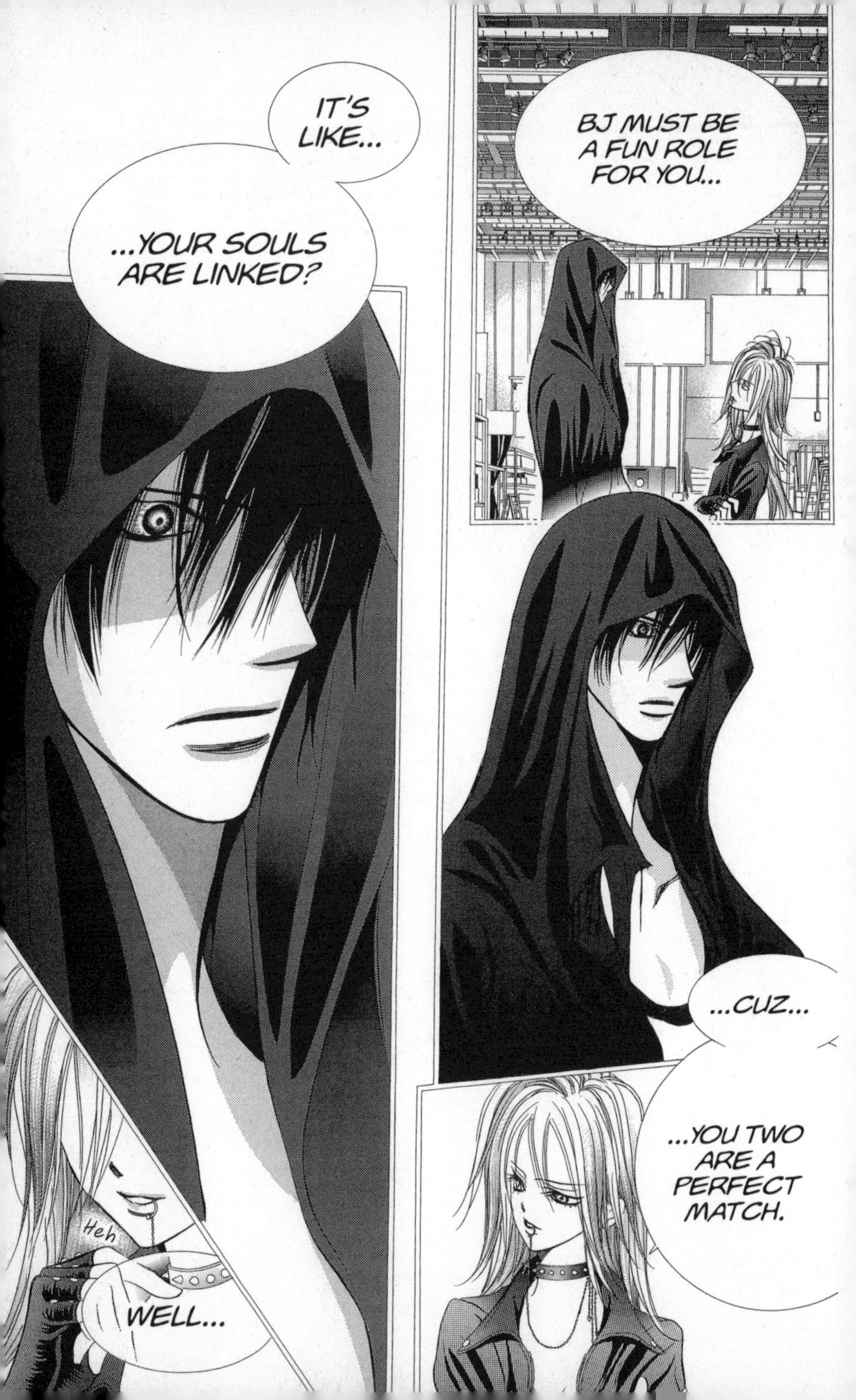
BJ MUST BE A FUN ROLE FOR YOU...
...CUZ...
...YOU TWO ARE A PERFECT MATCH.
IT'S LIKE...
...YOUR SOULS ARE LINKED?
Heh
WELL...

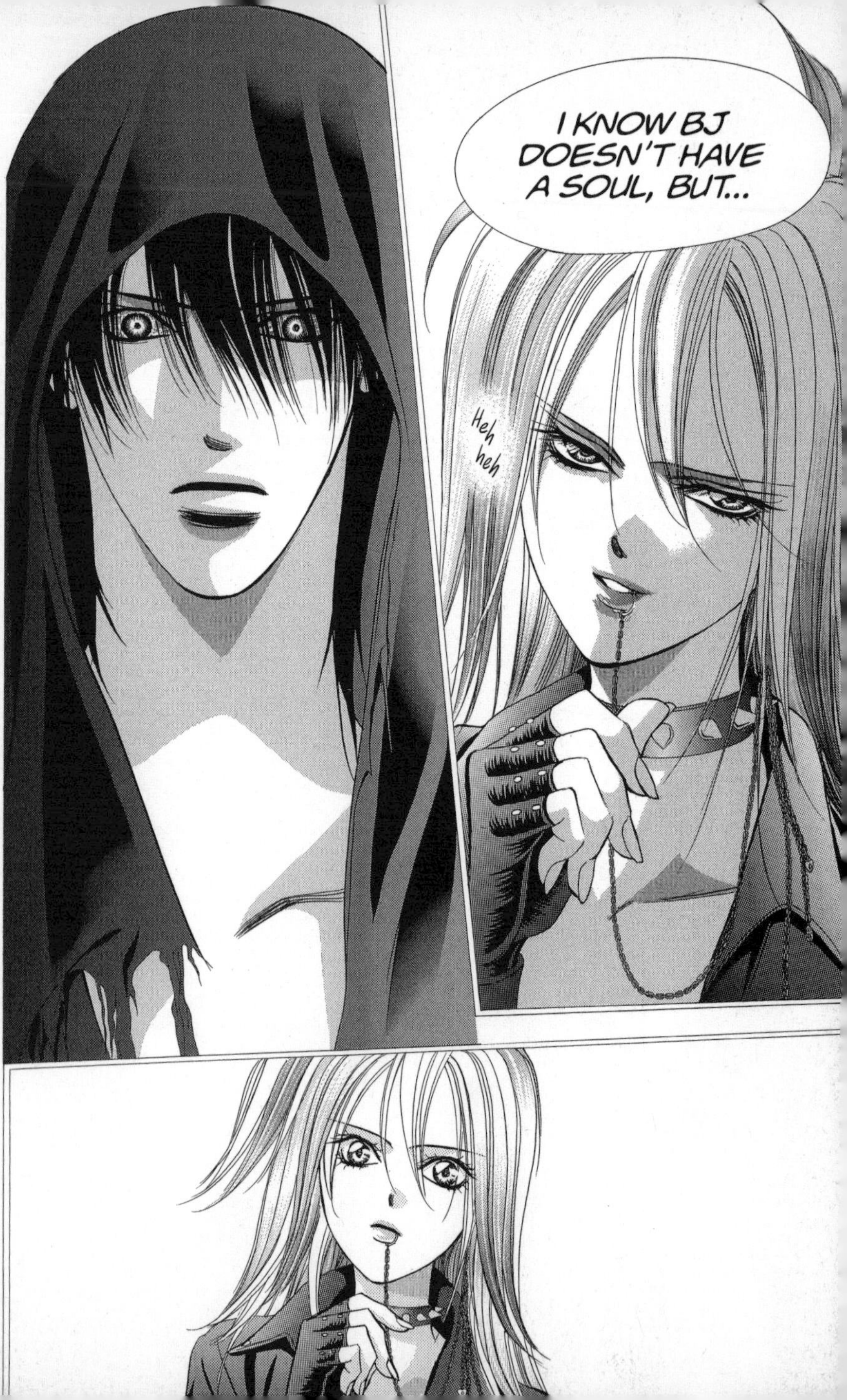
I KNOW BJ DOESN'T HAVE A SOUL, BUT...
Heh heh

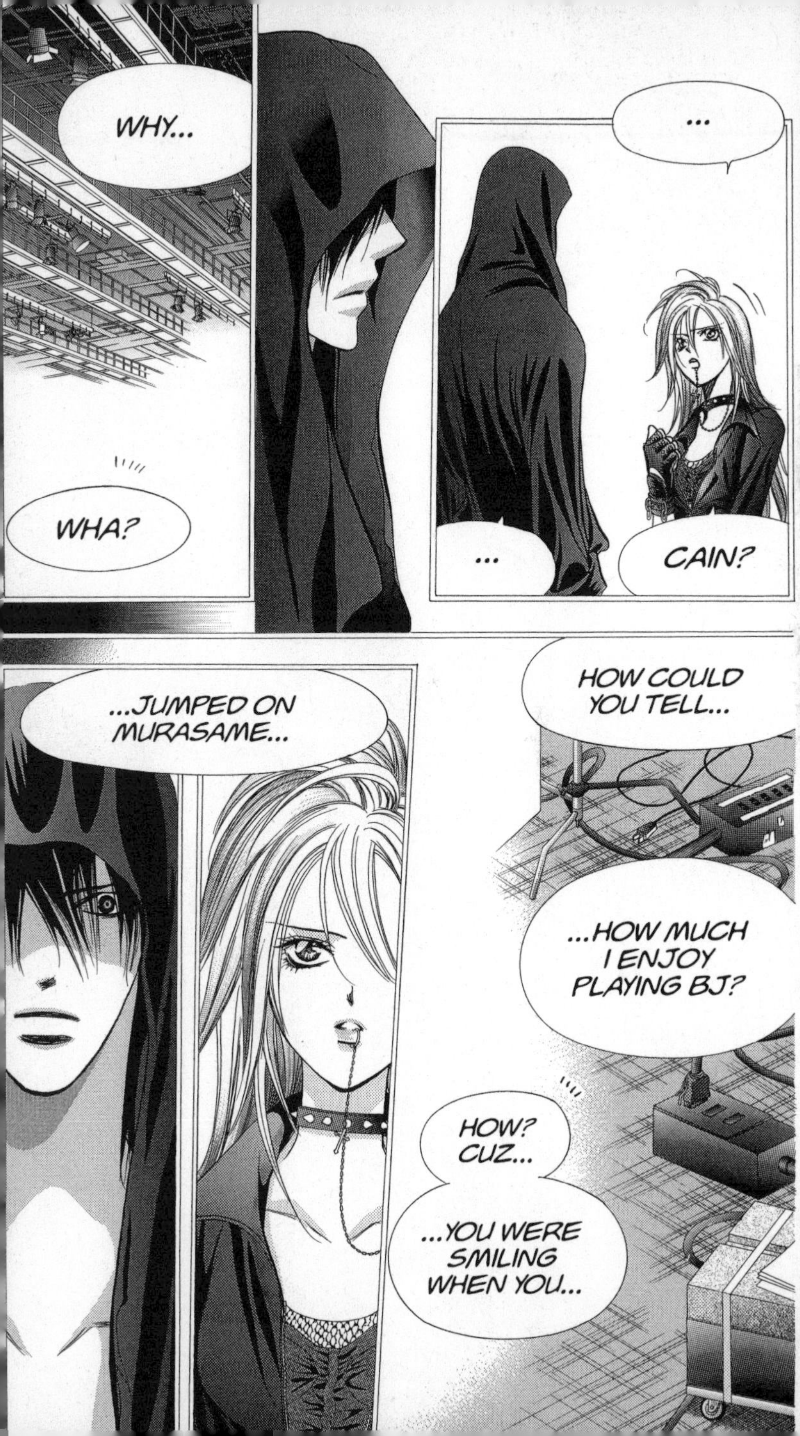
...
CAIN?
...
WHY...
WHA?
HOW COULD YOU TELL...
...HOW MUCH I ENJOY PLAYING BJ?
HOW? CUZ...
...YOU WERE SMILING WHEN YOU...
...JUMPED ON MURASAME...

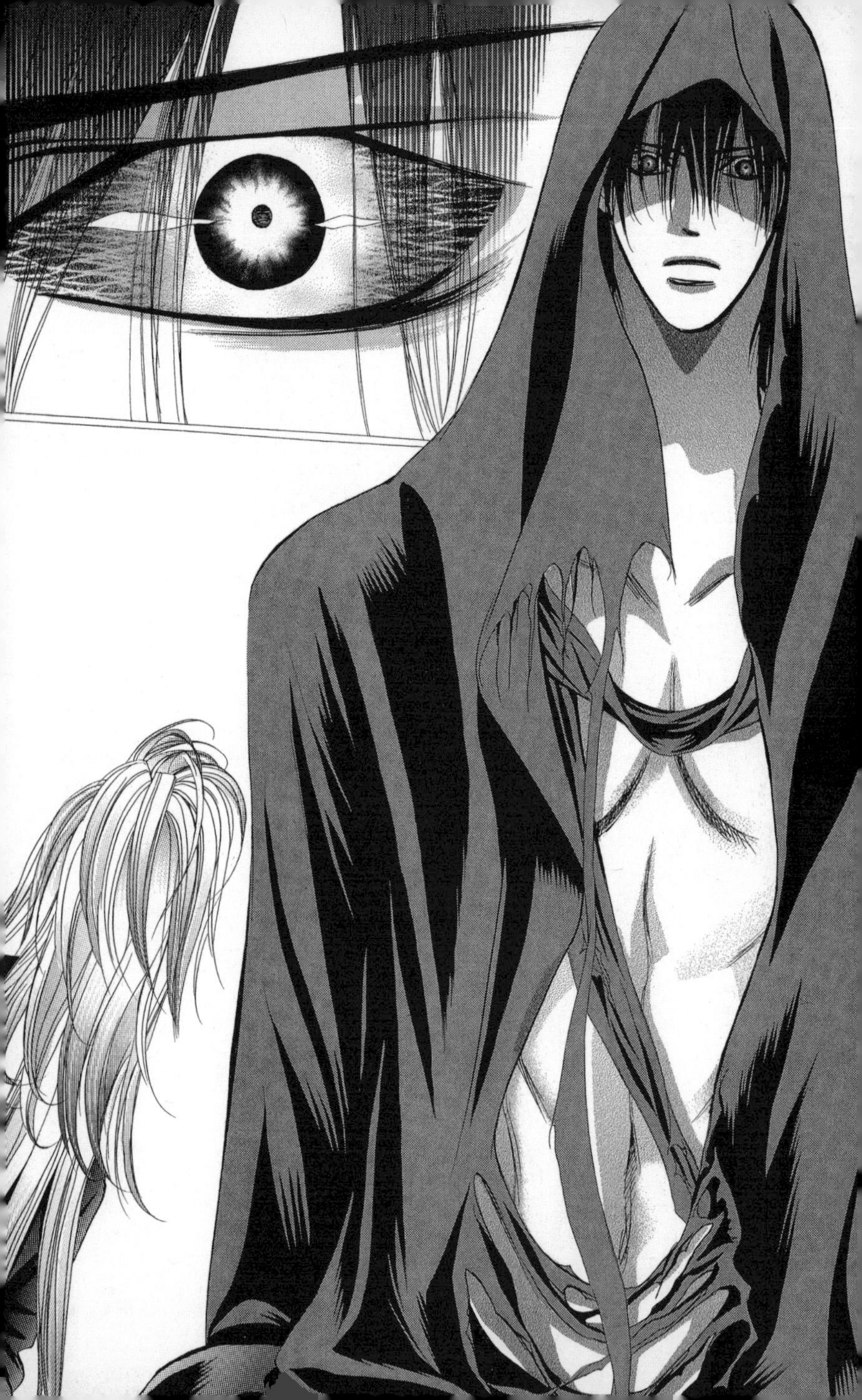

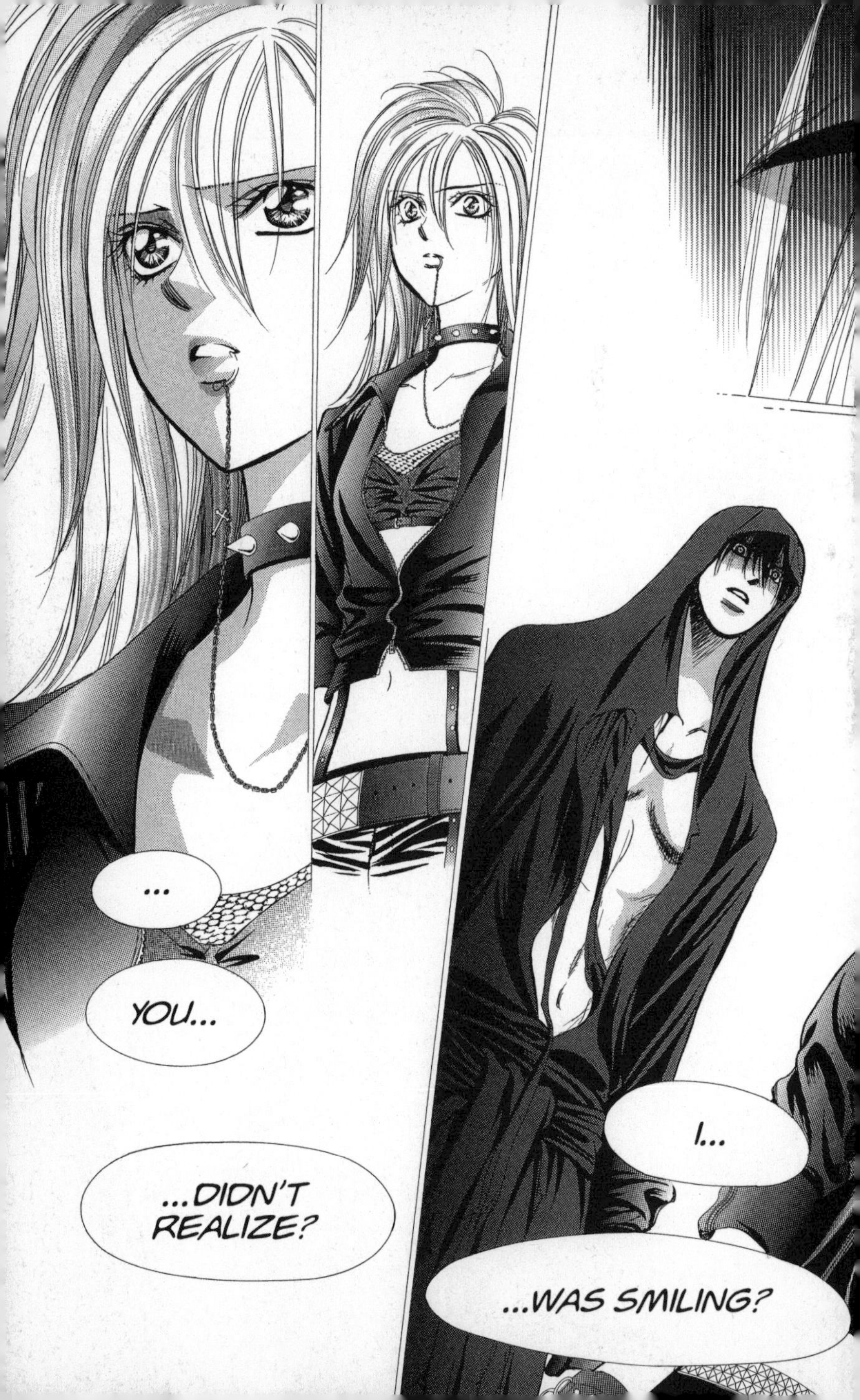
I...
...WAS SMILING?
...
YOU...
...DIDN'T REALIZE?

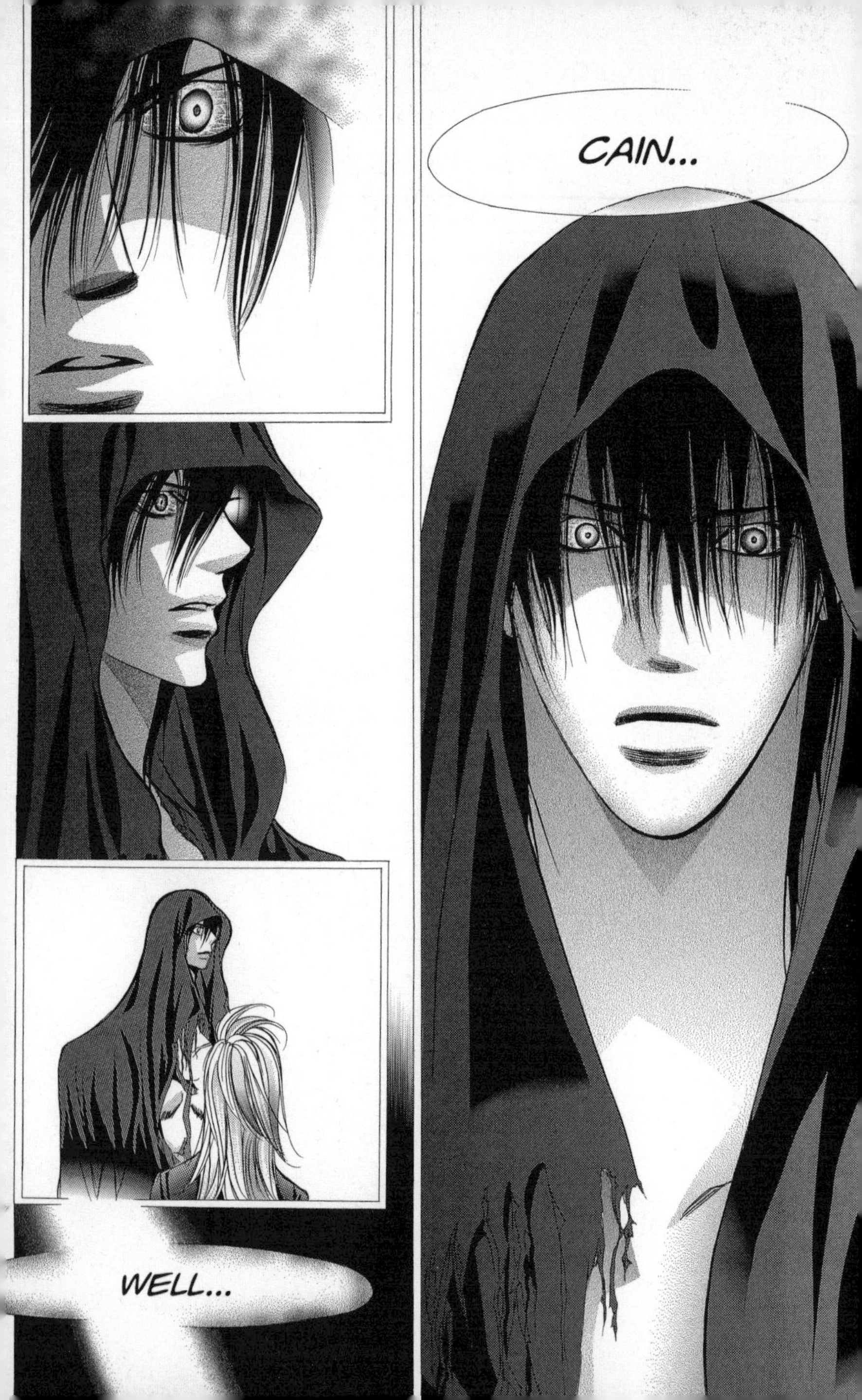
CAIN...
WELL...

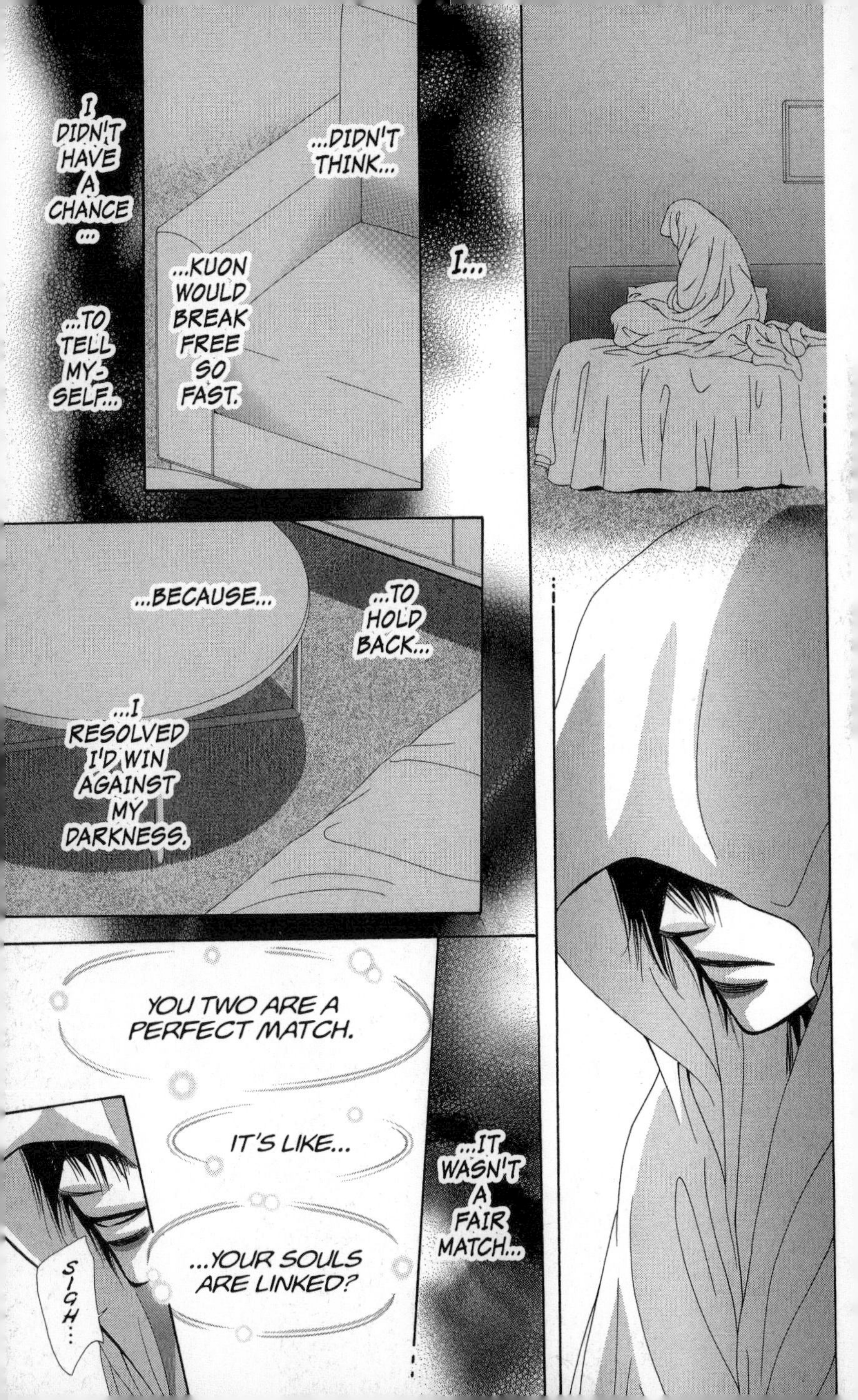
I...
...DIDN'T THINK...
...KUON WOULD BREAK FREE SO FAST.
I DIDN'T HAVE A CHANCE...
...TO TELL MY-SELF...
...TO HOLD BACK...
...BECAUSE...
...I RESOLVED I'D WIN AGAINST MY DARKNESS.
YOU TWO ARE A PERFECT MATCH.
IT'S LIKE...
...YOUR SOULS ARE LINKED?
SIGH...
...IT WASN'T A FAIR MATCH...

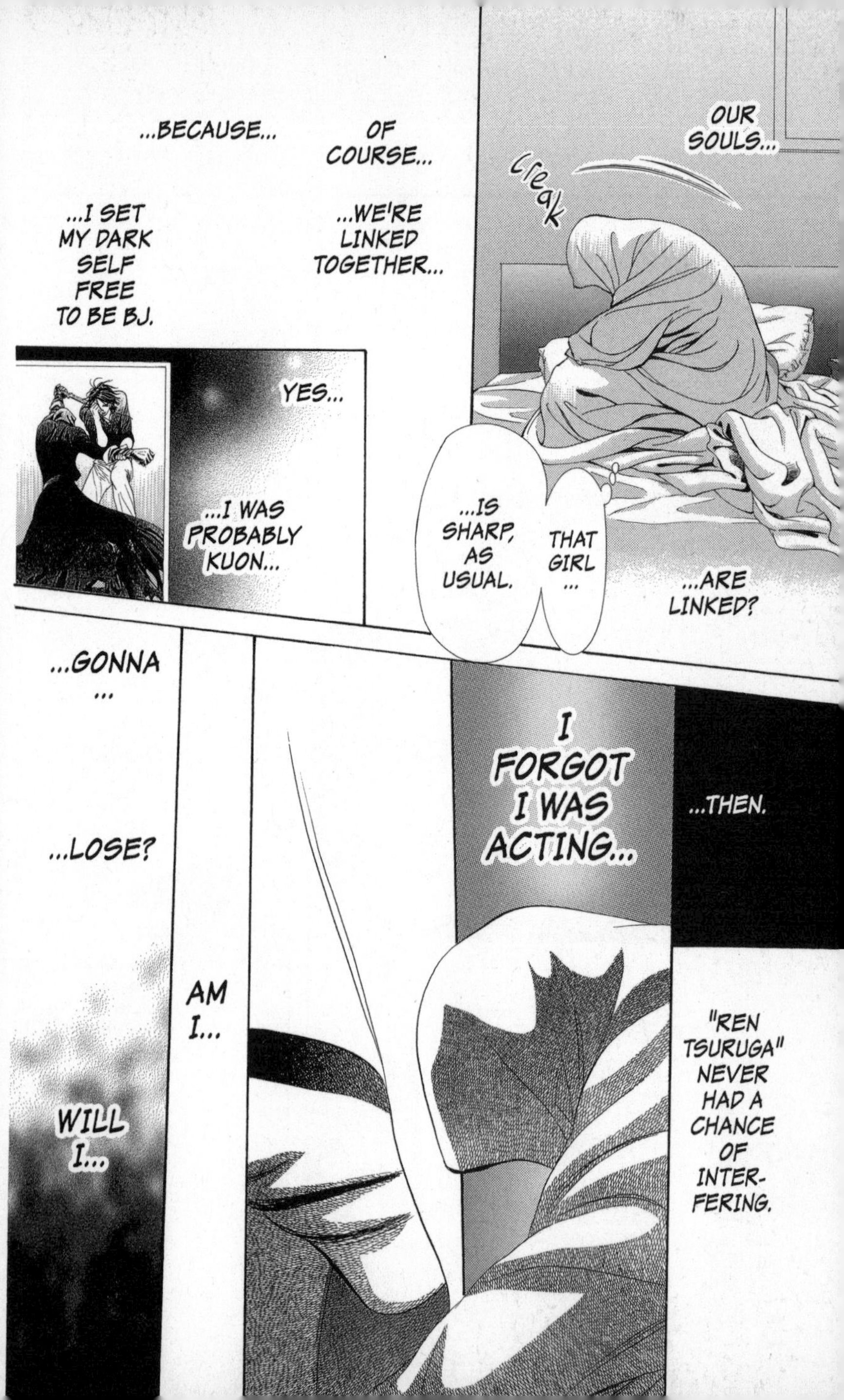
OUR SOULS...
creak
...ARE LINKED?
THAT GIRL ...
...IS SHARP, AS USUAL.
OF COURSE...
...WE'RE LINKED TOGETHER...
...BECAUSE...
...I SET MY DARK SELF FREE TO BE BJ.
YES...
...I WAS PROBABLY KUON...
I FORGOT I WAS ACTING...
...THEN.
"REN TSURUGA" NEVER HAD A CHANCE OF INTER-FERING.
AM I...
...GONNA ...
...LOSE?
WILL I...

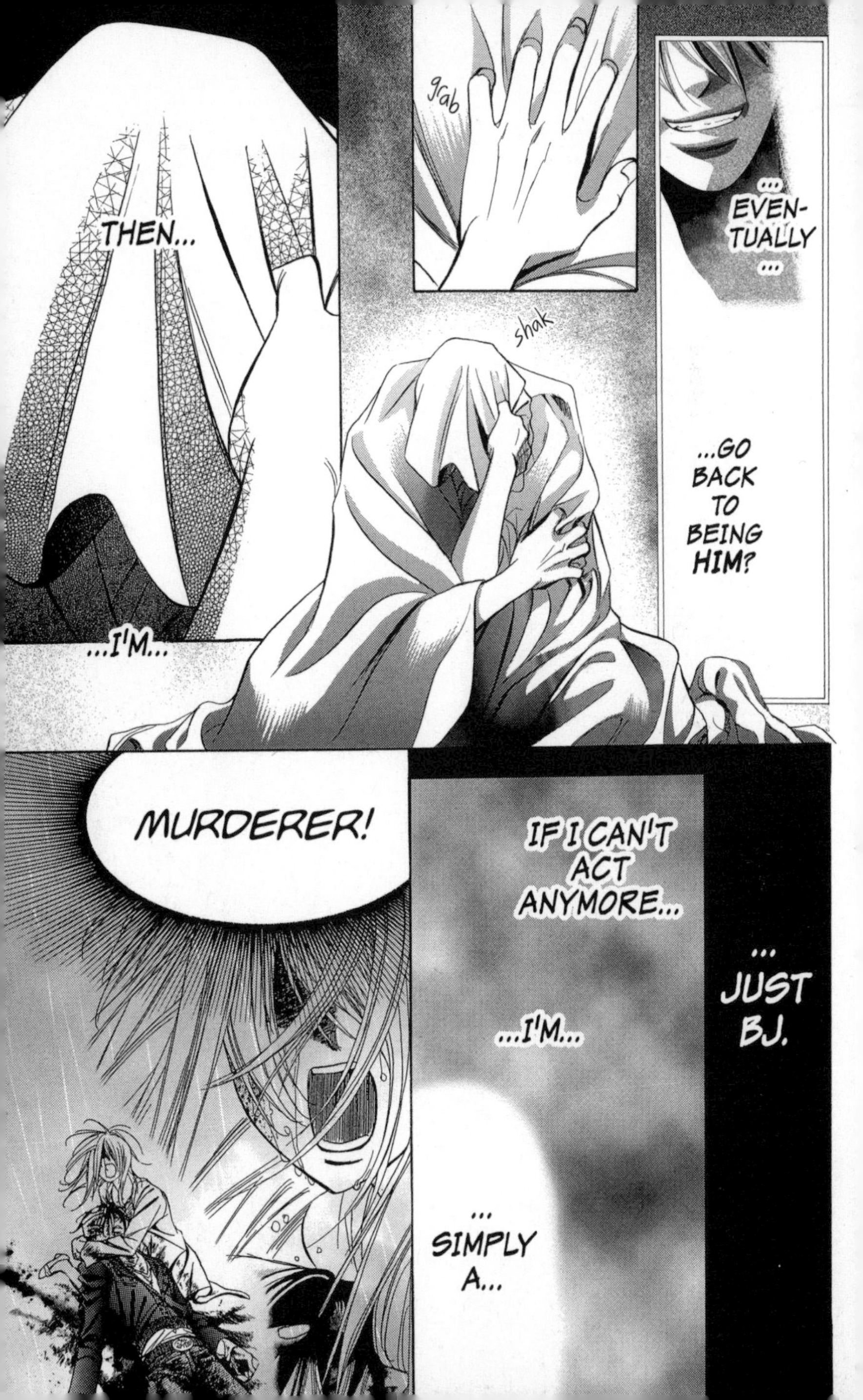
...EVENTUALLY...
...GO BACK TO BEING HIM?
grab
shak
THEN...
...I'M...
IF I CAN'T ACT ANYMORE...
...I'M...
...SIMPLY A...
...JUST BJ.
MURDERER!

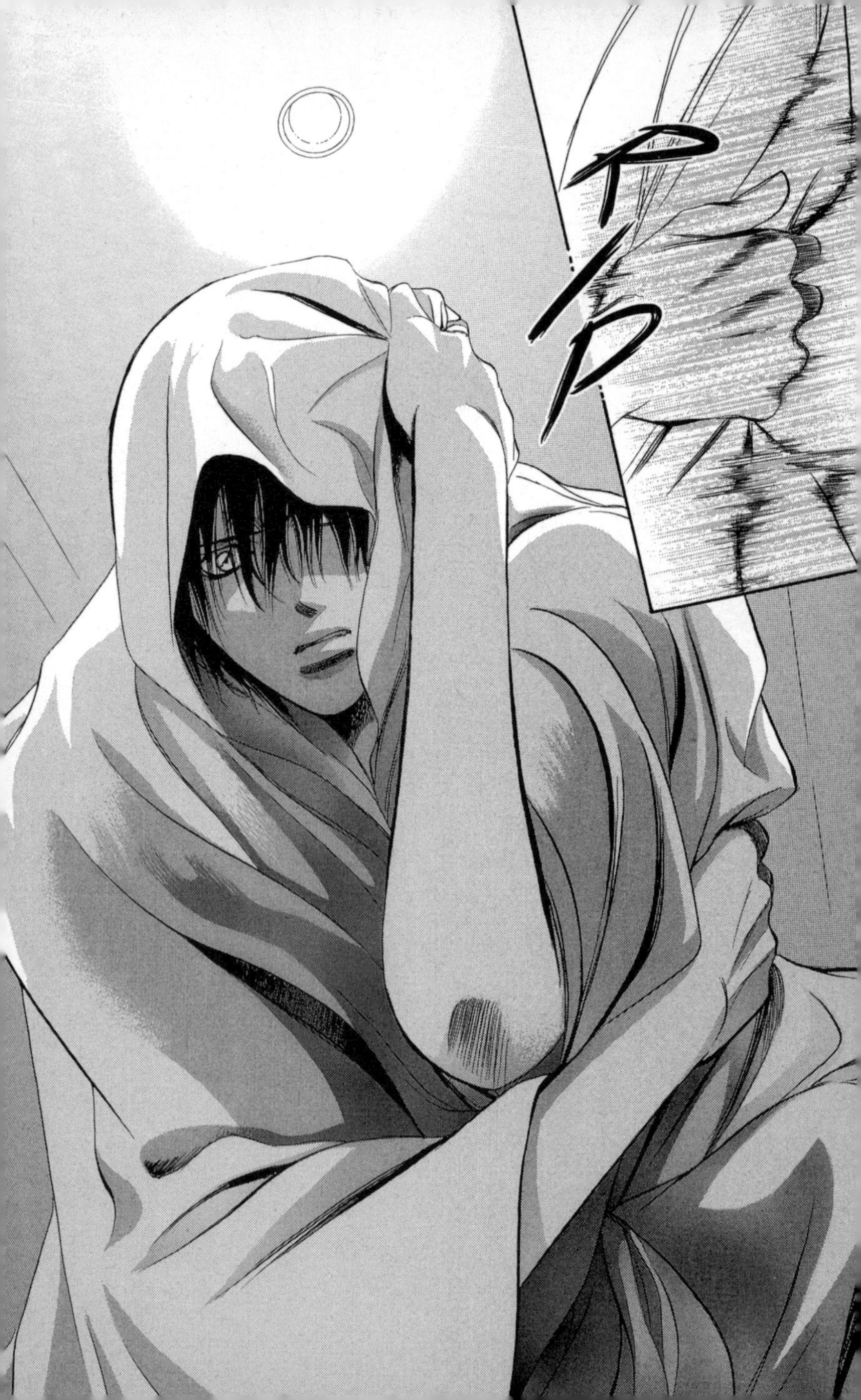
RIP

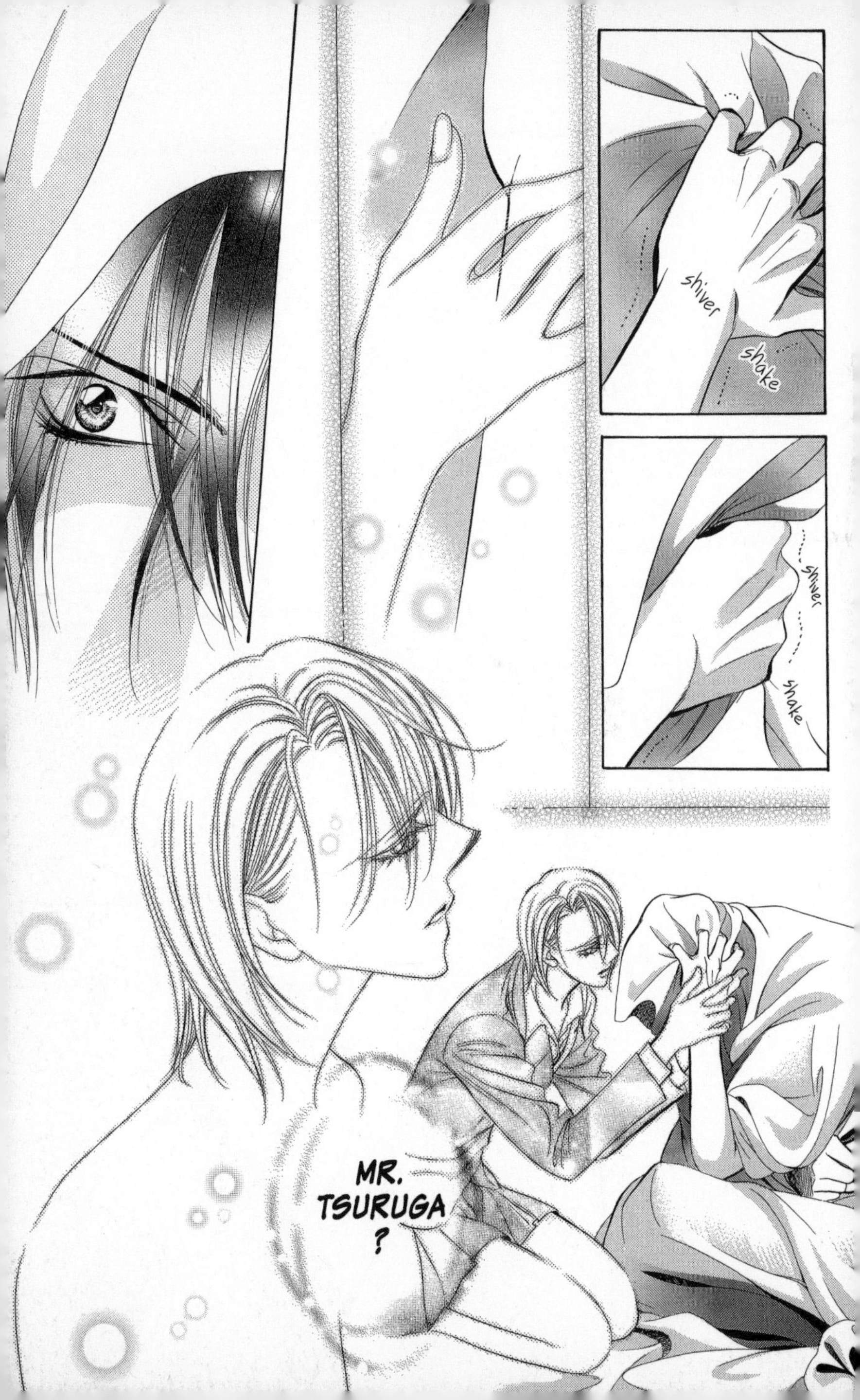
shiver
shake
shiver
shake
MR. TSURUGA ?

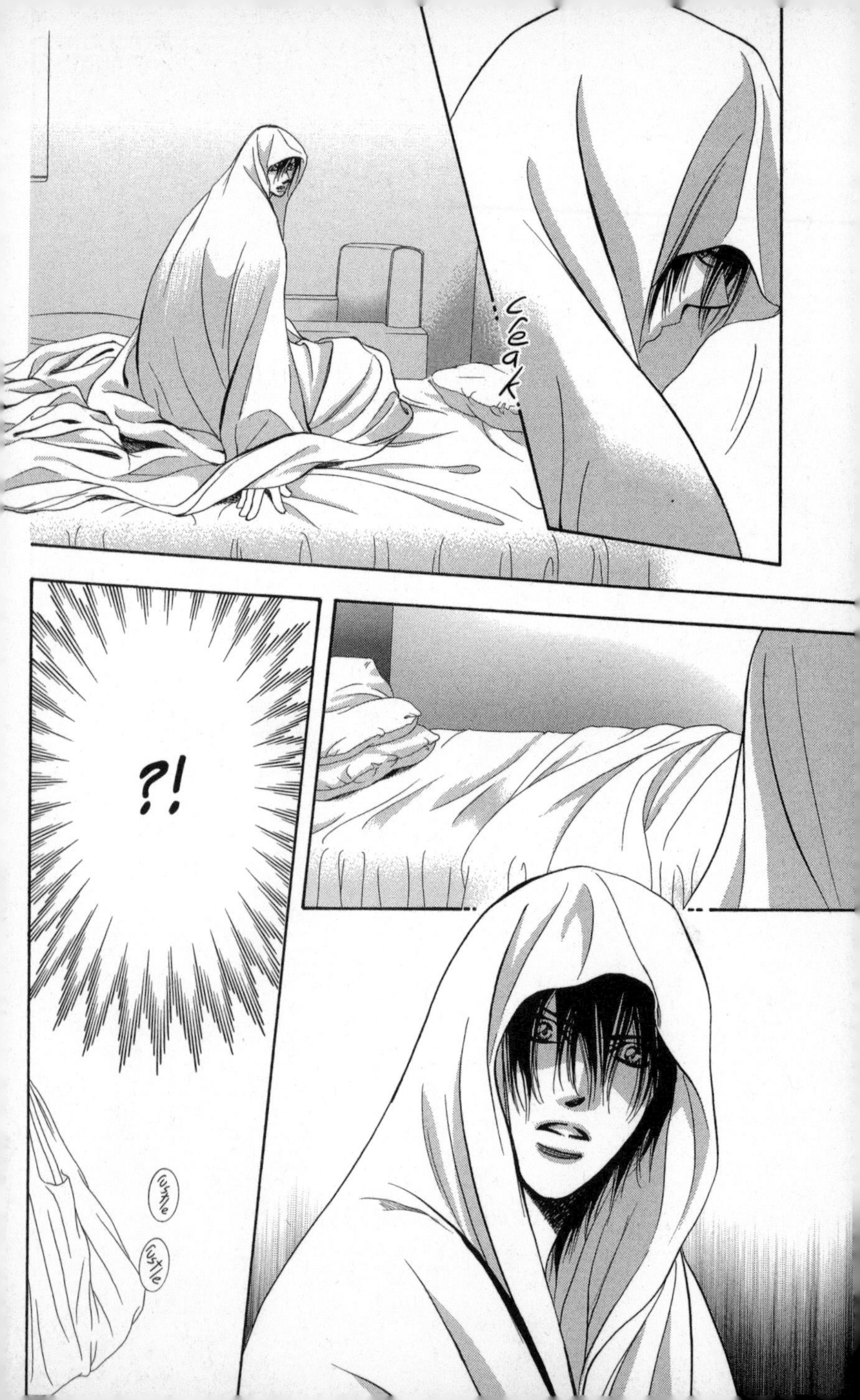
creak
?!
rustle
rustle

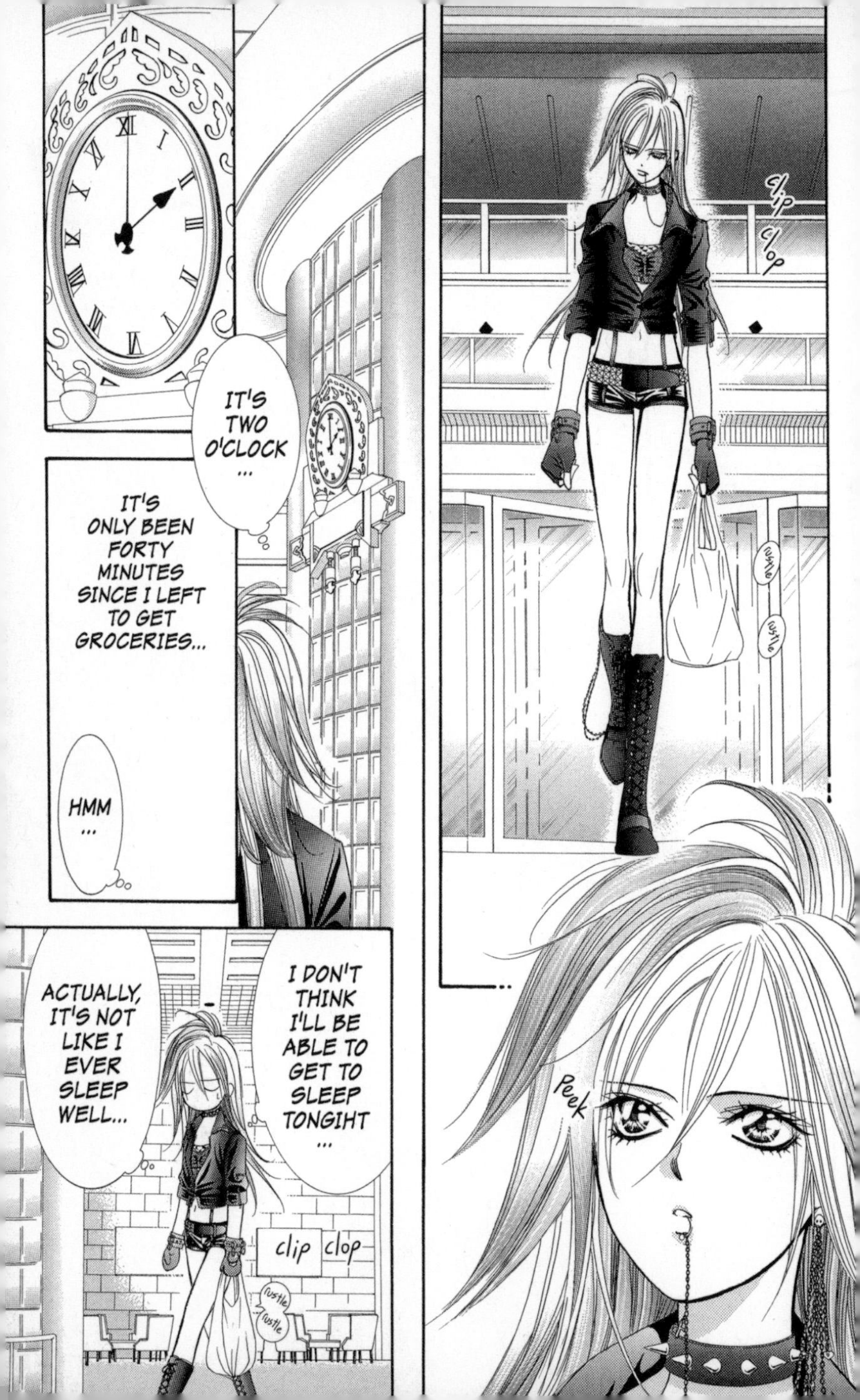
clip clop
rustle
rustle
!
...
Peek
IT'S TWO O'CLOCK ...
IT'S ONLY BEEN FORTY MINUTES SINCE I LEFT TO GET GROCERIES...
HMM ...
I DON'T THINK I'LL BE ABLE TO GET TO SLEEP TONGIHT ...
ACTUALLY, IT'S NOT LIKE I EVER SLEEP WELL...
clip clop
rustle
rustle

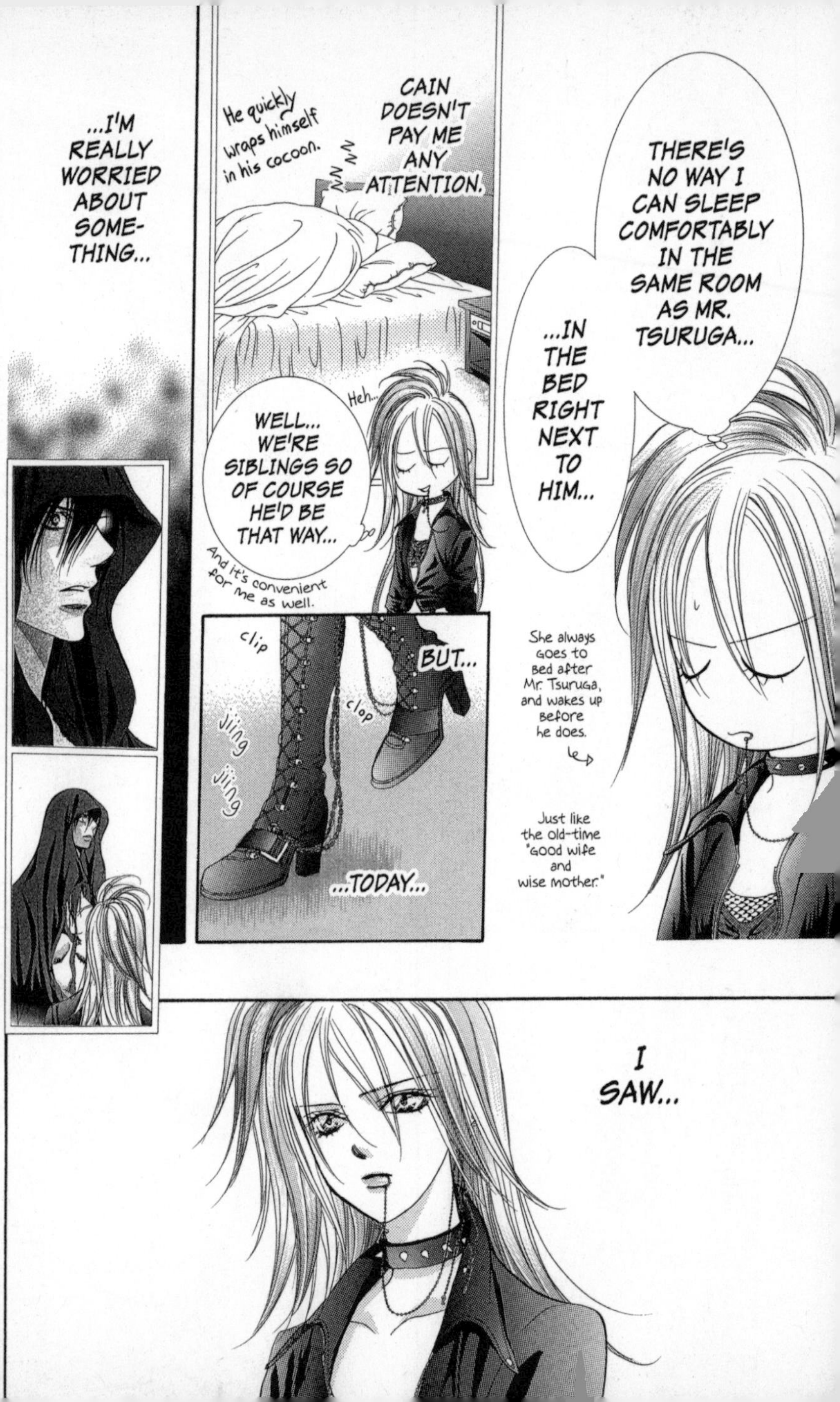
THERE'S NO WAY I CAN SLEEP COMFORTABLY IN THE SAME ROOM AS MR. TSURUGA...
...IN THE BED RIGHT NEXT TO HIM...
She always goes to bed after Mr. Tsuruga, and wakes up before he does.
Just like the old-time "good wife and wise mother."
CAIN DOESN'T PAY ME ANY ATTENTION.
He quickly wraps himself in his cocoon.
ZZZ
Heh...
WELL... WE'RE SIBLINGS SO OF COURSE HE'D BE THAT WAY...
And it's convenient for me as well.
BUT...
clip
clop
jiing jiing
...TODAY...
...I'M REALLY WORRIED ABOUT SOME-THING...
I SAW...

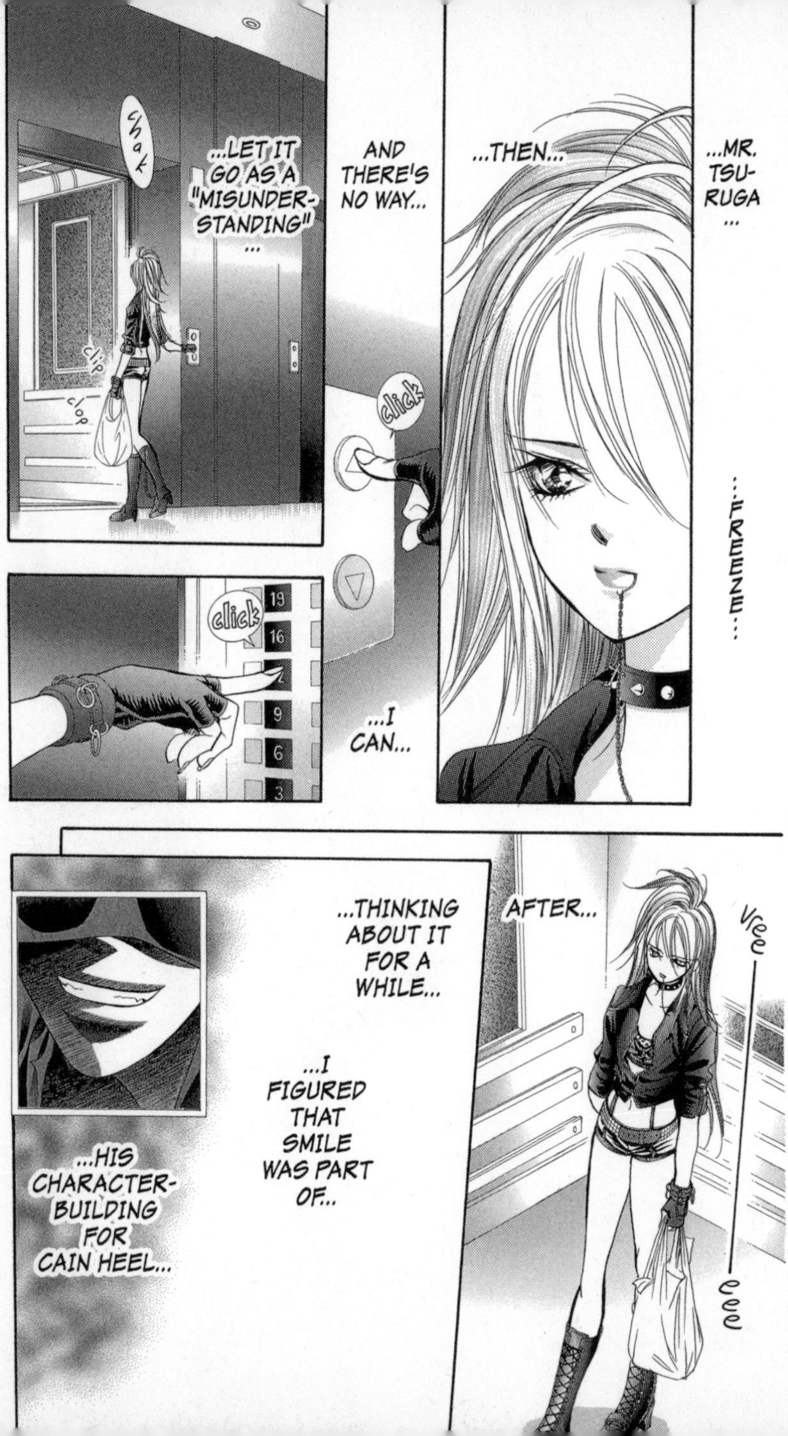

...MR. TSU-RUGA...
...FREEZE...
...THEN...
AND THERE'S NO WAY...
click
...I CAN...
click
...LET IT GO AS A "MISUNDER-STANDING"...
shak
clip
clop
AFTER...
vree—eee
...THINKING ABOUT IT FOR A WHILE...
...I FIGURED THAT SMILE WAS PART OF...
...HIS CHARACTER-BUILDING FOR CAIN HEEL...

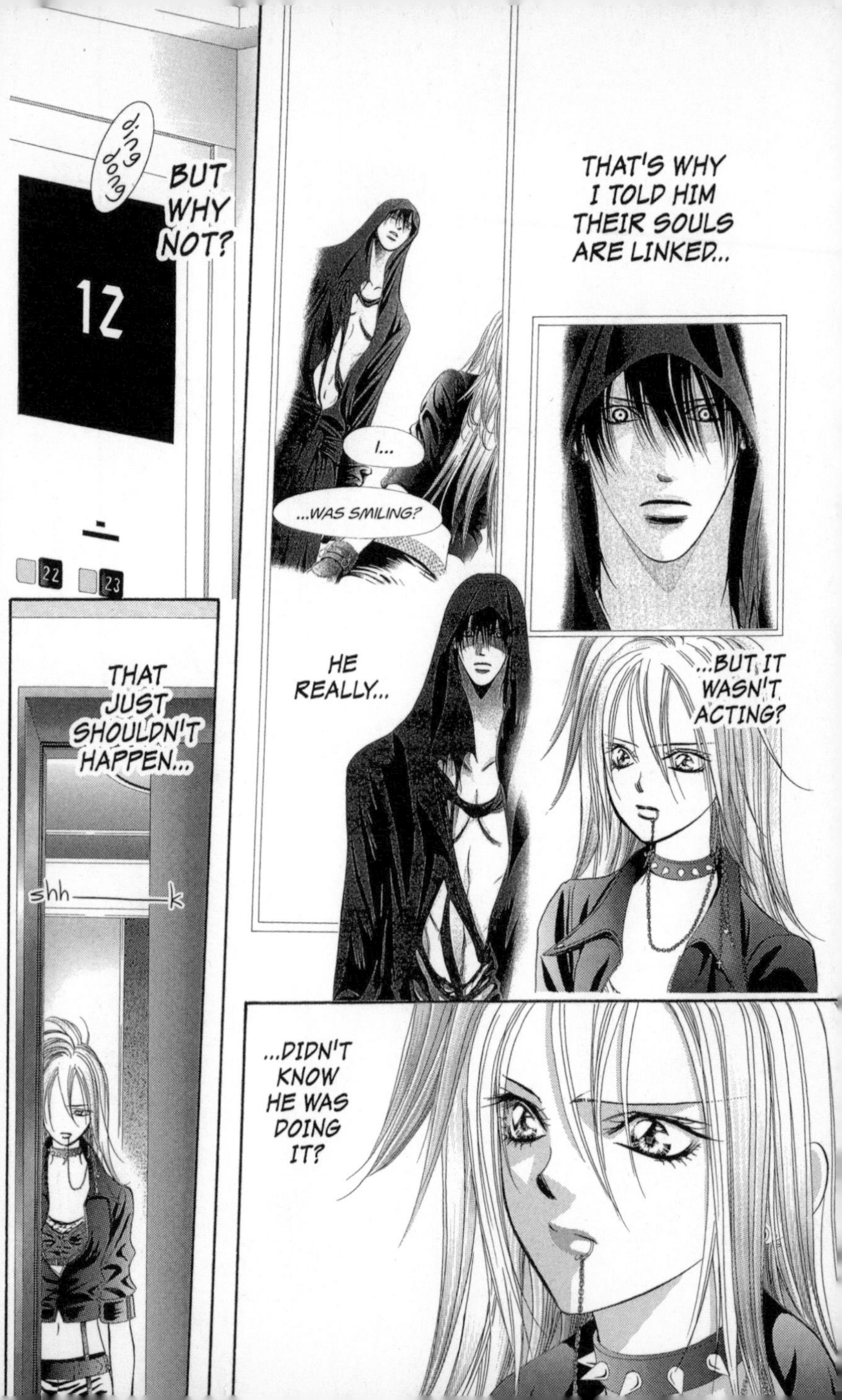
THAT'S WHY I TOLD HIM THEIR SOULS ARE LINKED...
I...
...WAS SMILING?
...BUT IT WASN'T ACTING?
HE REALLY...
...DIDN'T KNOW HE WAS DOING IT?
ding dong
BUT WHY NOT?
12
22
23
THAT JUST SHOULDN'T HAPPEN...
shh——k

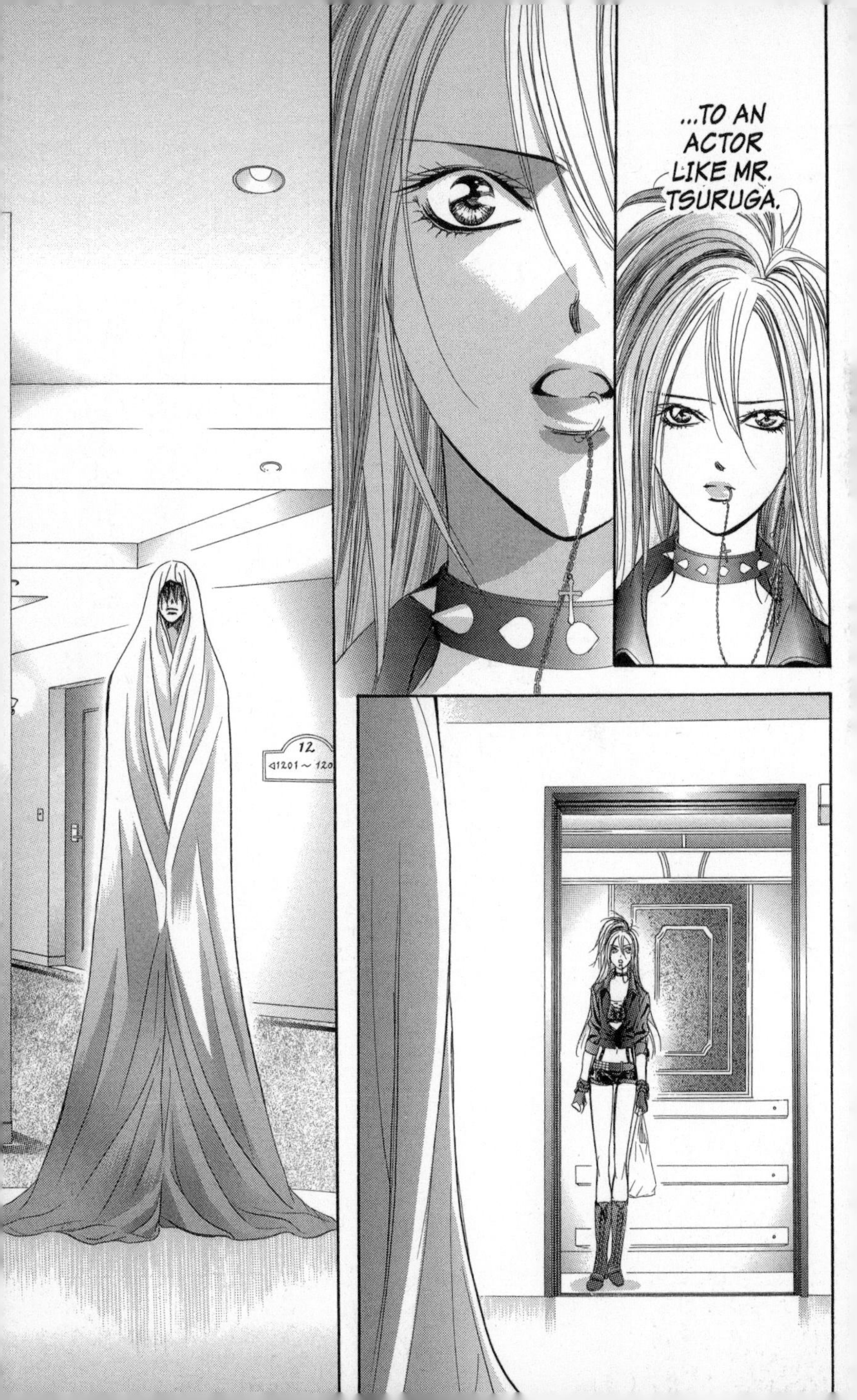
...TO AN ACTOR LIKE MR. TSURUGA.
12
◁1201 ~ 120

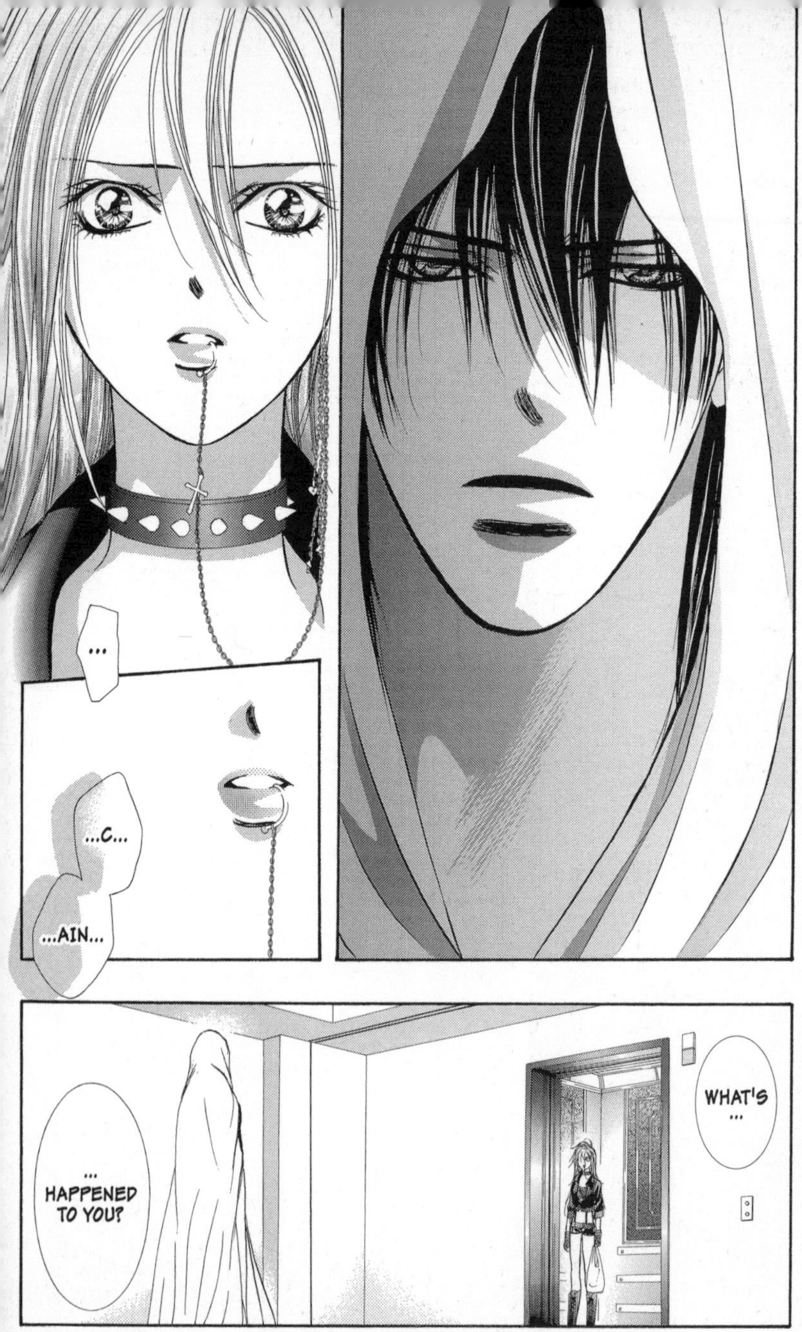
...
...C...
...AIN...
WHAT'S ...
... HAPPENED TO YOU?

End of Act 180

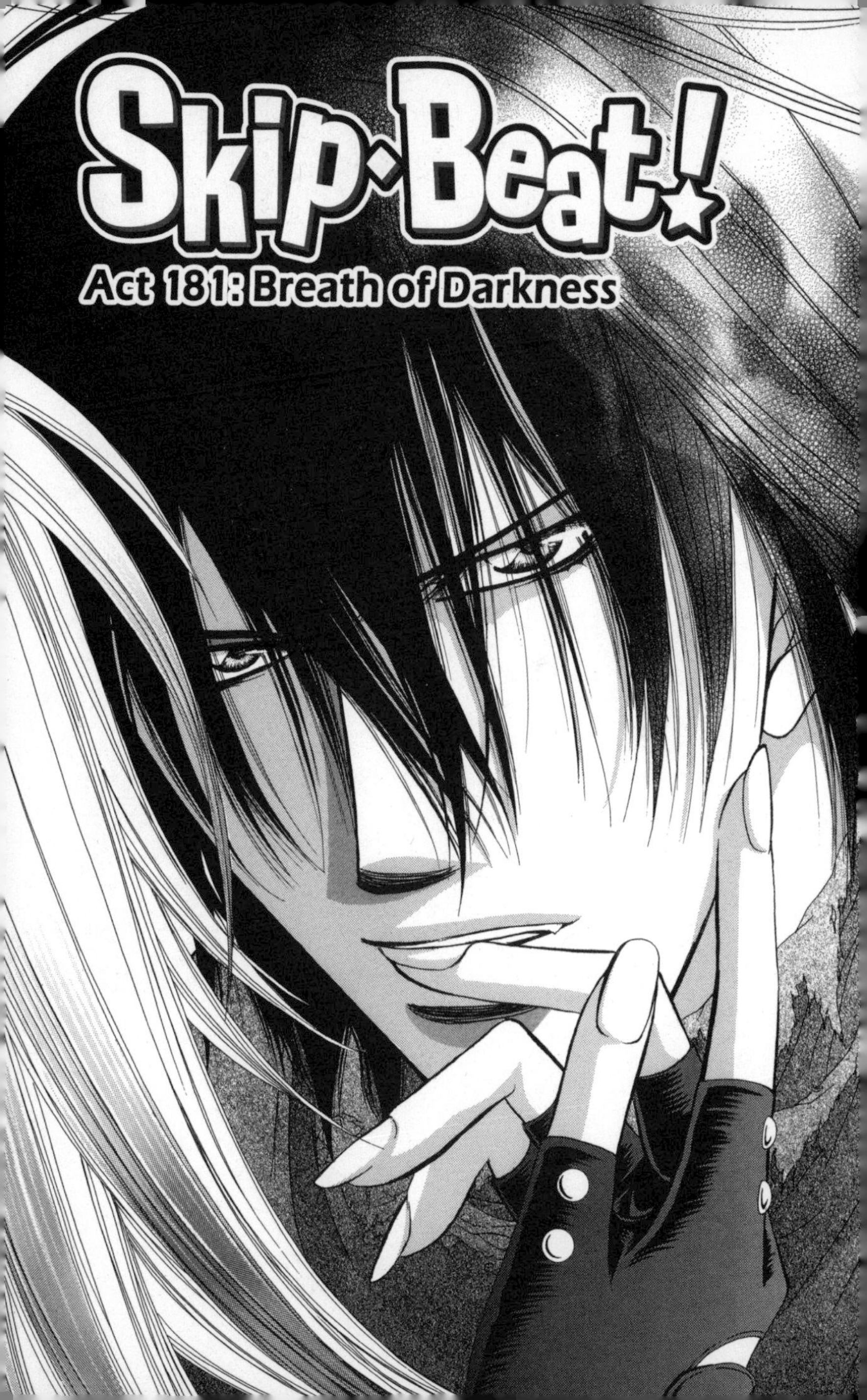
Skip·Beat!
Act 181: Breath of Darkness

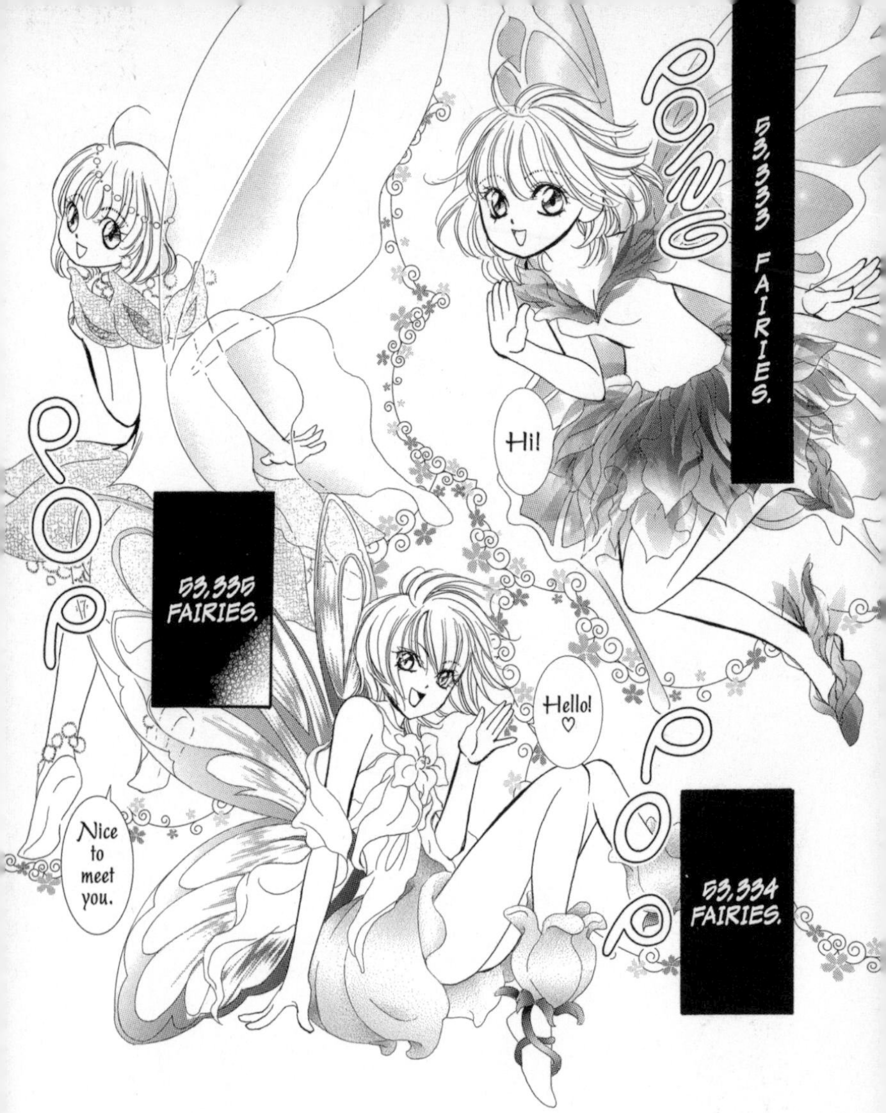
53,333 FAIRIES.
POING
Hi!
53,334 FAIRIES.
POP
Hello! ♡
53,335 FAIRIES.
POP
Nice to meet you.

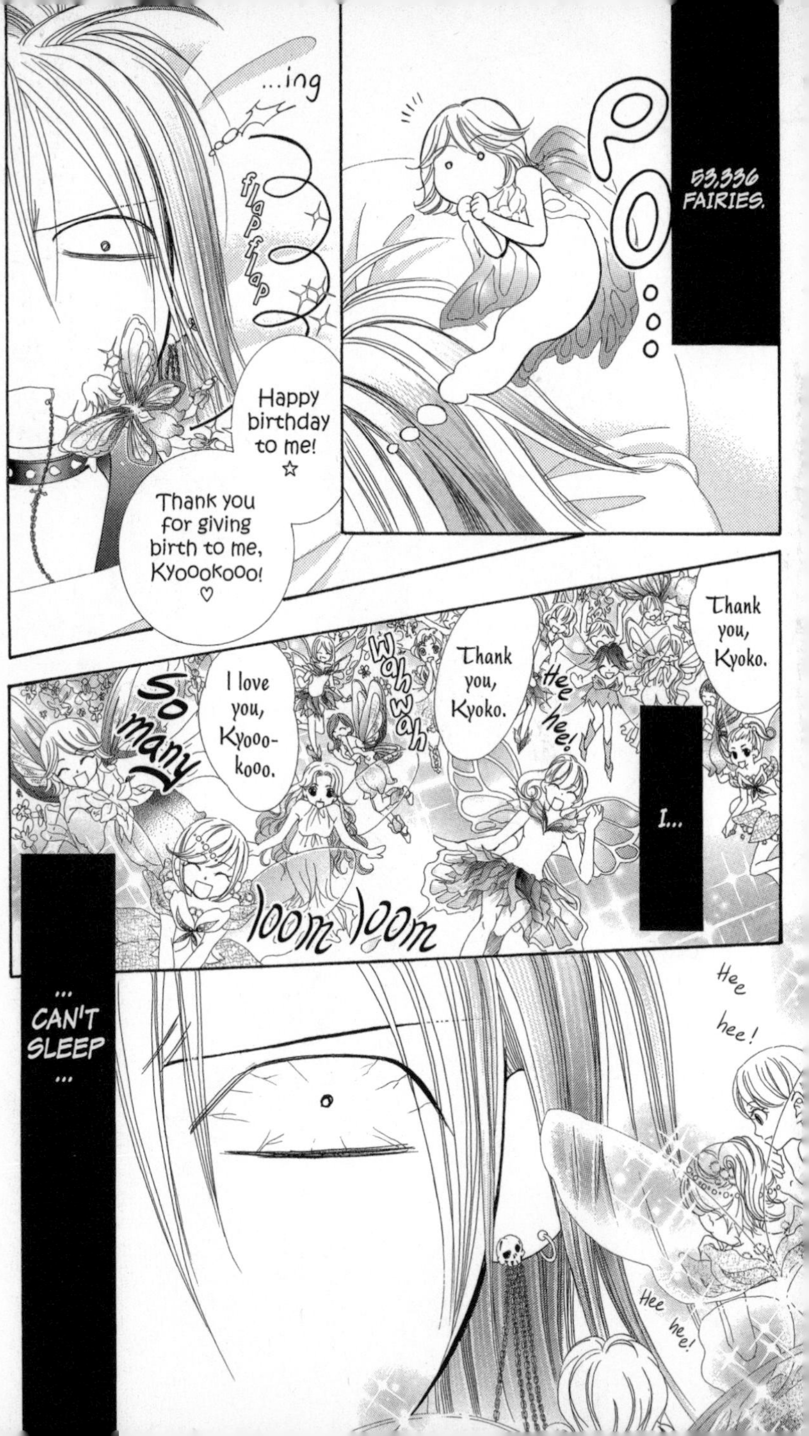
53,336 FAIRIES.
Poooo
...ing
flapflap
Happy birthday to me! ☆
Thank you for giving birth to me, Kyoookooo! ♡
Thank you, Kyoko.
I...
Hee hee!
Thank you, Kyoko.
Wahwah
I love you, Kyooo-kooo.
So many
loom loom
Hee hee!
Hee hee!
...CAN'T SLEEP...

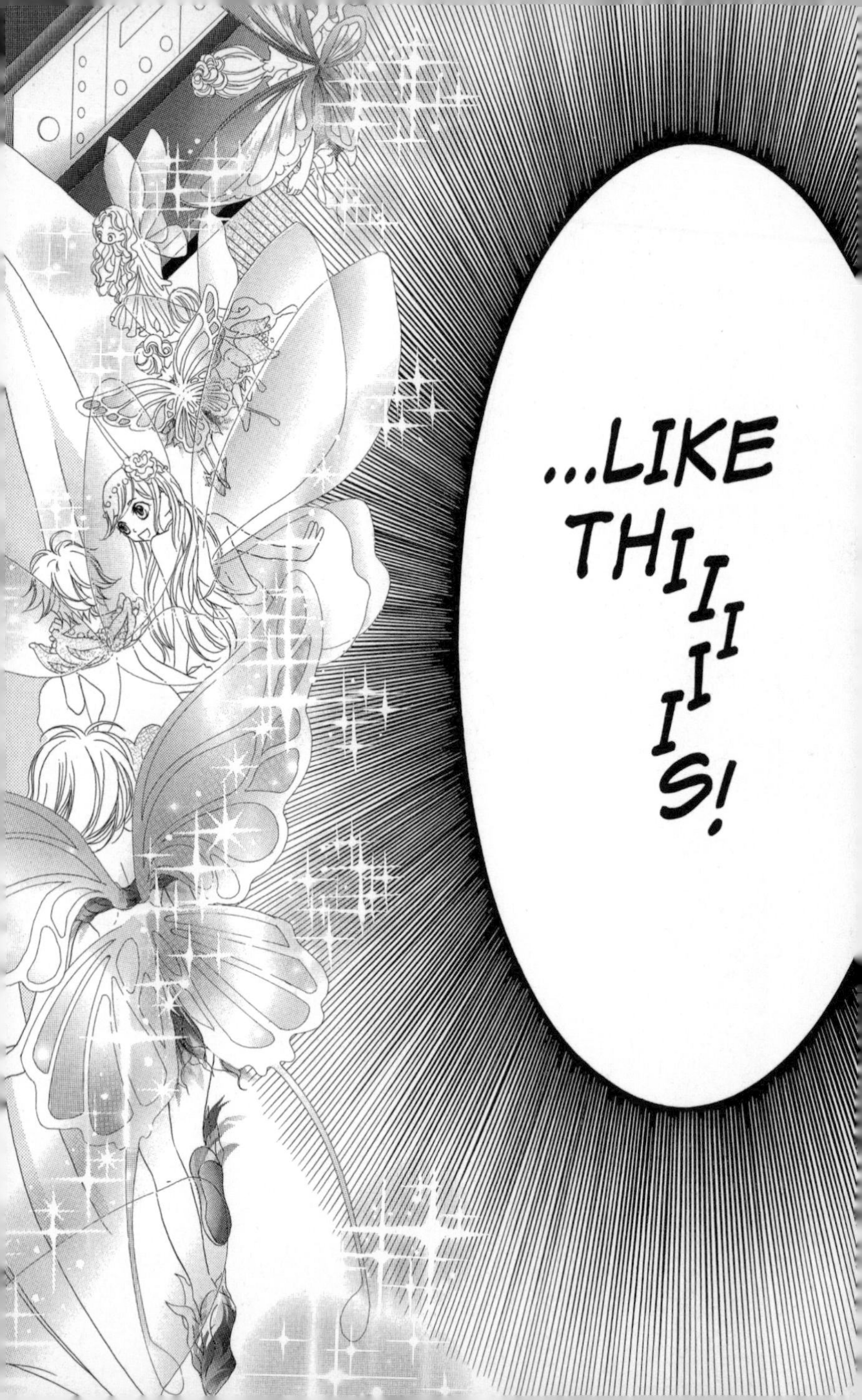
...LIKE THIIIIIS!

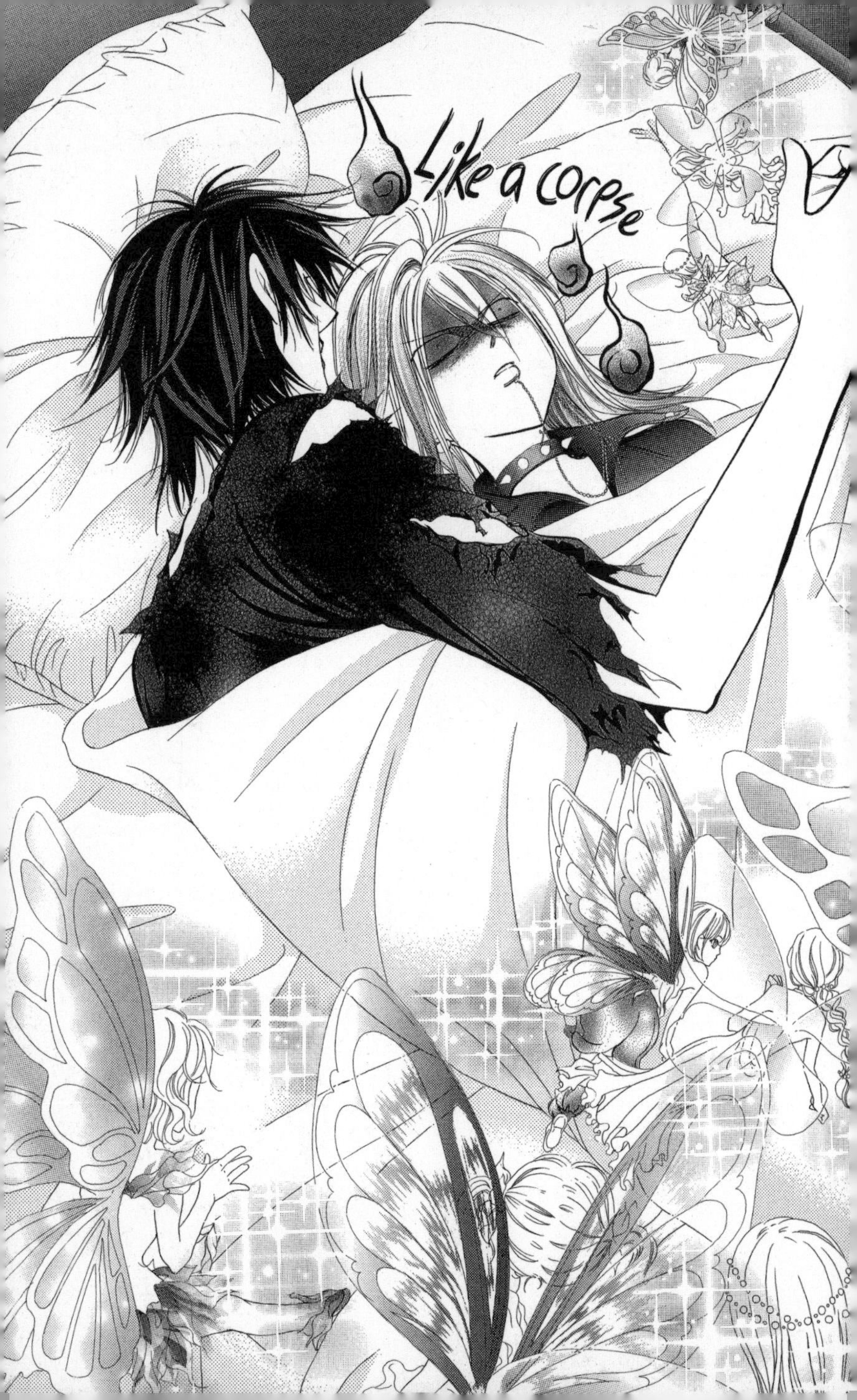
Like a corpse

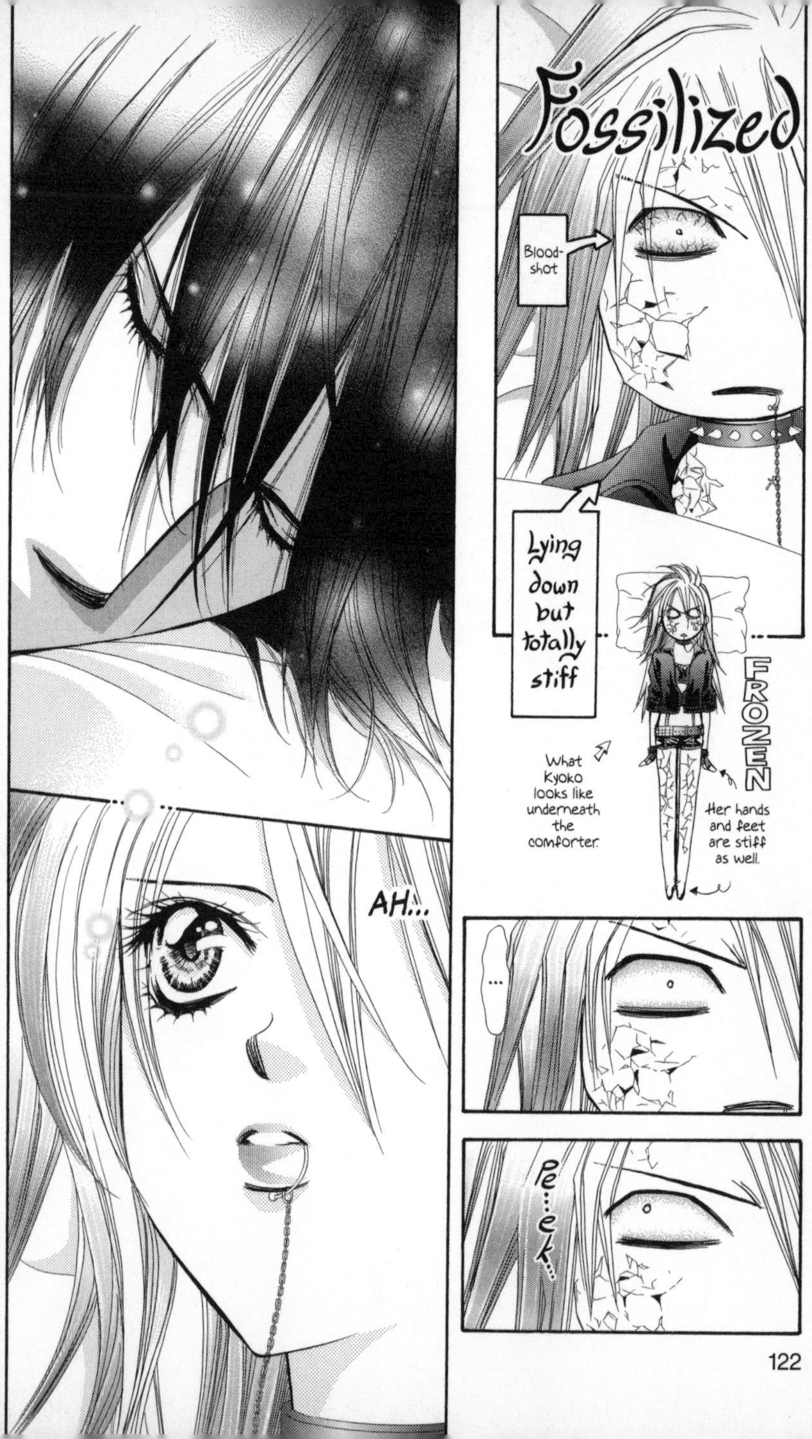
Fossilized
Blood-shot
Lying down but totally stiff
FROZEN
What Kyoko looks like underneath the comforter.
Her hands and feet are stiff as well.
...
Pe...ek...
AH...

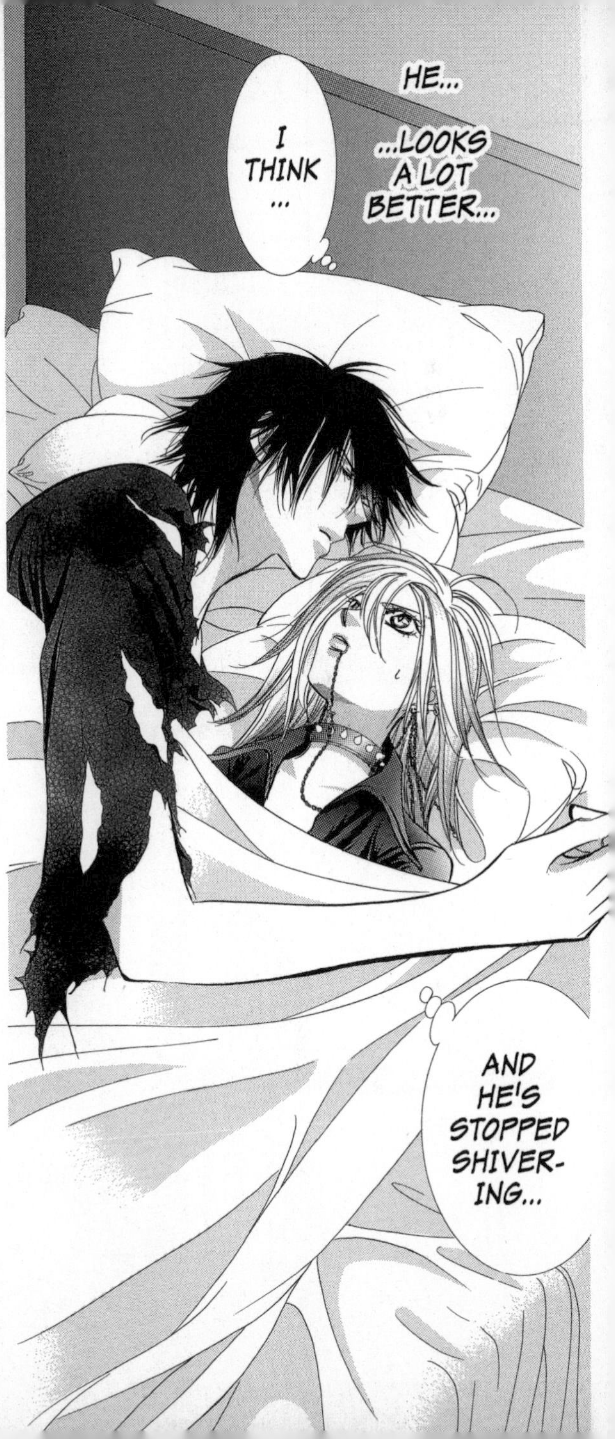
HE...
...LOOKS A LOT BETTER...
I THINK ...
AND HE'S STOPPED SHIVER-ING...

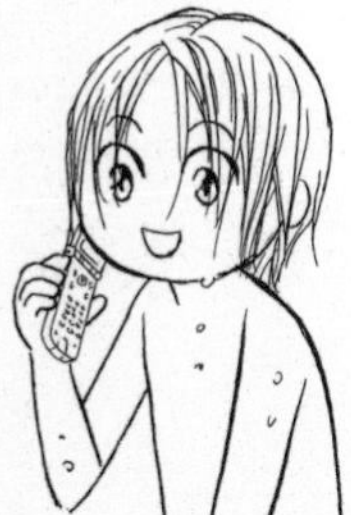

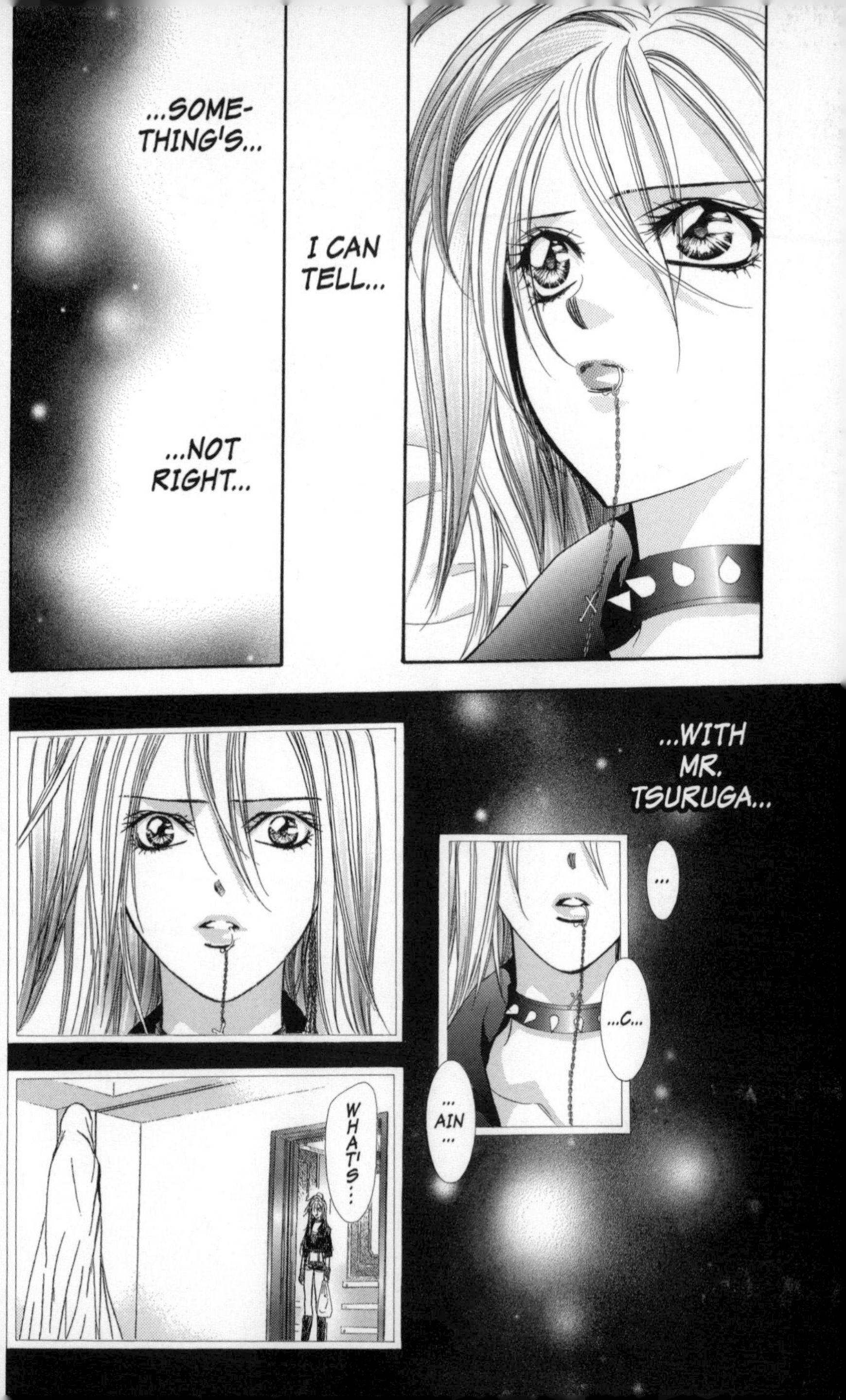
I CAN TELL...
...SOME-THING'S...
...NOT RIGHT...
...WITH MR. TSURUGA...
...
...C...
...AIN...
WHAT'S...

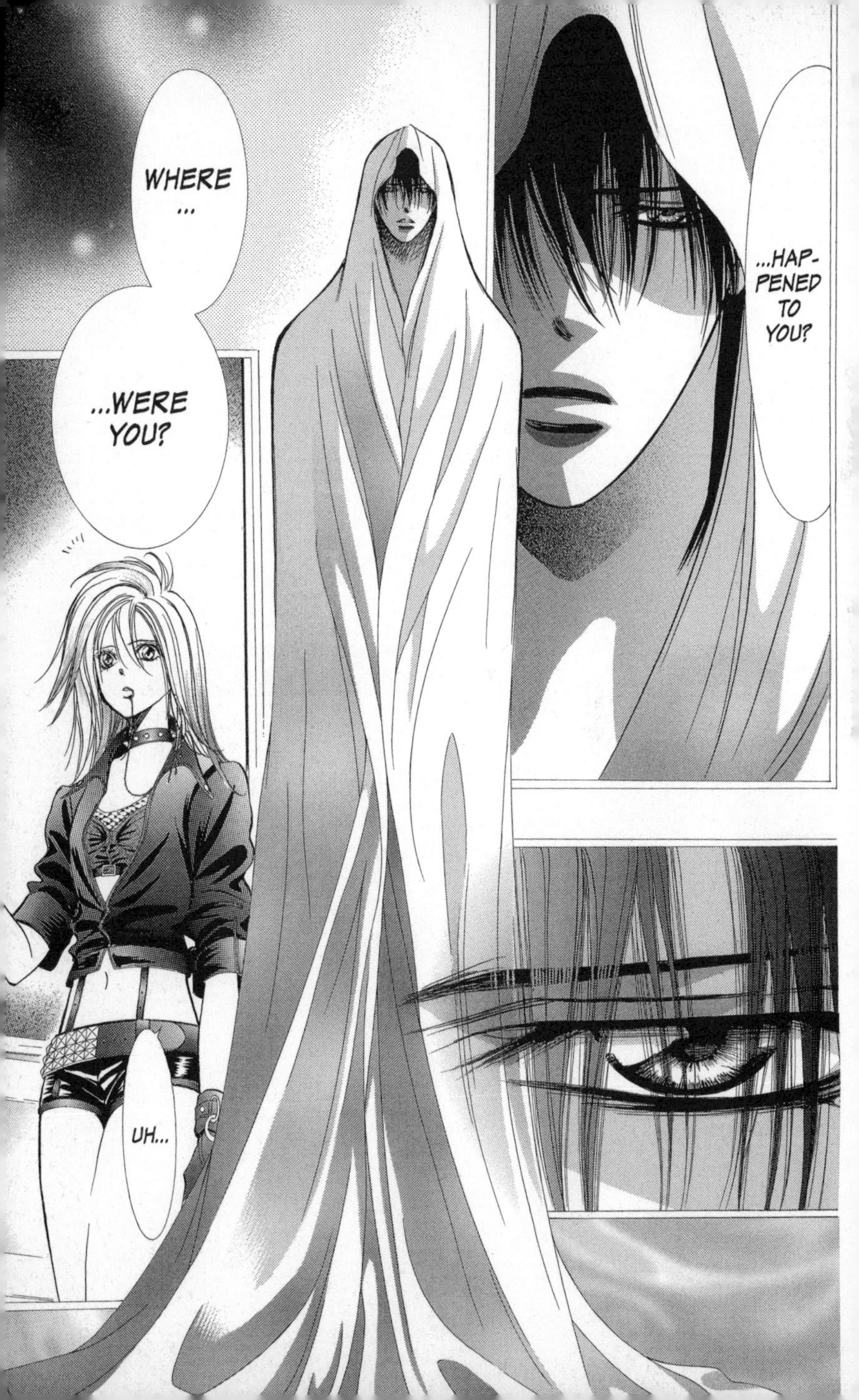
WHERE ...
...WERE YOU?
...HAP-PENED TO YOU?
UH...

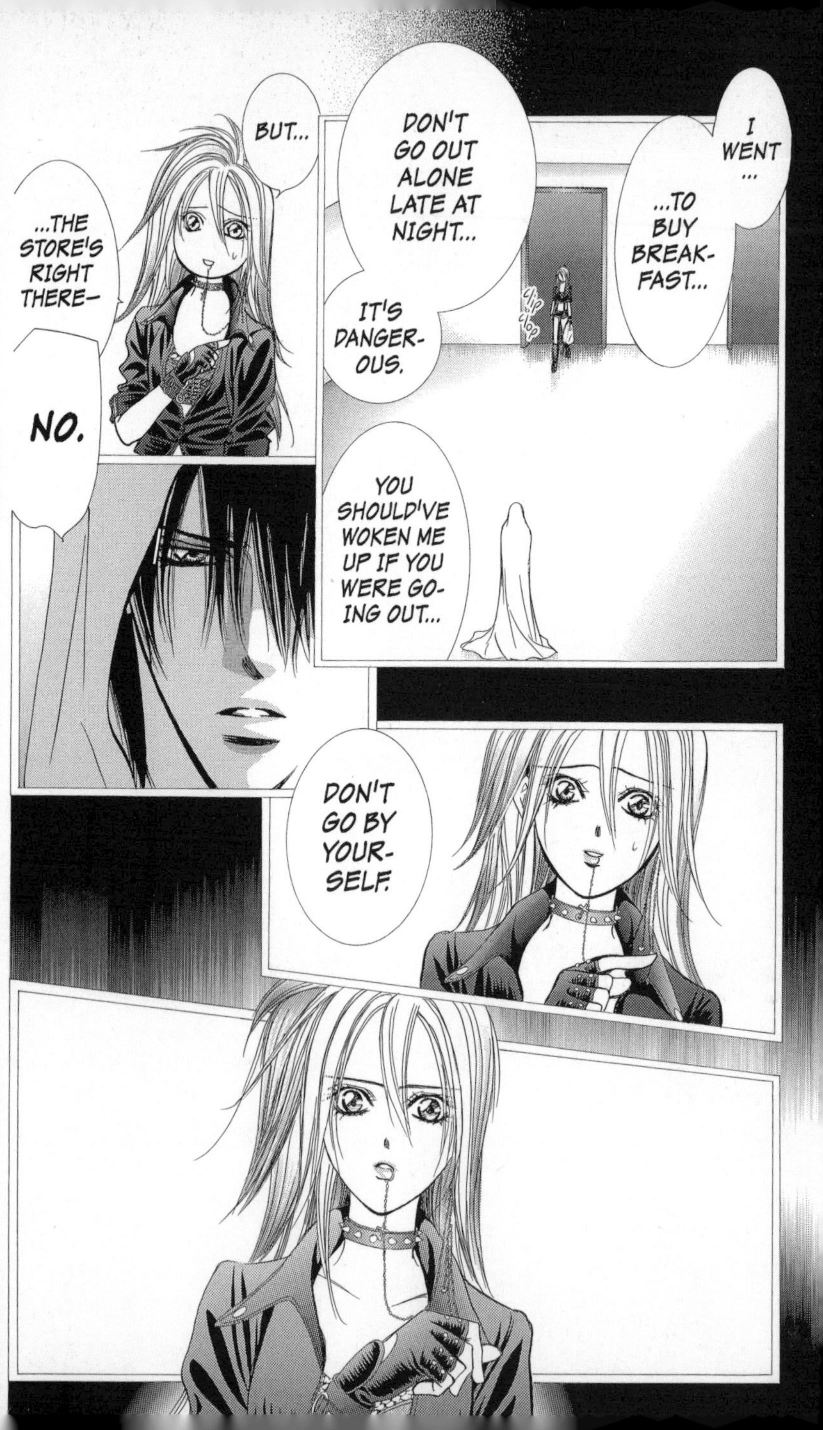
I WENT ...
...TO BUY BREAK-FAST...
DON'T GO OUT ALONE LATE AT NIGHT...
IT'S DANGER-OUS.
clip clop
YOU SHOULD'VE WOKEN ME UP IF YOU WERE GO-ING OUT...
BUT...
...THE STORE'S RIGHT THERE–
NO.
DON'T GO BY YOUR-SELF.

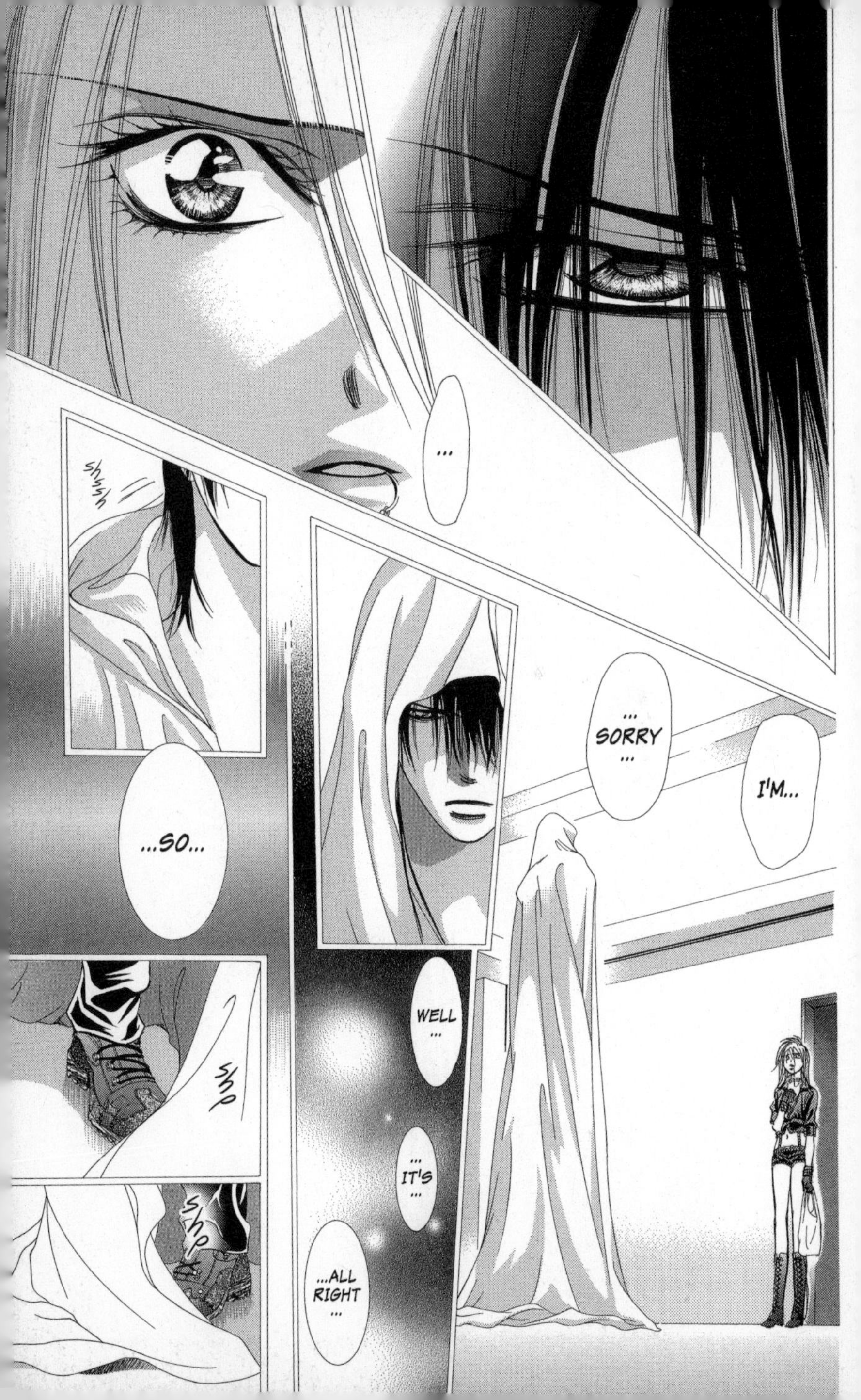
...
I'M...
...SORRY...
shhh
...SO...
shp
shp
WELL...
...IT'S...
...ALL RIGHT...

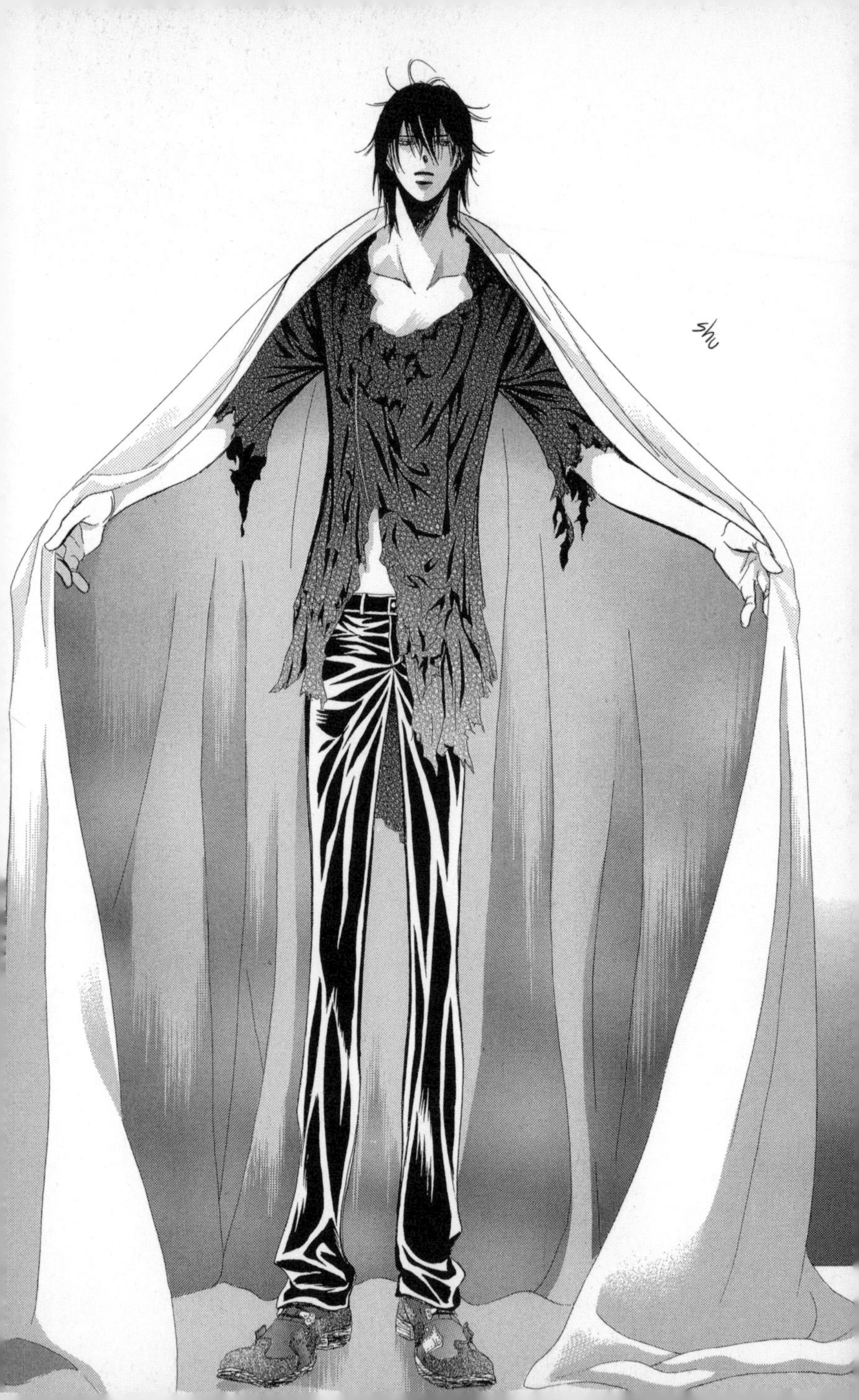
shu

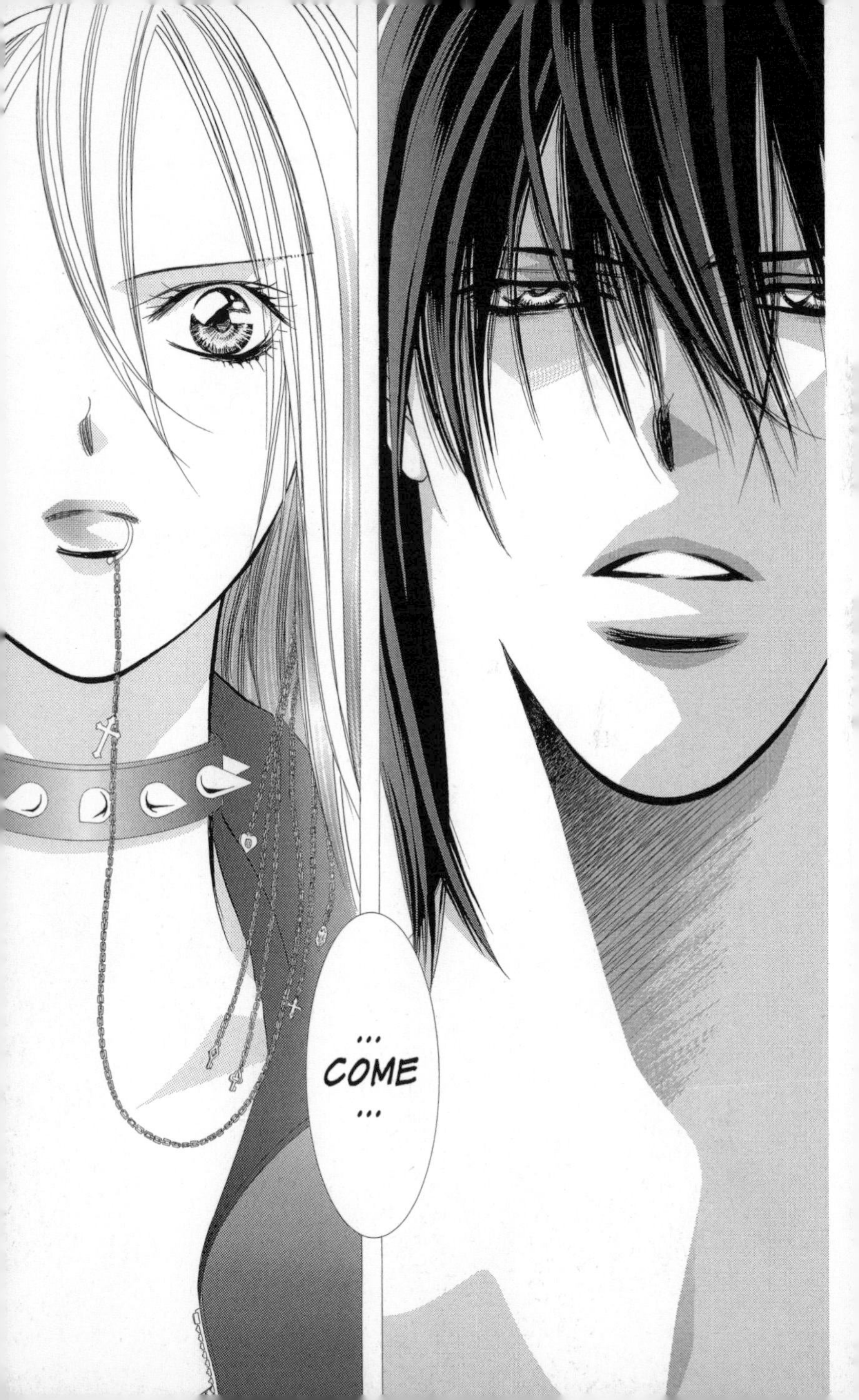
...COME...

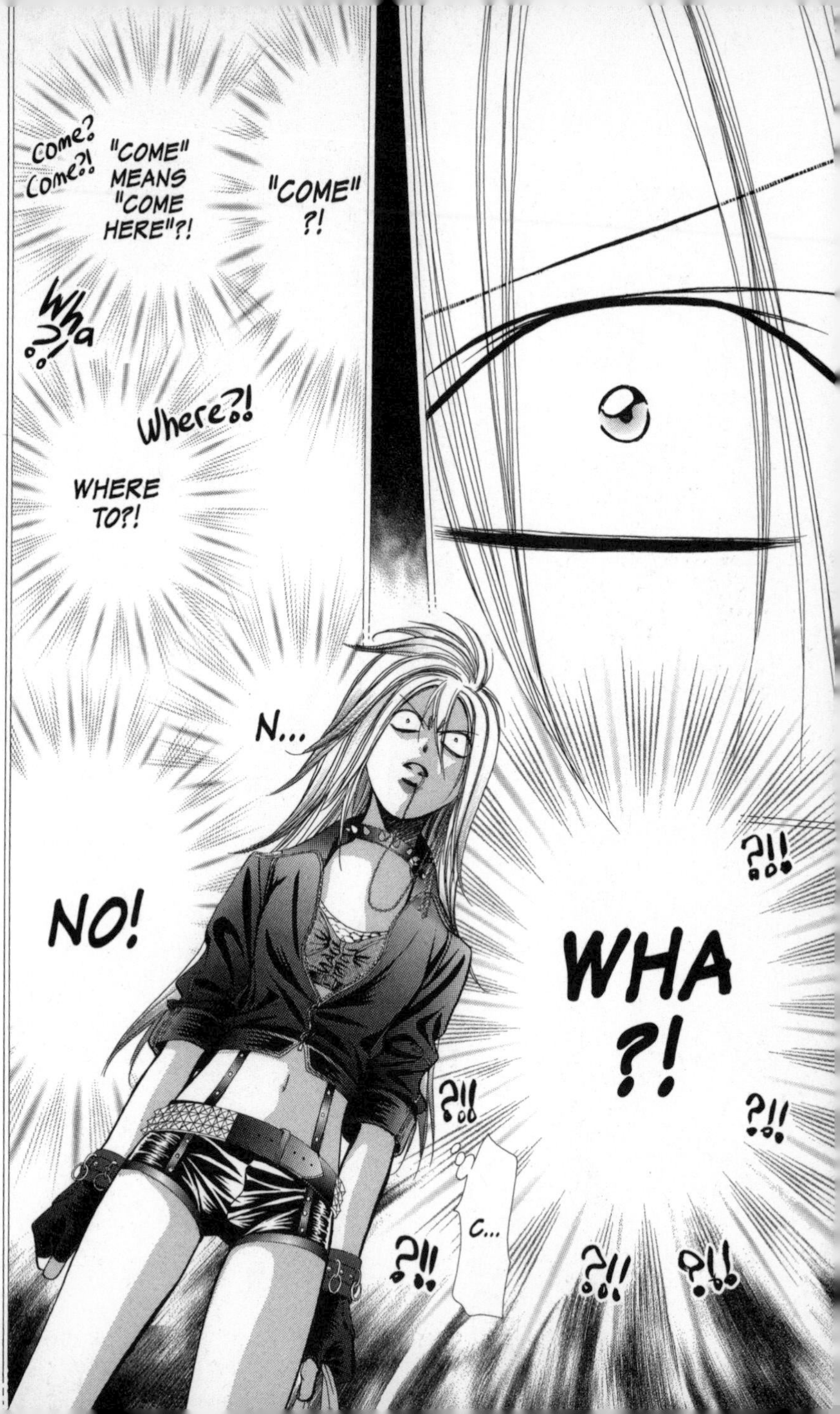
"COME" ?!
"COME" MEANS "COME HERE"?!
Come? Come?!
Wha?!
Where?!
WHERE TO?!
?!!
WHA ?!
?!!
?!!
?!!
?!!
?!!
C...
N...
NO!

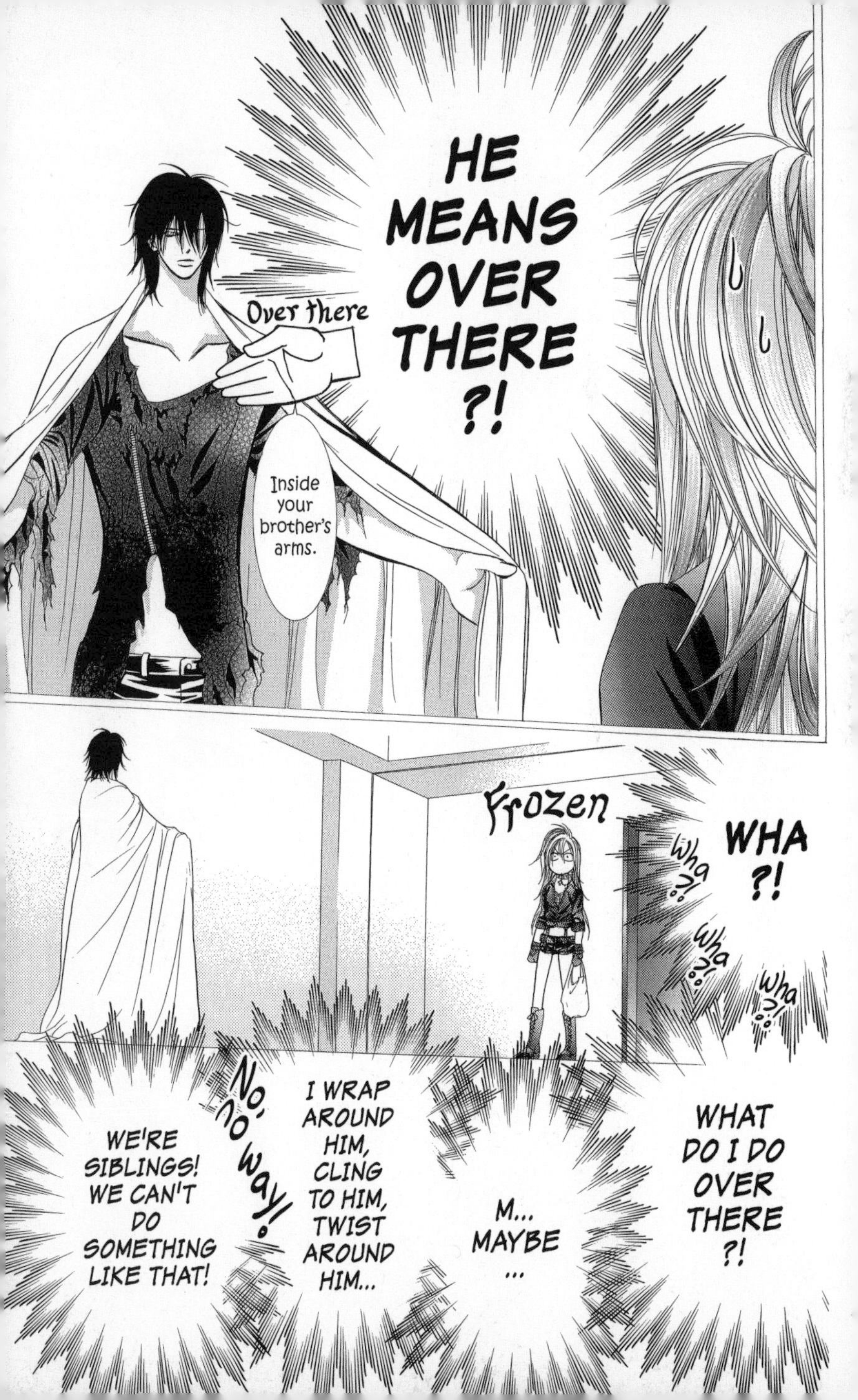
Over there
Inside your brother's arms.
HE MEANS OVER THERE ?!
WHA ?!
Wha ?!
Wha ?!
Wha ?!
Frozen
WHAT DO I DO OVER THERE ?!
M... MAYBE ...
I WRAP AROUND HIM, CLING TO HIM, TWIST AROUND HIM...
No, no way!
WE'RE SIBLINGS! WE CAN'T DO SOMETHING LIKE THAT!

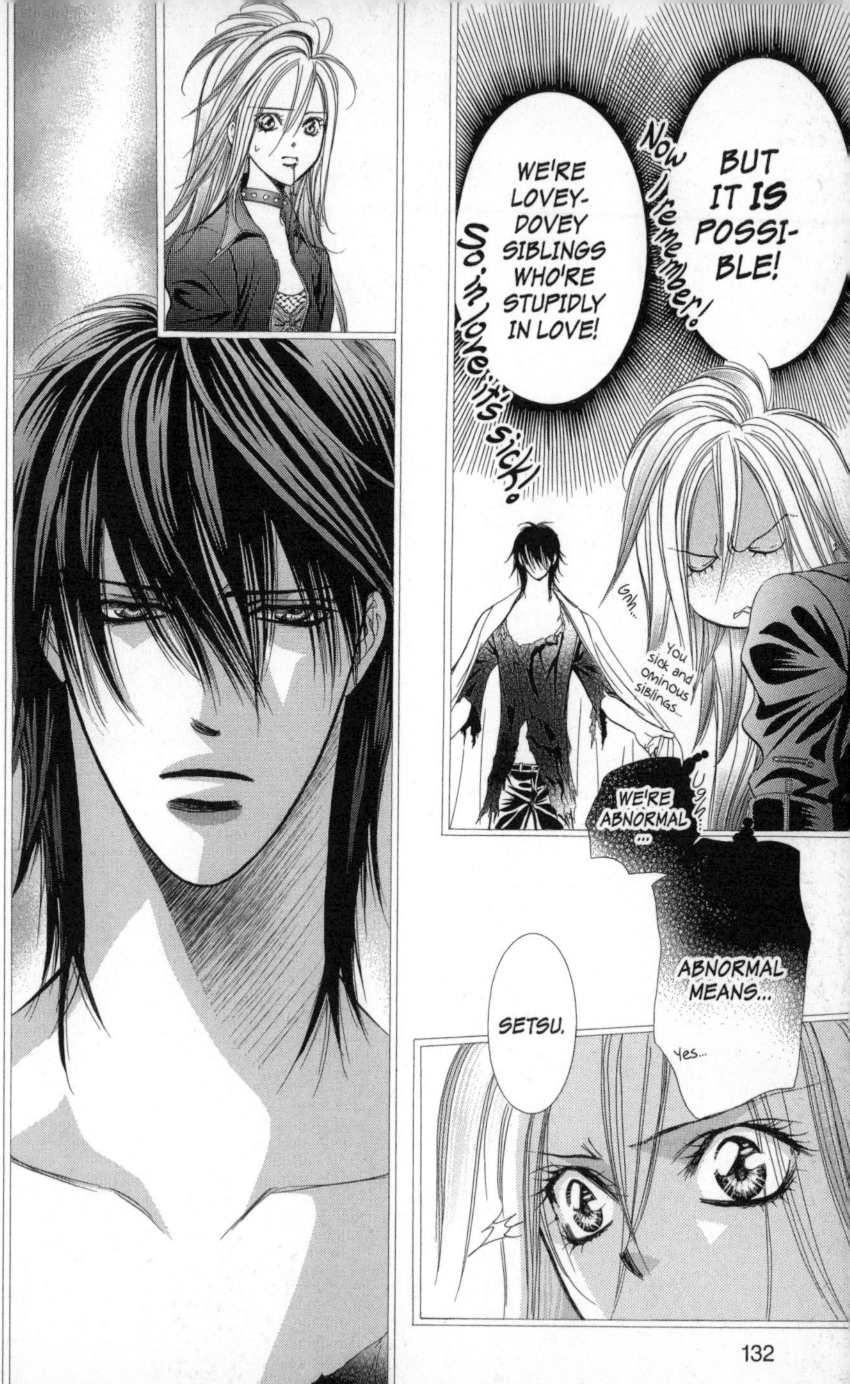
BUT IT IS POSSIBLE!
Now I remember!
WE'RE LOVEY-DOVEY SIBLINGS WHO'RE STUPIDLY IN LOVE!
So in love it's sick!
Gnh...
You sick and ominous siblings...
Ugh...
WE'RE ABNORMAL...
ABNORMAL MEANS...
Yes...
SETSU.

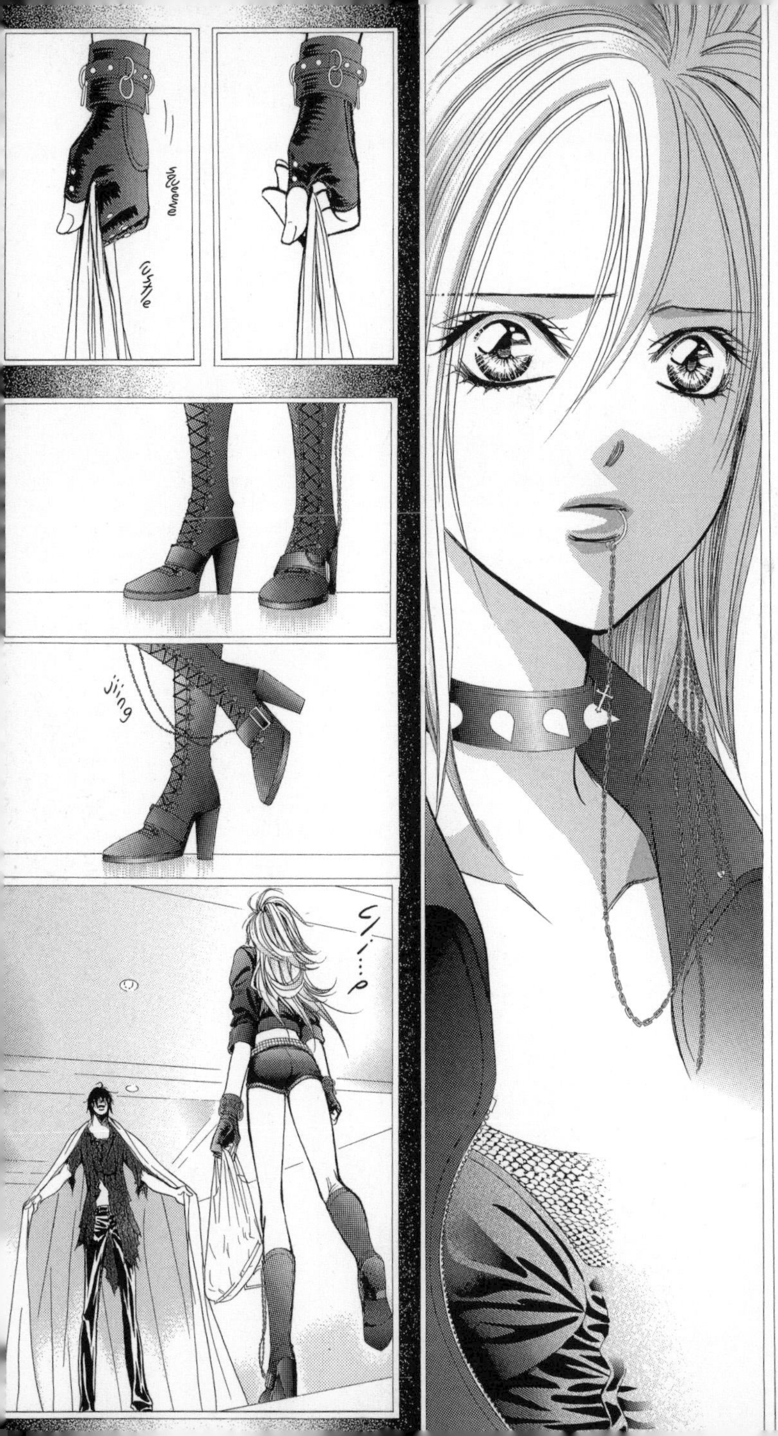
squeeze
rustle
jiing
cli...p

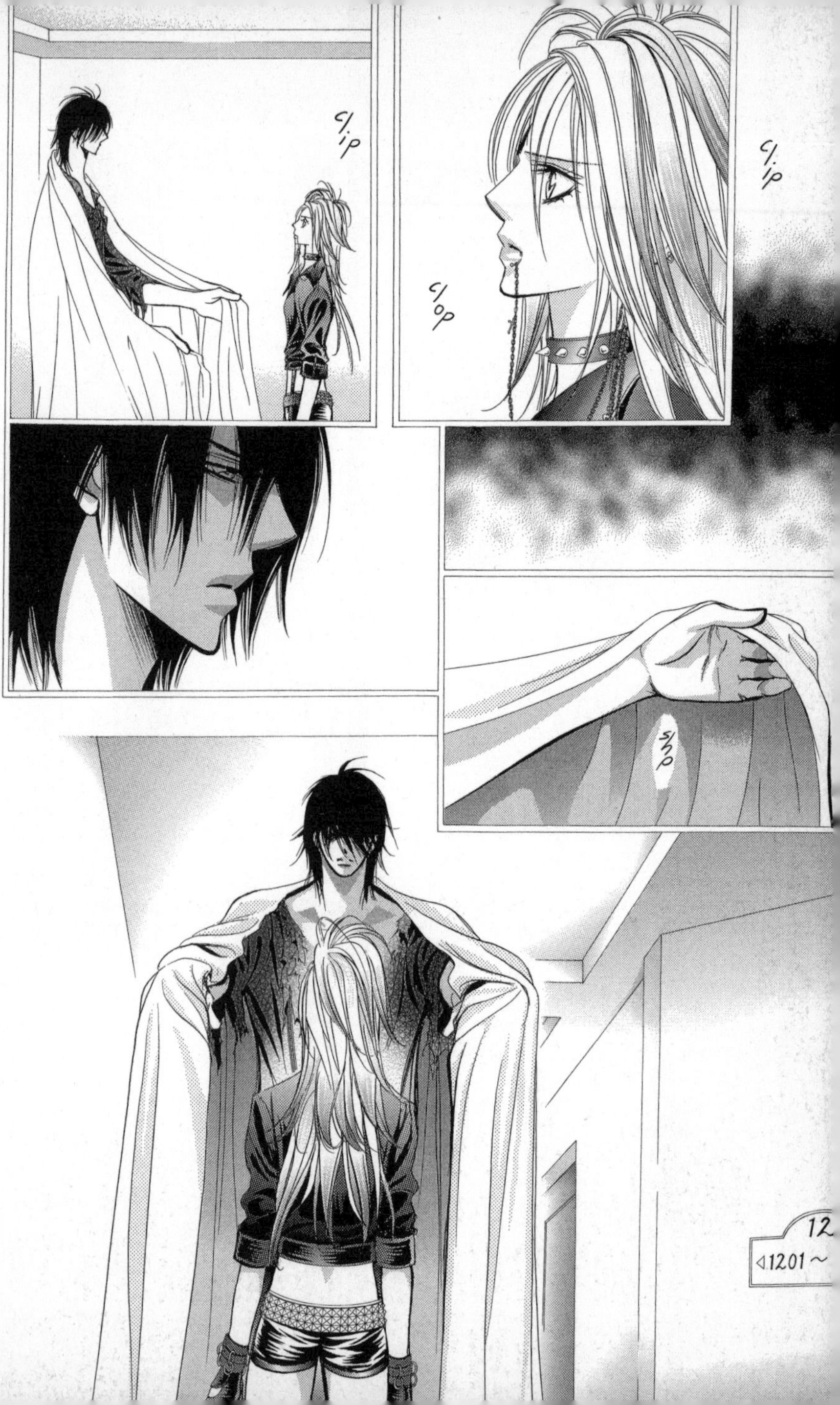
clip
clop
clip
slip
12
◁1201 ~

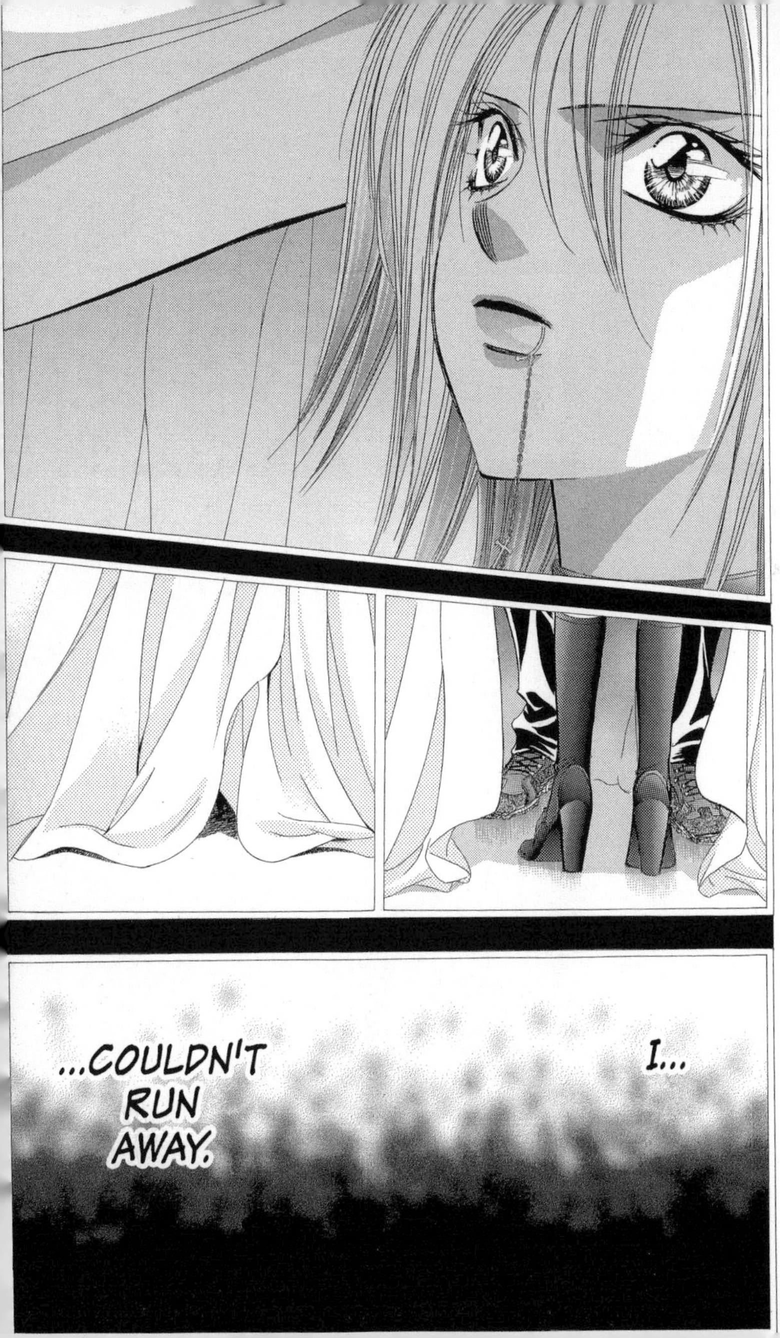
I...
...COULDN'T RUN AWAY.

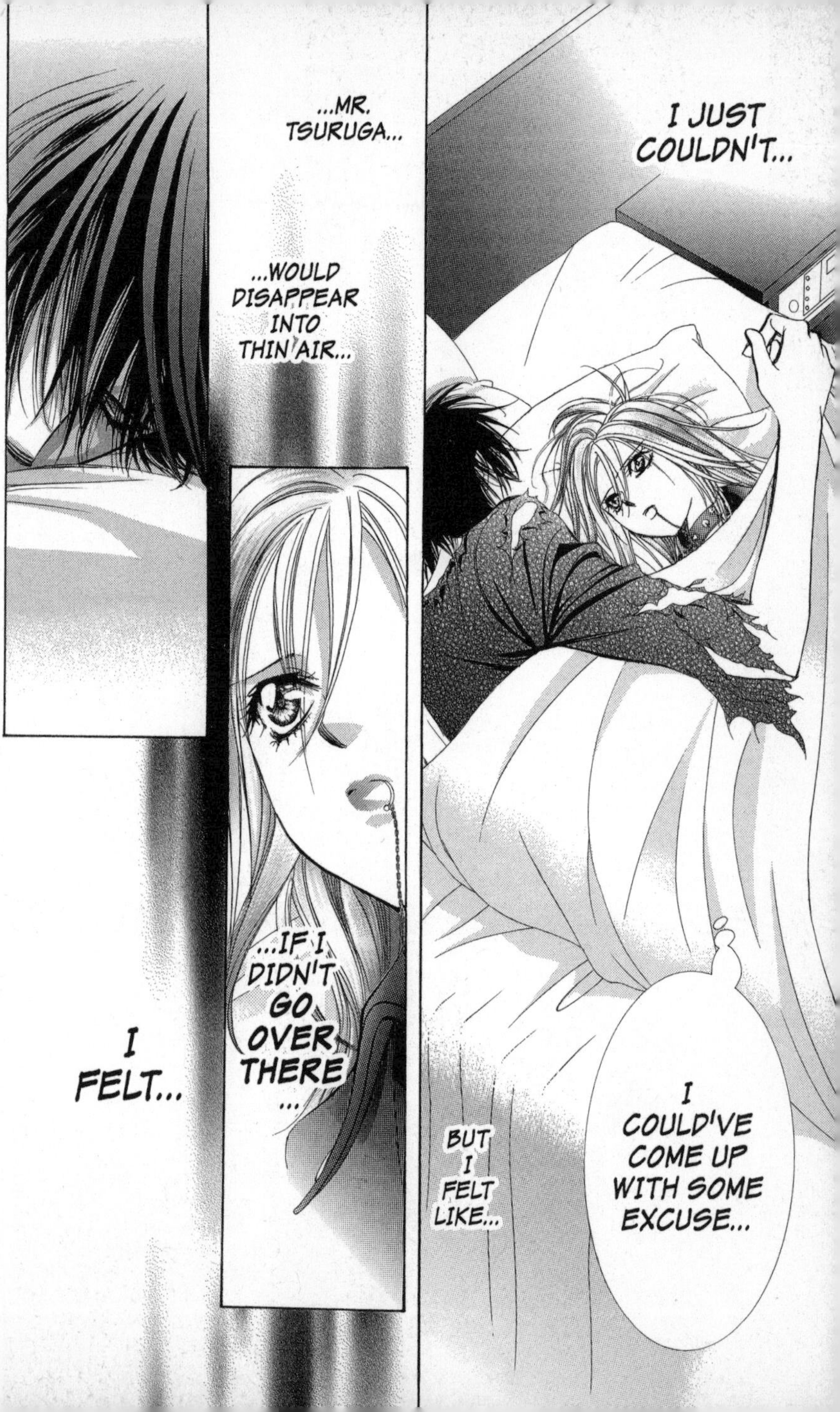
I JUST COULDN'T...
I COULD'VE COME UP WITH SOME EXCUSE...
BUT I FELT LIKE...
...MR. TSURUGA...
...WOULD DISAPPEAR INTO THIN AIR...
...IF I DIDN'T GO OVER THERE...
I FELT...

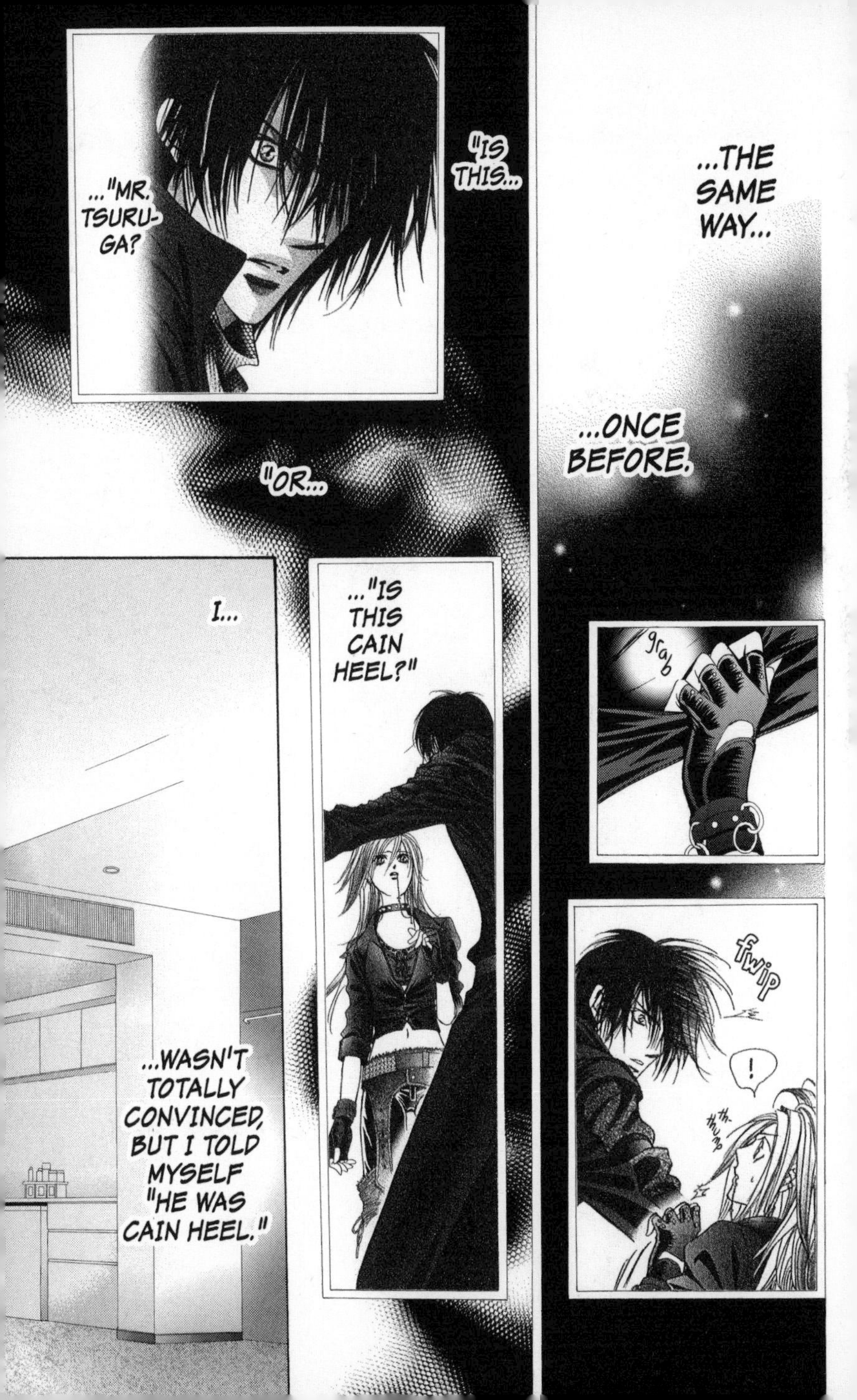
...THE SAME WAY...
...ONCE BEFORE.
grab
fwip
!
"IS THIS...
..."MR. TSURUGA?
"OR...
..."IS THIS CAIN HEEL?"
I...
...WASN'T TOTALLY CONVINCED, BUT I TOLD MYSELF "HE WAS CAIN HEEL."

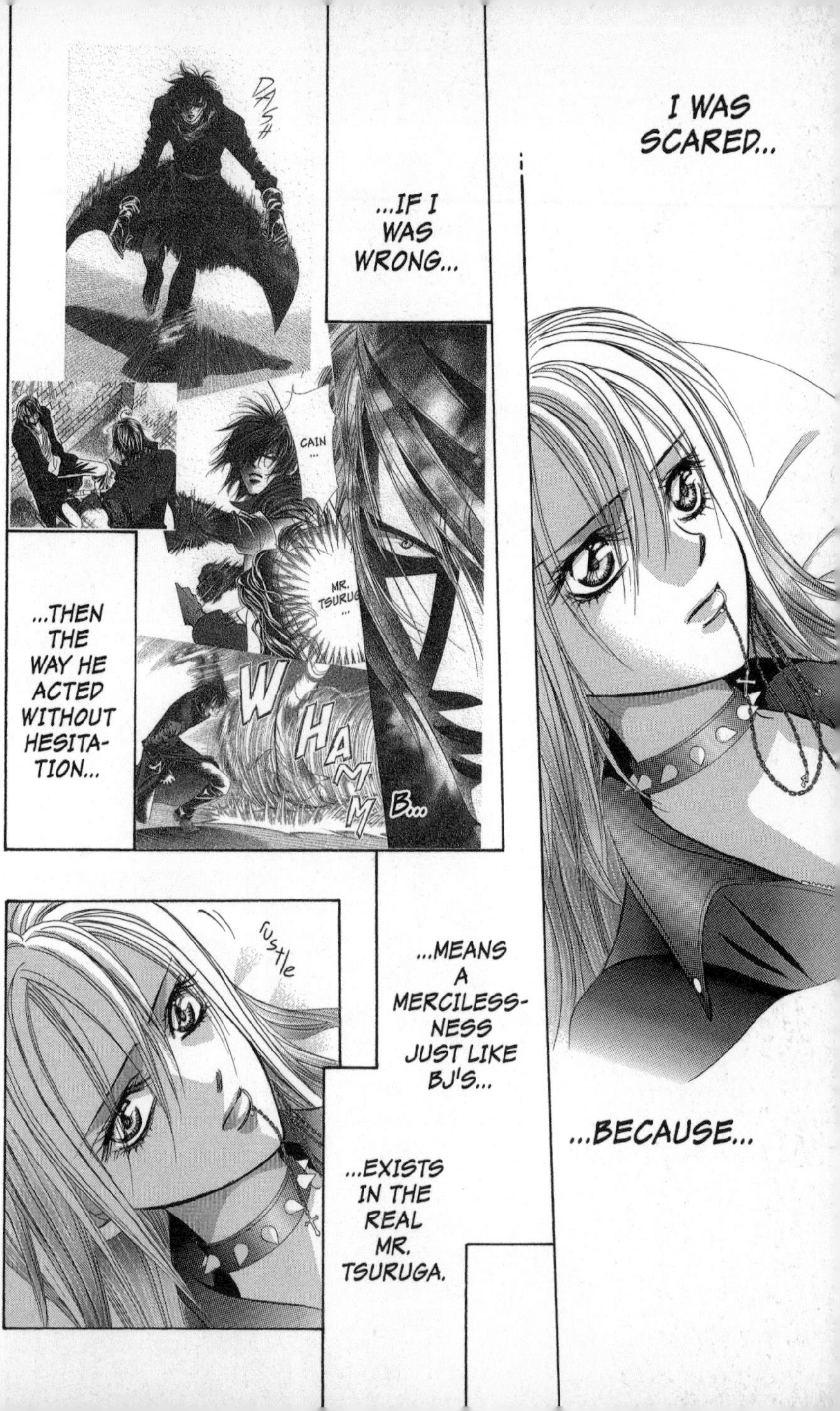
I WAS SCARED...
...BECAUSE...
...IF I WAS WRONG...
DASH
CAIN ...
MR. TSURUGA ...
WHAMM
B...
...THEN THE WAY HE ACTED WITHOUT HESITATION...
...MEANS A MERCILESSNESS JUST LIKE BJ'S...
rustle
...EXISTS IN THE REAL MR. TSURUGA.

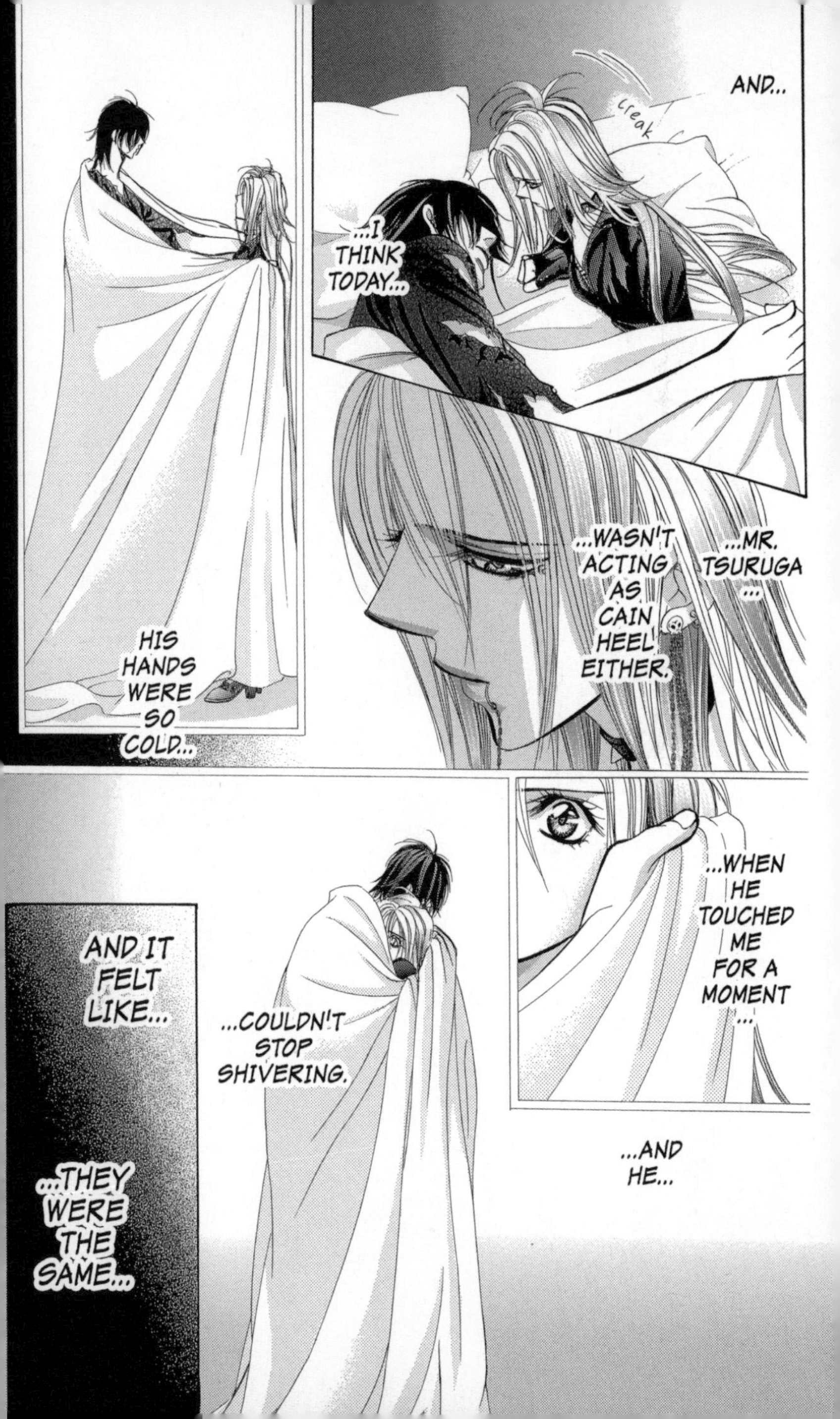
AND...
creak
...I THINK TODAY...
...MR. TSURUGA...
...WASN'T ACTING AS CAIN HEEL EITHER.
HIS HANDS WERE SO COLD...
...WHEN HE TOUCHED ME FOR A MOMENT...
...AND HE...
...COULDN'T STOP SHIVERING.
AND IT FELT LIKE...
...THEY WERE THE SAME...

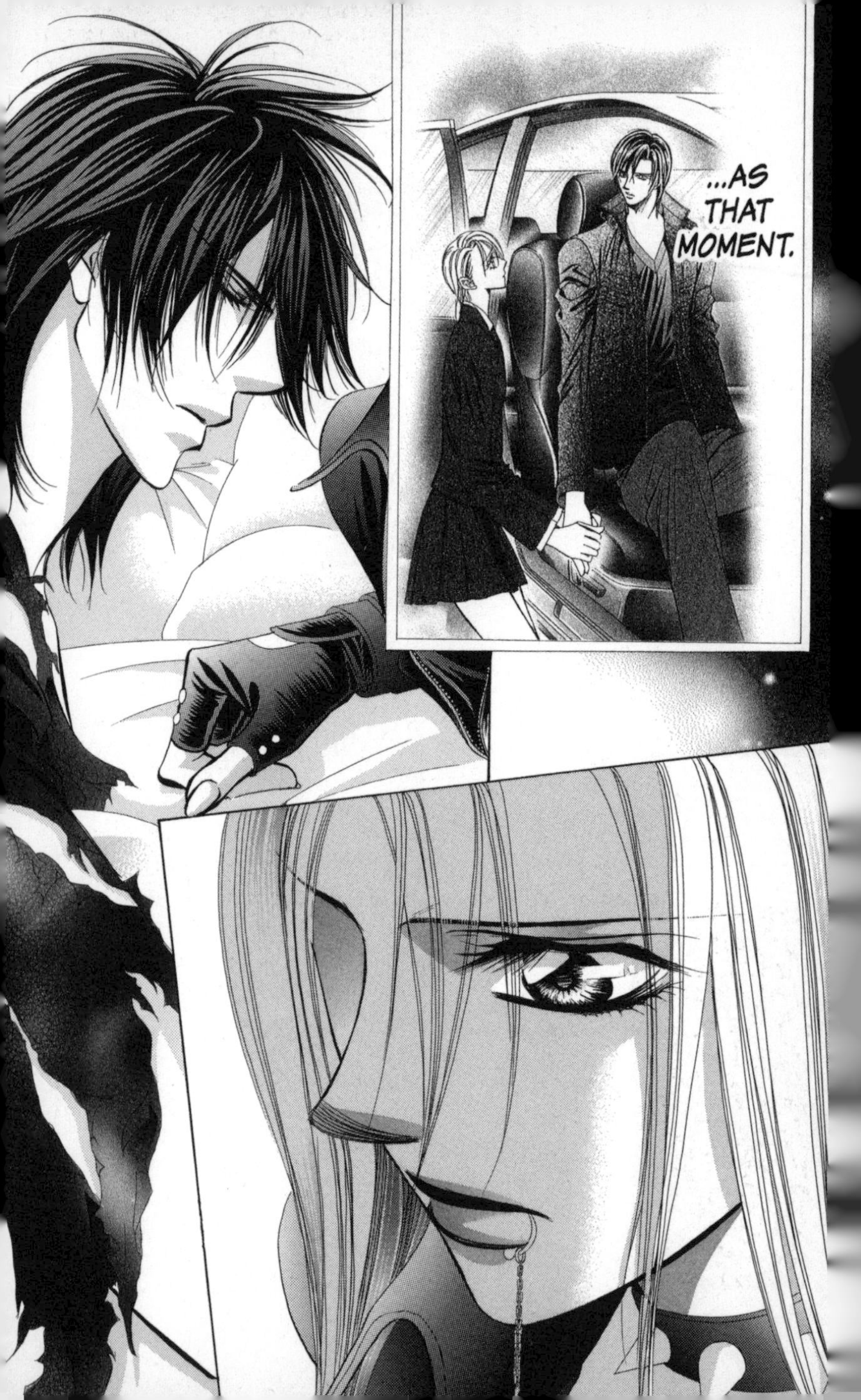
...AS
THAT
MOMENT.

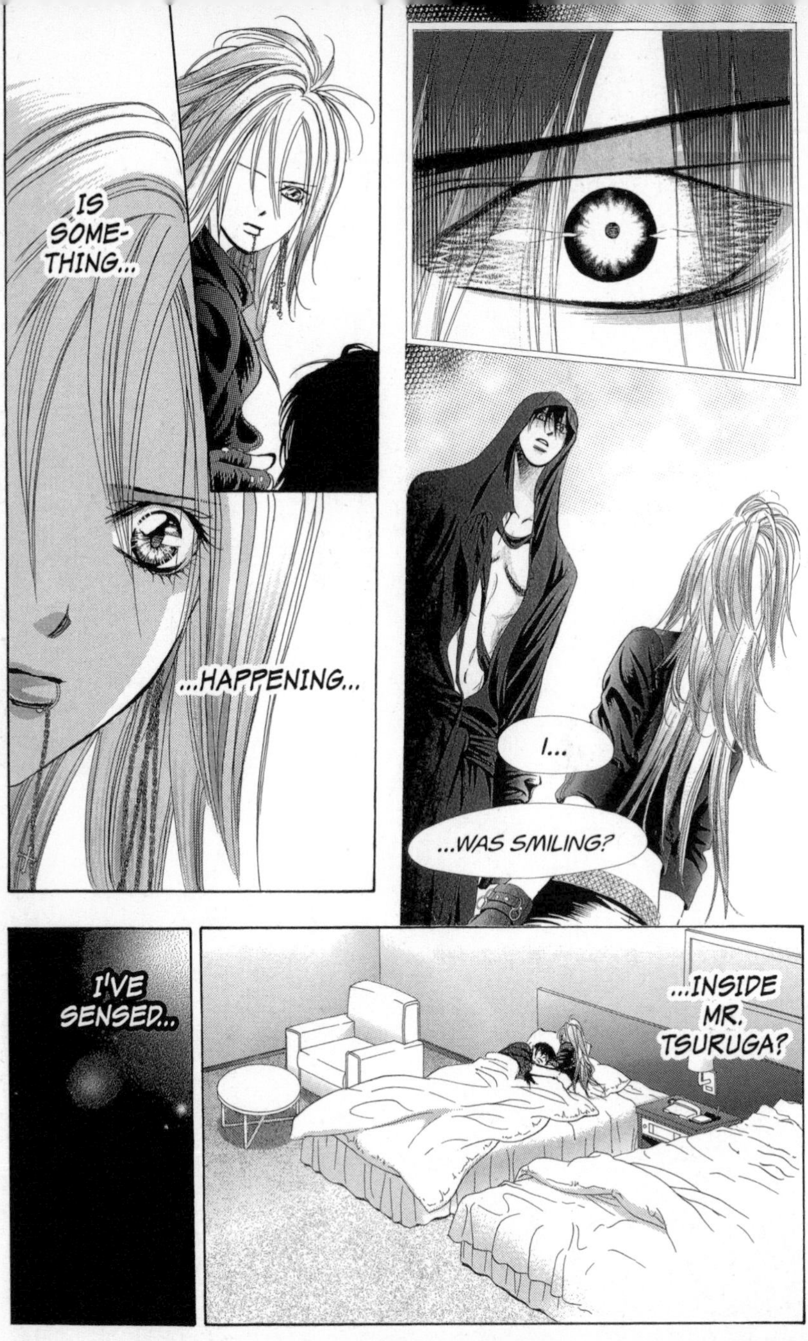
I...
...WAS SMILING?
IS SOMETHING...
...HAPPENING...
...INSIDE MR. TSURUGA?
I'VE SENSED...

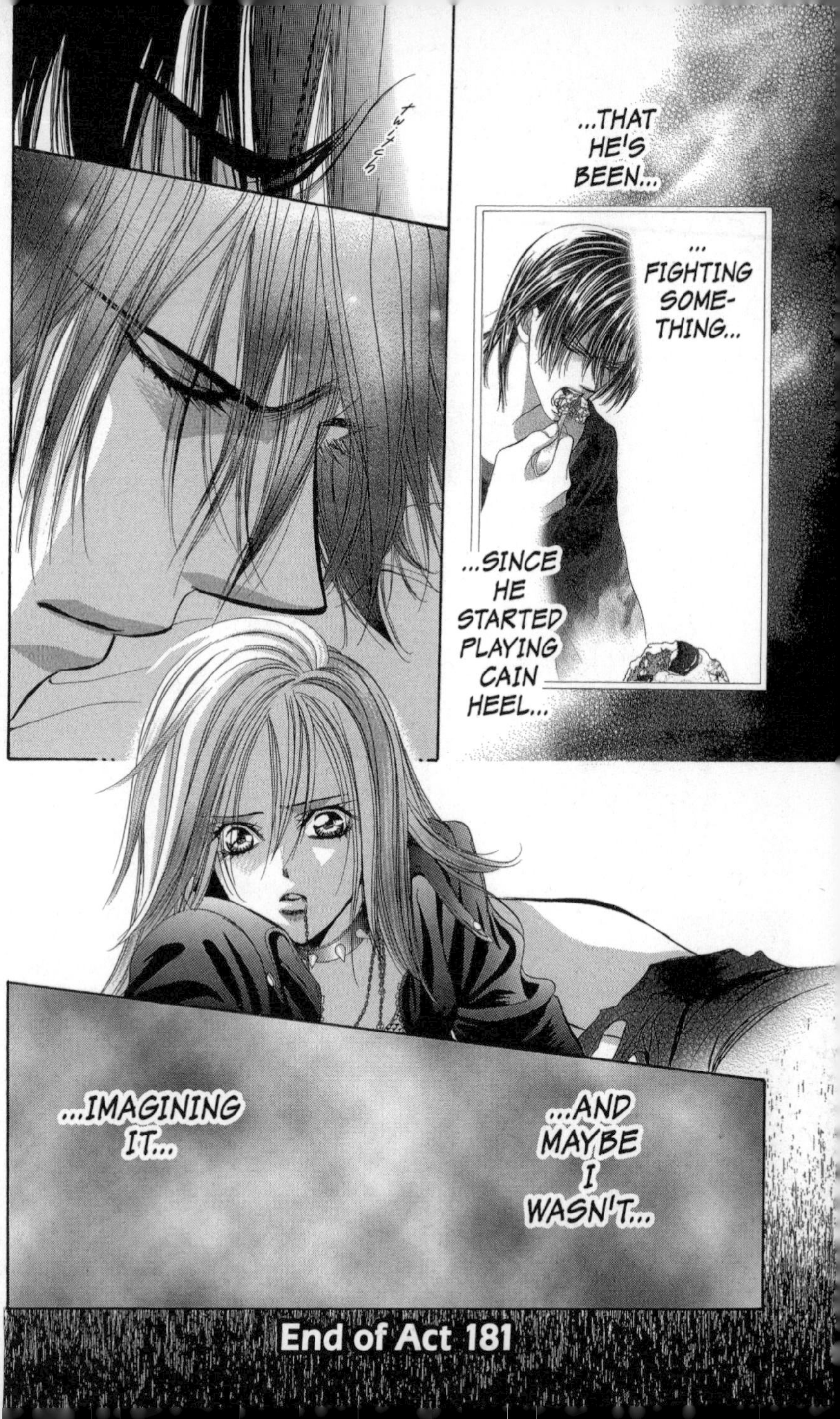
...THAT HE'S BEEN...
... FIGHTING SOME-THING...
...SINCE HE STARTED PLAYING CAIN HEEL...
twitch
...AND MAYBE I WASN'T...
...IMAGINING IT...
End of Act 181

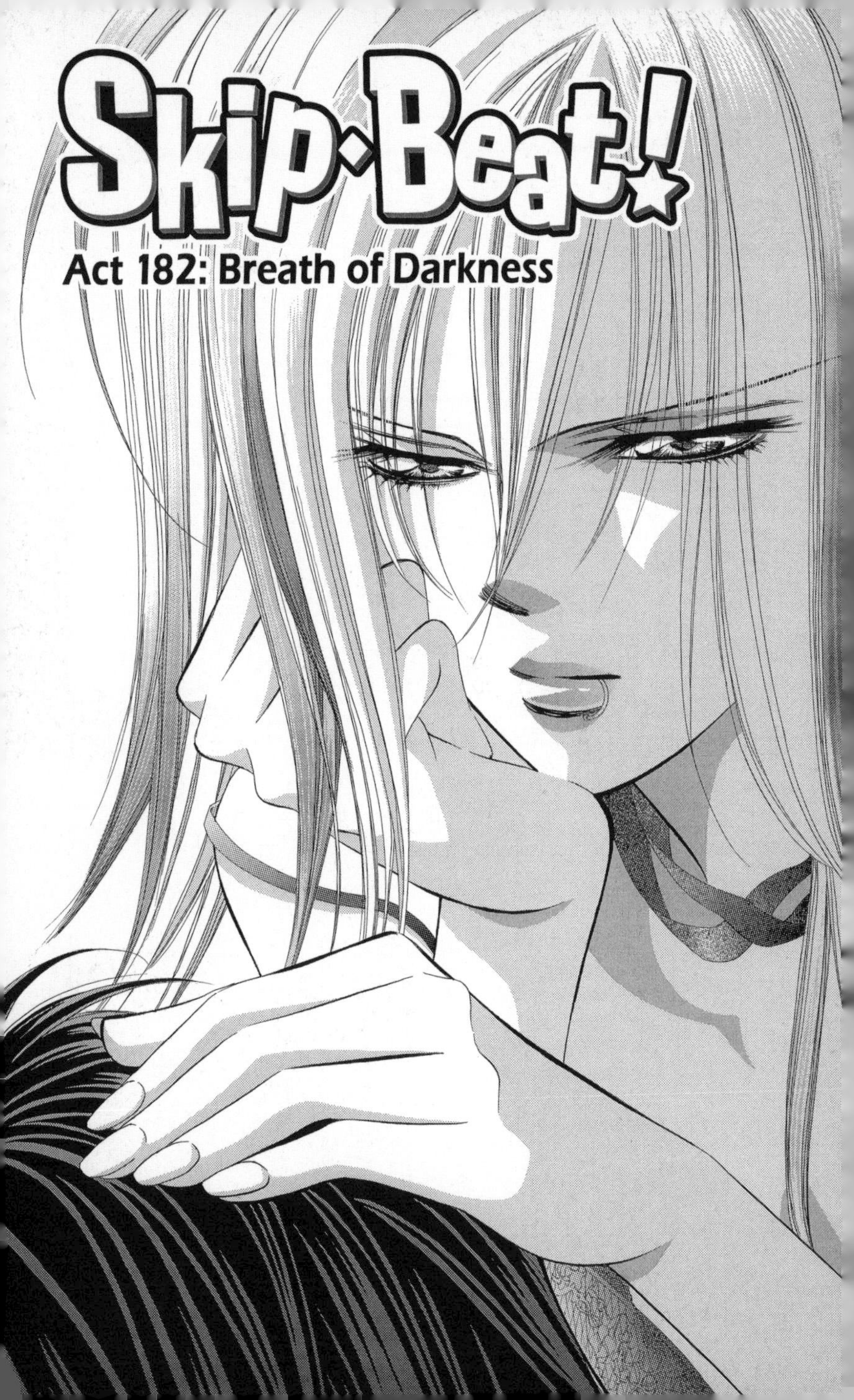
Skip·Beat!
Act 182: Breath of Darkness

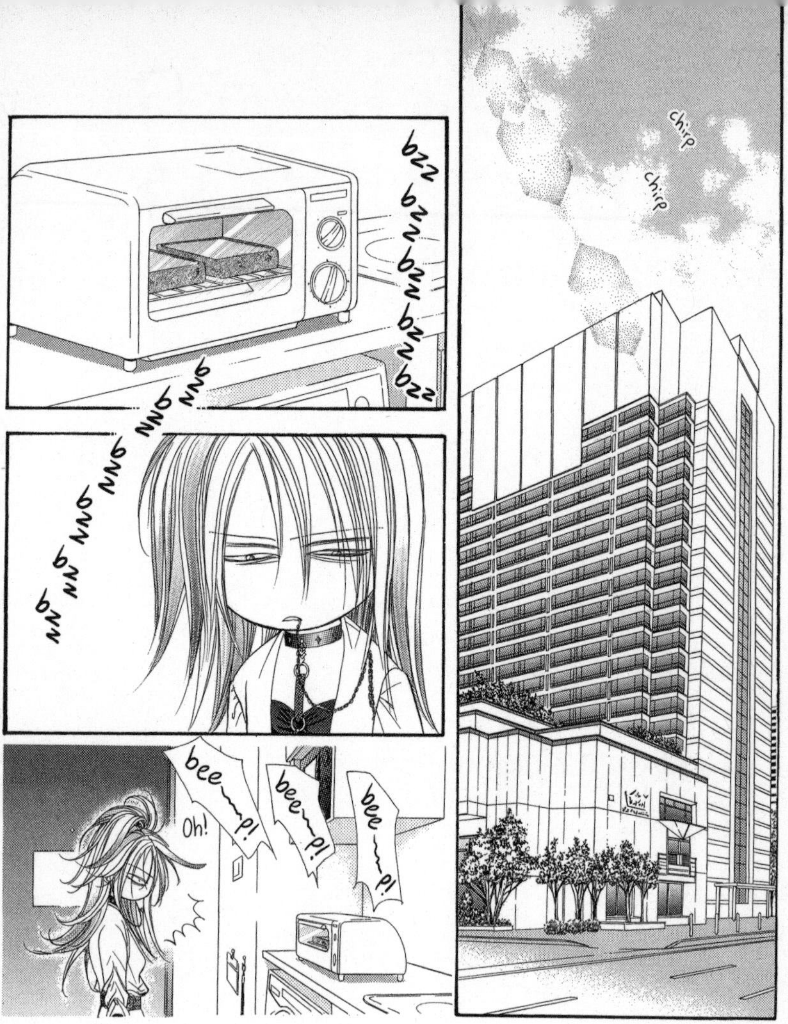
chirp
chirp
bzz bzz bzz bzz bzz
gnn gnn gnn bzz bzz
bee—p!
bee—p!
bee—p!
Oh!

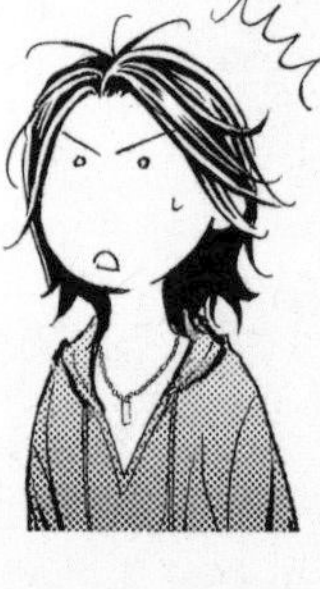

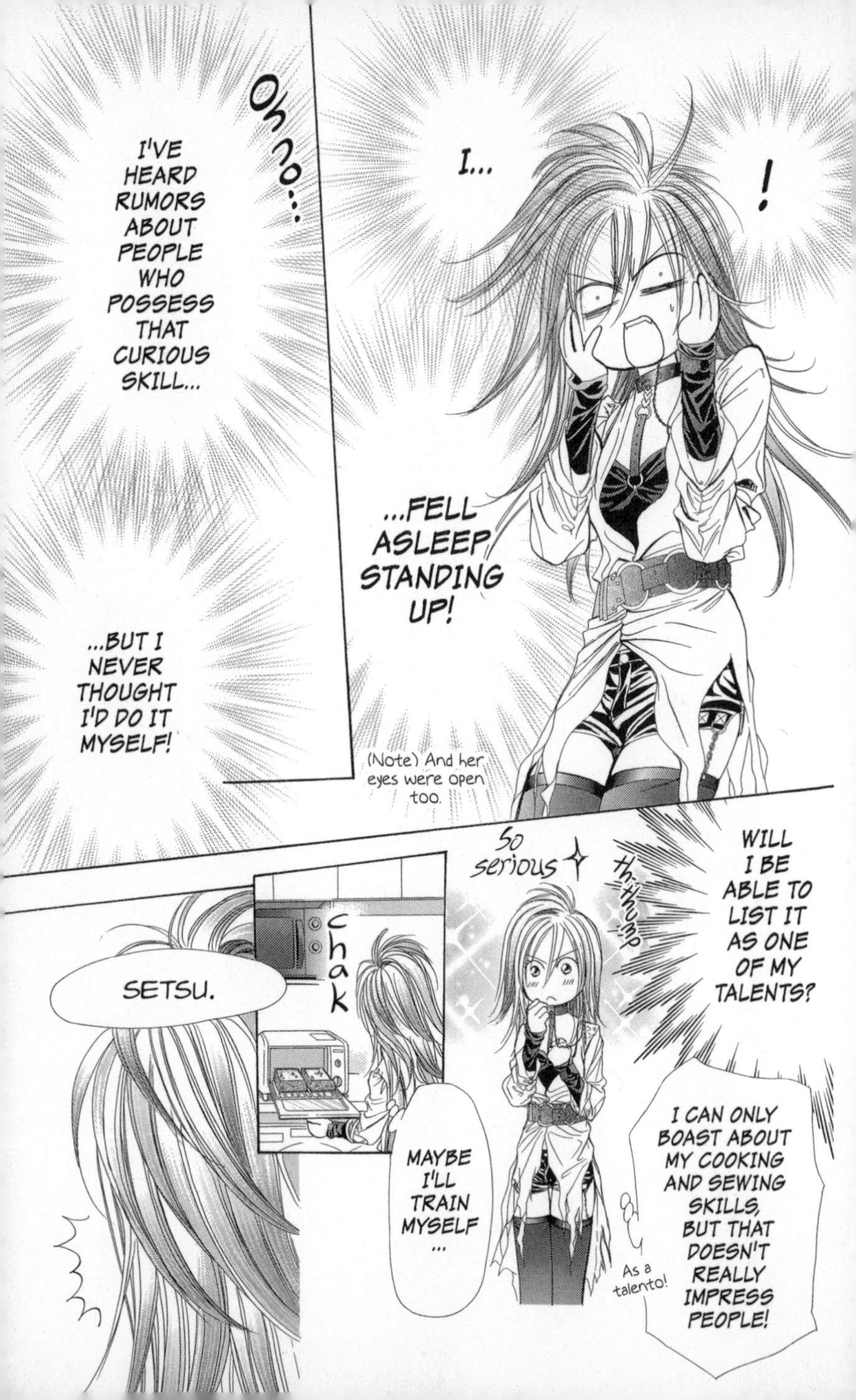
I...
!
...FELL ASLEEP STANDING UP!
(Note) And her eyes were open too.
Oh no...
I'VE HEARD RUMORS ABOUT PEOPLE WHO POSSESS THAT CURIOUS SKILL...
...BUT I NEVER THOUGHT I'D DO IT MYSELF!
So serious
th-thump
WILL I BE ABLE TO LIST IT AS ONE OF MY TALENTS?
I CAN ONLY BOAST ABOUT MY COOKING AND SEWING SKILLS, BUT THAT DOESN'T REALLY IMPRESS PEOPLE!
As a talento!
MAYBE I'LL TRAIN MYSELF...
chak
SETSU.

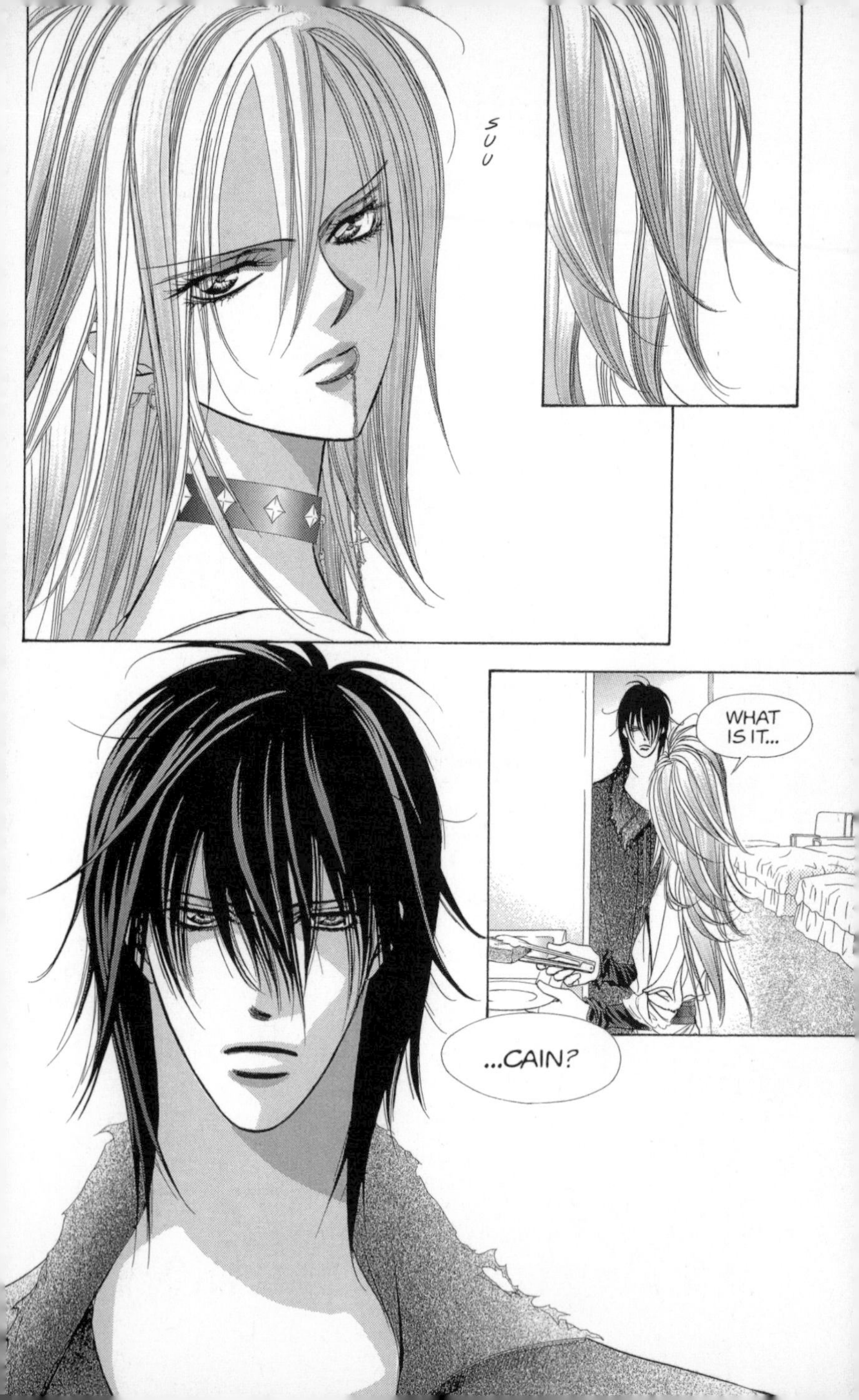
SUU
WHAT IS IT...
...CAIN?

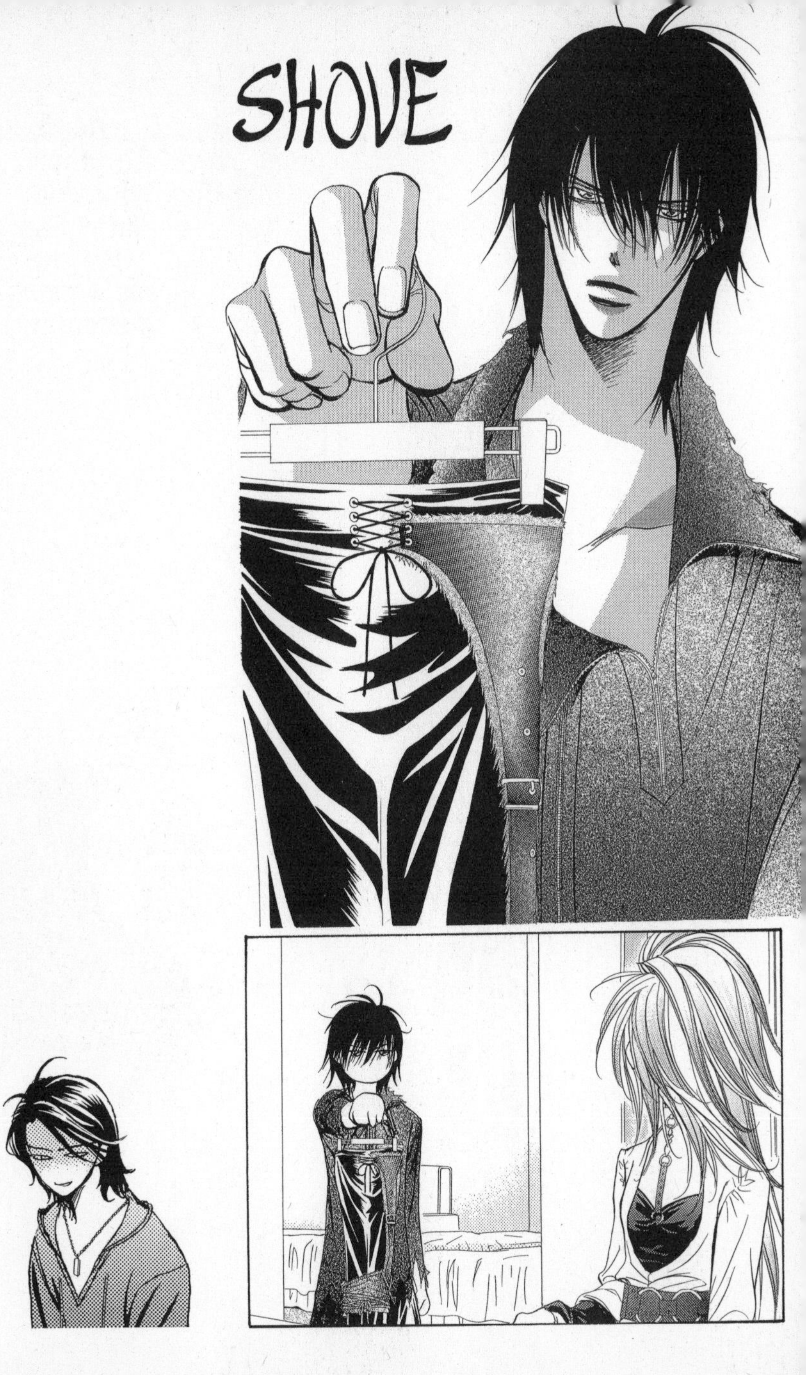
SHOVE

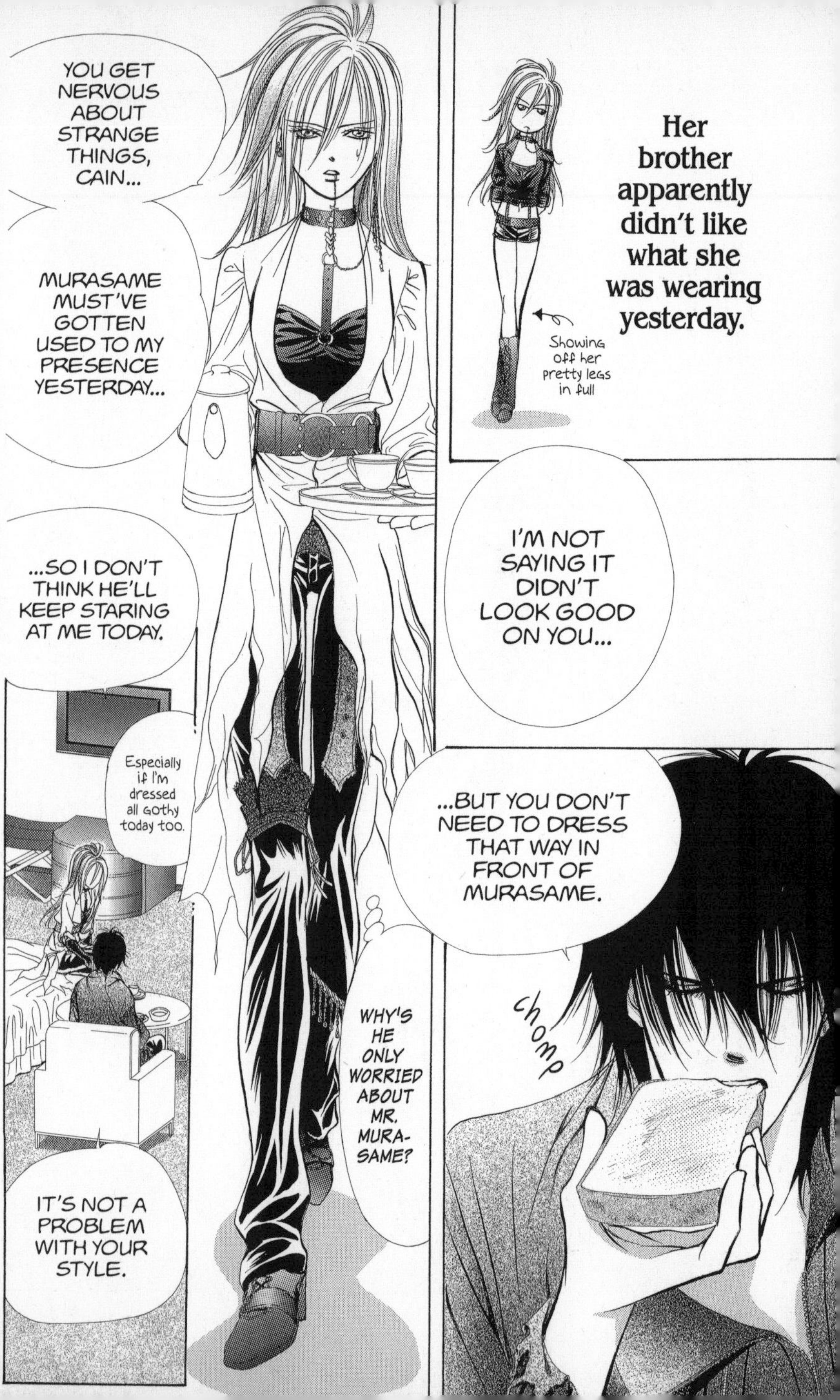
Her brother apparently didn't like what she was wearing yesterday.
Showing off her pretty legs in full
I'M NOT SAYING IT DIDN'T LOOK GOOD ON YOU...
...BUT YOU DON'T NEED TO DRESS THAT WAY IN FRONT OF MURASAME.
chomp
YOU GET NERVOUS ABOUT STRANGE THINGS, CAIN...
MURASAME MUST'VE GOTTEN USED TO MY PRESENCE YESTERDAY...
...SO I DON'T THINK HE'LL KEEP STARING AT ME TODAY.
Especially if I'm dressed all Gothy today too.
WHY'S HE ONLY WORRIED ABOUT MR. MURA-SAME?
IT'S NOT A PROBLEM WITH YOUR STYLE.

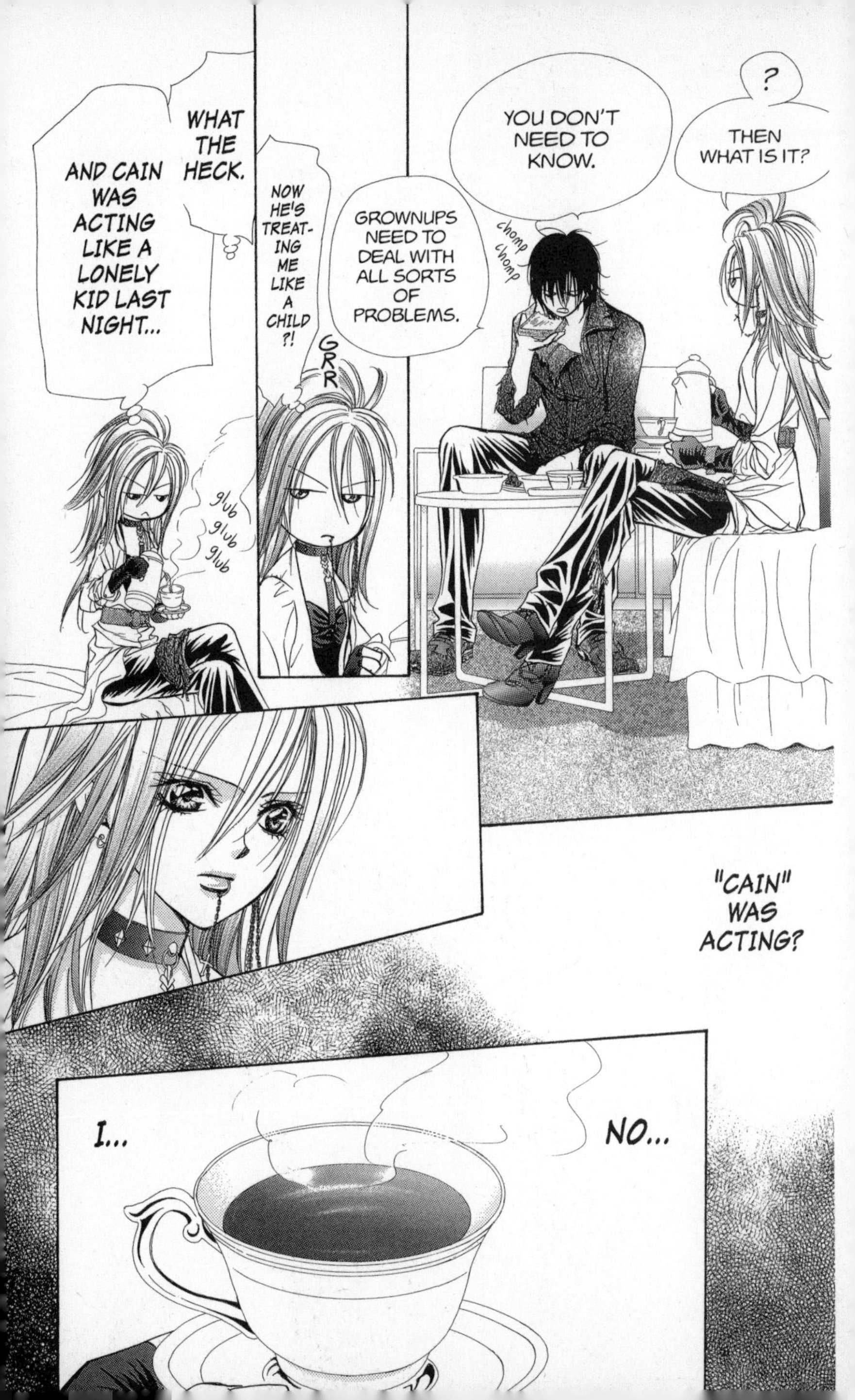
?
THEN WHAT IS IT?
YOU DON'T NEED TO KNOW.
chomp chomp
GROWNUPS NEED TO DEAL WITH ALL SORTS OF PROBLEMS.
NOW HE'S TREAT-ING ME LIKE A CHILD?!
GRR
WHAT THE HECK.
AND CAIN WAS ACTING LIKE A LONELY KID LAST NIGHT...
glub glub glub
"CAIN" WAS ACTING?
NO...
I...

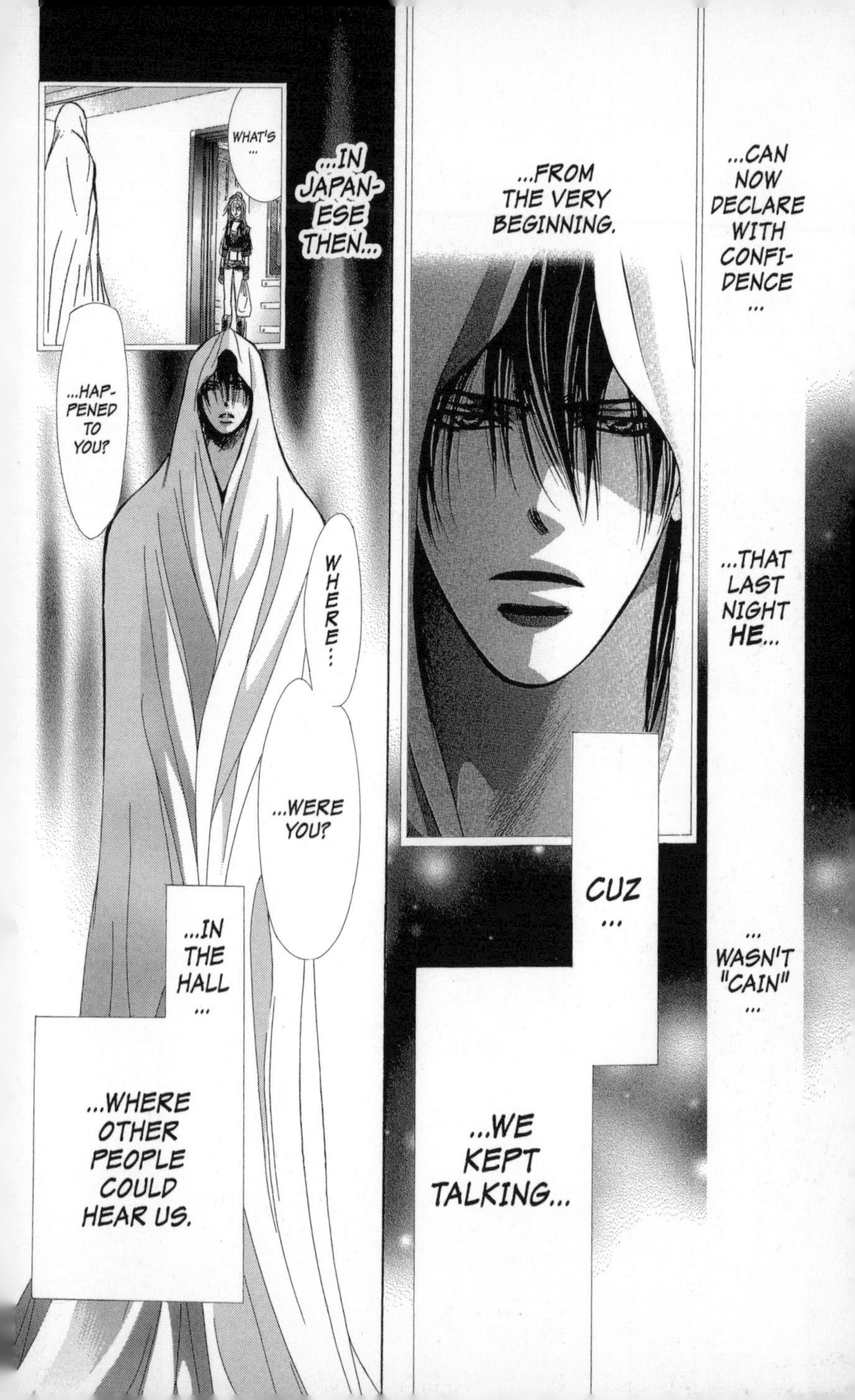
...CAN NOW DECLARE WITH CONFIDENCE...
...THAT LAST NIGHT HE...
...WASN'T "CAIN"...
...FROM THE VERY BEGINNING.
CUZ...
...WE KEPT TALKING...
...IN JAPANESE THEN...
WHAT'S...
...HAPPENED TO YOU?
WHERE...
...WERE YOU?
...IN THE HALL...
...WHERE OTHER PEOPLE COULD HEAR US.

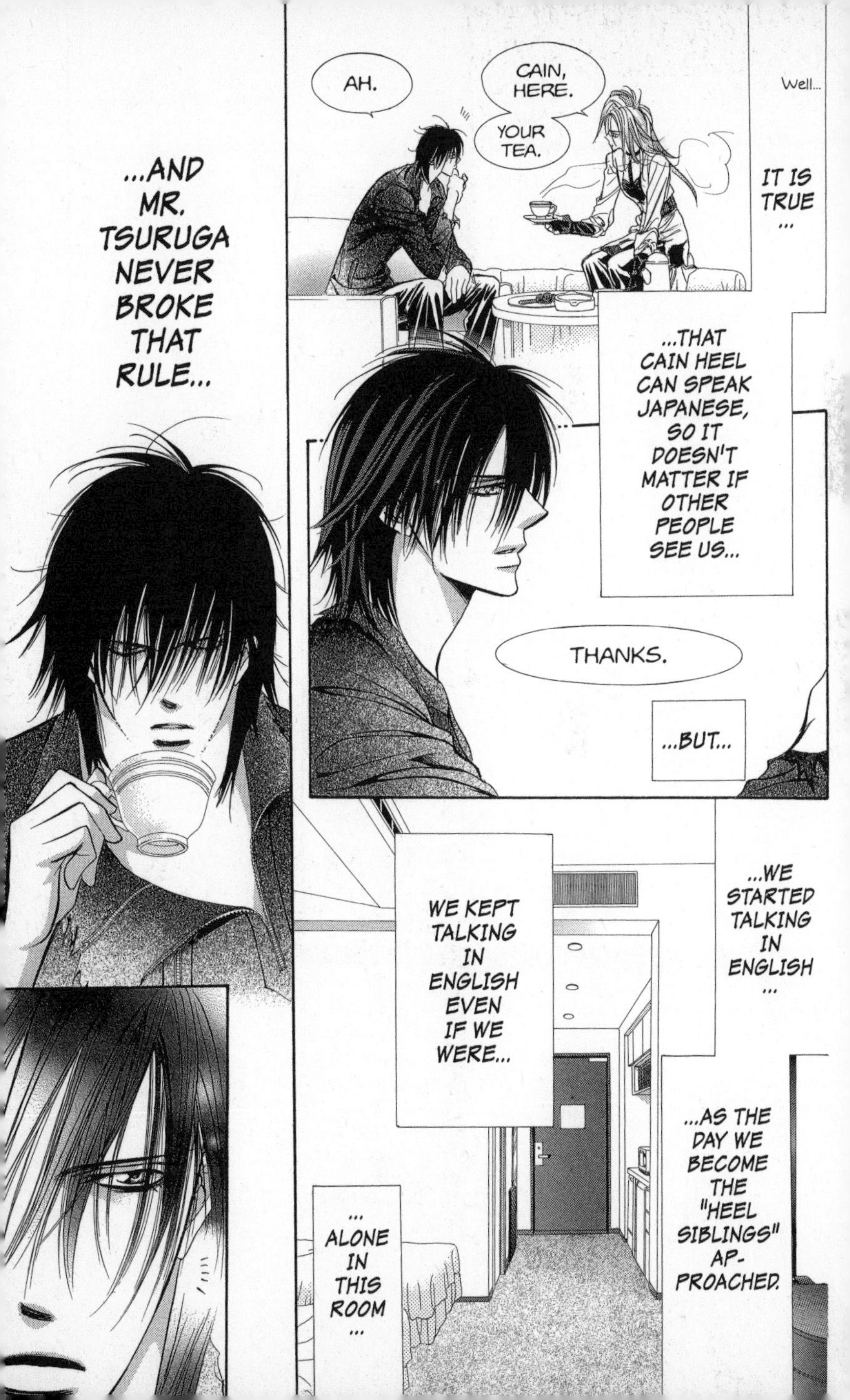

Well...
IT IS TRUE ...
CAIN, HERE.
YOUR TEA.
AH.
...THAT CAIN HEEL CAN SPEAK JAPANESE, SO IT DOESN'T MATTER IF OTHER PEOPLE SEE US...
THANKS.
...BUT...
...WE STARTED TALKING IN ENGLISH ...
...AS THE DAY WE BECOME THE "HEEL SIBLINGS" AP-PROACHED.
WE KEPT TALKING IN ENGLISH EVEN IF WE WERE...
... ALONE IN THIS ROOM ...
...AND MR. TSURUGA NEVER BROKE THAT RULE...

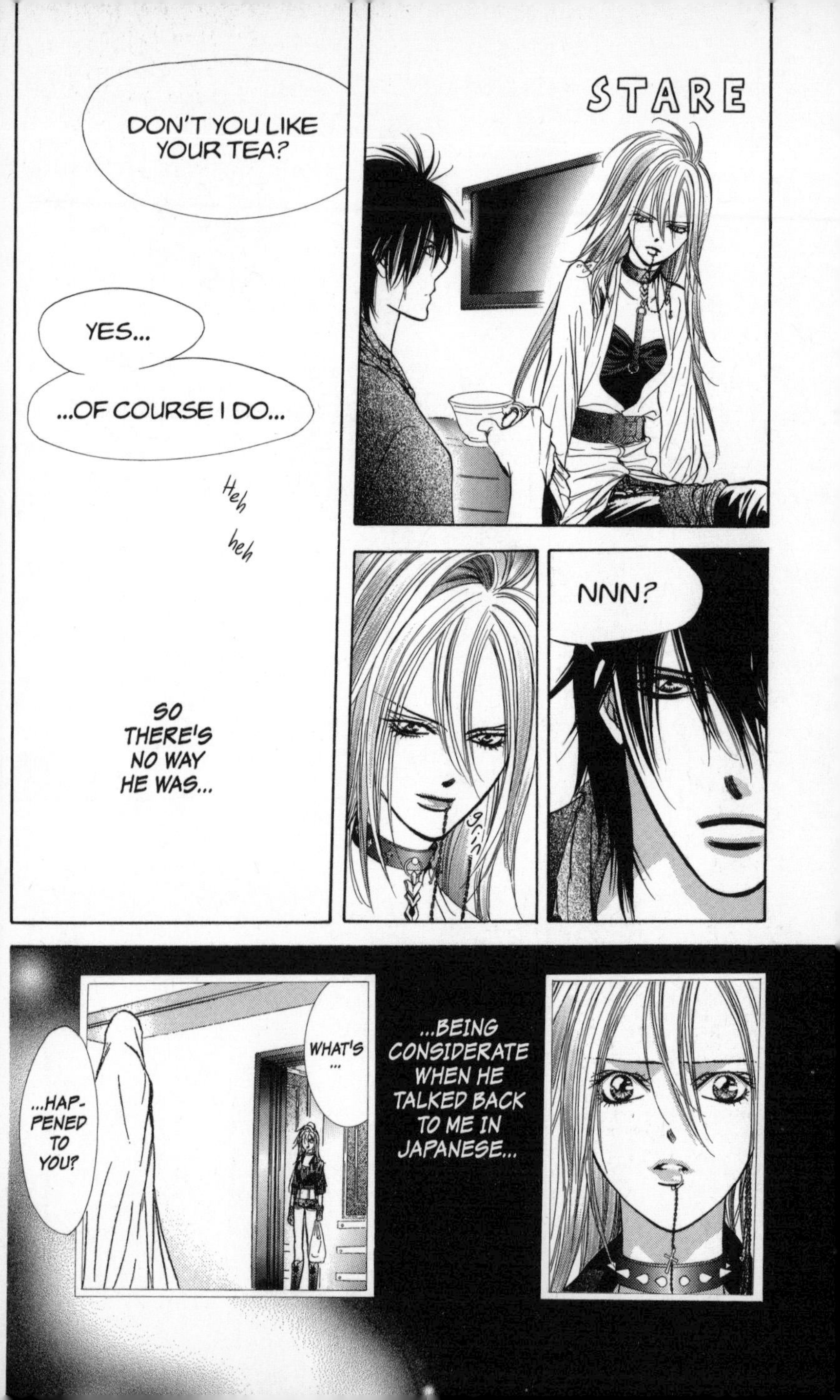
STARE
NNN?
grin
DON'T YOU LIKE YOUR TEA?
YES...
...OF COURSE I DO...
Heh heh
SO THERE'S NO WAY HE WAS...
...BEING CONSIDERATE WHEN HE TALKED BACK TO ME IN JAPANESE...
WHAT'S...
...HAP-PENED TO YOU?

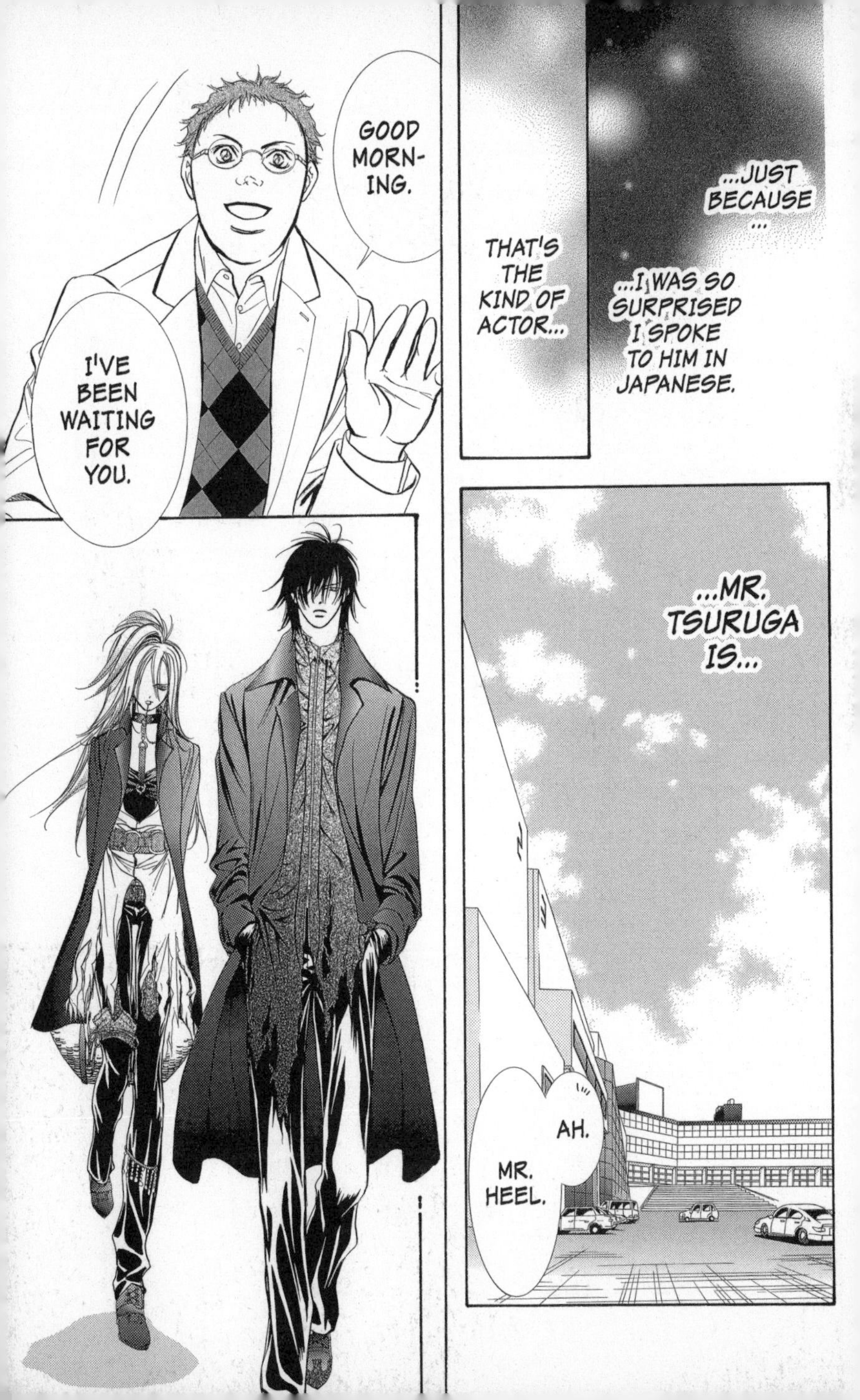
...JUST BECAUSE ...
...I WAS SO SURPRISED I SPOKE TO HIM IN JAPANESE.
THAT'S THE KIND OF ACTOR...
...MR. TSURUGA IS...
AH.
MR. HEEL.
GOOD MORN-ING.
I'VE BEEN WAITING FOR YOU.

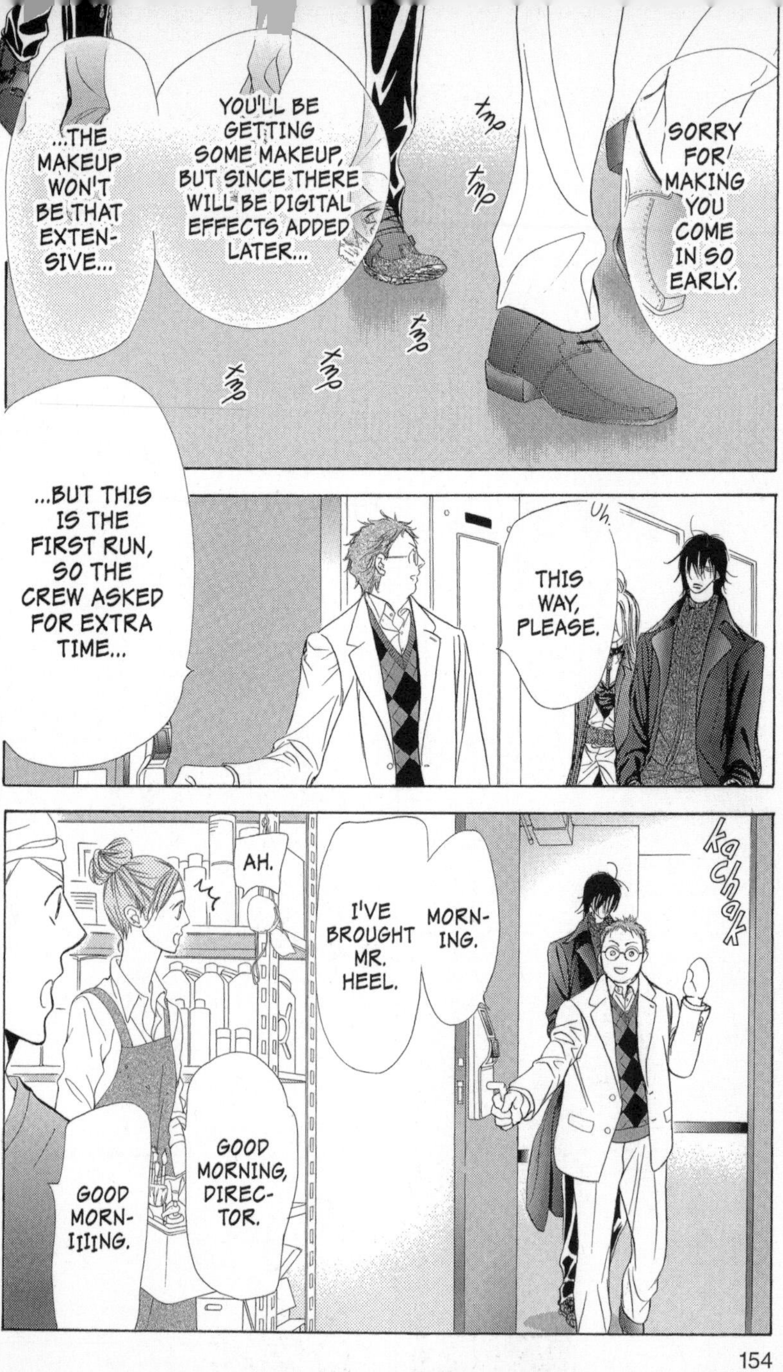
SORRY FOR MAKING YOU COME IN SO EARLY.
tmp
tmp
YOU'LL BE GETTING SOME MAKEUP, BUT SINCE THERE WILL BE DIGITAL EFFECTS ADDED LATER...
...THE MAKEUP WON'T BE THAT EXTEN-SIVE...
tmp
tmp
tmp
Uh.
THIS WAY, PLEASE.
...BUT THIS IS THE FIRST RUN, SO THE CREW ASKED FOR EXTRA TIME...
kachak
MORN-ING.
I'VE BROUGHT MR. HEEL.
AH.
GOOD MORNING, DIREC-TOR.
GOOD MORN-IIIING.

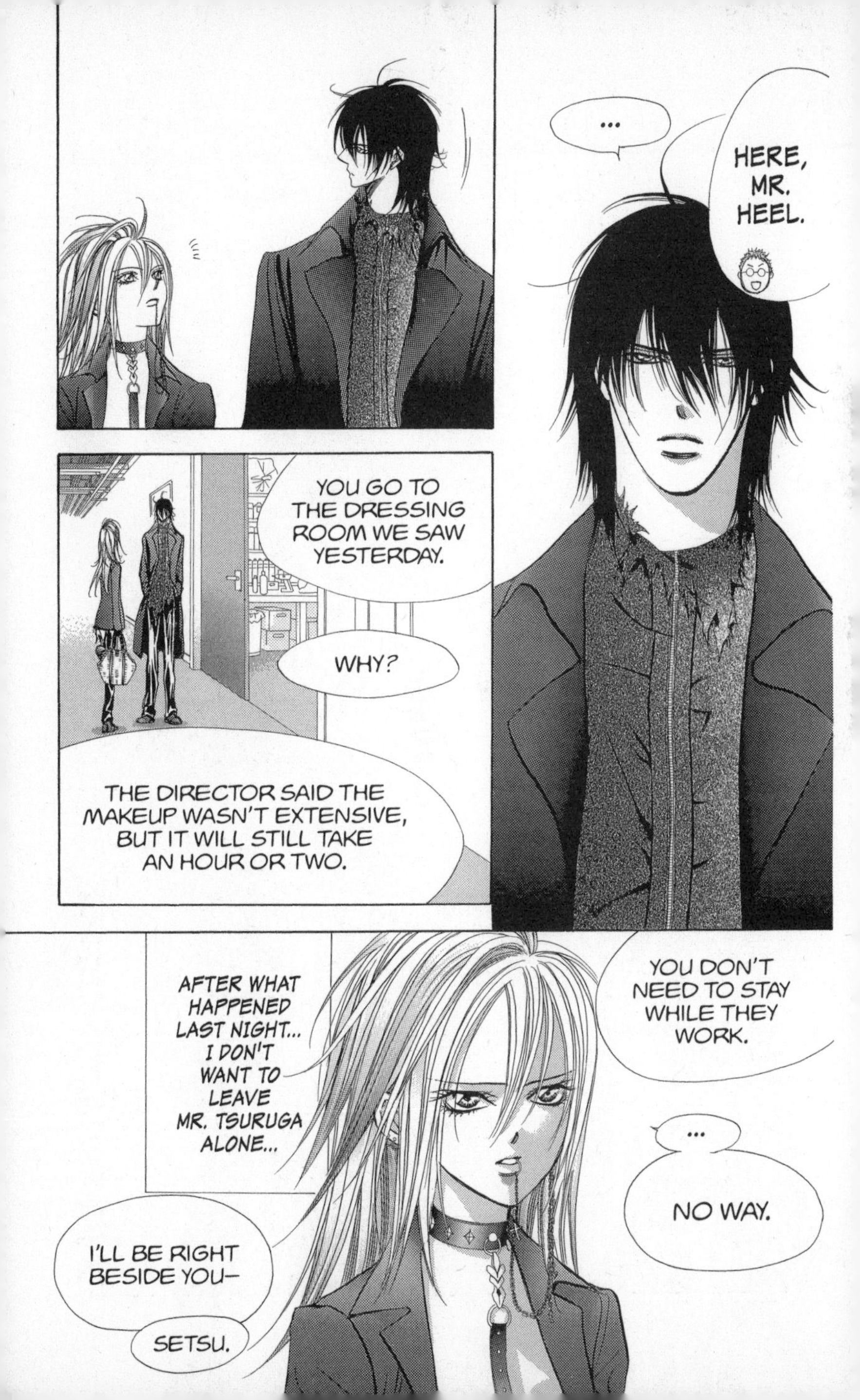
HERE, MR. HEEL.
...
YOU GO TO THE DRESSING ROOM WE SAW YESTERDAY.
WHY?
THE DIRECTOR SAID THE MAKEUP WASN'T EXTENSIVE, BUT IT WILL STILL TAKE AN HOUR OR TWO.
YOU DON'T NEED TO STAY WHILE THEY WORK.
AFTER WHAT HAPPENED LAST NIGHT... I DON'T WANT TO LEAVE MR. TSURUGA ALONE...
...
NO WAY.
I'LL BE RIGHT BESIDE YOU—
SETSU.

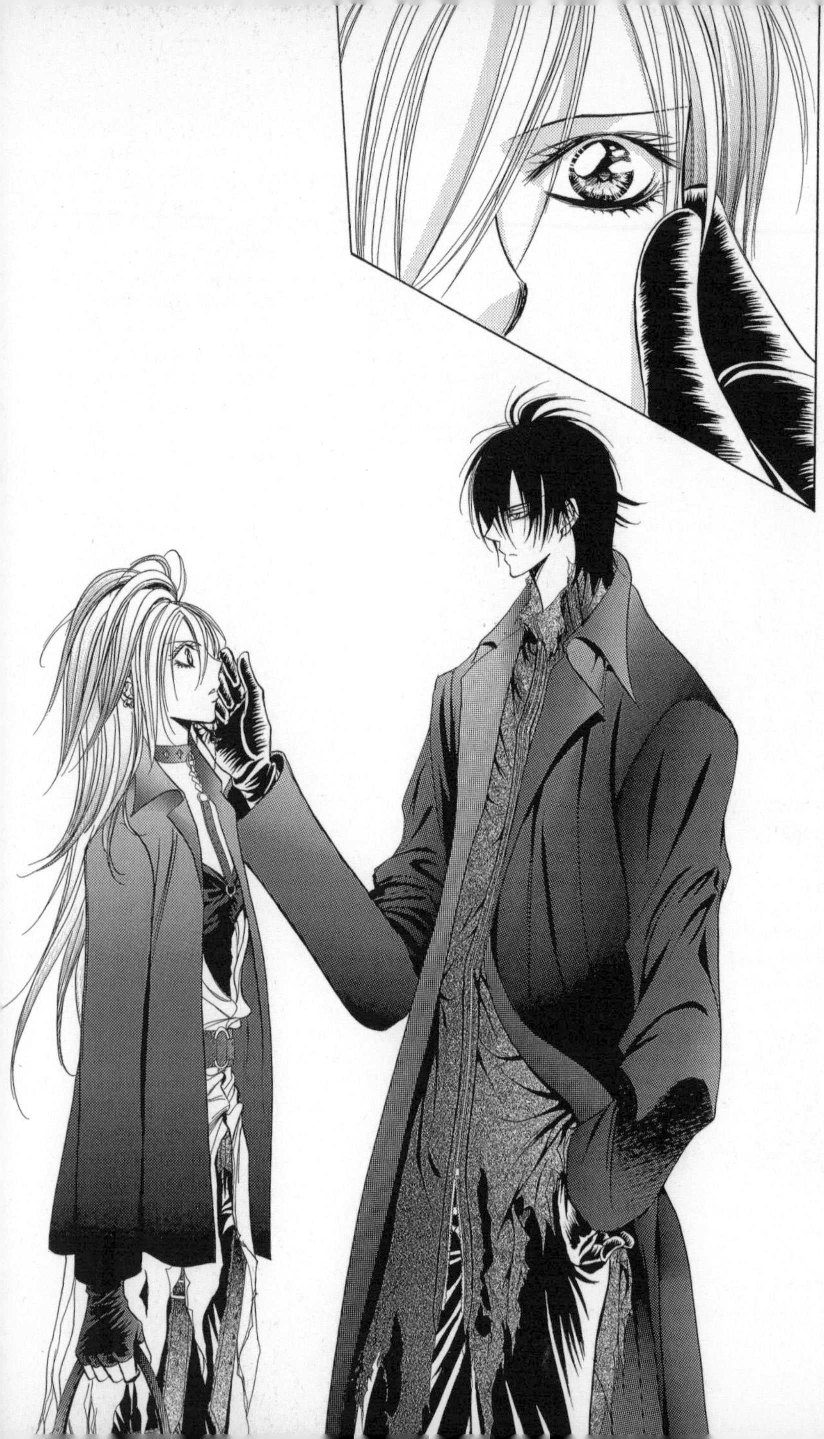

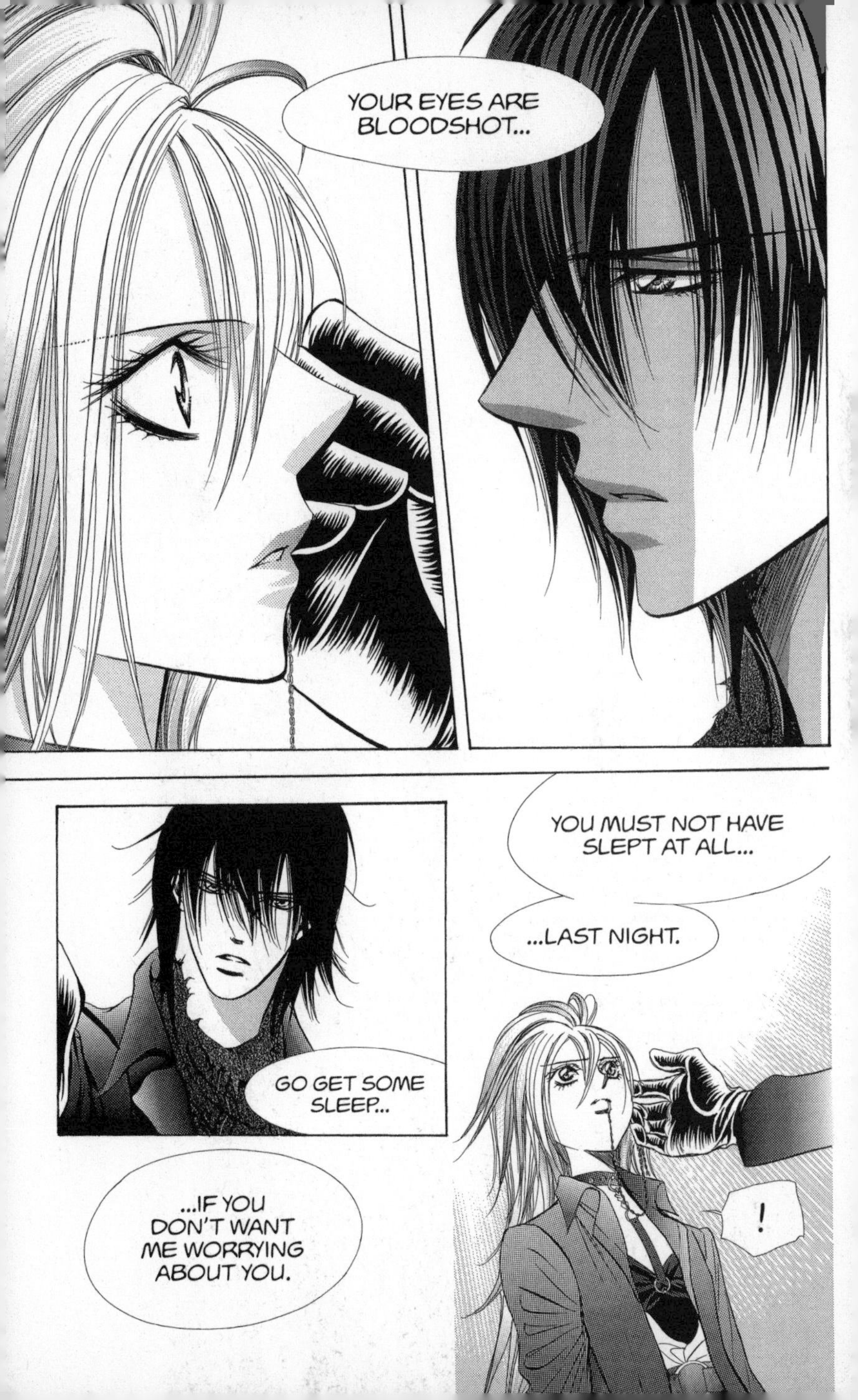
YOUR EYES ARE BLOODSHOT...
YOU MUST NOT HAVE SLEPT AT ALL...
...LAST NIGHT.
!
GO GET SOME SLEEP...
...IF YOU DON'T WANT ME WORRYING ABOUT YOU.

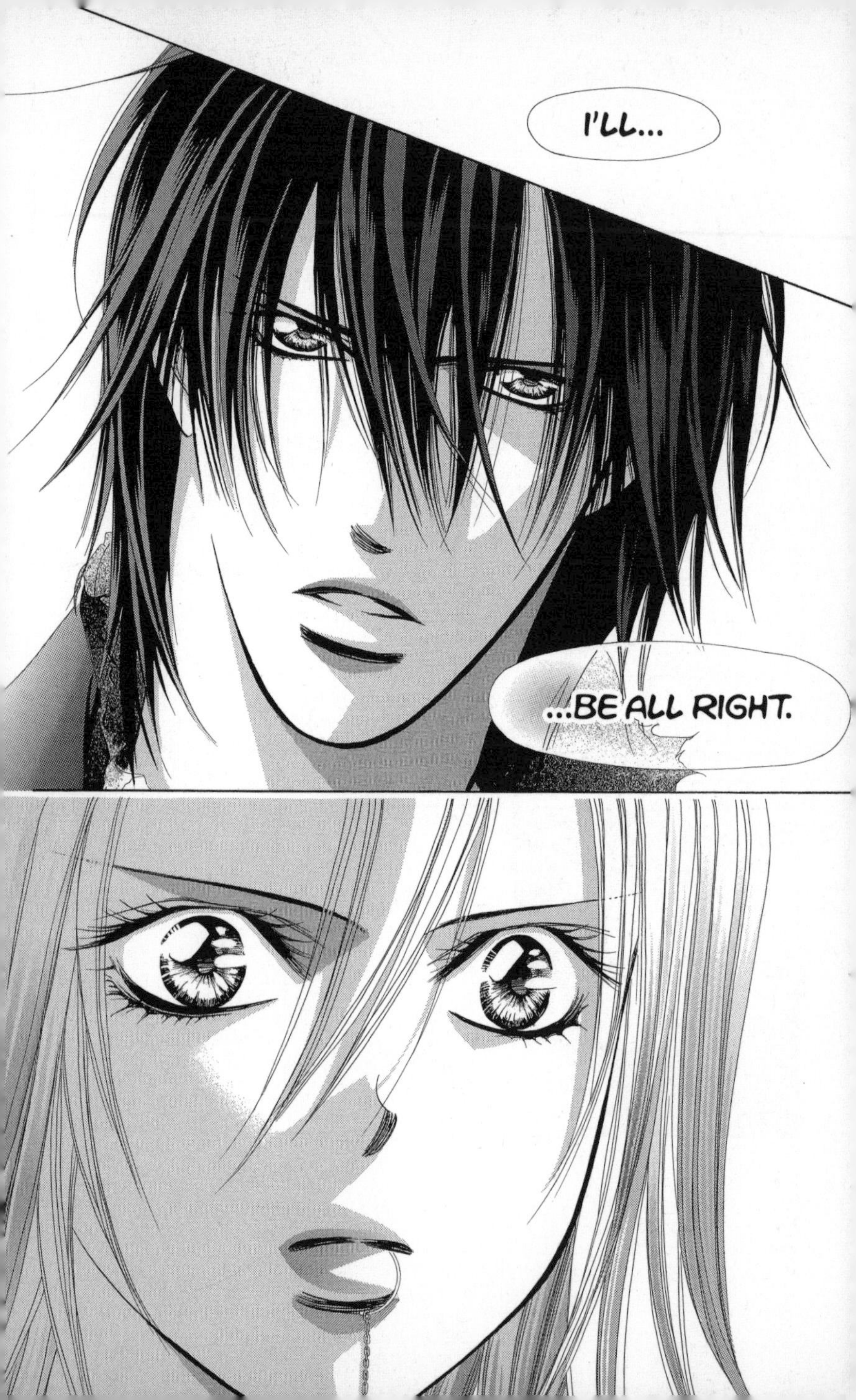
I'LL...
...BE ALL RIGHT.

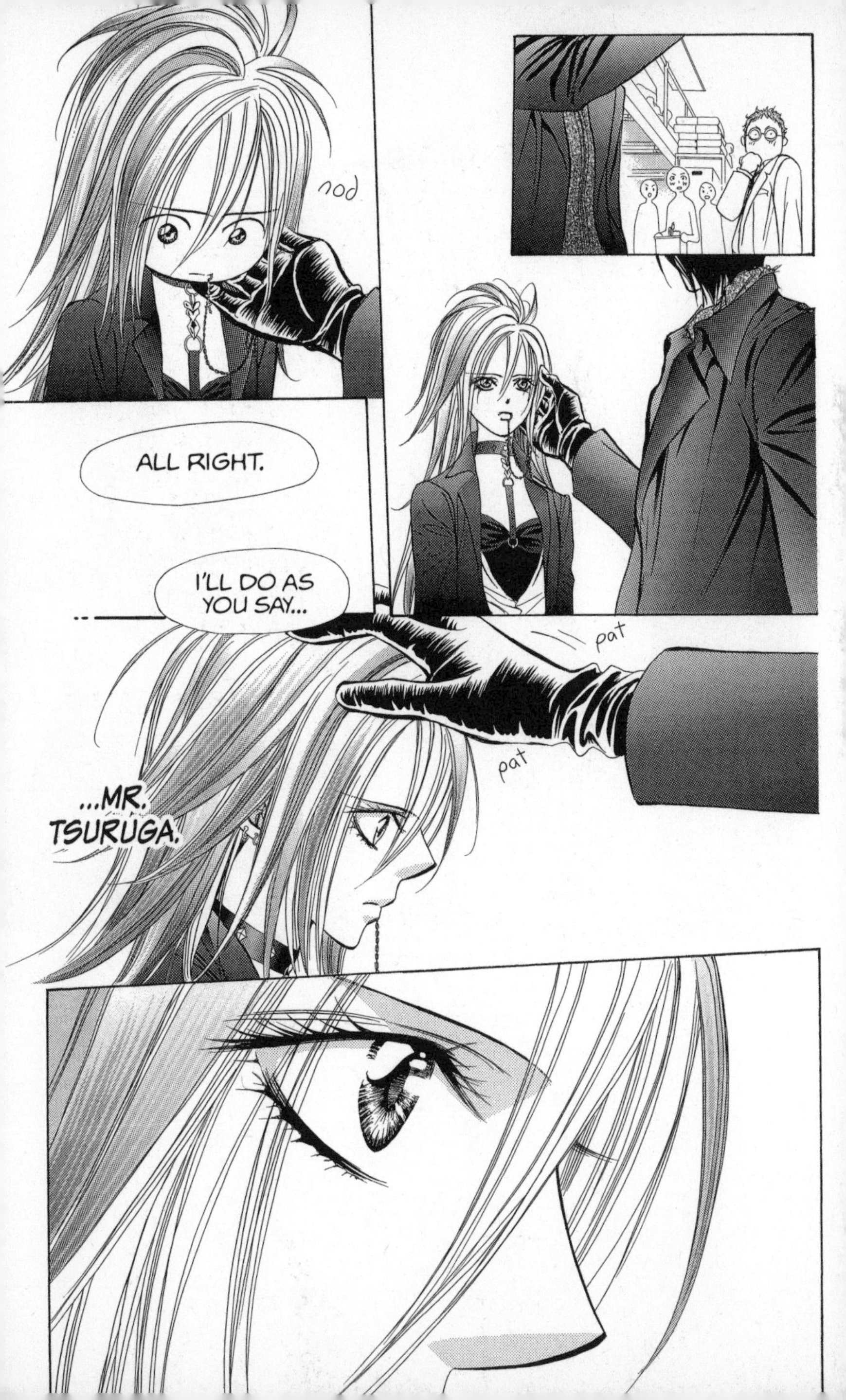
nod
ALL RIGHT.
I'LL DO AS YOU SAY...
pat
pat
...MR. TSURUGA.

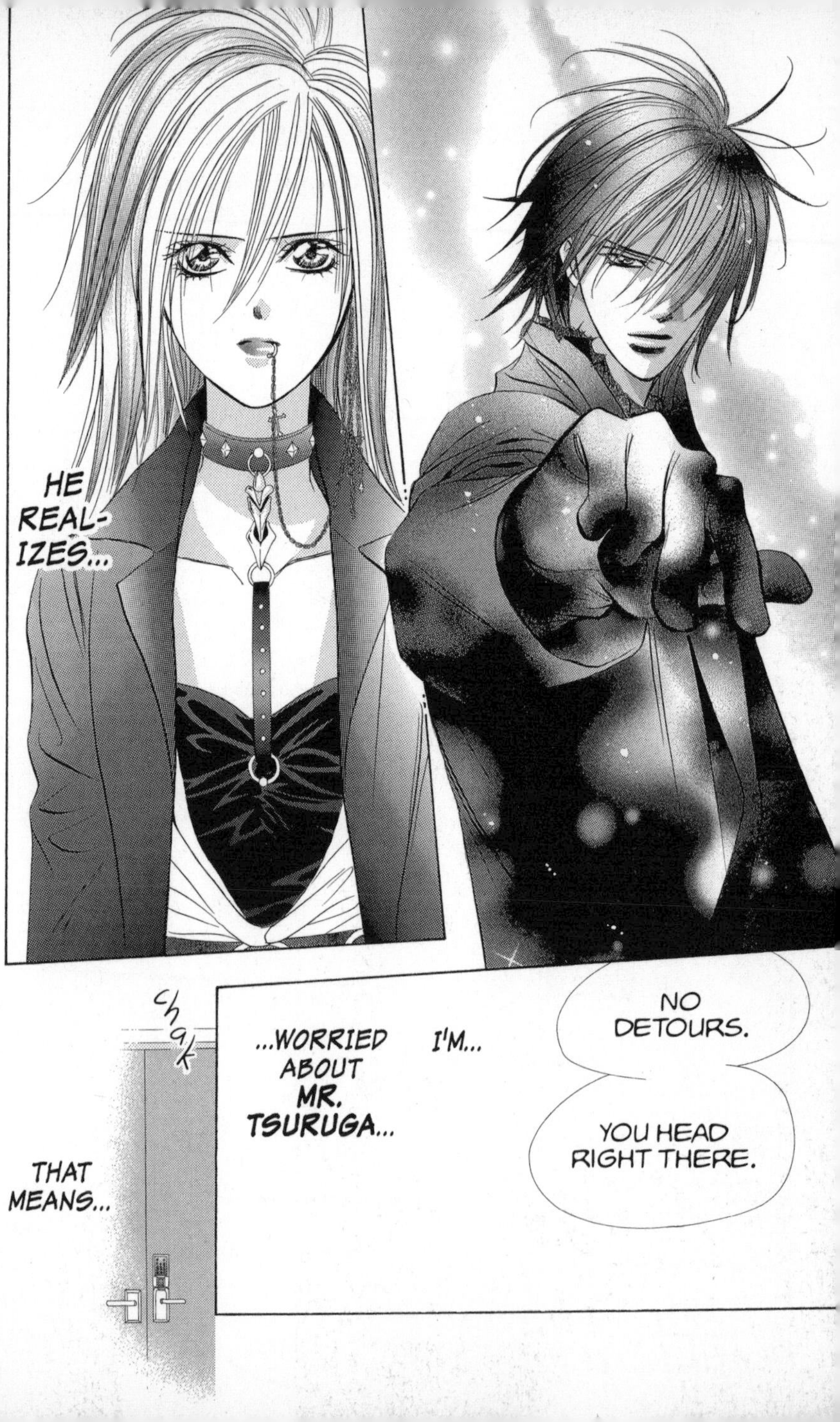
HE REALIZES...
NO DETOURS.
YOU HEAD RIGHT THERE.
I'M...
...WORRIED ABOUT MR. TSURUGA...
chak
THAT MEANS...

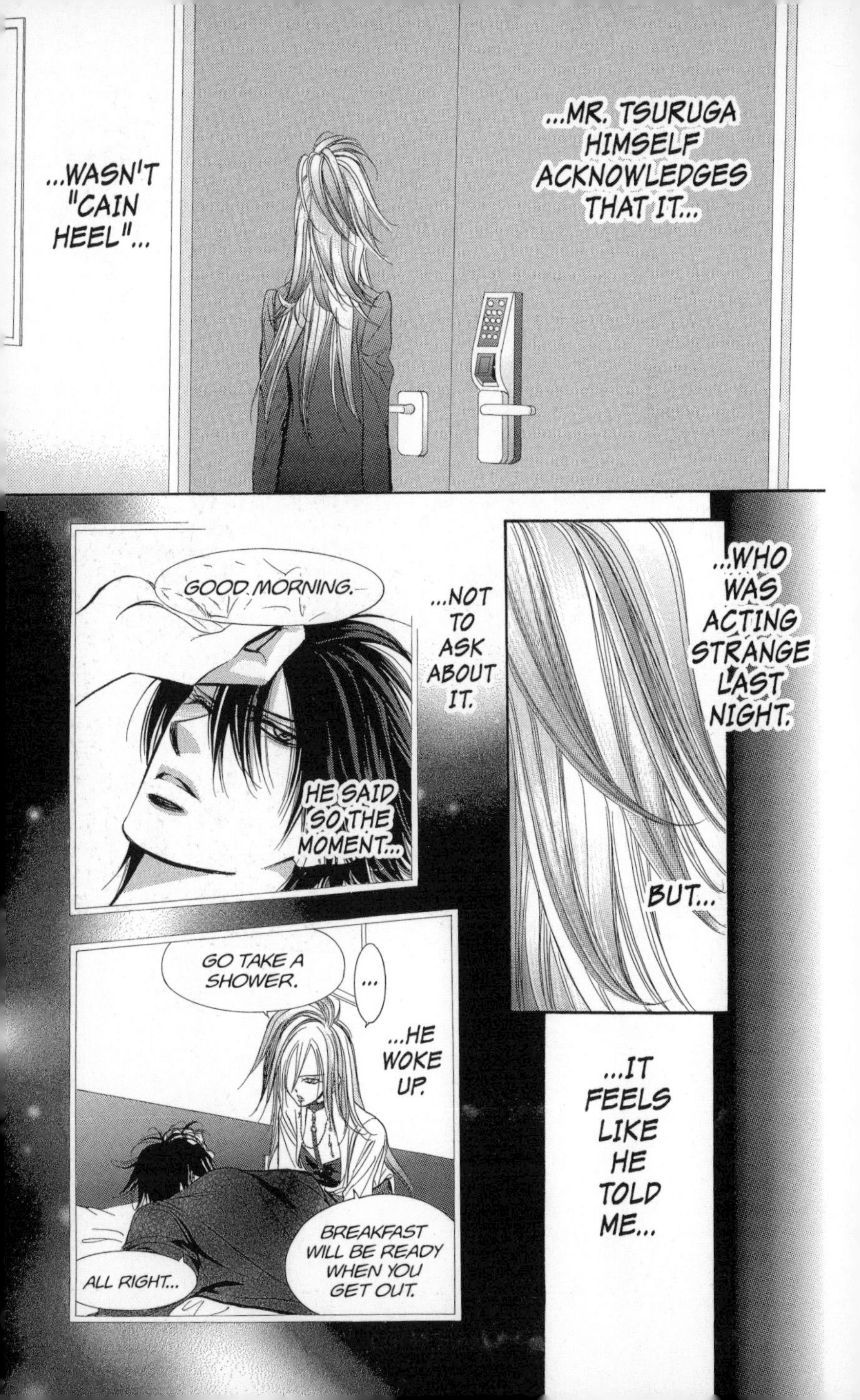

...MR. TSURUGA HIMSELF ACKNOWLEDGES THAT IT...
...WASN'T "CAIN HEEL"...
...WHO WAS ACTING STRANGE LAST NIGHT.
BUT...
...IT FEELS LIKE HE TOLD ME...
...NOT TO ASK ABOUT IT.
GOOD MORNING.
HE SAID SO THE MOMENT...
GO TAKE A SHOWER.
...
...HE WOKE UP.
BREAKFAST WILL BE READY WHEN YOU GET OUT.
ALL RIGHT...

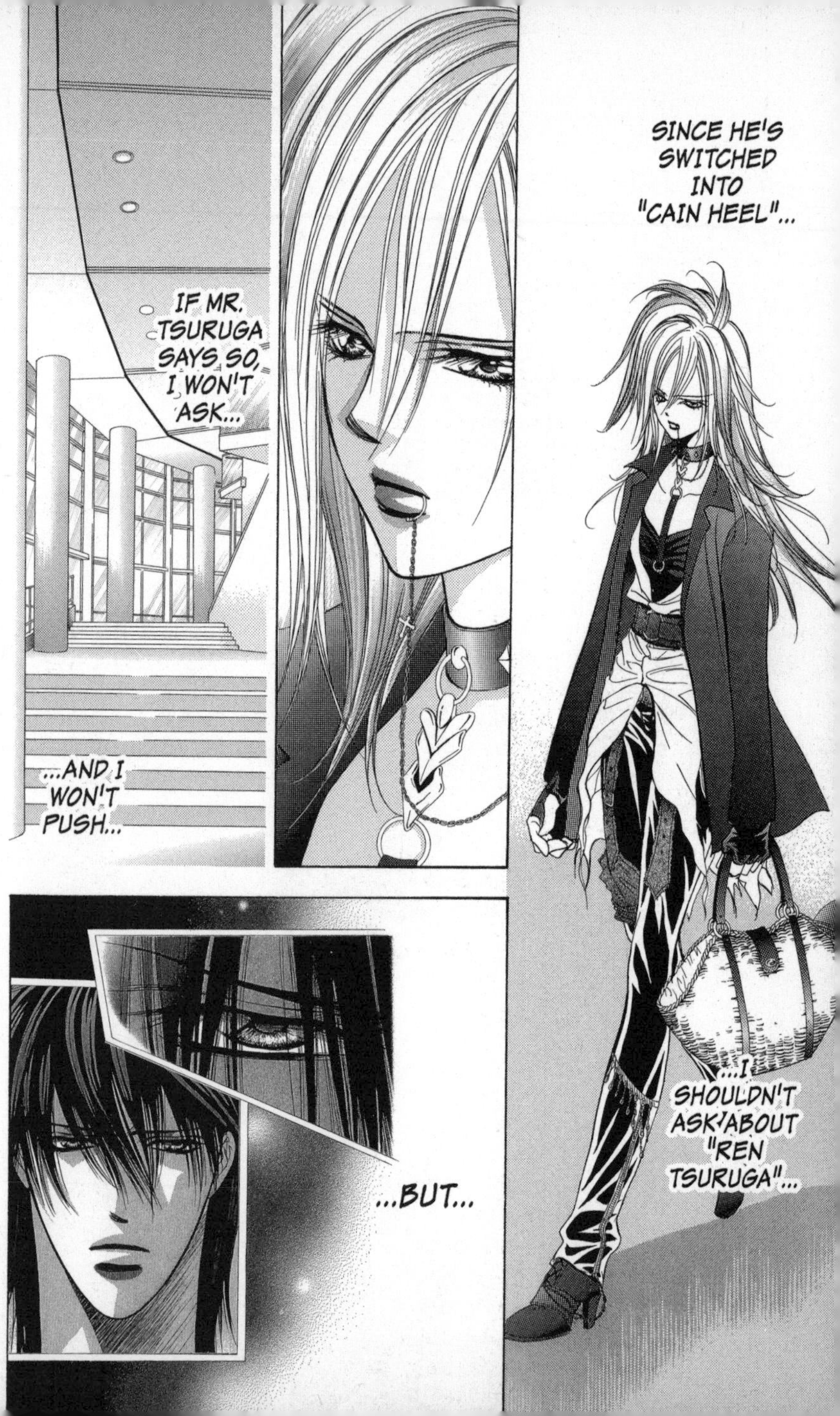
SINCE HE'S SWITCHED INTO "CAIN HEEL"...
...I SHOULDN'T ASK ABOUT "REN TSURUGA"...
IF MR. TSURUGA SAYS SO, I WON'T ASK...
...AND I WON'T PUSH...
...BUT...

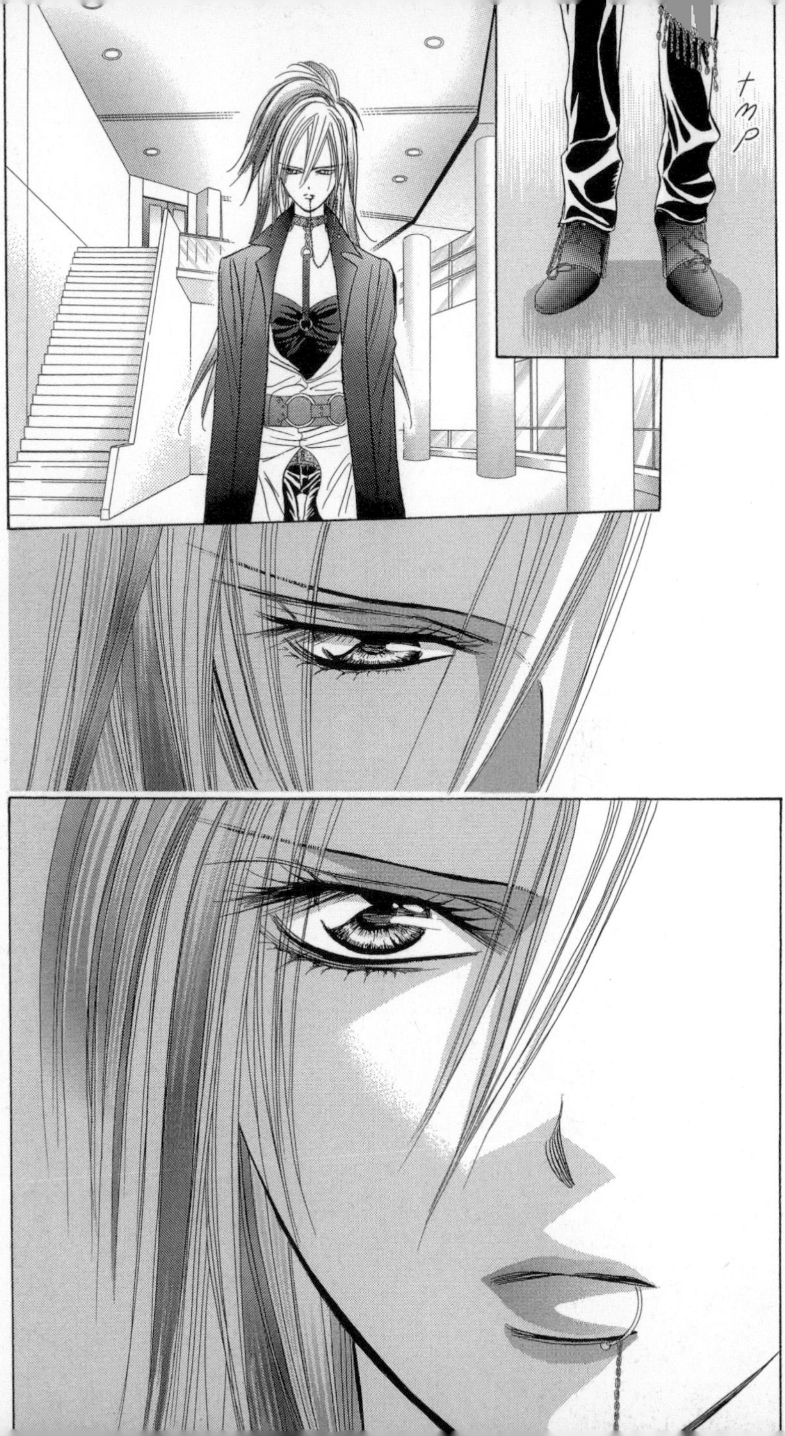
tmp

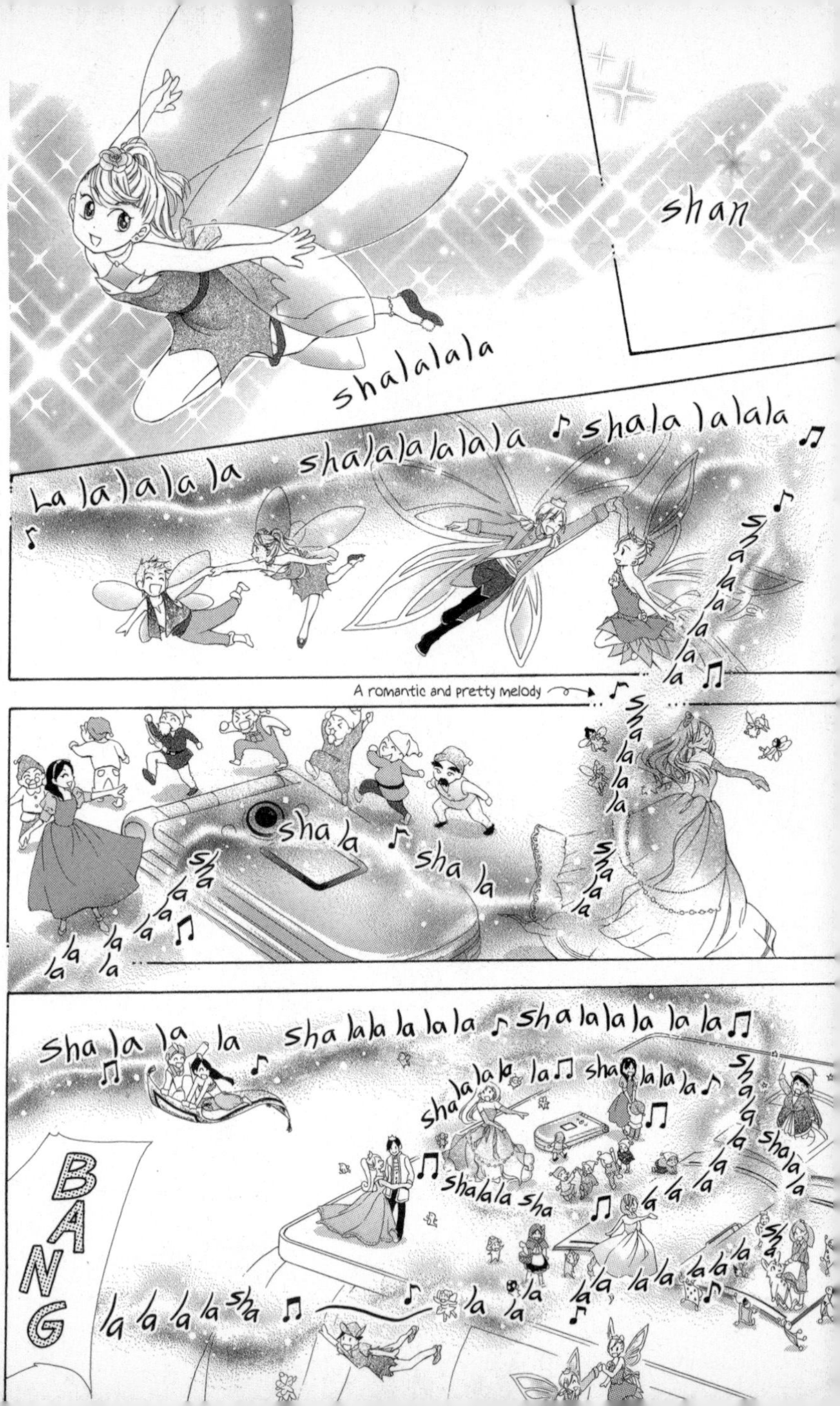
shan
shalalala
shala lalala ♪
shalalalalala ♪
La la la la la la ♪
shalalalalala ♫
A romantic and pretty melody
♪ shalalalala
shalala
sha la ♪ sha la
shalalalala ♫
sha la la la ♪ sha la la la la la ♫
sha la la la la la la ♪ sha la la la la la la ♫
shalalala la ♫ sha la la la la ♪
shalalalala shalala
shalala sha ♫
la la la la la la la la la la ♪
la la la la sha ♫ ♪ la la la la ♪
BANG

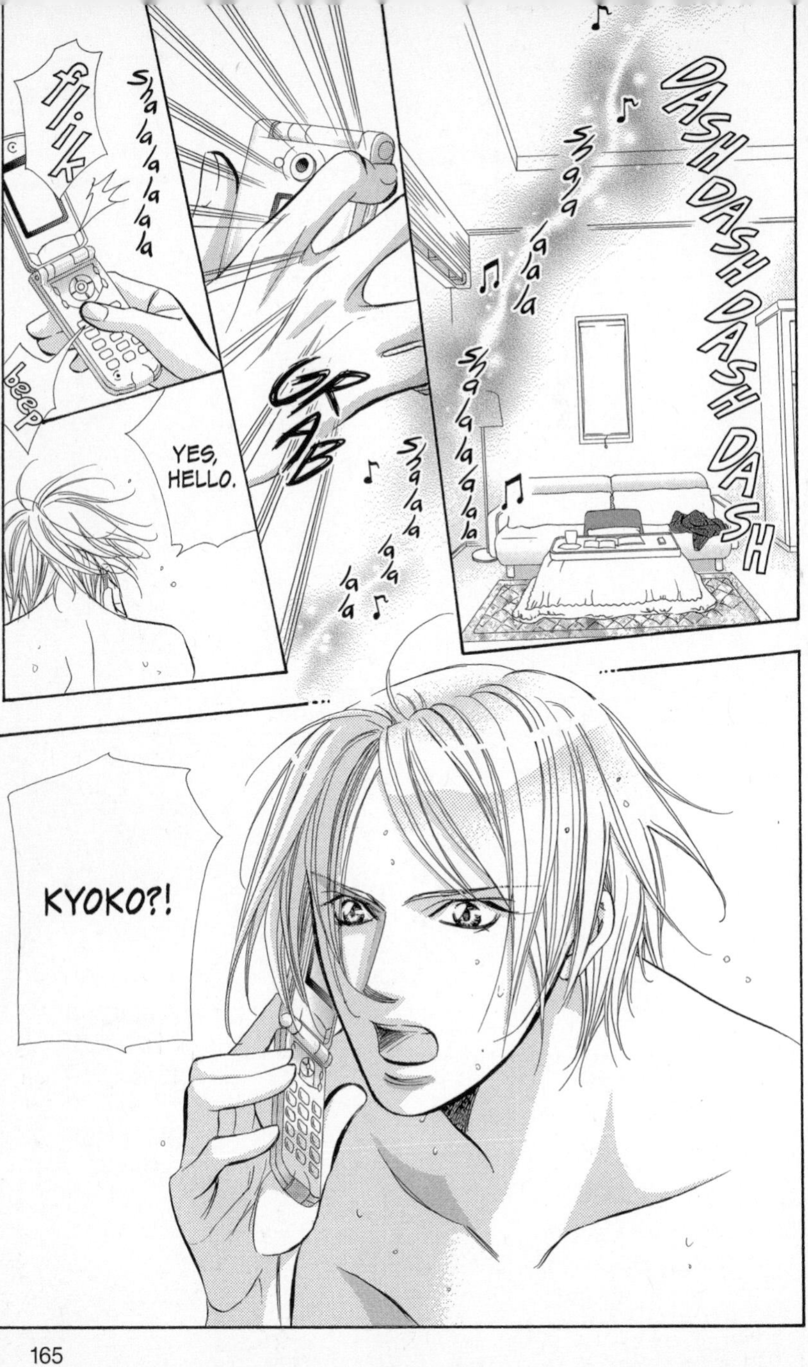
DASH DASH DASH DASH
Sha la la la la
Sha la la la la la la
GRAB
Sha la la la la la la
flik
Sha la la la la la la
beep
YES, HELLO.
KYOKO?!

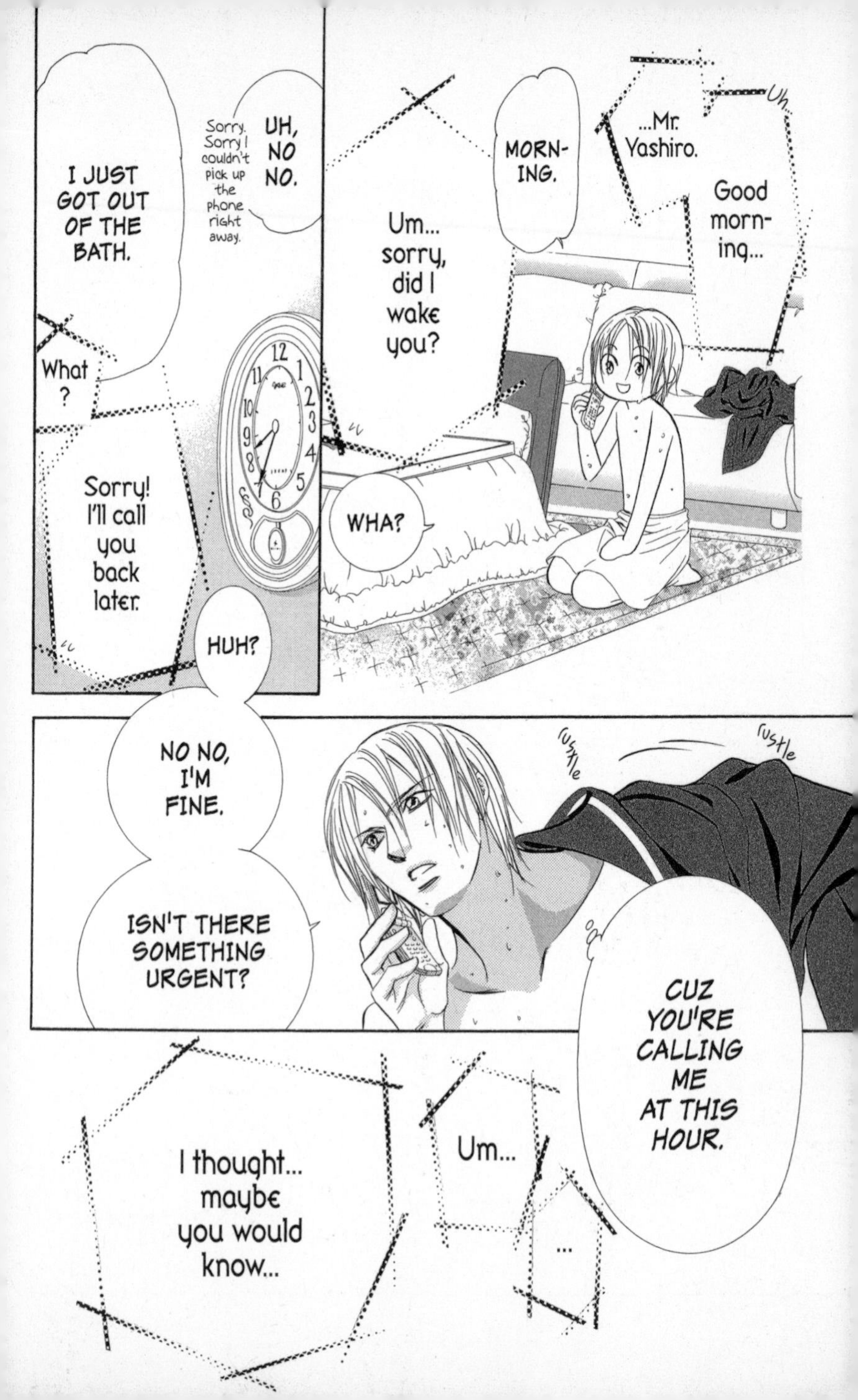
Uh
...Mr. Yashiro.
Good morning...
MORNING.
Um... sorry, did I wake you?
WHA?
UH, NO NO.
Sorry. Sorry I couldn't pick up the phone right away.
I JUST GOT OUT OF THE BATH.
What?
Sorry! I'll call you back later.
HUH?
rustle
rustle
NO NO, I'M FINE.
ISN'T THERE SOMETHING URGENT?
CUZ YOU'RE CALLING ME AT THIS HOUR.
...
Um...
I thought... maybe you would know...

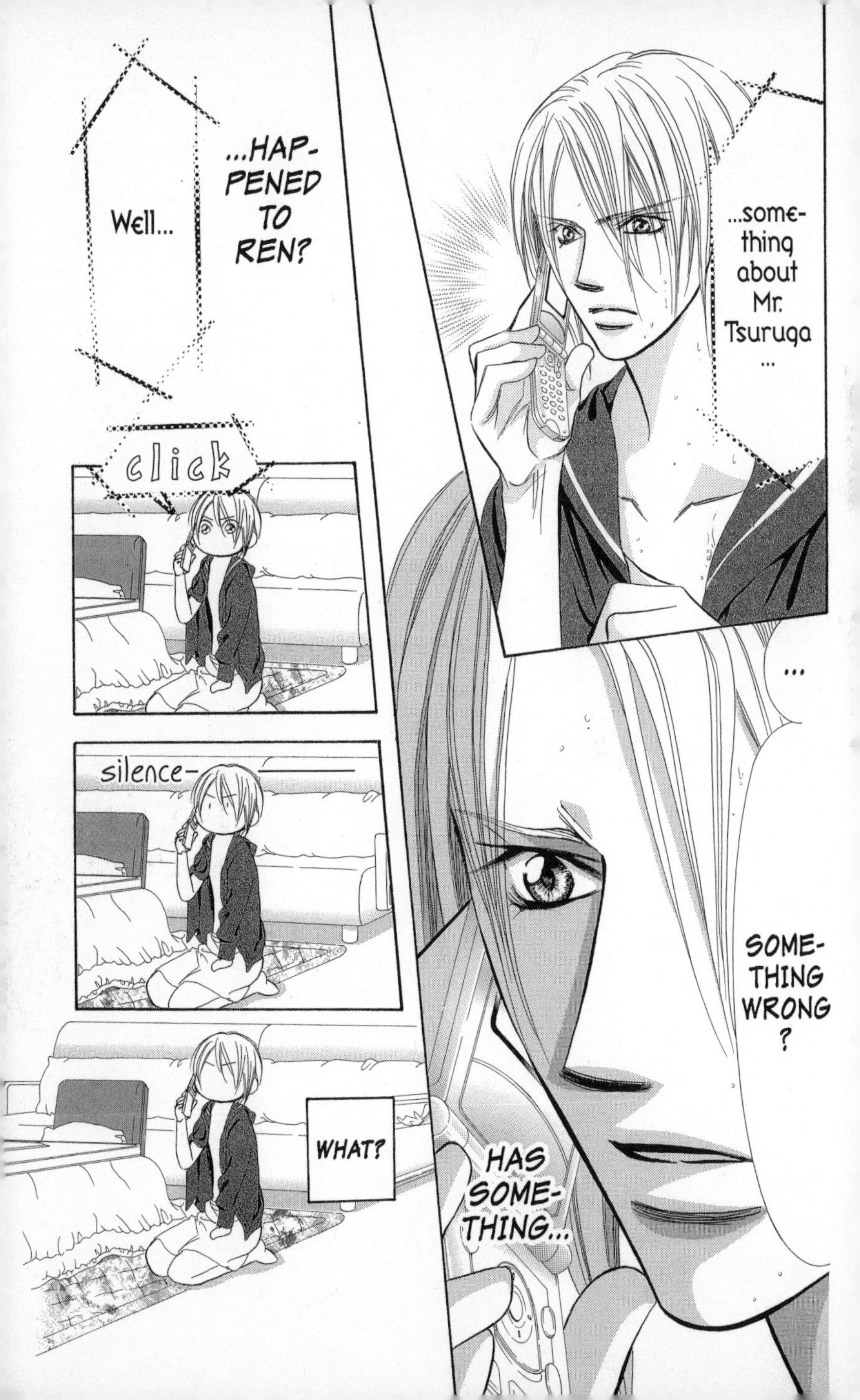

...some-
thing
about
Mr.
Tsuruga
...
...
SOME-
THING
WRONG
?
HAS
SOME-
THING...
...HAP-
PENED
TO
REN?
Well...
click
silence-
WHAT?

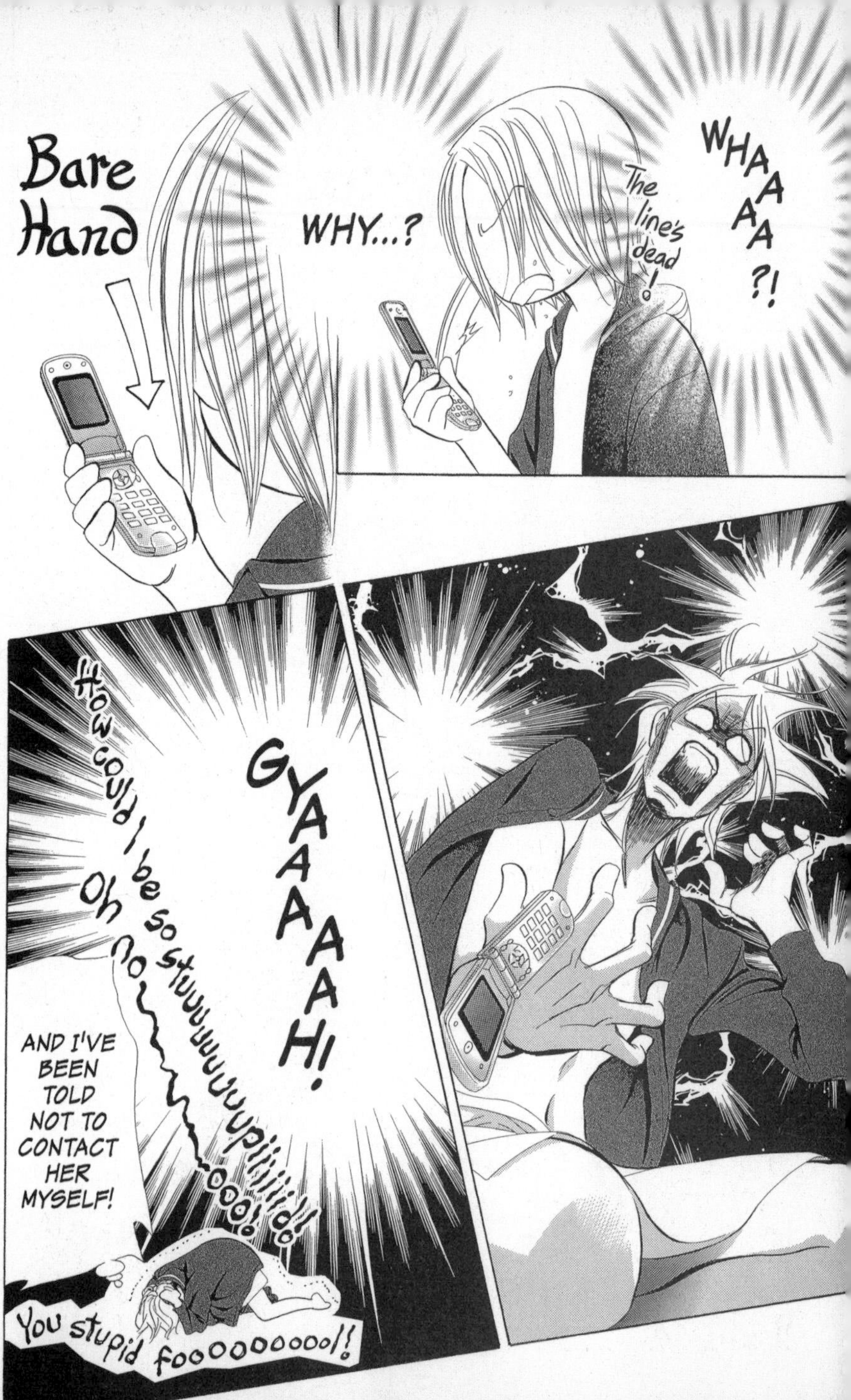
WHAAAAA?!
The line's dead!
WHY...?
Bare Hand
GYAAAAAAH!
How could I be so stuuuuuuuuuupiiiiid!
Oh no no~ooo!
AND I'VE BEEN TOLD NOT TO CONTACT HER MYSELF!
You stupid fooooooooool!

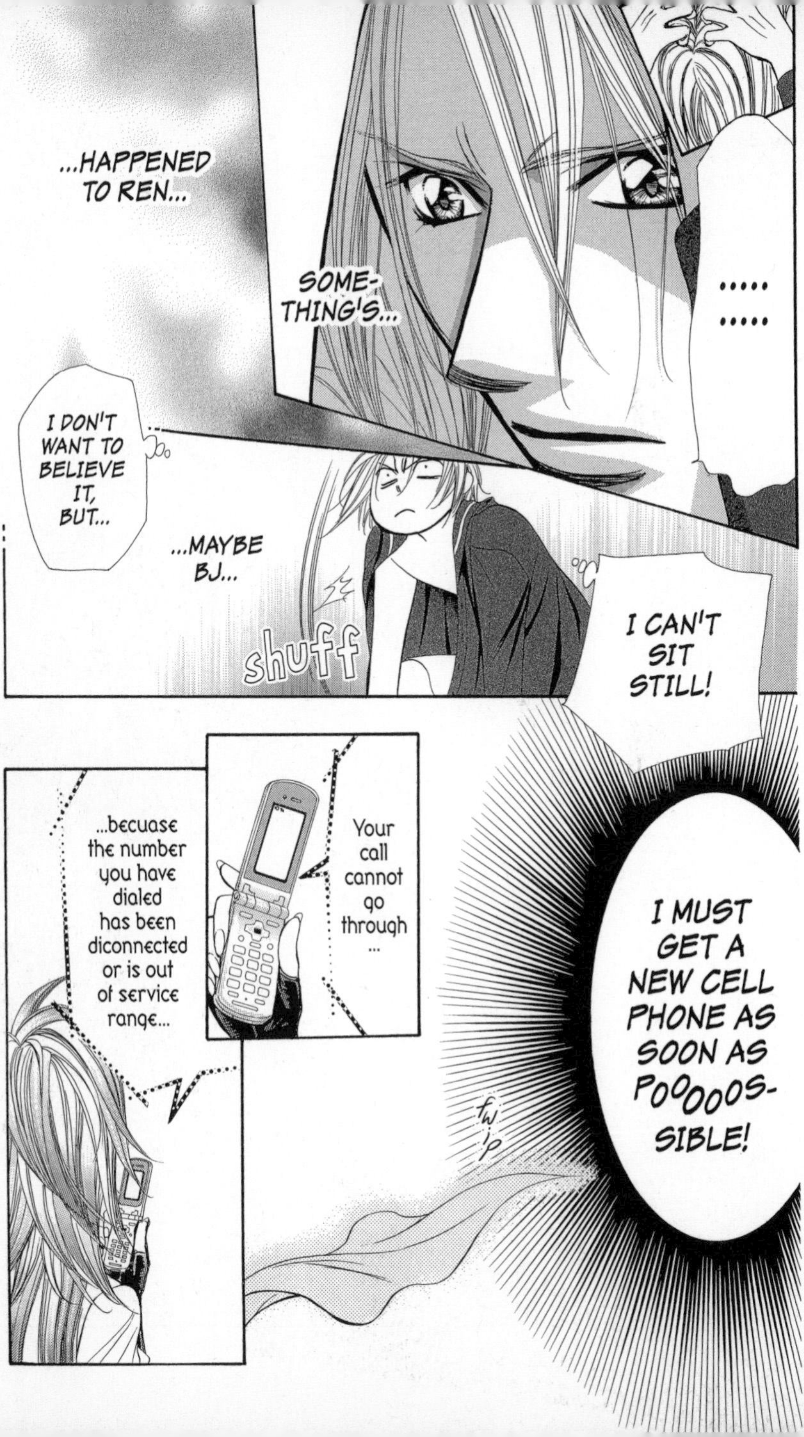
.....
.....
SOME-THING'S...
...HAPPENED TO REN...
I DON'T WANT TO BELIEVE IT, BUT...
...MAYBE BJ...
shuff
I CAN'T SIT STILL!
I MUST GET A NEW CELL PHONE AS SOON AS POOOOOS-SIBLE!
FWIP
Your call cannot go through ...
...becuase the number you have dialed has been diconnected or is out of service range...

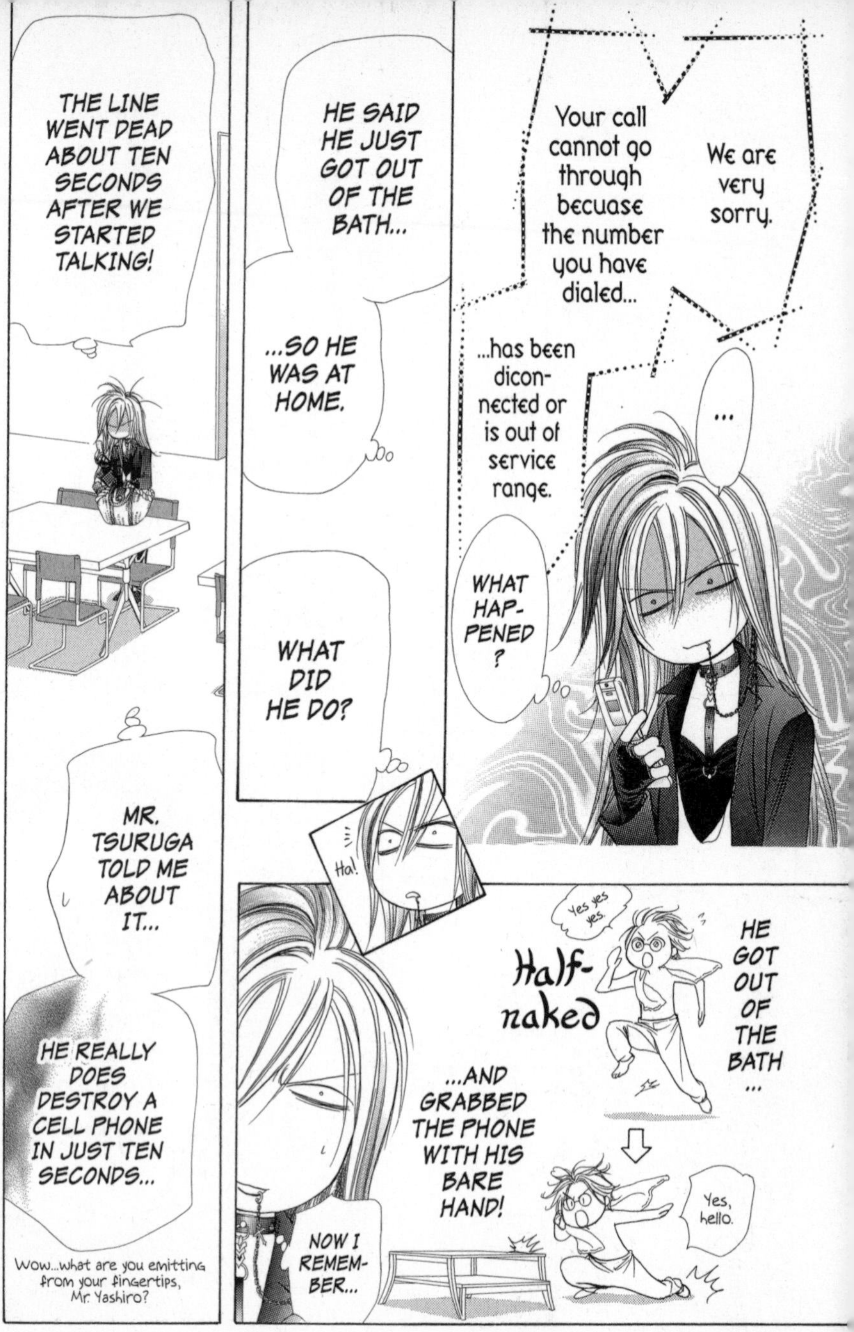

Your call cannot go through becuase the number you have dialed...
We are very sorry.
...has been dicon-nected or is out of service range.
...
WHAT HAP-PENED?
HE SAID HE JUST GOT OUT OF THE BATH...
...SO HE WAS AT HOME.
WHAT DID HE DO?
Ha!
HE GOT OUT OF THE BATH...
Yes yes yes.
Half-naked
...AND GRABBED THE PHONE WITH HIS BARE HAND!
Yes, hello.
NOW I REMEMBER...
THE LINE WENT DEAD ABOUT TEN SECONDS AFTER WE STARTED TALKING!
MR. TSURUGA TOLD ME ABOUT IT...
HE REALLY DOES DESTROY A CELL PHONE IN JUST TEN SECONDS...
Wow...what are you emitting from your fingertips, Mr. Yashiro?

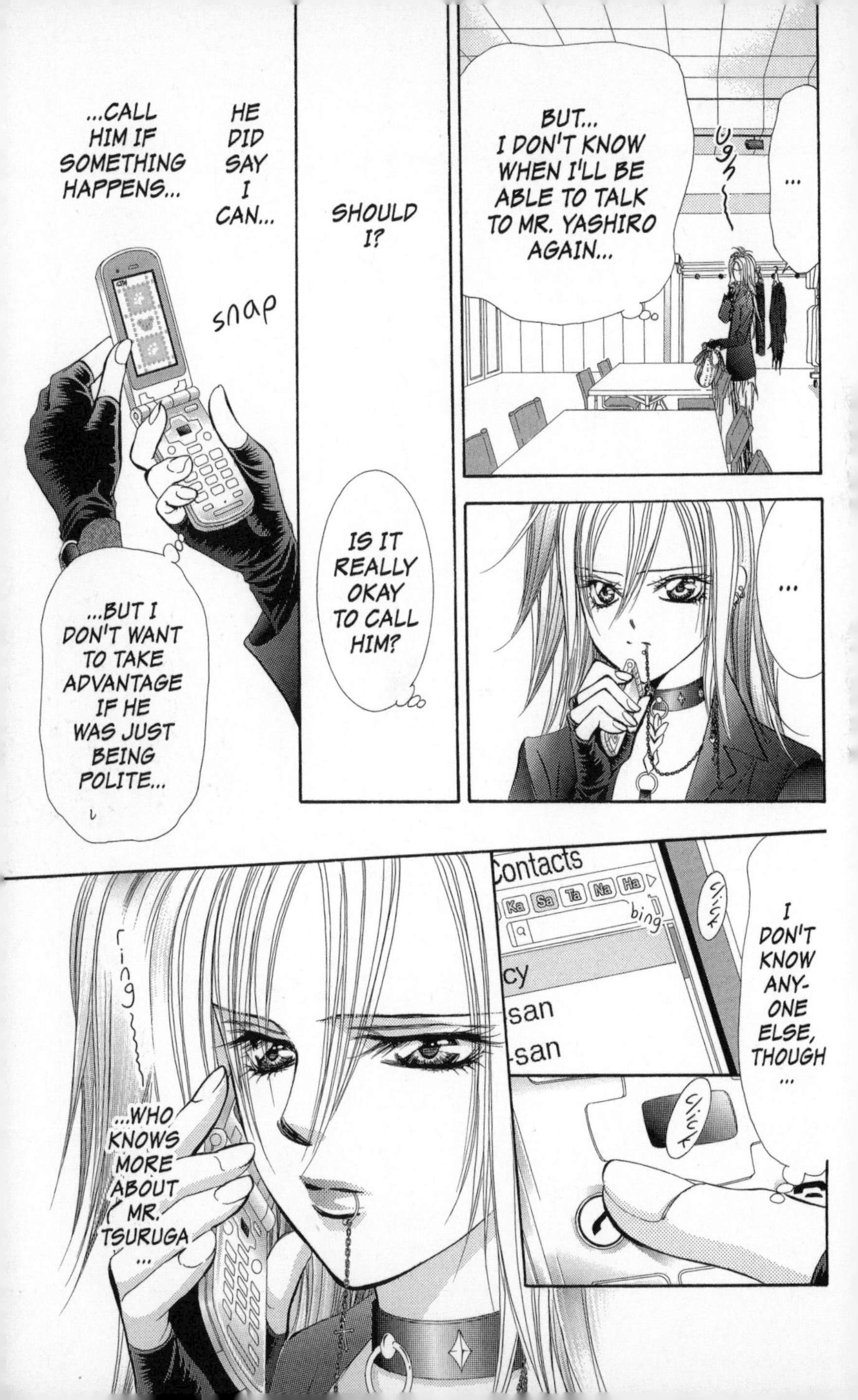
...
ugh~
BUT... I DON'T KNOW WHEN I'LL BE ABLE TO TALK TO MR. YASHIRO AGAIN...
...
SHOULD I?
IS IT REALLY OKAY TO CALL HIM?
HE DID SAY I CAN...
...CALL HIM IF SOMETHING HAPPENS...
snap
...BUT I DON'T WANT TO TAKE ADVANTAGE IF HE WAS JUST BEING POLITE...
I DON'T KNOW ANY-ONE ELSE, THOUGH...
click
Contacts
Ka Sa Ta Na Ha
bing
cy
-san
-san
click
ring~
...WHO KNOWS MORE ABOUT MR. TSURUGA...

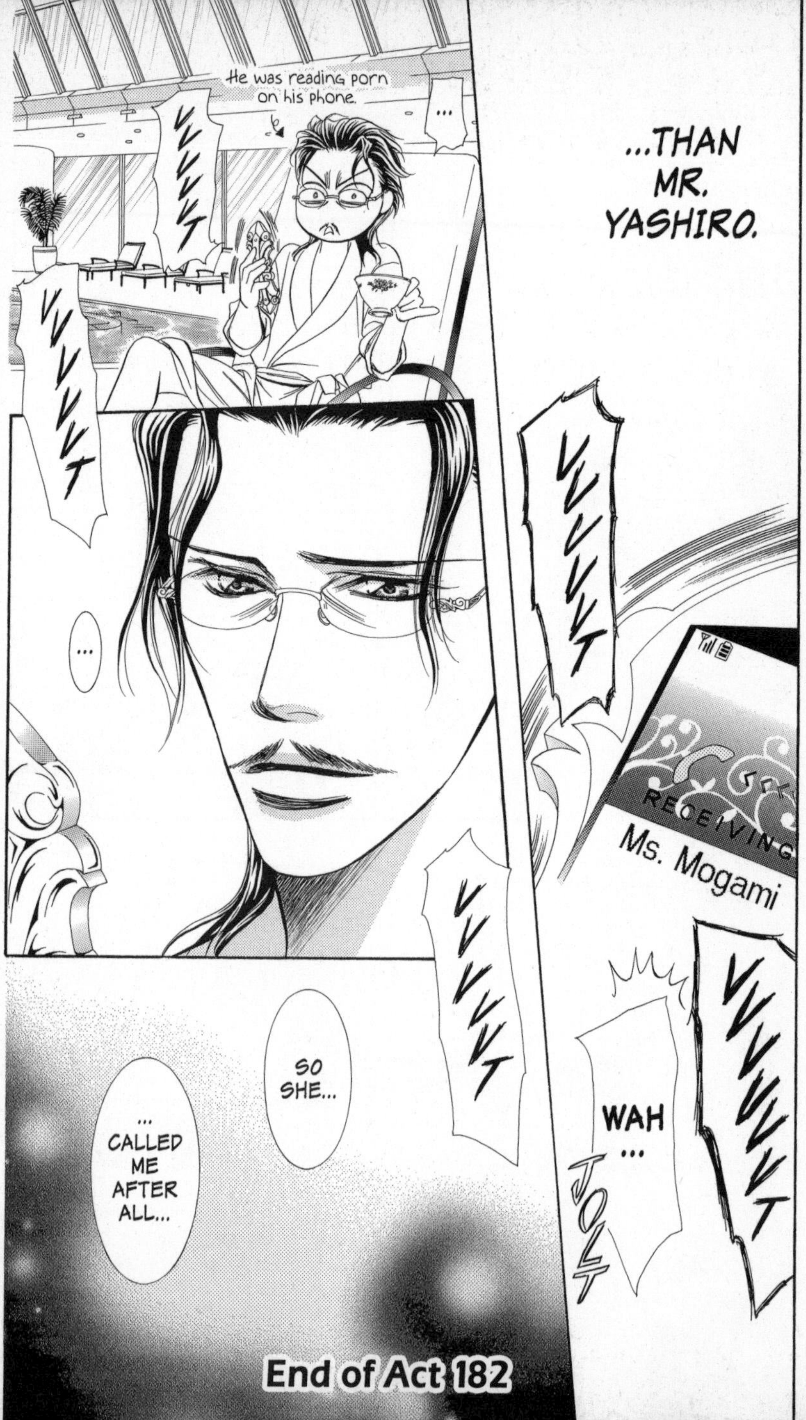
...THAN MR. YASHIRO.
VVVVVT
RECEIVING
Ms. Mogami
VVVVVT
WAH...
JOLT
He was reading porn on his phone.
...
VVVVVT
VVVVVT
...
VVVVVT
SO SHE...
...CALLED ME AFTER ALL...
End of Act 182

Skip-Beat! End Notes

Everyone knows how to be a fan, but sometimes cool things from other cultures need a little help crossing the language barrier.

Page 6, panel 1: Murasame's jacket
The long jacket with kanji inscription is a typical style for *yanki*, a type of Japanese delinquent.

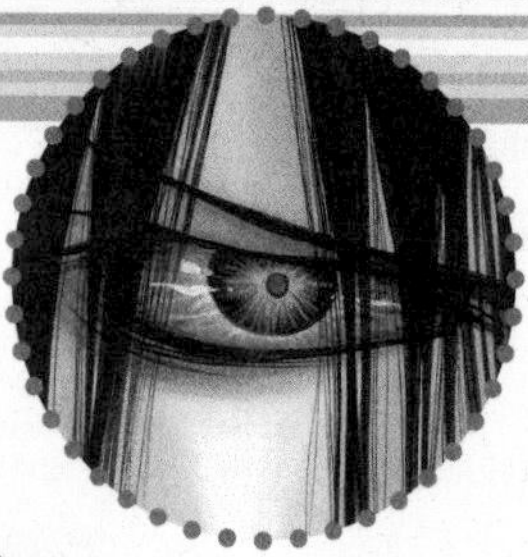

Yoshiki Nakamura is originally from Tokushima Prefecture. She started drawing manga in elementary school, which eventually led to her 1993 debut of *Yume de Au yori Suteki* (Better than Seeing in a Dream) in *Hana to Yume* magazine. Her other works include the basketball series *Saint Love*, *MVP wa Yuzurenai* (Can't Give Up MVP), *Blue Wars* and *Tokyo Crazy Paradise*, a series about a female bodyguard in 2020 Tokyo.

SKIP·BEAT!

Vol. 30

Shojo Beat Edition

STORY AND ART BY YOSHIKI NAKAMURA

English Translation & Adaptation/Tomo Kimura
Touch-up Art & Lettering/Sabrina Heep
Design/Ronnie Casson
Editor/Pancha Diaz

Printed in the U.S.A.

Published by VIZ Media, LLC
P.O. Box 77010
San Francisco, CA 94107

www.viz.com

www.shojobeat.com

10 9 8 7 6 5 4 3 2 1
First printing, February 2013

RATED T FOR TEEN

PARENTAL ADVISORY
SKIP·BEAT! is rated T for Teen and is recommended for ages 13 and up. This volume contains a grudge.
ratings.viz.com

SURPRISE!

You may be reading the wrong way!

It's true: In keeping with the original Japanese comic format, this book reads from right to left—so action, sound effects, and word balloons are completely reversed. This preserves the orientation of the original artwork—plus, it's fun! Check out the diagram shown here to get the hang of things, and then turn to the other side of the book to get started!

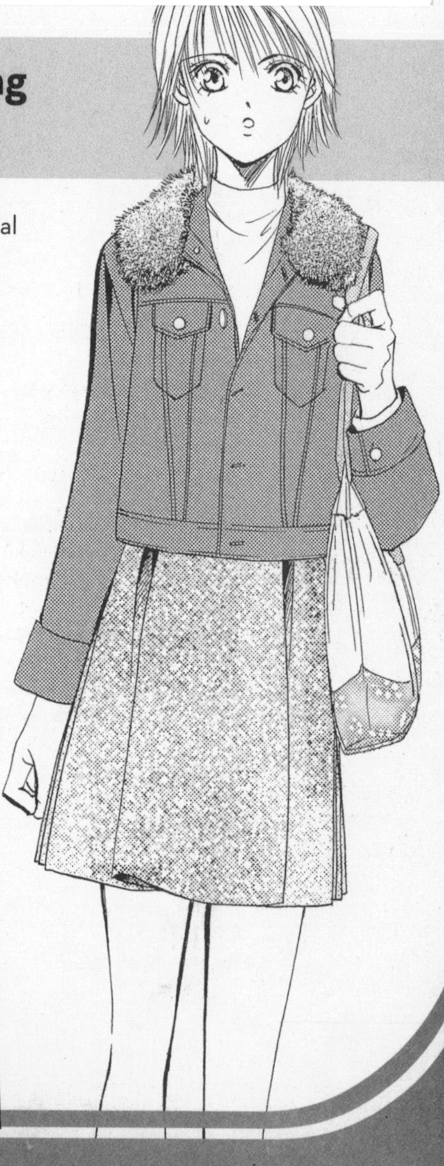

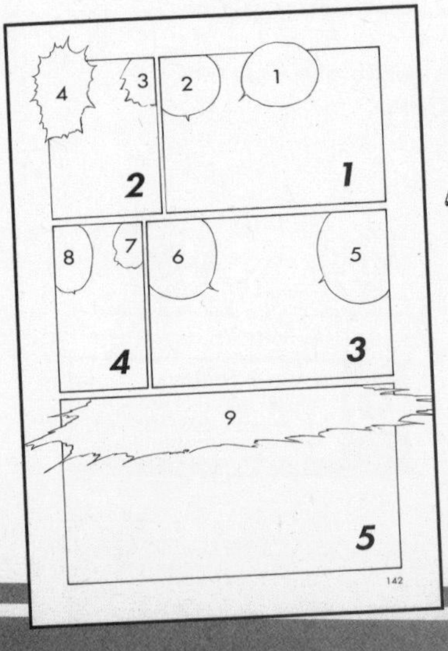
1
1
2
3
4
2
5
6
3
7
8
4
9
5